EMPIRE, EMERGENCY ا
INTERNATIONAL LAW

What does it mean to say we live in a permanent state of emergency? What are the juridical, political and social underpinnings of that framing? Has international law played a role in producing or challenging the paradigm of normalised emergency? How should we understand the relationship between imperialism, race and emergency legal regimes? In addressing such questions, this book situates emergency doctrine in historical context. It illustrates some of the particular colonial lineages that have shaped the state of emergency, and emphasises that contemporary formations of emergency governance are often better understood not as new or exceptional, but as part of an ongoing historical constellation of racialised emergency politics. The book highlights the connections between emergency law and violence, and encourages alternative approaches to security discourse. It will appeal to scholars and students of international law, colonial history, postcolonialism and human rights, as well as policy-makers and social justice advocates.

JOHN REYNOLDS is a Lecturer in International Law at the National University of Ireland, Maynooth. His work focuses on the operation of law in contexts of conflict, crisis and coloniality. He teaches and writes on international law, social justice and critical legal theory with particular emphasis on race, imperialism and global North/South dynamics.

EMPIRE, EMERGENCY AND INTERNATIONAL LAW

JOHN REYNOLDS

National University of Ireland, Maynooth

CAMBRIDGE
UNIVERSITY PRESS

CAMBRIDGE
UNIVERSITY PRESS

University Printing House, Cambridge CB2 8BS, United Kingdom

One Liberty Plaza, 20th Floor, New York, NY 10006, USA

477 Williamstown Road, Port Melbourne, VIC 3207, Australia

314-321, 3rd Floor, Plot 3, Splendor Forum, Jasola District Centre, New Delhi - 110025, India

79 Anson Road, #06-04/06, Singapore 079906

Cambridge University Press is part of the University of Cambridge.

It furthers the University's mission by disseminating knowledge in the pursuit of
education, learning and research at the highest international levels of excellence.

www.cambridge.org
Information on this title: www.cambridge.org/9781316623886
DOI: 10.1017/9781316779095

First published 2017
First paperback edition 2018

A catalogue record for this publication is available from the British Library

Library of Congress Cataloging in Publication data
Names: Reynolds, John, 1981–
Title: Empire, emergency, and international law / John Reynolds.
Description: Cambridge [UK] ; New York : Cambridge University Press, 2017. |
Includes bibliographical references and index.
Identifiers: LCCN 2017012108 | ISBN 9781107172517 (Hardback)
Subjects: LCSH: Emergencies–Law and legislation. | Human rights and international law. |
Imperialism. | War and emergency powers. | BISAC: LAW / International.
Classification: LCC K4700 .R49 2017 | DDC 342/.062–dc23
LC record available at https://lccn.loc.gov/2017012108

ISBN 978-1-107-17251-7 Hardback
ISBN 978-1-316-62388-6 Paperback

Empire has created the time of history. Empire has located its existence not in the smooth recurrent spinning time of the cycle of the seasons but in the jagged time of rise and fall, of beginning and end, of catastrophe. Empire dooms itself to live in history and plot against history. One thought alone preoccupies the submerged mind of Empire: how not to end, how not to die, how to prolong its era.

J.M. Coetzee, *Waiting for the Barbarians*

CONTENTS

Foreword *by* Antony Anghie   *page* ix

Prologue   1

PART I   TRADITIONS OF THE OPPRESSED   5

1 **Emergency, Colonialism and Third World Approaches
   to International Law**   7
   On the Concept of History   9
   On Perpetual Emergency   12
   On the Spectre of Colonialism   16
   On Theory and Method: Third World Approaches   20

2 **Racialisation and States of Emergency**   36
   The Spectre of Race   38
   Legality, Exception and Inclusion/Exclusion   46
   Emergency and Racial Sovereignty   56
   The Racialisation of International Law   65

3 **Emergency Doctrine: A Colonial Account**   68
   Martial Law: 'Province and Purpose'   71
   Legislative Normalisation: Codifying Emergency Powers   77
   The Political Economy of Emergency   93
   Emergency as Governance   104

PART II   EMPIRE'S LAW   109

4 **Emergency Derogations and the International
   Human Rights Project**   111
   The Post-war Context   113
   From European Empire to European Convention on Human Rights   117
   Universalising the State of Emergency   123
   The European Convention in the Colonies   128

5   Kenya: A 'Purely Political' State of Emergency   138
    Rehearsing the Emergency   144
    Performing the Emergency   149
    Mystifying Mau Mau: The Racialised Construction of a
    Diseased Mind   156
    Purely Political International Law   161

6   The Margin of Appreciation Doctrine: Colonial
    Origins   170
    The Cyprus Case   171
    The Troubles   178
    The Belmarsh Case   184
    A Third World Alternative?   189
    Imperialism Redux   191

PART III   THE COLONIAL PRESENT   193

7   Palestine: 'A Scattered, Shattered Space of Exception'? 195
    Palestine as Space of Exception   198
    The Law in These Parts: Settlement, Sovereignty, Emergency 213
    Israel's Emergency Modalities   221
    'Intent to Regularise': Emergency on Trial   236

8   Australia: Racialised Emergency Intervention   244
    The 'Intervention' in the Northern Territory   245
    Traces of Racial History   251
    Law, Land and Settler Sovereignty   260

9   International Law, Resistance and 'Real' States of
    Emergency   266
    The Limits and Possibilities of (International) Law   268
    Scripts of Resistance   273
    Real States of Emergency   286

    Bibliography   289
    Acknowledgements   314
    Index   317

FOREWORD

The question of 'emergency' and its relationship to the law has now been the subject of extensive scholarship spanning political theory, philosophy, human rights and international and constitutional law. Much of this has been produced in response to developments since the tragic events of 11 September 2001, and a great deal of it focuses on events and theorising in the West, sometimes returning to Roman times to explain the origins and character of emergency rule. Dr Reynolds takes a different approach, exploring instead the development and operation of emergency rule in colonial territories, and the enduring influence of this model on emergency law and indeed, international law. His book examines 'imperial emergency rule' – it could in fact be termed a global history of imperial emergency rule – in a number of different contexts, encompassing both colonial and ostensibly post-colonial states. Dr Reynolds thus connects together accounts of emergency that are often treated separately: colonial emergencies, the impact of these emergencies on the drafting of international legal instruments and contemporary settler colonialism. It is by drawing on this range of diverse yet related materials and case studies that Dr Reynolds provides such a far-reaching and incisive account of the complexities of 'imperial emergency rule' and how it has shaped, and continues to shape, emergency law everywhere.

The concept of 'racialised emergency' – and its characteristics, elaborations, variations, operations – is one of the principal themes by which Dr Reynolds connects his materials. He offers here a sustained study of the racialised character of imperial emergency governance which was broadly and generally justified on the basis that the 'normal' rule of law needed to be suspended because of the supposedly barbaric nature of the natives. Further, Dr Reynolds attempts to study emergency rule from below, from the perspective of those who are subjected to it. It is by elaborating and developing this approach that he challenges the clichéd claim that we are now living in unprecedented times in which the exception has become the norm. By focusing on the experiences of those often overlooked by history, Dr Reynolds persuasively points out that this has long been the case for millions of people who are living under emergency rule and have done so for decades.

In these cases, emergency rule becomes normalised, so much so that this version of emergency itself produces a complex set of regulations which create a simulacrum of the rule of law and rhetorically mimics its attributes. Notably further, imperial emergency rule has an important economic dimension and is directed at dispossessing peoples marked as racially other from their lands. The natural resistance of these people to their immiseration is then represented as a confirmation of their barbaric and inhuman nature, which again justifies the expansion of emergency rule and ongoing violence against them. Emergency rule must extend even further, to govern these people, and it then filters into everyday life. What we then observe is the 'banality' of emergency, this in contrast to the dramatic and singular events (such as 9/11) that trigger formal declarations of a state of emergency.

One of the key issues raised by this book is precisely the disturbing extent to which emergency has become so entrenched in the everyday operations of the law that in some respects the two regimes become indistinguishable. Emergency is inherent in the idea of law itself. Indeed, it generates law. Even when emergency is succeeded by a set of laws which make some claim to restore normality these laws are inevitably marked by structural changes imposed under the emergency. As a result, a residue of emergency remains even in the 'normal' law but the rhetoric shifts to some version of the importance of 'adapting to novel threats'. Current attempts to legalise drone strikes and expand the concept of self-defence through the 'unable or unwilling' test are adorned in the language of 'balance', 'necessity', 'proportionality' and 'law' itself. They are presented as universally binding and applicable principles of general international law, rather than exceptional, emergency measures. Once again, however, their likely target as in the time of emergency is the racialised other, the failed state, the inherently violent barbarian.

Dr Reynolds modestly and carefully points out that the paradigm he elaborates in such detail cannot account for every dimension of the complex phenomenon of emergency; and yet, there is a great deal he illuminates in this book which combines erudition with superbly clear writing. Racialised emergency, after all, is now prevalent in the West itself. What began as 'colonial emergency' has gone global. And his study of the economic dimensions of emergency is surely relevant to appreciating the plight of the tribal peoples and peasants expelled from their lands in countries intent on achieving 'development'. As Dr Reynolds argues, however, emergency produces resistance from below, and an understanding of how precisely emergency operates is crucial to this project of contestation. Dr Reynolds' book offers one such incisive understanding. It is an eloquent and valuable book which provides enduring insights into a pervasive feature of our times.

Antony Anghie

~

Prologue

I arrived at a time when the 'troubles' in the north of Ireland had descended to a relative low point – the H-block hunger strikes and Thatcher's intransigence. It was a somewhat disorienting experience growing up in an Irish state that was so close to, and yet in many ways so far removed from, the state of emergency through which the north of our small island was living. We tried to express solidarity with our northern cousins, but could fathom little of their lived experience of checkpoints, curfews and clashes. The *tiocfaidh ár lá*[1] graffiti sprinkled on walls and sheds around the Dublin mountains in which I grew up seemed inspirational and pointless in equal measure. Partition had bred and institutionalised a strange kind of postcolonial alienation. The conflict across the border and the impact of British emergency measures existed only in the abstract to us, but formed a constant background soundtrack to our lives – radio bulletins and the evening news, the idle chat of grown-ups down the shops. As children, we got to know all the jargon, all the big words of the north's emergency: gerrymandering and abstentionism, collusion and supergrasses, diplock courts and internment.

I started secondary school on 1 September 1994, the morning after the Provisional IRA ceasefire was called. In his introductory class, our history teacher emphasised the significance of the news: we were witnessing a momentous development in the life of the nation. He used it as a hook on which to hang the central themes of the 'Irish history' section of the curriculum: our island's sagas of colonialism, partition and sectarianism; the institutionalisation of difference and the tradition of oppression. The other section, 'European history', would be about rival monarchs and great 'discoveries'; religious wars and world wars and cold wars. There was scant, if any, mention of other traditions of the oppressed: in Asia,

---

[1] An Irish republican slogan: 'our day will come'.

1

Africa, Australia or the Americas. Colonial emergency rule seemed to be something specific to the north of Ireland.

A decade later, studies in international law led me to Palestine for several years, and from there to South Africa as part of a research project on the laws of apartheid. In both of those contexts – utterly distinct in place and context, yet hauntingly similar in some respects – emergency law etched its way into my consciousness as deeply implicated in settler colonial processes of dispossession and subjugation. The simple but significant practical effects of the apartheid emergency laws are evident in Mandela's recounting of his arrest, while already in detention, in 1960:

> "Nelson Mandela," the officer said, "I arrest you under the powers vested in me by the Emergency Regulations." We were not to be released at all, but rearrested under the terms of what we only then discovered was a State of Emergency. Each of us in turn was released for mere seconds, and then rearrested. We had been arrested illegally before the State of Emergency; now we were being properly arrested under the State of Emergency that came into force at midnight.[2]

The effect of the state of emergency, as such, is that of rendering lawful an otherwise unlawful exercise of state power. Mandela himself implicitly acknowledges the premise of the state of emergency in describing his re-arrest as 'proper'; that is, legally mandated.

As I studied the histories and evolution of the South African and Israeli emergency laws and began to understand this as a hallmark of settler sovereignty and colonial governmentality that was certainly not unique to the north of Ireland, the global 'war on terror' had ushered in what we were told was an exceptional scenario, unprecedented in modern history. Critics of the Bush administration warned that we were witnessing the crystallisation of a potentially perpetual discharge of executive power in a manner not previously countenanced in a liberal democratic order. The amorphous war was almost immediately cast as temporally indefinite, likely to extend beyond our own lifetimes. There was seemingly ubiquitous reference to Weimar and Nazi jurist Carl Schmitt's adage that '[s]overeign is he who decides on the exception . . . He decides whether there is an extreme emergency as well as what must be done to eliminate it'.[3] After all, 'what could offer better proof of the cogency of Schmitt's central problematic than the world's most powerful

---

[2] Nelson Mandela, *The Long Walk to Freedom* (London: Abacus, 1994) 285.

[3] Carl Schmitt, *Political Theology: Four Chapters on the Concept of Sovereignty* (1922) (George Schwab trans., Cambridge, MA: MIT Press, 1985) 5, 7.

state asserting its sovereignty by declaring a state of emergency?'[4] This in turn prompted recitals of the maxim that 'the state of exception has *become* permanent and general; the exception has *become* the rule'.[5] The prevailing zeitgeist framed the idea of permanent emergency as a pioneering departure from what went before. It had become the 'new paradigm';[6] the 'new normal'.[7]

But that sense of novelty was and is misleading. This book stems in part from my frustration with such narratives of newness, animated by a sense that some of the predominant assumptions permeating contemporary legal discourse on states of emergency have been marked by a certain ahistoricism when it comes to imperialism. The book has three main aims, broadly mirrored by the three parts into which it is structured. First, it seeks to illustrate some of the particular colonial lineages that have helped shape the concept of the state of emergency, and to emphasise that contemporary formations of emergency governance are often better understood not as new or exceptional, but as part of an ongoing historical constellation of emergency politics. Second, it demonstrates the direct influence of colonial legal traditions on the normative content of contemporary international law in relation to emergency doctrine and human rights derogation provisions. Third, it appraises the continuing legacy of these colonial legal traditions through contemporary settler colonial contexts where emergency powers are deployed in a racialised fashion. With such emergency interventionism facilitated by international law's doctrine, and unsanctioned by its institutions, we are forced to reckon with fundamental questions about the nature of law and its relation to physical and structural violence.

---

[4] Mark Neocleous, 'The Problem with Normality: Taking Exception to "Permanent Emergency"' (2006) 31 *Alternatives* 191, 192.

[5] Michael Hardt and Antonio Negri, *Multitude: War and Democracy in the Age of Empire* (New York: Penguin, 2004) 7. Emphasis added.

[6] Franz Schurmann, 'Emergency Powers – The New Paradigm in Democratic America', *New California Media* 23 December 2002.

[7] Jess Whyte, 'The New Normal', *Signature*, 18 March 2005.

PART I

Traditions of the Oppressed

The tradition of the oppressed teaches us that the 'state of emergency' in which we live is not the exception but the rule.

Walter Benjamin

Walter Benjamin, 'On the Concept of History (1940)' in *Selected Writings, Vol. 4: 1938–1940* (Harry Zohn trans., Howard Eiland & Michael W. Jennings eds., Cambridge, MA: Harvard University Press, 2003) 392.

Emergency, Colonialism and Third World Approaches to International Law

It is, by now, a familiar mantra: we live in a permanent state of emergency. When the French government declared a state of national emergency in November 2015, following mass shooting and suicide bombing attacks in Paris, this was no dramatic new departure. In the larger scheme of things, it represented a continuance of established state security policy. Following the lead set by the British government over decades of habitual practice, France issued notices of derogation from its legal obligations to protect civil rights and political freedoms.[1] The mainstream human rights view suggests that such formal derogation from an international treaty sends 'a credible signal that rights restrictions are necessary and temporary, and that the government has publicly committed itself to returning to full compliance with its treaty-based pledge to respect civil and politics liberties'.[2] The rolling French derogations, however, are couched in typically vague and open-ended terms which fail to specify with any degree of precision the nature or scope of the derogation. This unveils the hollowness of those liberal legalist

---

[1] The emergency was extended and renewed by the French parliament in November 2015 (for three months), in February 2016 (for a further three months), in May 2016 (for a further three months), in July 2016 (for a further six months) and in December 2016 (for a further six months, and likely to be extended again). France submitted according notices of derogation from the European Convention on Human Rights and the International Covenant on Civil and Political Rights. Notes Verbales from the Permanent Representation of France to the Council of Europe, dated 24 November 2015, 25 February 2016, 25 May 2016, 22 July 2016 and 21 December 2016, respectively. Depository Notifications from the Permanent Representation of France to the United Nations under Article 4(3) of the International Covenant on Civil and Political Rights, dated 23 November 2015, 25 February 2016, 22 July 2016 and 21 December 2016, respectively. UN Docs. C.N.703.2015.TREATIES-IV.4 (31 December 2015), C.N.538.2016.TREATIES-IV.4 (29 July 2016), C.N.565.2016.TREATIES-IV.4 (1 August 2016), and C.N.984.2016.TREATIES-IV.4 (9 January 2017), respectively.

[2] Emilie M. Hafner-Burton, Laurence R. Helfer and Christopher J. Fariss, 'Emergency and Escape: Explaining Derogations from Human Rights Treaties' (2011) 65:4 *International Organization* 673, 681.

rationales of necessity, balance, temporariness and judicial oversight.
A French parliamentary commission of inquiry had concluded by July
2016 that the state of emergency's initial 'limited impact' on public
security had 'quickly dissipated'.[3] And yet 'France's addiction to its state
of emergency' continued.[4] For a bourgeois racial state apparatus, the
point of the emergency paradigm lies not so much in its practical efficacy
as it does in its capacity to perpetuate a sense of siege that justifies
domination of its marginalised others.

From the outset, the state of emergency in France was swiftly (and
unsurprisingly) characterised by its repressive function. Emergency
powers were mobilised to shut down street demonstrations during the
United Nations Conference on Climate Change in December 2015 and to
issue assigned residence orders against environmental activists without
charge or conviction. Coercive measures were also imposed under the
emergency to restrict the activities of groups designated as 'radical left' by
the French authorities, even where those authorities acknowledged that
the targeted groups and their members did not present any threat to
national security.[5] French administrative courts and the Council of State
rejected appeals by environmental and left-wing activists against the
unjustness of these emergency measures. The government proceeded to
cast the net of emergency powers widely enough to shut down labour
rights demonstrations, as well as to introduce drastic counter-terrorism
provisions into the permanent criminal codes.

The predominant effect of the emergency law, however, has been the
discriminatory and intimidatory persecution of Muslims in France:
'young people belonging to Arab or African minorities, particularly
Maghrebis in low-income areas and housing projects'.[6] For those subjected to the widespread and invasive house raids, searches and arrests
without warrants under the state of emergency, the 'emergency measures
follow a blindfolded strategy. They primarily target Muslims, often

---

[3] Assemblée Nationale, 'Rapport fait au nom de la commission d'enquête relative aux
moyens mis en œuvre par l'État pour lutter contre le terrorisme depuis le 7 janvier
2015', N° 3922, 5 juillet 2016.

[4] Nadim Houry, 'Breaking France's Addiction to its State of Emergency', *Open Democracy* ,
13 March 2017.

[5] Amnesty International, *Upturned Lives: The Disproportionate Impact of France's State of
Emergency*, AI Index EUR 21/3364/2016 (London: Amnesty International, 2016) 18–19.

[6] Didier Fassin, 'Short Cuts', 38:5 *London Review of Books* 23 (March 2016). Fassin
highlights the fact that the 'selective application of the state of emergency' by French
security forces is paralleled by a rise in far-right aggression against Muslims and mosques.

without any foundation.'[7] In this, and in the related French military interventions in Iraq and Syria, the echoes of empire continue to reverberate. The roots of the particular emergency legal framework mobilised by the French state in 2015 are located in Algeria in 1955,[8] and in the colonial emergency powers there which were imported back into mainland France by 1961. Arab Muslims in France were similarly the target then – of curfews and other emergency measures initially, and ultimately of the police massacre of those who defied the curfew to demonstrate in Paris on 17 October 1961.[9] In the post-colonial dynamic that has pertained since then, the continued marking out of racialised communities in France (like in Britain and elsewhere) as suspect is nothing new. Yet the narrative of newness resonates through the post-2001 language of the globalised war on terror and the repeated depictions of France's 'new normal'.[10] I invoke France here as my point of departure for the broader analysis in this book simply as the latest instance in which this 'new normal' paradigm has been projected. In thinking about what a global history of emergency rule might look like, however, the scenario of expansive emergency powers being used to stifle political movements and civil liberties is best understood more as normal, less as new.

On the Concept of History

The state of emergency, as a juridical–political form, can take on a range of different technical and ontological characteristics depending on the constitutional and epistemological tradition in which it is located. There has been much work done analysing and theorising martial law, the state of exception, emergency legislation, *l'état de siège* and other forms as they have manifested in various contexts – from Roman law doctrine to the response to the 1908 earthquake in Reggio Calabria; from the Weimar

---

[7] *Ibid.*, 7. Of 3,289 searches recorded by February 2016, only five resulted in referral to the anti-terrorism prosecutor. Commission Nationale Consultative Des Droits De l'Homme, 'Statement of Opinion on the State of Emergency', 18 February 2016, §.16.

[8] *Loi n° 55-385 du 3 avril 1955 relatif à l'état d'urgence.* The full range of France's emergency law regimes are detailed further at the beginning of Chapter 3.

[9] Jean-Paul Brunet, *Police Contre FLN: Le drame d'octobre 1961* (Paris: Flammarion, 1999); Jean-Luc Einaudi, *La bataille de Paris: 17 octobre 1961* (Paris: Seuil, 1991).

[10] Letta Tayler, 'France's Emergency Powers: The New Normal', *Human Rights Watch*, 2 August 2016; Nic Robertson, 'Europe on the Edge: The New Normal', *CNN*, 28 July 2016; Martin Reardon, 'Paris and the New Normal', *Al-Jazeera*, 14 November 2015.

Constitution in inter-war Germany to the Patriot Act in 'forever war' USA, and so on. And within this analysis come the recitals of the permanent state of emergency: the amorphous wars against non-state terrorism; the cyclical crises of global capitalism; the series of 'natural' disasters that become ever more unnatural as we continue to mangle the planet's ecology; the migrant crisis, so-called, that fortress Europe has constructed for itself. As such, Walter Benjamin's description of the state of emergency as the rule rather than the exception is as relevant today as when he wrote it more than seventy-five years ago. But with each iteration, the perpetual emergency is reincarnated as something unprecedented – as the *new* paradigm, the *new* normal – thereby giving rise to the need for new (more repressive) legal powers for the state apparatus.

This sense of newness is misplaced. Benjamin's aphorism, from his eighth thesis on the concept of history, has been cited regularly in the post-2001 homeland security context to illustrate the idea of the exception *becoming* the rule with each new crisis event. The permanent emergency is typically framed as a novel paradigm shift in which traditional normalcy/emergency lines of distinction have now become blurred. This is often done, however, without sufficient appreciation of the full ambit of Benjamin's exegesis. It is the particular experiences and struggles that constitute the *tradition of the oppressed* which teach us that the state of emergency is convention, not exception – and that the supposedly new normal is in fact part of a continuing historical constellation of emergency control mechanisms. The widespread 'amazement that the things we are experiencing are "still" possible' is not grounded in historical consciousness or philosophical thought.[11] The permanence of the emergency is revealed to us not through the prevailing situation – whether that of capitalism's Great Depression and fascism's states of exception in Benjamin's inter-war context, or the global counter-terrorism paradigm, environmental disasters and periodic fiscal crises of our early twenty-first-century context – but through the tradition of the oppressed, who have been consistently subject to emergency rule as a form of political, cultural and economic subordination. Benjamin's concept of history is history not as linear sequence of past events, but as catastrophic constellation, as ever-blowing storm that continually infuses and reconditions our present and future. In this sense, the structural nature of the state of emergency is best understood through a historical

---

[11] Benjamin, 'On the Concept of History', 392.

materialist analysis of imperial and state power as embedded racial and class rule, rather than through any reactive and reductive analysis of 'new' contemporary events. To get to the nub of emergency power, we must immerse ourselves in the ongoing history of the oppressed and the generational struggles of the downtrodden as '[t]he subject of historical knowledge'.[12]

In seeking guidance from such history and its subaltern voices, this book offers an argument for the deconstruction of emergency governance as a colonial legal technique that has been absorbed into the lexicon of international law. It aims to make a contribution to the struggle against normalised emergency repression by recuperating scripts of resistance from traditions of the oppressed. The book sets out to situate emergency doctrine – as it applies across the institutional and constitutional planes of international relations, national security and political economy through to the more mundane registers of material existence – in colonial historical context, and to highlight the particular relevance of this for international law and for still-evolving settler colonial environments. I seek to show that emergency law has been (and remains) deeply implicated in settler coloniality and related processes of occupation, dispossession and discrimination. The precedent of concerted emergency rule under European colonialism demonstrates, in this context, a certain historical myopia within those assumptions and narratives of novelty that have permeated early twenty-first-century debates. In probing the nature of the relationship between imperialism, race and emergency legal regimes, however, the story told here does not purport to speak definitively to every aspect of the state of emergency. No account of such a pervasive doctrine and multifarious practice can reasonably claim to do so. Emergency doctrine, that 'mixture of history, politics and emotion',[13] cannot be reduced to any single lineage or linear narrative. The contribution of this book will be to expound on particular colonial constellations in the historiography of the state of emergency, to drill down into its constitutive racial components and to highlight it as a widespread and normalised, often banal, experience.[14]

---

[12] *Ibid.*, 394.

[13] Joseph B. Kelly and George A. Pelletier, 'Theories of Emergency Government' (1966) 11 *South Dakota Law Review* 42.

[14] This is not to argue that the colonial template and legacy is all-encompassing. Contemporary power is increasingly diffuse, extending beyond state forms and manifesting in new modes of hegemony and dominance, even while much of its traditional apparatus remains present.

On Perpetual Emergency

With the attacks of 11 September 2001 and the ensuing onset of an expanded and globalised 'war on terror', the world was ushered into what was painted as an unprecedented scenario in modern history. Against that backdrop, South African writer J.M. Coetzee reflected on the political nature of his early novels, in particular the extent to which his depiction in *Waiting for the Barbarians* of 'the Empire' and its state of emergency was rooted in the actual security policies of the apartheid regime in the 1970s. He recalled that the apartheid police could raid, arrest and detain at will. They were indemnified from legal recourse through the provisions of enabling emergency and security legislation: 'All of this and much more, in apartheid South Africa, was done in the name of a struggle against terror. I used to think that the people who created these laws that effectively suspended the rule of law were moral barbarians. Now I know they were just pioneers, ahead of their time.'[15]

One's place in the sequence of history as linear time is always relative, however. Apartheid South Africa's emergency laws may have appeared ahead of their time when considered in the shadow of the post-2001 security legislation to which Coetzee refers. But they were concurrent to similar special powers deployed by the British government in the north of Ireland, to Israel's consolidation of emergency measures in Palestine, and to the Pinochet regime's use of state of emergency mechanisms to wage free-market war on Chile's social structures. And those measures were themselves following in the footsteps of a larger series of continuities and correlations, particularly in colonial legal systems. By the late 1990s, some one hundred countries had been under a state of emergency in the preceding decade, encompassing three-quarters of the earth's surface.[16] From the perspective of some critical Third World international lawyers, the impact of this is all too concrete: 'emergencies, both conceptually and practically, have prevented the realization of basic human rights to millions of people in countries around the world.'[17] It also belies the diagnoses of the state of emergency as an unprecedented new paradigm attached to 'counter-terrorism' and security discourses *after* 2001. Emergency powers were universal and endemic, a standard

---

[15] J.M. Coetzee, *Diary of a Bad Year* (London: Harvill Secker, 2007) 171.

[16] 'The Administration of Justice and the Human Rights of Detainees: Question of Human Rights and States of Emergency', Report of Special Rapporteur Leandro Despouy, UN Doc. E/CN.4/Sub.2/1997/19, 23 June 1997, 44, paras. 180–181.

[17] Balakrishnan Rajagopal, *International Law from Below: Development, Social Movements and Third World Resistance* (Cambridge: Cambridge University Press, 2003) 177.

instrument of coercion and control, well before 2001. When it comes to international legal regulation of emergencies, the sceptical view is that states typically 'do not hew to the oversight mechanisms demanded by human rights treaties'; they invoke emergency powers, but in a manner of 'disguised emergency'.[18] Emergency doctrine and the language of crisis have been purposefully deployed by the security state to whittle away civil rights protections, to shrink the space for political dissent and to erode anti-discrimination norms.[19]

By grounding the thinking and theorising of emergency, exception and necessity in social and historical context, therefore, we begin to understand emergencies as wide-ranging, dynamic, managed and layered processes that unfold and evolve over time, rather than as sudden and short-lived anomalous moments. In models of emergency that demonstrate the normalisation of special powers over time through ongoing and proliferating lawmaking processes – as opposed to sporadic sovereign suspensions of law – we come to see the 'prosaic politics of emergency' and the 'banality of emergency'.[20] State and imperial violence is not exceptional. It is simply an expression of the association between sovereign power and its discourses of security, rooted in the claimed monopoly on legitimate violence. In the colonial arena, the function of the state of emergency was to maintain the legitimacy and legality of that violence where it was intensified, and to frame the grievances of anti-colonial resistance as irrational and illegitimate violence. Emergency powers were not only about detention and curfews; their socio-economic function is revealed through complicity in dispossession and (settler) colonial sovereignty: the alienation and expropriation of land that was initiated by conquest was in many instances continued and consolidated by (often banal)

---

[18] Fionnuala Ní Aoláin, 'The Cloak and Dagger Game of Derogation', in Evan Criddle (ed.), *Human Rights in Emergencies* (Cambridge: Cambridge University Press, 2016).

[19] Benjamin Authers and Hilary Charlesworth, 'The Crisis and the Quotidian in International Human Rights Law' (2014) 44 *Netherlands Yearbook of International Law* 19, 30.

[20] Leonard C. Feldman, 'The Banality of Emergency: On the Time and Space of "Political Necessity"' in Austin Sarat (ed.), *Sovereignty, Emergency, Legality* (Cambridge: Cambridge University Press, 2010) 138. This terminology, of course, borrows from Hannah Arendt's *Eichmann in Jerusalem: A Report on the Banality of Evil* (New York: Viking, 1963). Arendt's theory of the nature of totalitarian government and her description of individual 'cogs' in the administrative machinery of bureaucratised violence remain prescient. In a similar vein to the idea of the banality of emergency, Didier Fassin refers to 'petty states of exception' in the context of the policing of the urban poor in the French banlieues. Such petty states of exception are 'more numerous but also more threatening for democracies than is the grand state of exception in its Schmittian or Agambenian definition.' Didier Fassin, 'Petty States of Exception: Contemporary Policing of the Urban Poor', in Mark Maguire et al (eds.), *The Anthropology of Security* (London: Pluto, 2014) 104, 116.

emergency measures. Colonial sovereignty and emergency governance
are connected in a blueprint for implementing control over land and
resources, for disciplining labour and for discharging power over native
body and life itself. On this basis, and borrowing from Patrick Wolfe's
canonical explication of the structural nature of invasion and settler
colonialism,[21] I suggest that the state of emergency is similarly better
understood as structure rather than as event.

The underlying rationale for emergency doctrine as it has unfolded –
through population management and control, premised on a 'symbiosis
between law and the violence employed to maintain its authority'[22] – tends
to get lost in much of the contemporary debates, however. Substantial
analysis has revolved around the nature of the emergency's relationship
with the rule of law and the juridical order; the degree to which a state of
emergency involves a suspension or abandonment of 'normal' law. The
extent to which extraordinary powers should be allowed for in law, or
proscribed by law, remains a point of friction. Do such powers compromise the integrity of law by crossing a legal rubicon of sorts, or, conversely,
do they operate to uphold the very system of law itself? These questions
raise broader issues as to the epistemology of legal form and how the
protagonists of the rule of law/emergency debates read 'law' in often very
different ways. The notion of sovereignty on both the international and
constitutional law planes is also implicated, with Antony Anghie noting
that the 'enduring and perhaps unresolvable problem arises from the
paradox that the sovereign is both within and outside the law'.[23]

A historiography of emergency powers reveals their inscription over
time into law. British colonial emergency measures, in particular, were
marked by an emphasis on legalism that only deepened over the course
of the imperial project: the early export of martial law to the plantations;
the legislative codification of emergency powers in the nineteenth-
century colonies; the default declaration of states of emergency around
the empire in the 1940s and 1950s in a bid not to end, not to die, to
prolong its era. Colonial emergency doctrine lives on through its

---

[21] Patrick Wolfe, *Settler Colonialism and the Transformation of Anthropology: The Politics and Poetics of an Ethnographic Event* (London: Cassell, 1999) 2–3.

[22] A.W.B. Simpson, 'General Editor's Preface' to R.W. Kostal, *A Jurisprudence of Power: Victorian Empire and the Rule of Law* (Oxford: Oxford University Press, 2005), vii.

[23] Antony Anghie, 'Rethinking Sovereignty in International Law' (2009) 5 *Annual Review of Law and Social Science* 291, 306. This paradox of sovereignty reflects the problematic of international law writ large: how the law-creating sovereign can be compelled by that same law, or can extricate itself from its reach.

incorporation into the international legal corpus through various derogation regimes. The 'legitimating project of Western legality and its
strained application to colonial exigencies'[24] can be seen as part of a
totalising complex, in which emergency powers are not merely episodic
and exceptional, but themselves form part of the legal order. In reflecting
on how we have arrived at the point where the language, logic and
process of emergency are so embedded, therefore, I explore how emergency doctrine – as it is now understood – crystallised within colonial
legal systems from the early nineteenth century onwards. Its enduring
implications are substantiated by the continuities and mimicries we see
in various 'post-colonial'[25] forms, including within liberal international
legal projects. International human rights law now offers an ostensible
non-discrimination rhetoric when it comes to states of emergency. While
exemptions from certain rights are facilitated by international law in
contexts of self-declared public emergencies, derogation measures should
'not involve discrimination solely on the ground of race, sex, language,
religion or social origin'.[26] Lived experiences and state practice, by
contrast, show that emergency measures and race often continue to
remain intimately entwined.

   The policy of retaining emergency measures in a 'post-emergency'
context also remains a regular feature of the national security legal
landscape. I will show later in the book how this was done in the final
pre-independence years in Kenya, and how this process is currently
underway in Palestine and Australia. In his reading of the proliferation
of British anti-terrorism legislation enacted since the late 1990s, Nasser
Hussain describes a structural shift in the law away from traditional
conceptions of emergency powers as reactive and temporary, towards
an understanding of securitisation and security law as part of a larger,
permanent 'methodology of governance'.[27] Hussain emphasises certain
mechanisms – the increasing use of (racialised) classifications of persons
in the law, the emergence of intensely bureaucratic and administrative

---

[24] Nasser Hussain, *The Jurisprudence of Emergency: Colonialism and the Rule of Law* (Ann
   Arbor: University of Michigan Press, 2003) 135.
[25] This terminology is adopted with reservation, wary of the over-simplification inherent in
   the implied temporal break from the colonial, discussed further below. 'Post-colonial' is
   used here in general terms to denote the period after the end of formal European rule in
   colonised territories. 'Postcolonial', by contrast, will be used in reference to postcolonial
   theory and related intellectual movements and scholarship.
[26] Article 4(1), International Covenant on Civil and Political Rights.
[27] Nasser Hussain, 'Hyperlegality' (2007) 10 *New Criminal Law Review* 514, 515.

facets of emergency law, the use of special tribunals and commissions – that contribute to 'hyperlegality' at work.[28] This hyperlegality typifies the contemporary security state and its 'multiplication of laws and legal categories'.[29] Related to this is the militarisation of policing and the seepage of armed conflict categorisations into domestic legal contexts via the counter-terrorism paradigm. Judith Butler shows that, in settings from Gaza to Ferguson, where the category of civilian is eviscerated and if civilians 'are now recast as security risks, or threats, or if their bodies are understood as weaponised, the sphere of civic protection is displaced by the protocols of war'.[30] Measures conceived and deployed in a war-time context are absorbed into domestic law enforcement. The policing of black lives, as well as the management of borders and economies, becomes militarised. Heightened security powers are normalised, urban police forces are kitted out in full riot gear with military-grade weapons, constitutional protections are abrogated and the legal regime systematic-ally endeavours to retract the rights it is ostensibly obligated to defend.[31] Through all of this we can trace a process whereby emergency/military doctrines which developed in colonial/conflict contexts to control native/ enemy bodies are written into international law and ultimately univer-salised and localised as acceptable.

On the Spectre of Colonialism

The question of whether, and in what ways, colonial history is germane to contemporary international political and legal debates remains a point of contestation.[32] For many, colonialism is an anomaly of the past, now corrected by processes of universalism and of no further relevance as a conceptual category. Brad Roth, for example, describes colonialism as a 'legal aberration' and argues that critiquing contemporary norms as

---

[28] *Ibid.*

[29] David Lloyd, 'Settler Colonialism and the State of Israel: The Example of Palestine/Israel' (2012) 2:1 *Settler Colonial Studies* 59, 75.

[30] Judith Butler, 'Human Shields' (2015) 3:2 *London Review of International Law* 223, 238.

[31] *Ibid.*, 239.

[32] Anne Orford, 'The Past as Law or History? The Relevance of Imperialism for Modern International Law' in Emmanuelle Jouannet, Hélène Ruiz-Fabri and Mark Toufayan (eds.), *Droit international et nouvelles approches sure le tiers-monde: entre répétition et renouveau* (Paris: Société de Législation Comparée, 2013) 97–118.

reflective of patterns of Western domination is redundant.[33] In contrast, Third World scholars show such a position to be analytically naïve and politically bankrupt. Reflecting on Frantz Fanon's view of imperial history as ineluctably connected with violence, Anghie concludes that it is 'crucial to argue that imperialism has *always* governed international relations, rather than seeing imperialism as having ended with formal decolonization'.[34] The stakes here are high, given the extent to which the modern Western state and the contemporary international order have pinned their legitimacy on a democratic and universal rupture from historic patterns of domination and exclusion. Such a rupture is, in many regards, a fiction. In the legal domain, the influence of imperialism continues to percolate: from securitisation and military intervention to migration, development and the environment; from the structural biases built into international trade and investment law for the benefit of the global North to the ongoing use of colonial-era laws as mechanisms of repression within the global South.

When it comes to emergency law specifically, contemporary reality cannot be viewed in isolation from colonial history. While analogous doctrines may be traced back to pre-modern times, the doctrine of emergency assumed a position of such centrality to governance in the British empire, in particular, as to be unavoidable. It has been avoided and absent, however, in much of the legal scholarship on the state of emergency.[35] Hussain is a notable exception here, providing a compelling account of the jurisprudence of martial law and the state of emergency in British India which demonstrates the role of the emergency legal form at the heart of colonial policy.[36] This brings to mind Fanon's rebuttal of any perceptions of French exceptionalism in Algeria, in which he showed that the violence of French militarism in the empire was by no means anomalous; it was structural and systemic. Emergency powers, far from

---

[33] Brad Roth, 'Governmental Illegitimacy and Neocolonialism: Response to Review by James Thuo Gathii' (2000) 98 *Michigan Law Review* 2056, 2065.

[34] Antony Anghie, *Imperialism, Sovereignty and the Making of International Law* (Cambridge: Cambridge University Press, 2005) 309. Emphasis in original.

[35] Some important critical works notwithstanding, which I will draw on in the chapters that follow. See, for example, Hussain, *The Jurisprudence of Emergency*; Kostal, *A Jurisprudence of Power*; A.W.B. Simpson, *Human Rights and the End of Empire: Britain and the Genesis of the European Convention* (Oxford: Oxford University Press, 2001). For a survey of related historical scholarship on the nature of colonial legal governance, see, for example, Lauren Benton, 'Constitutions and Empires' (2006) 31 *Law & Social Inquiry* 177.

[36] Hussain, *The Jurisprudence of Emergency*.

being deviant aberrations from a liberal norm, are 'generalized' as part of a 'pattern of police domination, of systematic racism, of dehumanization rationally pursued'; apparently 'monstrous practices' implemented under the state of emergency, such as torture, are 'inherent in the whole colonialist configuration'.[37] Third World international lawyers develop this line of analysis in showing how emergency doctrine was bound up in 'the racist ideology of colonialism and the pragmatic need to discredit Third World resistance'; a fear of mass anti-colonial movements, in this regard, 'served as the central reason for the imposition of emergencies in the colonies'.[38]

The appropriateness of the 'colonial' and 'post-colonial' frames will continue to be contested, while many more emergency situations are not easily bracketed as one or the other. Israel, in a declared state of emergency since its inception in 1948, is a case in point: it is at once a post-colonial territory and a colonising state, characterised by some as a 'post-colonial colony'.[39] Racialised emergencies in settler colonial societies – whether in Alabama,[40] apartheid South Africa,[41] or Australia[42] – often do not fit neatly within the temporal assumptions of the post-colonial. Settler colonialism is of course a persistent and persisting structure. The place of Italy's declared 'nomad emergency'[43] on the spectrum of coloniality is also ambiguous: a European state formed in the nineteenth century deploying emergency laws in the twenty-first century to control an ethnic group present in the

---

[37] Frantz Fanon, 'Algeria Face to Face with the French Torturers' in Frantz Fanon, *Toward the African Revolution: Political Essays* (Haakon Chevalier trans., New York: Grove Press, 1970) 64 (published originally in French in *El Moudjahid*, N° 10, September 1957).

[38] Rajagopal, *International Law from Below*, 179.

[39] See, for example, Joseph Massad, 'The Post-Colonial Colony: Time, Space, and Bodies in Palestine/Israel' in Fawzia Afzal-Khan and Kalpana Seshadri-Crooks (eds.), *The Pre-occupation of Postcolonial Studies* (London: Duke University Press, 2000) 311–346.

[40] Patrick O. Gudridge, 'Emergency, Legality, Sovereignty: Birmingham, 1963' in Sarat (ed.), *Sovereignty, Emergency, Legality*, 72–119.

[41] On apartheid's emergency laws, see, for example, Gilbert Marcus, 'Civil Liberties Under Emergency Rule' in John Dugard, Nicholas Haysom and Gilbert Marcus (eds.), *The Last Years of Apartheid: Civil Liberties in South Africa* (New York: Foreign Policy Association, 1992) 32–54.

[42] Northern Territory National Emergency Response Act 2007, No. 129 of 2007; Deirdre Howard-Wagner, 'From Denial to Emergency: Governing Indigenous Communities in Australia' in Didier Fassin and Mariella Pandolfi (eds.), *Contemporary States of Emergency: The Politics of Military and Humanitarian Interventions* (New York: Zone Books, 2010).

[43] Nando Sigona, 'The Governance of Romani People in Italy: Discourse, Policy and Practice' (2011) 16:5 *Journal of Modern Italian Studies* 590; Amnesty International, *Italy: 'Zero Tolerance for Roma'* (London: Amnesty International, 2011) 10–23.

territory since the fourteenth century. Likewise Britain's protracted jurisprudence of emergency in its annexed colony in the north of Ireland. The
international state of emergency underlying the global 'war on terror' is
infused with many of the hallmarks of colonial relations in a purportedly
post-colonial world, and thus also sits uneasily between these parameters.
This gives rise to definitional questions around the concpetual and material
paradigms in which states of emergency are performed.

Much work has been done theorising and problematising the complex
and contested categories of the 'colonial' and the 'post-colonial', as well as
derivatives represented by the 'neo-colonial', the 'auto-colonial', the 'self-
colonial' and so on.[44] The concomitant ruptures and continuities inherent
in the overlap between such categories are captured well by Gayatri Spivak's
pronouncement that '[w]e live in a post-colonial neo-colonized world'.[45]
Postcolonial theory has long been occupied by the politics of syntax,
periodisation and categorisation. If the structural conditions created by
colonialism continue to dispossess and marginalise colonised peoples –
whether Indigenous communities in settler colonial societies or independent post-colonies on the global periphery – what does this imply for
assumptions that an identifiable endpoint has been passed, that we are
'post' colonialism? From whose perspective has colonialism ended? What is
implied by the reduction of non-European traditions in all of their diversity
to a generic 'pre-colonial' history? How do the coloniality of relations
between nations and the resultant race thinking intersect with other forms
of social relations – class, gender, religion – to produce a particular analysis
of power? Whilst these important questions will continue to be revisited,
what is important to note here is that across a diversity of temporal and
territorial spaces, whether framed in colonial, post-colonial, or neo-colonial
paradigms, the embedded dynamics of racialised power structures and
value systems persistently underpin states of emergency, even where overt
articulations and invocations of race have dissipated. Where 'direct colonialism has largely ended', as Edward Said puts it, imperialism 'lingers where
it has always been, in a kind of general cultural sphere as well as in specific
political, ideological, economic and social practices'.[46]

---

[44] See, for example, Aijaz Ahmad, 'Postcolonialism: What's in a Name' in Roman de la
Campa, E. Ann Kaplan and Michael Sprinker (eds.), *Late Imperial Culture* (London:
Verso, 1995).

[45] Gayatri Spivak, *The Post-Colonial Critic: Interviews, Strategies, Dialogues* (Sarah Harasym
ed. London: Routledge, 1990) 166.

[46] Edward W. Said, *Culture & Imperialism* (New York: Vintage, 1993) 9.

With this in mind, the manifestations of emergency doctrine in the context of hegemonic control systems can be contextualised in related and often overlapping paradigms that constitute the colonial constellation. The foundational paradigm is *the colonial past*, relating to emergency laws and powers implemented in a situation of direct colonial rule in European empires. The reverberations continue, however, through *the colonial present*, relating to emergency legal regimes that are inextricably linked to the ideology and architecture of ongoing settler colonisation processes. Emergency doctrine has also evolved in the wider geopolitical context of *the imperial present*, relating to state of emergency discourse as it pertains to global counter-terrorism policy and international political economy dynamics. In addition, evoking Spivak's paradigm of *the post-colonial neo-colonial present*, we can locate the continuities, reproductions and transplantations of colonial emergency rule within the legal and policy frameworks of former colonies and metropoles, as well as of settler colonial societies. In examining states of emergency across this broad colonial constellation, the overarching conceptual approach and sensibility that frames this book is that of Third World Approaches to International Law (TWAIL).

On Theory and Method: Third World Approaches

The form and content of what I refer to broadly as emergency modalities[47] may vary substantially across the categories and chronologies of coloniality that I have broadly demarcated above, but certain common elements can be identified running through the historical continuum, along an axis of conquest and control. The impact of racialised emergency rule is felt most intensely, of course, by its others: the colonised native, the suspect community, the Indigenous people; oppressed minorities and wretched majorities of the earth who remain peripheral to the exploitation of land and resources and to flows of transnational capital. In historical terms, many of these constituencies can be seen as emanating in different forms from beneath the extended

---

[47] With this, my intention is to capture the diversity of forms that emergency takes in different settings, encompassing various types of laws and legal constructs (statutory legislative acts, constitutional provisions, court decisions, executive decrees, military orders, emergency powers, martial law, derogations) and the institutions charged with implementation or oversight of same (special courts, military tribunals, emergency administrative bodies, international monitoring bodies).

banner of the 'Third World'. Following the lead of anti-colonial and postcolonial scholars, I understand the Third World not in the sense of a place or fixed demographic, but a project – an anti-imperial and anti-racist project; a social and political consciousness that bands together a diversity of actors through their common marginalisation by the particularities of global North hegemony.[48] This project encompasses a liberation struggle against colonial governance, and a class struggle against the structures of neoliberal globalisation, widely articulated now through the concept of the 'global South'.[49]

The nomenclature of the Third World (as well as that of the global South) is as susceptible to contestation as any label that purports to encompass and unify the heterogeneity of peoples that, in the global vista, account for 'most of the world'.[50] Given its Cold War origin as a modern 'Third Estate' of sorts, peripheral to the dominant industrialised worlds of a bipolar North,[51] the concept of the Third World is subject to critique as anachronistic and obsolete. In this critique, it does not reflect contemporary geographic distributions of subaltern populations or the complicity of the elites of the South in all of the exploitation and inequality that the current international political and economic order entails. The Third World, it is argued, is but 'a tattered remnant of another time'.[52] For some, it fails to adequately speak to the place in

[48] See, for example, Frantz Fanon, *The Wretched of the Earth* (1961) (Constance Farrington trans., London: Penguin, 1967); Vijay Prashad, *The Darker Nations: A People's History of the Third World* (New York: New Press, 2007). For an alternative take, and penetrating discussion of Third-Worldist ideology in relation to capitalism and socialism, Western media cultivation of 'Three Worlds Theory', and the contradictions of 'non-alignment', see Aijaz Ahmad, *In Theory: Classes, Nations, Literatures* (London: Verso, 1992) 287–318.

[49] Vijay Prashad, *The Poorer Nations: A Possible History of the Global South* (London: Verso, 2012).

[50] Partha Chatterjee, *The Politics of the Governed: Reflections on Popular Politics in Most of the World* (New York: Columbia University Press, 2004).

[51] The term 'Third World', *le tiers-monde*, originates in the writing of French anti-colonial intellectuals. See Alfred Sauvy, 'Trois Mondes, Une Planète', 118 *L'Observateur*, 14 August 1952; Georges Balandier (ed.), *Le Tiers-Monde: Sous-développement et développement* (Paris: Presses Universitaires de France, 1961).

[52] R.B.J. Walker, 'Space/Time/Sovereignty' in Mark E. Denham and Mark Owen Lombardi (eds.), *Perspectives on Third World Sovereignty: The Postmodern Paradox* (London: Macmillan, 1996) 15. It bears noting here that 'Third World' also acquired a pejorative connotation in Western media and political discourse, used as a synonym for poverty, disease, corruption and uncivilised barbarity. Such deprecatory usage remains common in right-wing and reactionary rhetoric in the West. See, for example, Patrick J. Buchanan, *State of Emergency: The Third World Invasion and Conquest of America* (New York: Thomas Dunne, 2006).

contemporary world systems of the former Soviet sphere (sometimes designated as the Second World), or does not fully account for the plight of Indigenous peoples within the global North or South (the Fourth World). These are valid concerns. Contemporary understandings of 'Worlds designated as Third'[53] may also be imagined in a more plural and inclusive conceptual sense, however, signifying not just the former colonial territories – historically bound together and defined (by Eurocentric visions) as uncivilised spaces ripe for conquest, exploitation and 'development' – but all communities on the receiving end of the political, economic and cultural impacts of imperial relations. The Third World project, by that or any other name, remains concerned with inequalities primarily between North and South, but increasingly also within North and South[54]:

> Unnecessary importance is often attached to the end of the cold war. The growing north-south divide is sufficient evidence, if any were needed, of the continuing relevance of the category 'third world'. Its continuing usefulness lies in pointing to certain structural constraints that the world economy imposes on one set of countries as opposed to others. ... However, the presence or absence of the third world, it is worth stressing, is not something that is either to be dogmatically affirmed or completely denied. It is not to be viewed as an either/or choice in all contexts. The category 'third world' can coexist with a plurality of practices of collective resistance. Thus, regional and other group identities do not necessarily undermine aggregation at the global level. These can coexist with transregional groupings and identities. In the final analysis, the category 'third world' reflects a level of unity imagined and constituted in ways which would enable resistance to a range of practices which systematically disadvantage and subordinate an otherwise diverse group of people.[55]

---

[53] Vanja Hamzić, 'Mir-Said Sultan-Galiev and the Idea of Muslim Marxism: Empire, Third World(s) and Praxis' (2016) 37:11 *Third World Quarterly* 2047.

[54] For an expansive theorising of the lived history of the South encompassing the experiences of Indigenous peoples in North America, for example, see Amar Bhatia, 'The South of the North: Building on Critical Approaches to International Law with Lessons from the Fourth World' (2012) 14 *Oregon Review of International Law* 131. For a brief reflection on this theme in the context of the Canadian Truth and Reconciliation Commission's 2015 finding that the state of Canada engaged in systematic cultural genocide against its Indigenous populations, see Asad Kiyani, John Reynolds and Sujith Xavier, 'Symposium Foreword: Third World Approaches to International Criminal Law' (2016) 14:4 *Journal of International Criminal Justice* 915.

[55] B.S. Chimni, 'Third World Approaches to International Law: A Manifesto' (2006) 8 *International Community Law Review* 3, 4–6. See also Sundhya Pahuja's 'A Note on the Use of "Third World"', in Sundhya Pahuja, *Decolonising International Law: Development, Economic Growth and the Politics of Universality* (Cambridge University Press, 2011) 261.

Chimni emphasises the importance of distinguishing between the political concept of the Third World and the ruling elites of former colonised nations that have bought into prevailing rules of global governance and transnational capital. Given those elites' neglect of the welfare of the peoples of the South and their failure to address the class and gender divides that fester within, there is 'an obvious dialectic between struggles inside third world countries and in external fora'.[56] With creeping 'peripheralisation of the centre'[57] taking an increasing hold in certain quarters, and a sense that 'all nations now face political, social, and economic challenges once typical of the Third World',[58] the Third World analytic frame is arguably more, not less, relevant. For Eyal Weizman, '[g]lobalization takes the periphery straight to the center, the frontier between the First and Third worlds starts running through the middle of world cities'.[59] This implies the enduring importance of a consciousness of the experiences, struggles and traditions of the oppressed of the Third World. This is a crucial component of any attempt to historicise (from a global perspective) the doctrine of emergency, and to deconstruct its coloniality. As Karen Mickelson puts it, '[t]he "Third World" terminology itself may appear out-of-date, but its very contingency, involving an insistence on history and continuity, may in fact be one of its strengths.'[60]

In the field of international law, emphasis on this notion of the Third World, whether understood in purely historical context or as a conceptual frame of ongoing relevance, opens up the horizon of TWAIL:

> The Third World is a political reality . . . a stream of historical experiences across virtually all non-European societies that has given rise to a particular voice, a form of intellectual and political consciousness. Although there is wide diversity among Third World societies, the term is historicized as part of a strategic paradigm for resistance and liberation. The

---

[56] Chimni, 'Third World Approaches to International Law: A Manifesto', 7.

[57] John Reynolds, 'Peripheral Parallels?: Europe's Edges and the World of Bandung' in Luis Eslava, Michael Fakhri and Vasuki Nesiah (eds.), *Bandung, the Global South, and International Law: Critical Pasts and Pending Futures* (Cambridge: Cambridge University Press, 2017).

[58] David Kennedy, 'Law and the Political Economy of the World' (2013) 26 *Leiden Journal of International Law* 7, 10.

[59] Eyal Weizman, 'Military Options as Human Planning', interview with Philipp Misselwitz in Eduardo Cadava and Aaron Levy (eds.), *Cities without Citizens* (Philadelphia, PA: Slought Books, 2003) 195.

[60] Karin Mickelson, 'Rhetoric and Rage: Third World Voices in International Legal Discourse' (1998) 16 *Wisconsin International Law Journal* 360.

"Third World" must therefore be understood as a direct attack on the
Western hegemony of the globe. TWAIL is the expression of this confrontation in the discipline, theory, and practice of international law.[61]

Best understood as a political grouping of loosely affiliated international
legal scholars, TWAIL can be seen in its broad construction as encompassing both theoretical and methodological dimensions. Offering a
materialist and postcolonial critique of international law as well as
important contributions to the science of method in international legal
studies (if not a systematic methodology itself), it is an academic school
with an activist bent that coheres around a broadly unifying set of ideas.[62]
TWAIL comprises an engaged community of intellectuals seeking to
flesh out a radical epistemology capable of liberating international law
from its imperial and elitist shackles.[63] This approach to legal scholarship
is marked by a commonality of convictions revolving around certain core
tenets: that international law is deeply rooted in the political, cultural and
economic backdrop of the European imperial project, and that colonial
patterns persist within the structures, institutions and norms of international law. As such, colonial legal concepts are not only crucial to
understanding the past evolutions of international law, but have retained
a formative role in contemporary international law. Subordination of the
periphery by imperial centres has been facilitated by the law itself. The
primary thrust of TWAIL is to understand and deconstruct the role of
international law in creating and perpetuating racialised hierarchies and
structural material inequalities. TWAIL then attempts to construct and
present alternative conceptions and structures of international legal
governance that unsettle festering colonial power dynamics and give
shape to transformative and liberationist tactics within the architecture
of international law.[64] As a movement of scholars, TWAIL is open about
this normative purpose and emancipatory agenda.

TWAIL scholarship has thus endeavoured to identify areas where
such racial and material hierarchies remain – buttressed by supposedly

---

[61] Makau Mutua, 'What is TWAIL?' (2000) 94 *American Society of International Law Proceedings* 31, 35–36.
[62] For related discussion, see Obiora Chinedu Okafor, 'Critical Third World Approaches to International Law (TWAIL): Theory, Methodology, or Both?' (2008) 10 *International Community Law Review* 371, 376–378.
[63] Richard Falk, 'Foreword: Third World Approaches to International Law (TWAIL) Special Issue' (2016) 37:11 *Third World Quarterly* 1943, 1944.
[64] Mutua, 'What is TWAIL?', 31.

anodyne international legal norms and institutions[65] – and to amplify historically silenced Third World vocals in international debate. Leading TWAIL voices in this regard identify two distinct generations of Third World international law scholarship, very much informed by the prevailing geopolitical context.[66] The first generation of Third World jurists and scholars emerged as African and Asian nations rode the wave of decolonisation into the arenas of international law and international relations from the 1950s to 1970s.[67] Their intention was to reform and reconstruct the existing order of classic international law, famously described in this context by Algerian diplomat and jurist Mohammed Bedjaoui as 'a set of rules with a geographical bias (it was a European law), a religious-ethical inspiration (it was a Christian law), an economic motivation (it was a mercantilist law) and political aims (it was an imperialist law)'.[68] Third World scholars began to challenge the parochial and celebratory historical narrative of international law as written by their Western counterparts. Their own narrative, by contrast, evoked a counter-hegemonic critique of the system, with a radical transformation agenda. Now that the decolonised states had a voice and vote in the United Nations General Assembly, it was hoped that a more democratic

---

[65]   Antony Anghie, 'What is TWAIL: Comment' (2000) 94 *American Society of International Law Proceedings* 39.

[66]   Antony Anghie and B.S. Chimni, 'Third World Approaches to International Law and Individual Responsibility in Internal Conflicts' (2003) 2 *Chinese Journal of International Law* 77. For a thoughtful critique of this generational 'splitting' of TWAIL scholarship, see George Galindo, 'Splitting TWAIL' (2016) 33:3 *Windsor Yearbook of Access to Justice* 39.

[67]   Foundational texts include: J.J.G. Syatauw, *Some Newly Established Asian States and the Development of International Law* (The Hague: Martinus Nijhoff, 1961); S.P. Sinha, *New Nations and the Law of Nations* (Leiden: Martinus Nijhoff, 1967); M.T. Al-Ghunaimi, *The Muslim Conception of International Law and the Western Approach* (The Hague: Martinus Nijhoff, 1968); R.P. Anand, *New States and International Law* (Delhi: Vikas, 1972); T.O. Elias, *Africa and the Development of International Law* (Leiden: Sijthoff, 1972); T.O. Elias, *New Horizons in International Law* (Leiden: Sijthoff, 1979); U.O. Umozurike, *International Law and Colonialism in Africa* (Enugu: Nwamife, 1979). From the early years of Third World engagement in critical international legal scholarship, some European scholars transcended the geographical divide and made pioneering contributions. See, for example, C.H. Alexandrowicz, *An Introduction to the History of the Law of Nations in the East Indies (16th, 17th and 18th Centuries)* (Oxford: Clarendon Press, 1967).

[68]   Mohammed Bedjaoui, 'Poverty of the International Order' in Richard Falk, Friedrich Kratochwil and Saul H. Mendlowitz (eds.), *International Law: A Contemporary Perspective* (Boulder: Westview Press, 1985) 153. Bedjaoui served on the bench of the International Court of Justice from 1982 to 2001.

international legal order could be attained so as to redress the imbalance and exclusion that had long underwritten North–South relations. Emphasis was placed on the fact that pre-colonial societies were neither strangers nor averse to the idea of international law.[69] The exploitative and disempowering hierarchies that had crystallised with the joining of international law to the hip of the European colonial project were to be abrogated by harnessing the transformative potential of international law to take into account the needs and aspirations of the peoples of the newly independent states and to advance their political and economic agendas. The aim was thus not simply to repudiate the existing international legal order but to produce a truly universal and participatory international law. Attempts were made 'to formulate a new approach to sources doctrine by arguing that General Assembly resolutions passed by vast majorities had some binding legal effect'.[70] Structural reform of the global economy – the crucial accompaniment to political independence – was envisioned in the form of a New International Economic Order.[71]

---

[69] Citing their predecessors' identification of the common adherence to forms of international law among ostensibly very different societies, Anghie and Chimni refer us to the fact that 'non-European societies had developed sophisticated rules relating, for example, to the law of treaties and the laws of war'. Anghie and Chimni, 'Third World Approaches to International Law and Individual Responsibility', 80. Alexandrowicz's study of the law of nations in the East Indies, for example, informs such challenges to the idea that the non-Western world was unfamiliar with international legal practices in the pre-colonial era. Alexandrowicz, *An Introduction to the History of the Law of Nations*. Chimni also cites, by way of example, Judge Weeramantry's opinion in the *Nuclear Weapons* case at the International Court of Justice detailing the presence of international legal norms and humanitarian laws in non-Western systems, as well as Judge Ammoun's references in the *Barcelona Traction* case to the importance of common ideals of prosperity and peace (rather than protection of the economic activities of industrialised powers) as the primary objective of a universal international law. B.S. Chimni, 'The Past, Present and Future of International Law: A Critical Third World Approach' (2007) 7 *Melbourne Journal of International Law* 499, 501. The pitfalls inherent in such arguments – of falling into the trap of reproducing Eurocentric versions of what international law is, 'in the vein of "they, too, had an international law" and thus of feeding the West's universalising discourses' – are highlighted in Martti Koskenniemi, 'Histories of International Law: Dealing with Eurocentrism' (2011) 19 *Rechtsgeschicte* 152, 168.

[70] Anghie and Chimni, 'Third World Approaches to International Law and Individual Responsibility', 81, citing, inter alia, Georges Abi-Saab, 'The Development of International Law by the United Nations' in Frederick Snyder and Surakiart Sathirathai (eds.), *Third World Attitudes to International Law: An Introduction* (Dordrecht: Martinus Nijhoff, 1987).

[71] General Assembly Resolution 3201 (S-VI), Declaration on the Establishment of a New International Economic Order, UN Doc. A/Res/S-6/3201, 1 May 1974. See Mohammed Bedjaoui, *Towards a New International Economic Order* (Paris: UNESCO, 1979).

While discrete advances were made, such as with the consolidation of the doctrine of permanent sovereignty over natural resources,[72] attempts to democratise the international legal system and empower the General Assembly were generally stilted by positivist arguments relating to sources and consent.[73] The New International Economic Order, meanwhile, failed to gain traction in the face of the global North's economic interests and the hegemony of the Bretton Woods institutions. The principles of sovereign equality of states and non-intervention, given understandably significant weight by newly independent societies as a shield against imperial interference, came to also be used to mask systematic abuses of power in post-independence states.

In the face of such setbacks, any concerted collective Third World approach appeared to have retreated from view by the 1980s. It re-emerged, however, in the late 1990s, evolved and adapted to the shifting geopolitical sands and very much invigorated by the ground-breaking work of a new generation of Third World scholarship.[74] While this work

---

[72] General Assembly Resolution 1803 (XVII), 'Permanent sovereignty over natural resources', UN Doc. A/5217, 14 December 1962. See also common Article 1(2) of the international human rights Covenants, and the 1974 Charter of Economic Rights and Duties of States, General Assembly Resolution 3281, UN Doc. A/Res/29/3281, 12 December 1974. The doctrine of permanent sovereignty over natural resources has attained recognition as reflective of customary international law.

[73] Anghie and Chimni, 'Third World Approaches to International Law and Individual Responsibility', 81.

[74] Formative texts include: B.S. Chimni, *International Law and World Order: A Critique of Contemporary Approaches* (New Delhi: Sage, 1993); Obiora Okafor, *Re-defining Legitimate Statehood: International Law and State Fragmentation in Africa* (The Hague: Martinus Nijhoff, 2000); Antony Anghie, B.S. Chimni, et al., *The Third World and International Order: Law, Politics and Globalization* (Leiden: Martinus Nijhoff, 2003); Rajagopal, *International Law from Below*; Anghie, *Imperialism, Sovereignty*; James Thuo Gathii, *War, Commerce, and International Law* (New York: Oxford University Press USA, 2010). Third World scholars have also engaged in notable collaborative work with critical Western international lawyers. See, for example, Richard Falk, Balakrishnan Rajagopal and Jacqueline Stevens (eds.), *International Law and the Third World: Reshaping Justice* (London: Routledge-Cavendish, 2008); Anne Orford (ed.), *International Law and its 'Others'* (Cambridge: Cambridge University Press, 2006); Emmanuelle Jouannet, Hélène Ruiz-Fabri and Mark Toufayan (eds.), *Droit international et nouvelles approches sure le tiers-monde: entre répétition et renouveau* (Paris: Société de Législation Comparée, 2013). TWAIL special issues include: Richard Falk, Balakrishnan Rajagopal and Jacqueline Stevens (eds.), 'Reshaping Justice: International Law and the Third World' (2006) 27:5 *Third World Quarterly*; James Thuo Gathii (ed.), 'Special Issue on the Third World and International Law' (2007) 9:4 *International Community Law Review*; Karin Mickelson, Ibironke Odumosu and Pooja Parmar (eds.), 'Situating Third World Approaches to International Law (TWAIL): Inspirations, Challenges and Possibilities' (2008) 10:4

distinguishes itself from earlier assessments of the relationship between international law and the Third World – most notably through a decidedly more critical interrogation of the post-colonial nation-state – the core impetus of the preceding generation still resonates. Put in its most fundamental terms, this critical Third World approach 'gives meaning to international law in the context of the lived experiences of the ordinary peoples of the third world in order to transform it into an international law of emancipation'.[75] Those lived experiences in recent years have given rise to a plethora of issues of concern, including continuing conditions of 'underdevelopment', structural biases in the global economic order, contemporary formations of empire, questions of international environmental justice, regulation of trade and investment, and discourses of culture, gender and human rights.

Underpinning, in some shape or form, all of the TWAIL scholarship on these issues are questions of racialisation, with colonialist convictions of cultural superiority (expressed across a range of guises from benevolent 'civilising mission' narratives to unconcealed racism) critiqued for continuing to efface the claims and contributions of non-Europeans. The centrality of race – through its derivative civilised/uncivilised binaries – to the self-definition of the discipline of international law (as the law of 'civilised nations'[76]) is as relevant to the political economy of material inequalities as it is to more overt imperial violence. Particular emphasis is placed on the idea that colonial power dynamics and legal concepts were and remain integral to the formation and development of modern Western legalism and, in turn, international legal norms. Included in this, I argue, is the doctrine of emergency, which has its own story to tell of colonial origins and evolution, civilised/savage binaries and post-colonial continuities and replications.

International Community Law Review; Ardi Imseis (ed.), 'Third World Approaches to International Law and the Persistence of the Question of Palestine' (2009) 15 *Palestine Yearbook of International Law*; B.S. Chimni (ed.), 'Special Issue: Third World Approaches to International Law' (2011) 3:1 *Trade, Law and Development*; Michael Fakhri (ed.), 'TWAIL: Capitalism and the Common Good' (2012) 14:1 *Oregon Review of International Law*; Usha Natarajan, John Reynolds, Amar Bhatia and Sujith Xavier (eds.), 'TWAIL: On Praxis and the Intellectual' (2016) 37:11 *Third World Quarterly*. For a 'tentative' bibliography of TWAIL literature up to 2011, see James Thuo Gatthi, 'TWAIL: A Brief History of its Origins, its Decentralized Network, and a Tentative Bibliography' (2011) 3:1 *Trade, Law and Development* 26, 49–64.

[75] Chimni, 'The Past, Present and Future of International Law', 499–500.

[76] Article 38(1)(c), Statute of the International Court of Justice.

This book, then, endeavours to navigate the extensive discourse on states of emergency and emergency doctrine, guided by TWAIL sensibilities. The TWAIL perspective is instructive in reading historical and contemporary patterns of emergency doctrine on a number of levels. It speaks to the specific role of emergency law in the context of the broader racialised control function of law in the colonial project, as well as to the bearing that the colonial experience of states of emergency may have had on the evolution of Western liberal legalism and jurisprudence and, by consequence, on the doctrinal corpus of international law. It helps chart the legacy of emergency doctrine as it developed in colonial spaces and manifests today in a variety of different spaces (including established settler colonial societies, zones of ongoing colonisation, occupied territories, former imperial metropoles, and formally independent post-colonies). It allows us to understand the ways in which the reach of states of emergency extends beyond the traditional sites and forms of international and constitutional law (courts, parliaments, legislation, human rights commissions) to the banal and everyday planes of material existence (land, livestock, ID cards, building permits, water metres, trade union membership). Through this prism, the manner by which the administrative and bureaucratic violence of emergency has become an embedded feature of oppression can be examined.

*

The first part of this book continues in the following two chapters to lay out the theoretical and historical vista for my reading of emergency doctrine. Chapter 2 seeks to understand the relationship between the state of emergency and racial sovereignty as mutually constitutive. The execution of sovereignty in the colony, through a temporally unconstrained emergency rule that suffocates the colonised within law's controlling grasp, is explored with reference to processes of racialisation. This seeks to fill an analytical lacuna in emergency law discourse when it comes to questions of race, a shortcoming which is symptomatic of a broader disciplinary malaise:

> One of the more remarkable features of contemporary international relations and international law is the disappearance of race—and its related concepts of 'civilized'/'uncivilized'—as a term which is central to the self-definition of the discipline. ... Despite the absence of such distinctions in contemporary international law, racialized hierarchies persist and are furthered by ostensibly neutral international law and institutions.[77]

---

[77] Anghie, 'What is TWAIL: Comment', 39. See further, for example, Ediberto Román, 'A Race Approach to International Law (RAIL): Is There a Need for Yet Another Critique

Of course, not all states of emergency are implemented in a racially discriminating manner.[78] Racial dynamics have, however, been sufficiently prevalent as to be an identifiable underlying component of emergency doctrine. Colonial and post-colonial histories are replete with racially inflected emergency measures, although such racialisation is not unique to suppression in the colony or securitisation in the post-colony. States of emergency born outside of situations of state security or political violence have similarly witnessed the targeting of particular racial groups by liberal democratic state authorities (as the experiences of African-Americans in the aftermath of Hurricane Katrina in New Orleans, for example, so aptly demonstrate).

Chapter 3 proceeds to map the emergence of the doctrine of emergency from a colonial historical vantage point. I trace the origins of the modern conception of the state of emergency to its genesis in English martial law, from where it swiftly embarked upon an evolutionary path that began with the export of English law to Britain's early empire conquests and underwent a series of 'colonial mutations'.[79] Special powers were normalised in Ireland, India and beyond through the enactment of emergency legislative codes over the course of the nineteenth and early twentieth centuries. This culminated in governance by wholesale emergency powers across the empire during the 1940s and 1950s in a bid to suppress the revolts of national liberation movements. With emergency governmentality in the colonial context inherently tied to forms of political domination and control, the impacts of the state of emergency were largely contingent on race. I draw on a range of historical material to illuminate how the emergency was constructed under colonial legal systems as part of an institutionalisation of difference and the shoring up of authority over the native other. Here, anti-colonial resistance and agency – themes that percolate through the book – come

of International Law' (2000) 33:4 *University of California Davis Law Review* 1519; Makau Mutua, 'Critical Race Theory and International Law: The View of an Insider-Outsider' (2000) 45 *Villanova Law Review* 841, noting that in the post-Cold War triumph of markets and Western hegemony, 'the rules of "international governance" have been exposed anew as inequitable, oppressive, destructive and hierarchically ordered by race'.

[78] Emergency powers are often deployed by ruling regimes against political dissidents on the basis of ideology, as was the case under a number of Latin American dictatorships and military juntas between the 1960s and the 1980s. Emergency measures deployed in economic contexts are generally marked primarily by their class dynamics, albeit often with significant overlap between class and race.

[79] Hussain, *The Jurisprudence of Emergency*, 2.

into confrontation with emergency powers. My key argument in this context relates to the place of emergency law in the construction and consolidation of imperial sovereignty. Building on this, it is possible to interrogate the extent to which dualistic conceptions of the rule of law and the state of emergency – and the ambivalent and illimitable spaces between and beyond – shaped the practice of colonial governance. This leads us on to gauge the normative boomerang effect of colonial practice on constitutional and international law discourse in the West. Aimé Césaire succinctly articulated such a 'boomerang effect of colonization' in the context of European fascism's repatriation of imperial racial theories and institution of colonial methods within Europe.[80] What we must ask, in that light, is not just how the relationships between sovereignty, emergency and rule of law cross-pollinate in the colonies, but also 'to what extent we are to read the colonial as an iteration of the modern'.[81]

With the focus to this point primarily on the racial elements of emergency doctrine, Chapter 3 also introduces its related class and political economy elements, and the particular role played by states of emergency in sustaining and reinforcing economic structures. The ways in which race and class are interlaced with emergency powers can be seen from the evolution of capitalist world systems under the colonial trading companies. The reproduction of the language and logic of national emergency in the economic sphere serves to elide the conceptual divisions between physical war and class war, and between state security and socio-economic inequality.[82] This demonstrates the reach of emergency doctrine, in the wider context of international law, as a material project that 'unfolds on the mundane and quotidian plane through sites and objects which appear unrelated to the international'.[83]

With that in mind, Part II of the book attempts to navigate some of the interactions between the normalised features of colonial emergency rule and the content and jurisprudence of international law. Chapter 4 draws out the long shadow of colonialism to demonstrate the influence of the prevailing backdrop of late imperial wars on the normative framing of

---

[80] Aimé Césaire, *Discourse on Colonialism* (1955) (Joan Pinkham trans., New York: Monthly Review Press, 1972) 41.

[81] Hussain, *The Jurisprudence of Emergency*, 7.

[82] Mark Neocleous, 'From Martial Law to the War on Terror' (2007) 10:4 *New Criminal Law Review* 489, 507.

[83] Luis Eslava and Sundhya Pahuja, 'Between Resistance and Reform: TWAIL and the Universality of International Law' (2011) 3:1 *Trade, Law & Development* 103, 109.

international human rights law. The post-war international human rights legal order of treaties and tribunals narrates itself as a response to the 'unimaginable atrocities' and 'odious scourge' of the fascism that had gone before. This was the doctrinal and institutional becoming of the 'never again' mantra. International human rights, that is, represent the progressive response to the very state of exception that totalitarianism had instituted and operationalised. Yet the proliferating states of emergency in the colonies had a significant influence on the framing of the major international human rights conventions that were formulated in response to Europe's state of exception. The drafting of the European Convention on Human Rights and the International Covenant on Civil and Political Rights got underway in the late 1940s. In the early drafts of these treaties, there was no mention of states of emergency; no mention of the possibility of derogation from the legal obligations to be undertaken by states. The drafting process, however, took place amidst an upsurge of anti-colonial revolt around the British empire. The Colonial Office sent communiqués to governors in the colonies with the decree that declarations of emergency were to be the default response to native opposition. There were states of emergency imposed in twenty-nine British colonial territories in total from 1946 onwards. The list reads like an A to Z of the empire, from Aden to Zanzibar. These were simply the latest images in the transmission of colonial emergency that had flashed up in Ceylon in 1848 or Jamaica in 1865 or Amritsar in 1919. This was emergency governance as a technique of control and population management, but one that allowed a particular formulation of legal order to be preserved. The British government's insistence on the insertion of emergency derogation clauses into the human rights treaties, detailed in Chapter 4 through a review of the drafting records, reflects this experience.

Imagine Benjamin's angel of history[84] looking back from the newly consecrated United Nations palaces in New York or Geneva in 1948. Where the angel sees the arc of history as one single catastrophe, *we* see only the latest link in a chain of events before us. Amidst the ruins, the storm that we call progress – that in this instance we called universal human rights – propels us forward. And our endeavour in this moment of progress is merely to clear the most visible surface-layer debris left by fascism and war, not the thicker rubble stacked beneath by imperialism,

---

[84] Invoked in his description and interpretation of Paul Klee's *Angelus Novus* in Benjamin, 'On the Concept of History', 392.

which continues to keep piling wreckage upon wreckage all around. In this formative moment for international human rights law, the idea of emergency becomes constitutive of human rights and underpins the construction of a need for those rights to be balanced against or offset by security priorities. It generates the imperative for legal protection of rights, while at the same time providing the justification for their suspension. The centrality of emergency to the crystallisation of international human rights law also produces a crisis-driven conception of rights, which in turn feeds into the hierarchisation of rights (in which economic, social and cultural rights – not seen as entwined with moments of crisis or exception in the same way as civil and political rights – are rendered less urgent).[85]

Having secured treaty provision for states of emergency in the context of its global colonial emergencies, Britain lodged a whole host of derogations to exempt itself from human rights obligations in the colonies after the European Convention on Human Rights came into force in 1953. Chapter 5 explores perhaps the most notorious example of this – in Kenya, where brutality and torture in the internment camps was enabled by the state of emergency in place through the 1950s. Britain's declared emergency and derogation provided the legal grounds for the mass detention policy that underpinned this violence in the camps. I show that the legal emergency was extended by the colonial authorities – long after the conditions of emergency had receded to 'normalcy' in their own view – for the explicit purpose of maintaining the derogation under the European Convention on Human Rights. As such, the state of emergency in Kenya serves as an especially useful prism through which to analyse state practice and engagement with evolving international norms. Drawing on archival research, I examine the scope of Britain's emergency powers, from the acute violence of the camps to the quotidian aspects of livestock confiscation, and show the state of emergency as a planned and productive racialised process that was very much bound up in land policy and the preservation of colonial sovereignty.

Chapter 6 turns to the jurisprudence under the European Convention on Human Rights, where a small but significant body of European Court of Human Rights case law has developed on Article 15 derogations relating to emergency measures in contexts of colonial counter-insurgency and state security that include Cyprus, the north of Ireland

---

[85] Authers and Charlesworth, 'The Crisis and the Quotidian', 21.

and the preventive detention of Muslims in the post-2001 state of emergency. This jurisprudence is revealing of the nature of the interface between international legal institutions and domestic authorities. The Court has in some cases adjudged that certain powers and practices went too far in the context of the given emergency, but in each case the underlying declaration and enactment of the state of emergency itself was vindicated. The European Court constructed its 'margin of appreciation' doctrine for the very purpose of leaving discretion to the state to decide on the emergency. The derogation regime that was enshrined in human rights law evidences a failure to make any radical break from the constitutive role played by emergency in state conceptions of sovereignty, and can be seen as a release valve that significantly dilutes human rights law's counter-hegemonic potential.

Part III of the book appraises the continuing legacy of colonial legal traditions through contemporary settler colonial contexts where emergency powers are deployed. Chapter 7 grounds my theoretical discussion around emergency and racial sovereignty in the fractured lands of Palestine. Israel's multifarious emergency modalities are examined in this 'colonial present' setting where traditional territorial colonisation is fused with modern security biopolitics. The function of emergency law in the imposition and maintenance of sovereignty links Israeli practice vis-à-vis the Palestinians with other colonial encounters. Israel's juridical–security apparatus mimics European liberal legalism in presenting itself as generally accepting and embracing of human rights obligations, save in circumstances where particular illiberal measures are necessitated on security grounds. These measures, however, comprise such a pervasive patchwork of emergency legalities and modalities as to have permeated all spheres of Palestinian political, economic and cultural life. The British Mandate-era Defence (Emergency) Regulations were retained and applied to Arab-majority areas of Israel that were placed under military rule from 1948 to 1966, and to the occupied territories since 1967. The constitutional state of emergency declared in 1948 also remains in place in the Israeli legal system almost seventy years later. In the midst of this, Israel has invoked the emergency derogation option under international treaties to claim the legality of measures such as mass internment of Palestinians without trial. I articulate the dynamics of legality, emergency and sovereignty in Palestine/Israel in terms of 'repressive inclusion': a racially contingent inclusion within – and repression by – the juridical order. This evokes the suffocating hold of racialised emergency legal structures. The consequences for Palestinian lives and bodies have been severe; the alienation of land and fragmentation of territory have been acute.

Chapter 8 moves to the settler colonial setting of Australia's Northern Territory where, since 2007, the federal government has been engaged in an 'emergency intervention' into Indigenous communities. While presented as a child protection measure, this state of emergency has involved an interference with Indigenous lands, lives, labour and bodies that outstrips and belies its stated purpose of children's welfare. It has in some aspects been militarised, and in all aspects heavily racialised. The Australian state made no attempt to conceal this. In imposing the emergency legislation, it explicitly suspended the application of the Racial Discrimination Act and its anti-racism protections in the Northern Territory. Through the performance of this 'social' emergency, we see again the versatility of the state of emergency as a legal construct, and the expansive ways in which it continues to be mobilised as a tool of settler colonial governmentality.

Chapter 9 concludes the book by considering the limits and possibilities imbued in the language and discursive process of law as both a constraining and an enabling device; a vehicle of domination for states seeking to consolidate security apparatuses through emergency doctrine, but potentially also a site of resistance for subjugated groups seeking to loosen the bind of emergency rule. The permanence of the normalised emergency renders the norm/exception distinction illusory and calls for the imagining of radical alternatives to disrupt the entrenched balance of power. In this light, the concluding chapter thinks about the scope for resistance to hegemonic modes of emergency governance in recuperating the traditions and emancipatory politics of the oppressed.

2

Racialisation and States of Emergency

Late twentieth and early twenty-first-century legal scholarship on states of emergency and exception has been marked, perhaps more than anything else, by its resuscitation of Carl Schmitt[1] and its attempts to theorise sovereign action within or beyond the liminal spaces of a juridical order.[2] While such conceptual mapping is instructive for our understanding of the interactions between sovereignty, law and exception, it cannot in itself fully encapsulate and elaborate the contours of emergency legal doctrine. In particular, certain lingering blind spots with regard to colonial history and questions of race and racialisation are denoted by the Eurocentric nature of Schmitt's writings on the exception, a trait which endures in the work of Giorgio Agamben and other contemporary Western theorists. The analytic frames of biopolitics, bare life and states of exception have not, overall, been sufficiently attentive to the significance of race and colonialism. My understanding and analysis of the state of emergency is guided by the need, as I see it, for scholarship in this field to be more cognisant of the ways in which Eurocolonial

---

[1] David Luban details the rise in Schmitt's prevalence in statistical terms, with his figures indicating that the number of law review references to Schmitt during the 1980–1990 period was multiplied by a factor of 23 during the 1990–2000 period, and by 84 during the 2000–2010 period. David Luban, 'Carl Schmitt and the Critique of Lawfare' (2010) 43 *Case Western Reserve Journal of International Law* 457, 468.

[2] For an overview of such 'inside/outside' or 'legal/extra-legal' debates, see Nomi Claire Lazar, *States of Emergency in Liberal Democracies* (Cambridge: Cambridge University Press, 2009) 136–162. See also, for example, Austin Sarat (ed.), *Sovereignty, Emergency, Legality* (Cambridge: Cambridge University Press, 2010); Victor V. Ramraj (ed.), *Emergencies and the Limits of Legality* (Cambridge: Cambridge University Press, 2008); Oren Gross and Fionnuala Ní Aoláin, *Law in Times of Crisis: Emergency Powers in Theory and Practice* (Cambridge: Cambridge University Press, 2006); Bruce Ackerman, 'The Emergency Constitution' (2004) 113 *Yale Law Journal* 1019; Oren Gross, 'Chaos and Rules: Should Responses to Violent Crises Always Be Constitutional?' (2003) 112 *Yale Law Journal* 1011; Oren Gross, 'The Normless and Exceptionless Exception: Carl Schmitt's Theory of Emergency Powers and the "Norm-Exception" Dichotomy' (2000) 21 *Cardozo Law Review* 1825.

thought and practice shaped the normalisation of emergency doctrine in occidental and international law.

In a bid to more clearly unmask the underlying purpose, legacies and effects of emergency doctrine, I examine the construct of the state of emergency as an often racialised component of sovereignty and governmentality. This is integral to understanding emergency politics, past and present, and illustrating the story of how states of emergency continue to operate, discriminate and alienate. The racial aspects of emergencies are illuminated by reference to European imperial history and colonial law's proliferation of emergency modalities. When British colonial authorities began legislating emergency measures to suppress anti-colonial agitation, those measures were deployed in line with institutionalised hierarchies based on constructed racial difference.

The central concern of this chapter, therefore, is with foregrounding the operation of the broad range of measures that are loosely and often tenuously united under the umbrella of emergency law as being, in the experiences of colonised peoples, a heavily racialised process. Such measures are embodied in the specific emergency powers and decrees promulgated by the (colonial) state on the basis of circumstances presented as a threat to its 'normal' (repressive) functioning. Regimes of emergency law, with their complex array of apparatuses and institutions, emerged as part of empire's 'polymorphous techniques of subjugation'.[3] Such measures are typically – but not necessarily, and perhaps less so over time as 'crisis coincides with normality and becomes, this way, just a tool of government'[4] – adopted under the auspices of a formally declared state of emergency, the specific form of which may vary across jurisdiction. In that sense, the malleability of the doctrine of emergency must be stressed. It is a distinctly 'elastic'[5] concept and technique that, in the context of the European colonial project, evolved in a multiplicity of forms which served to consolidate colonial sovereignty. In this evolution, the legal-administrative grid of emergency rule became bound up with the racialised structures of settler colonialism and imperial governance.

The racial pillar is, however, often absent from scholarly sketches of the architecture of states of emergency. The first section of this chapter

---

[3] Michel Foucault, 'Two Lectures' in Michel Foucault and Colin Gordon (eds.), *Power/Knowledge* (Colin Gordon et al. trans., New York: Pantheon Books, 1980) 96.

[4] Giorgio Agamben, 'For a Theory of Destituent Power', *Critical Legal Thinking*, 5 February 2014.

[5] H.P. Lee, *Emergency Powers* (Sydney: Law Book Co., 1984) 4.

addresses this absence, and some blind spots in the work of prominent critical theorists. It also conceptualises race and racialisation for the purposes of my analysis. The second section then considers the state of emergency as a site of legality. I argue that the state of emergency is ultimately defined by contingent inclusion within the law, more so than by conceptions of extra-legality or legal vacuum. The story of how emergency governance is institutionalised in colonial administration is a story of the role of law. The colonised are not excluded entirely from the sphere of law, but are rather embraced and enveloped in a suffocating hold by emergency legality. This is a legality that is marked by differentiation and stratification. Its evolution and application in the colonial context are underpinned by processes of racialisation and repression. The third section of the chapter deals with this relationship between emergency and racial sovereignty, while the final section anchors the analysis in connection to a broader racialisation of (international) law.

The Spectre of Race

In response to the preponderate theorising of norm/exception binaries and 'models of extra-legality'[6], Austin Sarat observes that 'it may be that existing scholarship is so caught up in the Schmitt/Agamben opposition of sovereignty and law that we have been inattentive to the myriad of ways in which law imagines, anticipates, and responds to emergencies, ways in which sovereign prerogative is either irrelevant or operates within the terrain of ordinary legal procedures'.[7] The result is a failure to adequately expose the full potential disposition of the doctrine of emergency as it has evolved; that is, as a protracted process of population management or domination. Focus on a conceptualisation of the state of emergency in dramatic sovereign decisionist or constitution-suspending terms elides the legislated, institutionalised and dispersed modalities that it has widely assumed, and overlooks the sculpting, moulding and refining of emergency powers over the passage of time. It is belied by daily

---

[6] See, for example, see Gross and Ní Aoláin, *Law in Times of Crisis*, 119–170.

[7] Austin Sarat, 'Toward New Conceptions of the Relationship of Law and Sovereignty under Conditions of Emergency' in Sarat (ed.), *Sovereignty, Emergency, Legality*, 3. On the nature of such forms of irresolution, the work of Michel Foucault is instructive. Golder and Fitzpatrick, for example, demonstrate the irresolute nature of 'Foucault's law', where a binary approach is rejected and perimeters are not absolute. Ben Golder and Peter Fitzpatrick, *Foucault's Law* (Abingdon: Routledge, 2009).

realities under entrenched and prolonged emergencies, which tend to be shaped less by the sudden imminence of existential threat, and more by the consolidation of restrictive measures as normalised banalities. Situations in which emergency regulations are implemented are 'almost never the sort of total emergencies that ... one might imagine from the theory',[8] as evidenced by the inapplicability of the 'ticking bomb' scenario beyond the curiously correlated worlds of legal/moral philosophy debates and jingoistic homeland security-inspired television productions.[9] Emergency modalities and practices emerge, evolve, ferment and normalise over periods spanning years and decades that long pre-date and outlast any hypothetical ticking bombs.

As I argue through this book, colonial rule is particularly revealing of the use of emergency powers not merely as a reactive mechanism to avert prevailing or impending crises, but as the performance of calculated pre-emptive measures infused into ongoing governance and designed to preserve sovereign power. One of the specific ways in which law has imagined, anticipated and responded is through the construction of emergency structures that exploit and reify racial difference. Emergency discourse underpins the routine violence of the law against racialised minority or migrant populations. Where premised on a perceived threat to state security emanating from a dangerous other, states of emergency in many instances feed into processes of social ordering based on broadly construed racial markers. Yet much of the critical theorising of the exception and the emergency has been relatively inattentive to the role of race and imperialism in constituting emergency politics and legal doctrine. To the extent that contemporary states of emergency and exception have been historicised, elements of the discourse and its protagonists are marked by a certain Eurocentrism. Agamben's genealogical mapping of the state of exception, for instance, is encased firmly within the Western political tradition, tracing the origins of the exception from Roman law doctrine through the French revolution and martial law

---

[8] Kim Scheppele, 'Legal and Extra-Legal Emergencies' in Keith E. Whittington, R. Daniel Kelemen and Gregory A. Caldeira (eds.), *The Oxford Handbook of Law and Politics* (Oxford: Oxford University Press, 2008) 165, 174.

[9] See, for instance, *24* (20th Century Fox Television, 2001–2010); Alan Dershowitz, *Why Terrorism Works: Understanding the Threat, Responding to the Challenge* (New Haven: Yale University Press, 2003); Fritz Allhoff, 'A Defense of Torture: Separation of Cases, Ticking Time-bombs, and Moral Justification' (2005) 19:2 *International Journal of Applied Philosophy* 243; cf. David Luban, 'Liberalism, Torture, and the Ticking Bomb' (2005) 91 *Virginia Law Review* 1425.

in England to the Weimar Republic and the Nazi regime, and modern juridico-political systems in Italy, Switzerland and the United States.[10] This particular bloodline of emergency that Agamben sketches, from ancient Rome to Article 48 of the Weimar Constitution, is, he claims, 'certainly correct'.[11] For Agamben, when it comes to the idea of security-driven emergency rule as 'a permanent technology of government', prior to the evolution of the contemporary security state '[t]he *only* clear precedent was the Nazi regime'.[12] He discusses eighteenth- and nineteenth-century France and England at length, but manages to bypass those countries' imperial enterprises, their inveterate states of emergency, and Third World experience under that colonial emergency rule.

Agamben presents *homo sacer*, a figure of archaic Roman law with a status situated outside both divine and human law: *hominis sacri* could not be sacrificed as their deaths were of no additional value to the gods, but they could nonetheless be disposed of with impunity – killed, but never murdered – as their lives were equally worthless to society.[13] Agamben transposes the figure of *homo sacer* (or 'life that does not deserve to live'[14]) to modernity through his marginalisation by the operation of sovereign power. *Hominis sacri* are encompassed as objects of sovereign power, but precluded from being its subjects. Socially conditioned states of suspended life and suspended death emerge to 'exemplify the distinction that Agamben offers between bare life and the life of the political being (*bios politikon*), where this second sense of "being" is established only in the context of political community'.[15] Agamben's paradigmatic state of exception, marked by conceptual binaries and zones of indistinction (inside/outside, norm/exception, public/private, zoē/bios), is defined as 'an inclusive exclusion (which thus serves to include what is excluded)' that produces bare life through sovereign violence.[16] In this sense, bare life is constituted through the construction

---

[10] Giorgio Agamben, *State of Exception* (2003) (Kevin Attell trans., Chicago: University of Chicago Press, 2005).

[11] Agamben, 'For a Theory of Destituent Power'.   [12] *Ibid.* Emphasis added.

[13] Agamben, *Homo Sacer: Sovereign Power and Bare Life* (1995) (Daniel Heller-Roazen trans., Stanford: Stanford University Press, 1998) 8–10, 71–74, 83.

[14] *Ibid.*, 136–143.   [15] Judith Butler, *Precarious Life* (London: Verso, 2004) 67.

[16] Agamben, *Homo Sacer*, 21. This notion is applied by Michelle Farrell in her exploration of torture in Coetzee's *Waiting for the Barbarians*. The barbarian (the excluded) is civilised (included) through subjection to torture. The act of torture 'signifies nothing other than the Empire's ability to render life bare and to inscribe the meaning of humanity upon the excluded body'. Michelle Farrell, *The Prohibition of Torture in Exceptional Circumstances* (Cambridge: Cambridge University Press, 2013) 249–250.

and performance of the space of the exception: a grey area between law and non-law that is conducive to exceptional practices characteristic of executive sovereign power.

The most extreme manifestation of such a space of the exception, for Agamben, is that of the 'camp'. The camps are not born out of ordinary law but out of the state of exception and martial law, with the inhabitants stripped of legal status in the eyes of their captors, and so completely deprived of their rights and prerogatives that no act committed against them could appear any longer as a crime. They are treated as *hominis sacri* by the sovereign power that incarcerates them; reduced to bare life. The primary site of inquiry and embodiment of the camp in Agamben's work is the Nazi *Lager*. He very briefly cites the Spanish *campos de concentraciones* in Cuba and British internment camps in South Africa. In those instances, 'a state of emergency linked to a colonial war is extended to an entire civil population'.[17] This is conspicuous as a rare and fleeting allusion to colonial history in Agamben's analysis. He does acknowledge the significance of the temporality of the state of emergency in his observation that since the Second World War, 'the voluntary creation of a permanent state of emergency (though perhaps not declared in the technical sense) has become one of the essential practices of contemporary states, including so-called democratic ones'.[18] With this move (framing it as a post-war phenomenon), however, Agamben simultaneously excises the element of entrenched emergency that had been a feature of legal systems and governance dynamics in the colonies. It also bears noting that while he draws on Hannah Arendt's work on Nazi racial policy in developing his theory of the exception, Agamben leaves aside central elements of her analysis that (following Third World writers such as Aimé Césaire[19]) situate the origins of European totalitarianism and 'race-thinking' in European colonialism.[20] In interrogating the exclusionary and repressive dynamics of sovereign power, Agamben's gaze is very much directed inwards at the effects of those dynamics as they manifest internally within the West, rather than looking further afield to excavate their roots in Europe's external imperial practices. More broadly, as Simone Bignall and Marcelo Svirsky highlight, Agamben's 'relative silence about colonialism' extends to a lack of engagement with postcolonial thinkers and their appraisals of Europe's politics of

---

[17] Agamben, *Homo Sacer*, 166.   [18] Agamben, *State of Exception*, 2.
[19] Césaire, *Discourse on Colonialism*, 35-46.
[20] Hannah Arendt, *The Origins of Totalitarianism* (New York: Meridian, 1958) 185–221.

domination.[21] Bignall and Svirsky's collection on *Agamben and Colonialism* implores us to engage in critical debates around states of exception in ways that are mindful of the rich histories of anti-colonial rebellion, respectful of the nuances of agency and its multiple forms, and conscious of advancing a transformative politics that resists the bind of hegemonic emergency rule.[22]

Similar concerns over Michel Foucault's work on biopolitics can be highlighted from the perspective of postcolonialism. In his depiction of a normative conception of power, Foucault neglects to delineate the social field from which the norm is generated, prompting Nasser Hussain to wonder whether 'this terrain [is] the recognizable unit of the nation-state, or a more politico-philosophical space of the "West"?'[23]

> Here the limits of Foucault's work for a history of emergency, particularly colonial emergency, begin to reveal themselves. Indeed, postcolonial critics who have embraced and been energized by Foucault's work have nonetheless noted the particular omissions of colony and empire from the epistemic shifts he so assiduously sought to document. This is not to be merely tendentious – no critic, after all, can be expected to cover everything – rather it is merely to note that despite Foucault's interest in the development of spaces of confinement, he never thoroughly investigated the construction of the epistemic space of the West itself as putatively self-contained and self-generative.[24]

With his attention fixed on the internal apparatuses of the European state, Foucault 'has little to say about the relation between the sovereignty of the state and the new forms of law, or the limits to the functioning of the normative itself'.[25] Like Agamben, Foucault does nonetheless open up a space for the conceptualisation of emergency in temporal terms. The temporally unbounded dimension of emergency became a firm feature of colonial legal systems over time. The trend away from sovereignty and Machiavellian conceptions of power towards 'the art of government', as identified by Foucault, coincided with rise of the European nation-state and its colonial expansion. Foucault alludes to this himself when he underlines the process of centralisation 'which, shattering the structures of feudalism, leads to the establishment of the great territorial,

[21] Simone Bignall and Marcelo Svirsky, 'Introduction' in Simone Bignall and Marcelo Svirsky (eds.), *Agamben and Colonialism* (Edinburgh: Edinburgh University Press, 2012) 3.
[22] *Ibid.*   [23] Hussain, *The Jurisprudence of Emergency*, 14.   [24] *Ibid.*   [25] *Ibid.*, 15.

administrative and colonial states'.[26] While not interrogating it directly, he is certainly aware of the parallel trajectories of the problem of government and the rise of the state and its colonial expansion. He proceeds to assert that '[t]he art of government could only spread and develop in subtlety in an age of expansion',[27] an expansion which we understand as both economic and territorial. This provides a useful point of departure for an analysis of the relationship between colonialism and emergency doctrine. With larger and increasingly resistant populations to manage in its overseas dominions, the colonial state came to require more sophisticated means of domination than military force alone. It was in this context that emergency powers were institutionalised and codified.

When it comes to race specifically, Alexander Weheliye takes up the baton, critiquing bare life and biopolitics discourse generally, and Agamben and Foucault specifically, for 'placing racial difference in a field prior to and at a distance from conceptual contemplation' so as to occlude race as a category of critical analysis and to divert attention from constructions of racial hierarchy and subjugations of the humanity of racialised subjects.[28] Arguing from a vantage point of black studies, Weheliye emphasises in response a 'layered interconnectedness of political violence, racialization, and the human', in which 'racialisation' is not a biological or cultural descriptor but 'a conglomerate of sociopolitical relations that discipline humanity' according to concerted processes of differentiation and hierarchisation.[29] In this rendering, racial logics produce regimented, institutionalised and militarised stratifications of human society.[30]

This underpins my understanding of race and racialisation in historical context. Over the centuries that European imperialism unfurled itself around the globe, modes of differentiating between human collectivities shifted. Earlier cultural, religious and territorial configurations of difference began to cede ground by the late eighteenth century to a pseudo-scientific discourse that framed race in genetic, biological and

---

[26] Michel Foucault, 'Governmentality' in Graham Burchell, Colin Gordon and Peter Miller (eds.), *The Foucault Effect: Studies in Governmentality* (Chicago: University of Chicago Press, 1991) 87.
[27] *Ibid.*, 97.
[28] Alexander G. Weheliye, *Habeas Viscus: Racializing Assemblages, Biopolitics and Black Feminist Theories of the Human* (Durham: Duke University Press, 2014).
[29] *Ibid.*
[30] Dylan Rodríguez, *Forced Passages: Imprisoned Radical Intellectuals and the U.S. Prison Regime* (Minneapolis: University of Minnesota Press, 2006) 11.

phenotypical terms, and gave rise to theories of scientific racialism.[31] Race is a specifically Eurocolonial creation of that time – tying physiognomy to cognitive capacity, and positing intrinsic hierarchies between the constructed races (with white European supremacy taken as given). Racialisation is linked to this, though it is a broader process. It is race put into socio-political action, but is prior to and not confined to biological conceptions of difference. Racialisation is 'an assortment of local attempts to impose classificatory grids on a variety of colonised populations, to particular though coordinated ends'.[32] Given the varying modes of colonialism in which regimes of domination are produced, racialisation itself is characterised by a diversity of forms. This reflects the 'socio-conceptual agility' of race[33] as the basis upon which a dominant group constructs a subordinate population as racially distinct so as to marginalise it politically and entrench its economic subjugation. Racial regimes are not ultimately defined by phenotype, but by historically produced notions of difference. Wolfe articulates this in terms of race constituting a 'trace of history', a process (not an ontology) that manifests across a range of racialising practices designed to maintain group-based modes of colonial domination over time.[34] These practices represent a coloniser's response to the threats arising from having to share social space with the colonised, and are typically intensified in the wake of a removal of physical separations (the frontier) or juridical barriers (slavery, citizenship exclusions) between the dominant and subordinated groups.[35] For Sherene Razack, race is also intimately entwined with place – not only the settler colony or the nation-state border, but also the park, the slum, the classroom and the mosque – and place becomes race through the law.[36]

---

[31] See, for example, Christine Bolt, *Victorian Attitudes to Race* (London: Routledge, 1971); Seymour Drescher, 'The Ending of the Slave Trade and the Evolution of European Scientific Racism' (1990) 14:3 *Social Science History* 415–450. The relevance of this in a context as recent as the state of emergency in Kenya in the 1950s will be discussed in Chapter 5.

[32] Patrick Wolfe, *Traces of History: Elementary Structures of Race* (London: Verso, 2016) 10.

[33] David Theo Goldberg, *Are We All Postracial Yet?* (Cambridge: Polity, 2015) 10. Goldberg has also argued for more specific conceptual mappings than 'racialisation', to take account of 'racial regionalizations'. Thus he speaks of the 'americanization, palestinianization, europeanization, latinamericanization, and southafricanization of racism(s), and by extension of race'. David Theo Goldberg, *The Threat of Race: Reflections on Racial Neoliberalism* (Oxford: Blackwell, 2009) 67–68.

[34] Wolfe, *Traces of History*, 7, 18.   [35] *Ibid.*, 14.

[36] Sherene H. Razack, 'When Place Becomes Race' in Sherene H. Razack (ed.), *Race, Space, and the Law: Unmapping a White Settler Society* (Toronto: Between the Lines, 2002) 1.

These historical and spatial lenses capture the multidimensional ways in which societies in particular places at particular historical junctures come to be structured by racial hierarchy. Constructs of race serve to sustain unequal social relations. The processes of racialisation by which subject groups are marked and managed – and by which inequalities and asymmetries of power are produced – have continued to proliferate across space and time, and have transcended conceptual and temporal oscillations in understandings of race and modes of coloniality. Irrespective of the formal abolition of slavery in the British empire in 1833, for example, race persisted and intensified as a central factor in British attitudes toward ongoing conquest and expansion. Continuities in racial attitudes and racial violence revealed themselves through colonial perceptions of the 'coolies' on plantations in India as a new breed of post-abolition slaves.[37] Certainty over the survival of racial domination beyond the framework of slavery can also be clearly detected in the writings of liberal colonialist (and Whig parliamentarian) Thomas Macaulay in 1827, regarding the question of whether to free a substantial number of African slaves from indentured labour in Caribbean sugar plantations.[38] As has been evocatively asserted (in rather gendered terms), 'with the nation torn between her conscience and her sweet tooth [Macaulay reassured her] that she could wash her Imperial skirts clean with Emancipation and still continue to enjoy the produce of her thriving colonies'.[39]

The diverse logics by which colonised populations have been racialised and co-opted can be seen in the contrast between Black/Negro bodies exploited for their labour and Red/Indigenous/Aboriginal territories expropriated for their land.[40] It can equally be seen in the similarities drawn between nineteenth-century African-Americans and twentieth-century European Muslims – two groups that are presented as similarly disposable and linked by analogous socio-political dynamics, despite the ostensible incongruity of comparing a distinctive racial-ethnic group with

[37] Elizabeth Kolsky, *Colonial Justice in British India: White Violence and the Rule of Law* (Cambridge: Cambridge University Press, 2010) 142–184.
[38] Thomas B. Macaulay, 'The Social and Industrial Capacities of Negroes' (1827), reprinted in *Race*, October 1971, 136.
[39] David Owen Williams, 'Racial Ideas in Early Victorian England' (1982) 5:2 *Ethnic and Racial Studies* 196.
[40] Wolfe, *Traces of History*, 3–4, noting the colour-coded triangulation of 'the application of Black people's labour to Red people's land producing the White man's property'.

a faith community.[41] The heterogeneity and malleability of race, as such, underpins its utility to imperialism. The ongoing continuities of these diverse racial logics can be seen in the targeting of suspect communities in colonial and post-colonial settings framed as emergencies. In such settings, states of emergency build on race's juridical function of conferring different legal statuses or entitlements across a range of social markers. Whilst the recipient of emergency measures varies across time and context – from 'criminal tribes' in colonial India to Catholics in partitioned Ireland and Muslims in metropolitan Britain; from Native Americans to Japanese-Americans and African-Americans; from Jews in Europe to non-Jews in Israel, non-Europeans in South Africa to non-Hindus in India – it is typically characterised by some form of racialisation.

I will explore the relationship between colonial sovereignty, emergency powers and racialisation in more detail in the third section of this chapter through the illustrative and diverse contexts of India and Ireland. Before that, we turn to debates around legality, exception and exclusion in the context of racialisation.

Legality, Exception and Inclusion/Exclusion

One of the central quandaries of debates on states of emergency and exception has been the extent of the presence or absence of law therein. Various expulsion theses and exception theses have been advanced to isolate the juridical from sovereign or executive prerogative in an emergency setting. In the context of martial law, for example, David Dyzenhaus notes the apparent contradictions of the norm/exception dynamic in his articulation of 'an absence of law prescribed by law under the concept of necessity – a legal black hole, but one created, perhaps even in some sense bounded, by law'.[42] In these terms he presents the 'conceptual puzzle' of martial law: that is, insofar as martial law involves the use of law to dissolve law so as to preserve legal order, can it really be understood as law? This remains a central question in debates over emergency powers and anti-terrorism laws, where the traditional dynamics of

---

[41] Ronald Judy, 'Democracy or Ideology' (2006) 33:3 *boundary 2* 35, 57; Weheliye, *Habeas Viscus*.

[42] David Dyzenhaus, 'The Puzzle of Martial Law' (2009) 59 *University of Toronto Law Journal* 1, 2.

martial law reside in less overt forms. Regardless of where we situate martial law or the state of emergency on the spectrum of legality, deciphering their underlying purpose is crucial to an understanding of their enduring legacies and effects.

For Agamben, within the 'double-structure' – of law on the one hand, and an absence of law (or governance through management) on the other – both elements co-exist while being driven to the extreme: 'Today we see how a maximum of anomy and disorder can perfectly coexist with a maximum of legislation.'[43] Framing governance through such a maximum of legislation opens up the space for us to view law and its institutions as part of the governmental apparatuses of security and domination. The proliferation of emergency laws and decrees in liberal democracies and authoritarian regimes alike is testament to this. The idea that law can ever recede entirely, therefore, is dubious. Regardless of how much credence is given to that possibility, it throws up significant conceptual questions that continue to animate debate. Does law have the capacity, through its presence or absence, to carve out territorialised zones of exception; to include and exclude; to humanise and dehumanise? In touching upon these foundational questions in the particular context of European colonialism, Anghie's work on the Spanish conquests provides a useful framing for us to situate emergency doctrine within such broader debates.

Anghie's argument, coming from a TWAIL perspective, is that we find in colonial and administered territories the difficulties of applying conventional doctrines of sovereignty; that is, of facilitating the 'distillation of a single will', 'the unitary, singular body animated by the spirit of sovereignty'.[44] In his discussion of the role of international law and institutions in creating and maintaining relations of domination between Western powers and non-self-governing territories, Anghie draws on Foucault's notion of new types of control and management in the stead of a unitary sovereign: 'It is in the non-European world that international law acquires a different form – and, indeed, creates new types of control and management.'[45] We can perceive the particular operation of law in

---

[43] Ulrich Raulff, 'An Interview with Giorgio Agamben' (2004) 5:5 *German Law Journal* 609, 611–612.
[44] Foucault, 'Two Lectures', 97. These lectures were the first two of a series of eleven later published in full in English as Michel Foucault, *Society Must Be Defended: Lectures at the Collège de France, 1975–76* (1997) (David Macey trans., London: Penguin, 2004).
[45] Anghie, *Imperialism, Sovereignty*, 190.

the colonies in terms described by Foucault, who endeavoured more generally 'to show the extent to which, and the forms in which, the law (not simply the law, but the whole complex of apparatuses, institutions and regulations responsible for their application) transmits and puts in motion relations that are not relations of sovereignty, but of domination'.[46]

The evolutionary path from the sovereign decisionism of martial law in medieval England to the normalisation and institutionalisation of emergency rule in the late British empire (which I map out in Chapter 3) mirrors this genealogy of the state – from a hierarchical state, 'born in the feudal type of territorial regime which corresponds to a society of laws', to an administrative state 'corresponding to a society of regulation and discipline', and finally a governmental state in which society is 'controlled by apparatuses of security'.[47] In this governmental state, the matrix of entrenched security politics reveals itself through its legislation, regulations, institutions, special powers and illiberal practices. As such, analogies between contemporary state of emergency discourse and colonial governance frameworks are perhaps more apt than the correlations of emergency with fascist/totalitarian executive decisionism that Agamben and others take up. As we will see, the idea of emergency as a technique of governance, rather than a temporary and exceptional reaction to a crisis, underpinned British policy in the empire. Given the quagmire arising for colonial officials disposed with a penchant for both imperial conquest and rule of law, the empire was a natural and inevitable incubation zone for the evolution of emergency governance. In order to justify a reliance on the use of force for the establishment and maintenance of domination, while simultaneously bequeathing the gift of British justice to the conquered territory, the colonial administration invoked emergency doctrine. This carved out room for manoeuvre while maintaining an overall semblance of legality. In the colonial space, in particular, the rule of law and the state of emergency must be understood as powerfully and intimately connected, mutually reinforcing. Emergency is not merely episodic and interruptive, contained beyond the otherwise smooth functioning of law, but is constitutive of that (uncontainable) law.

---

[46] Foucault, 'Two Lectures', 95–96.   [47] Foucault, 'Governmentality', 104.

In some of the debates around the nature of the state of exception, post-colonial theory lenses have been applied to deconstruct the way in which the exception crystallises in the colony. Such deconstruction typically points to the exclusion and (attempted) dehumanisation of the colonised population, the creation of zones in which political life is rendered unsustainable, and the inscription of control over native life – body, mind and territory. The colony is conceptualised as a space of exception, a zone of anomie in which the native's humanity is effaced through a process of exclusion from the law. This raises the spectre of the type of inclusion/exclusion debates that are salient to both emergency doctrine and colonial relations. Achille Mbembe, for example, reads Agamben's framing of the political-juridical structure of the camp in quite absolute terms, whereby 'the state of exception ceases to be a temporal suspension of the state of law. ... it acquires a permanent spatial arrangement that remains continually outside the normal state of law'.[48] Deeming concepts of biopower and biopolitics incapable of fully capturing modern configurations of sovereign power's absolute control over life, Mbembe goes a step further with his theory of necro-power and necropolitics. The notion of necropolitics is advanced to account for contemporary forms of subjugation of life to the power of death, and for the ways in which weapons are deployed with a view to maximising human death and destruction. More than mere biopolitical control over the body, or juridical reduction to a status less than equal, necropolitics connotes 'new and unique forms of social existence in which vast populations are subjected to conditions of life conferring upon them the status of *living dead*'.[49]

In making this move, Mbembe explicitly links necropower to both the colonial space and the state of exception. The conditions of living death, he argues, are most prevalent in the plantation and the colony, with colonial occupation combining biopolitical and necropolitical control over body and life. And in tracing the trajectories by which the state of exception entails a normative basis for the right to kill, Mbembe holds that power, in various guises, 'continuously refers and appeals to excep-tion, emergency, and a fictionalized notion of the enemy [and] labors to produce that same exception, emergency, and fictionalized enemy'.[50] Race is central to such production and to the exercise of necropower, underpinning a biological chasm between self and other; those to live and

---

[48] Achille Mbembe, 'Necropolitics' (2003) 15:1 *Public Culture* 11, 12–13.
[49] *Ibid.*, 40. Emphasis in original.   [50] *Ibid.*, 16.

those to die. This is explained with Mbembe's characteristic verve: race as
the ubiquitous shadow in Western political thought and practice, con-
stantly imagining the inhumanity of foreign peoples – the colonial
savages in particular. The language and logic of dehumanisation, exclusion and exception pervades his exposition of the colony:

> in modern philosophical thought and European political practice and
> imaginary, the colony represents the site where sovereignty consists
> fundamentally in the exercise of a power outside the law (*ab legibus
> solutus*) and where "peace" is more likely to take on the face of a "war
> without end."[51]

For Mbembe, the European imaginary posits the equality of all states
within the European juridical order which respect each other as civilised
enemies. In contradistinction to that order are the colonies and
frontiers: devoid of organised human societal formations; lacking regular
armies and equal sovereign enemies; inhabited by savages incapable
of distinguishing soldiers from criminals or of concluding peace.
Through this gaze:

> colonies are zones in which war and disorder, internal and external figures
> of the political, stand side by side or alternate with each other. As such,
> the colonies are the location par excellence where the controls and
> guarantees of judicial order can be suspended – the zone where the
> violence of the state of exception is deemed to operate in the service of
> "civilization." That colonies might be ruled over in absolute lawlessness
> stems from the racial denial of any common bond between the conqueror
> and the native. In the eyes of the conqueror, *savage life* is just another
> form of *animal life*, a horrifying experience, something alien beyond
> imagination or comprehension.[52]

In such a space of lawlessness, imperial warfare and governance are not
subject to legal rules or to institutional regulation. Certainly it is the case
that European powers typically departed from their own common law or
civil codes in their colonial territories. The story of the juridical order in
the colonies, however, is more complex and heterogeneous than one of
'absolute' lawlessness. Jörg Fisch, for one, insists in his account of the
colonial encounters on the centrality, rather than the absence, of legality:
'[t]here was probably no other empire building in history in which legal

---

[51] *Ibid.*, 23. On the *commandement* of the colonies rooted in 'a *régime d'exception* – that is, a
regime that departed from the common law', see also Achille Mbembe, *On the Postcolony*
(Berkeley: University of California Press, 2001) 29.
[52] Mbembe, 'Necropolitics', 24. Emphasis in original.

and moral justification played such an important part. The Europeans tried hard to legitimize their actions, to find a more solid legal foundation for what they did than simply refer to a right of conquest.'[53] The application of one particular juridical order within Europe 'does not mean that law, in a wider meaning, was absent from the process of expansion and from the relations between European and non-European political entities, or from the relations among the non-Europeans themselves'.[54] Fisch maintains that the European states themselves avowed the universal territorial validity of their rules. While the justifications offered for imperial outreach between the sixteenth and twentieth centuries have evolved – having comprised the quests to render the world first Christian, then civilised and now 'legally (but not at all materially) egalitarian, in the sense of the spread of democracy and human rights' – they are marked by a recurring missionary theme and a 'teleological view of history as a universalizing process'.[55] Law, as much as morality, has been integral to the articulation of those justifications and their execution outside of Europe. The role played by legal doctrines relating to trade, title, settlement and sovereignty illustrates this. My contention is that over time, emergency doctrine was increasingly central to the imperial governance process; emergency laws and powers constituted a particular form of legality rather than a vacuum of it.

Without engaging it directly, Anghie's work on Vitoria and Spanish colonisation of the Americas in the sixteenth century is aligned for the most part with the thrust of Fisch's analysis. In contrast to a dominant strand of thought among Vitoria's contemporaries (Juan Gines Sepulveda being the most prominent among them) that characterised the natives of the Americas as heathens and animals, barbarians standing outside of humanity and devoid of comparative rights, Vitoria himself recognised their humanity. For Anghie, this seemingly progressive inclusion of the Indigenous peoples within the realm of natural law, for which Vitoria is celebrated, produces a more dubious outcome. Vitoria's 'recognition of the humanity of the Indians has ambiguous consequences because it serves in effect to bind them to a natural law which, despite its claims to universality, appears derived from an idealised European view of the

---

[53] Jörg Fisch, 'The Role of International Law in the Territorial Expansion of Europe, 16th–20th Centuries' (2000) 3:1 *International Center for Comparative Law and Politics Review* 4, 4.
[54] *Ibid.*, 5.   [55] *Ibid.*

world'.[56] Falling short of the European standard of civilisation required to administer a legitimate state, the 'Indians' would violate this law by virtue of their very existence, identity and cultural practices. On the basis of such violation, Spanish prerogatives of travel, trade, just war, conquest and – ultimately – sovereignty are affirmed. Vitoria's humanising legal doctrine is thus one that inscribes to deprive, that includes to exclude,[57] or to repress. I will develop this notion of *repressive inclusion* further through my analysis of Israel's emergency modalities in Palestine in Chapter 7.

Samera Esmeir's compelling account of the relationship between modern law and the human in colonial Egypt points to a similar ambivalence in coloniser-colonised dynamics, this time in the context of British imperial law.[58] Following the Urabi revolution and Britain's military conquest of Egypt in 1882, the colonial state embarked upon a juridical venture of wholesale reform aimed at overhauling the legal system inherited from the pre-colonial Khedive. The mission was to emancipate Egyptians from the wanton and inhumane cruelties of Khedival rule, and to elevate them to a status of humanity perceived as previously lacking. Positive law was the force of modernity that would generate a rupture from the arbitrary violence of the past. Esmeir recounts how modern law engendered a concept of 'juridical humanity' that was rooted in sensibilities of humaneness and operated to inscribe the native Egyptian within the colonial rule of law. Through this particular narrative, the more general relationship between law and the human with regard to history, nature, sovereignty and violence is probed. Esmeir navigates a huge expanse of literature in the fields of colonial legal history, postcolonial theory, post-structuralist thought and more, but plots her own distinctive course through the relatively unchartered waters of legal narratives in British Egypt. The concept of juridical humanity both borrows from and departs from Hannah Arendt's articulation of the 'juridical person'.[59] Whereas in Arendt's account, violence is a product of *exclusion* (in the

---

[56] Antony Anghie, 'The Evolution of International Law: Colonial and Postcolonial Realities' (2006) 27:5 *Third World Quarterly* 739, 743. See also Anghie, *Imperialism, Sovereignty*, 13–31.

[57] Koskenniemi makes a similar claim: 'When the laws were extended to the native populations, their point was normally to create a status that was both inclusive but also exclusive.' Martti Koskenniemi, 'Colonial Laws: Sources, Strategies and Lessons?' (2016) 18 *Journal of the History of International Law* 248, 273.

[58] Samera Esmeir, *Juridical Humanity: A Colonial History* (Stanford: Stanford University Press, 2012).

[59] Arendt, *The Origins of Totalitarianism*, 447–455.

form of denationalisation, or in the camps' location outside of the 'normal' legal system), Esmeir's narration of Egypt's colonial story reads *inclusion* in the law as a hegemonic technique that facilitates its own brand of violence. The project of juridical humanity described and theorised by Esmeir thus connotes a type of inscription within the law that purports to enable a process of humanisation – as seen through a colonial lens – based on a liberal idealising of the 'rule of law'. Juridical humanity pulls the colonised into a domain of modernity that is fetishised in contrast to the arbitrary and inhumane nature of the pre-colonial order. The effect of colonial law's humane reforms is a process of rendering the natives – hitherto dehumanised by their own despotism – human through the law.

In a similar vein to Anghie's exposition of Vitoria, Esmeir's analysis shows that this inclusivity is not driven by benevolent designs at emancipation and equality on the part of the colonial state. Rather, the cultivation of juridical humanity embodies a more nuanced technique of inscribing Egyptians within the law as 'a technology of colonial rule and a modern relationship of bondage'.[60] Esmeir chronicles the humanising reforms that included the attempted elimination of torture, the abolition of the use of the *curbash* (whip), as well as decrees for more humane treatment of criminals, prisoners and animals. Here, 'the project of juridical humanity put pain and suffering to use'.[61] While colonial law's humanitarian intervention was effected through the reduction of suffering, Egypt was the subject of parallel thought processes of modernity that produced a domain of lawful, utilitarian, *humane* violence: 'Humanity is truly universalized when, in the colonies, pain is properly measured, administered, and instrumentalised. Only pain that serves an end is admitted. Useless, non-instrumental pain is rejected.'[62]

Under the imperial gaze, therefore, the inhumanity of pre-colonial violence lies not in the violence itself, but in its alleged arbitrariness. Juridical humanity, in Esmeir's reckoning, did not seek to prevent pain and suffering per se, but to eliminate the prescription of disproportionate or unproductive pain. Such instrumental suffering would often (though not always) assume the form of less overt modes of wounding than torture and whipping. Here, Esmeir's analysis of British reforms in Egypt takes its cue from Foucault's theorisation of certain features of liberal modernity – the abolition of public torture, criminal justice reforms, the

---

[60] Esmeir, *Juridical Humanity*, 285.   [61] *Ibid.*, 111.   [62] *Ibid.*, 142.

architecture of the panopticon – as new technologies of (bio)power directed more at the mind than the body. Esmeir is unconvinced and unsettled by law's instrumental means-end logic, and by the distinction between arbitrary cruelty and calculated productive humane violence. The impossibility of that distinction, in her final analysis, 'reveals all of the law's violence as arbitrary' and signals a 'collapse of ends into means'.[63] The structural contradictions within the law are thus revealed. Notably, Esmeir also elucidates the emergency modalities – martial law, military tribunals, special commissions – of British rule that produced a hybrid colonial liberal legal regime, split between its ideals of humanity and its factual violence. In my analysis, emergency doctrine is what allows it to straddle both.

Esmeir's reading of the British-Egyptian colonial archive convincingly demonstrates the thrust of juridical humanity as an attempt to frame the liberalism of colonial governance in juxtaposition to the violence of pre-colonial despotism. The form that this took – British officials ordering the cessation of torture and insisting on humane treatment of prisoners – did surpass some of the more vacuous rule of law platitudes propounded elsewhere, and disrupts the narrative of empire as unerringly dehuman-ising. The capacity of law to humanise or dehumanise is, however, itself contested and arguably better reflects intention than effect. Fanon, for one, acknowledges the *attempts* of colonial discourse to confiscate the humanity of the native but refuses to accept that such rhetoric is per-formative or that the colonial subject can be stripped of its agency. While violence in the colonies '*seeks* to dehumanize'[64] the native, 'he knows that he is not an animal ... he realizes his humanity ... he is treated as an inferior but is not convinced of his inferiority'.[65] That is, while the inequality between coloniser and native means that the conditions of life that the native enjoys may not be on her own terms, humanity itself is not something that can be juridically given or taken away. The endeav-ours of the state to craft humanity in a certain mould is part of a colonial

---

[63] *Ibid.*, 288–289.

[64] Jean-Paul Sartre, 'Preface' to Frantz Fanon, *The Wretched of the Earth* (1961) (Constance Farrington trans., London: Penguin, 1967) 16. Emphasis added.

[65] See Fanon, *The Wretched of the Earth*, 43, 53. Esmeir departs from Fanon on this point, but acknowledges her indebtedness to his work on the human and colonialism nonethe-less. For a rebuttal of the idea that slavery 'dehumanised' those enslaved, see, for example, Walter Johnson, 'To Remake the World: Slavery, Racial Capitalism, and Justice', *Boston Review*, 26 October 2016; Walter Johnson, *River of Dark Dreams: Slavery and Empire in the Cotton Kingdom* (Cambridge, MA: Harvard University Press, 2013) 207.

discourse that – through race and power dynamics – purports, ultimately unsuccessfully, to deprive the colonised of their voice.[66] Anti-colonial resistance, in this sense, can be understood as a response to the contradictions of colonial sovereignty.

I will return to resistance to emergency governance in this context in more detail later. For now, the pivotal aspects of the dialectics around spatial and juridical orders, inclusion and exclusion, humanisation and dehumanisation, are the interactions of legality and racialisation. Amidst the panoply and matrices of emergency regulations promulgated by the British colonial state in particular as European imperial history wore on, the colonies emerge as zones saturated by law; emergency law, but law nonetheless. The emergency modalities deployed serve as technologies of colonial governance that inscribed the native within the law, and effect control accordingly. In this reading, emergency law operates to bridge a divide that deepened over colonial time between the unfettered violence of conquest (in the colony) and an increasingly liberal idealising (in the metropole) of the rule of law as empire's gift. The banality and minutiae of emergency law exemplify an enterprise heavily inflected by a certain form of legality. It is thus a question not of the (presence or) absence of law, but of what type of law, with what structural biases. A situation not of outright exclusion from the realms of humanity or protection, but of suffocating inclusion *by* law. This is a racialised process, with colonial laws and emergency modalities 'intended to enable optimal extraction of value from foreign territories while disciplining populations that were felt as inferior and dangerous'.[67]

That said, the material presented for both theoretical and comparative reference – and the arguments extracted accordingly – cannot be uniform across colonial space and time. They need to be contextualised with reference to the particular social and political dynamics at play, and the temporal, constitutional and geographic variations of imperial rule and

---

[66] The question of the place of the subaltern voice – famously posed by Gayatri Spivak in the context of the banning of sati in India being narrated by (male) British colonial officials and Hindu leaders, rather than the women who would themselves practice sati – remains a formative one in postcolonial studies. Gayatri Chakravorty Spivak, 'Can the Subaltern Speak?' in Cary Nelson and Lawrence Grossberg (eds.), *Marxism and the Interpretation of Culture* (Basingstoke: Macmillan, 1988) 271–313. See also, for example, Edward W. Said, 'Representing the Colonized: Anthropology's Interlocutors' (1989) 15:2 *Critical Inquiry* 205.

[67] Koskenniemi, 'Colonial Laws', 251.

'colonial legal pluralism'.[68] One must leave room for an understanding
that is more complex or ambivalent than simple binaries, and that speaks
also to the underlying ideological motivations and consequences. This
becomes apparent when looking at the particular circumstances of states
of emergency in, for example, nineteenth-century India, twentieth-
century Kenya or twenty-first-century Palestine. One significant
common denominator, however, and this is where my exegesis of emergency doctrine aligns most closely with Mbembe's interpretation of the
state of exception, is in relation to the constitutive role played by racial
dynamics.

Emergency and Racial Sovereignty

The notion of emergency as a racialised enactment of sovereignty stems
from colonial contexts where the effects of a state of emergency were
inherently contingent on race (platitudes regarding equality and the
protection of loyal subjects of all races notwithstanding). Here, the
socio-historical formation of the doctrine of emergency is important;
states of emergency were not created in a void, and their effects have
fallen unevenly and disproportionately on racialised and minority
groups. They have indeed developed in a way that has led to the
construction of othered and suspect communities. Hussain's work
deftly demonstrates that in nineteenth-century India, general notions
of emergency – not simply specific moments of exception – were
imbricated in the legal reasoning and institutions of the colonial
state.[69] Indeed, the general contention I propound is that emergency
laws and powers – representing an important cog over time in the
machinery of the European expansionary project and its control of
native peoples – can be located on a continuum that evolved from
martial law in medieval England, through its export to the colonies and
the materialisation of emergency politics and lawmaking in the empire,
to the present day where similar narratives of emergency have been
adopted in post-colonies as well as retained by consolidated settler
colonial states and global imperial powers. The ubiquitous motif

---

[68] See generally Lauren A. Benton, *Law and Colonial Culture: Legal Regimes in World
History 1400–1900* (Cambridge: Cambridge University Press, 2002).

[69] This occurred in the context of what Hussain describes as the 'Manichaean racialism' of a
Victorian sensibility. Hussain, *The Jurisprudence of Emergency*, 48.

permeating this historiography is that of the creation of otherness,[70] the pinpointing of a racialised community as the object of the emergency measures.

An understanding of the racial element of sovereign engagement with crisis implies that the essence of the emergency is of more profound historical and social consequence than binary conceptions of legality and extra-legality. As discussed above, Agamben's *Homo Sacer* series, for all its insights in contesting and transcending the inside/outside debate and sharpening our understanding of law's liminal spaces, is constrained by the Eurocentrism and historical blind spots of its chosen methods, and a failure to fully address race. While rhetorically appealing for the purposes of unpacking political dynamics across universal planes, state of exception discourse may itself obscure the very uneven ways that the violence of law tends to operate. This raises the spectre of something more suffuse than norm and exception. Sumi Cho and Gill Gott, in their insightful portrait of the 'racial sovereign', imply that the failure of the project of liberal legal management of emergency powers lies in the fact that it 'discounts the Schmittean realist view of sovereignty, ironically, by engaging national security "concerns" at face value, irrespective of the long record of involuntary sacrifice fraudulently imposed upon racial minorities through declarations of emergency and threat'.[71] While a liberal constitutional theorist like Bruce Ackerman might acknowledge the identity-contingent limitations of any balancing test conducted in the face of construed security threats, in presenting his 'emergency constitution'[72] he 'stops short of offering any substantive constitutional protection against such abuses'.[73]

Cho and Gott offer a useful critique of what they describe as professionally risk-averse acceptance, evasion or collective reification of suspect and contingent sovereign projections (the 'war on terror', 'homeland security', 'Islamic' terrorism, and so on) in post-2001 scholarship on national security law. In doing so, they trace the socio-legal dynamic of emergency in the American context to a racially coded discourse of sovereignty that emerged from judicial engagement with the question

---

[70] On the 'othering' of the colonial native as 'the enemy of values', see Fanon, *The Wretched of the Earth*, 32.

[71] Sumi Cho and Gil Gott, 'The Racial Sovereign' in Austin Sarat (ed.), *Sovereignty, Emergency, Legality* (Cambridge: Cambridge University Press, 2010) 183.

[72] Ackerman, 'The Emergency Constitution'.

[73] Cho and Gott, 'The Racial Sovereign', 184.

of native rights and sovereignty in the nineteenth century.[74] Supreme
Court decisions such as that in *Cherokee Nations v. Georgia*,[75] which
rejected the claim of native sovereignty – casting the Cherokee instead as
a 'domestic dependent nation' – served to convert 'the legal equality
assumed by hundreds of treaties entered into by the United States and
native nations into a hierarchical and subjugationist relationship of ward/
guardian'.[76] This racially inflected conception of sovereignty was preserved in subsequent jurisprudence relating to early US ventures into
overseas imperialism. 'Unincorporated territories' such as Puerto Rico
were – like the Cherokee nation's 'domestic dependent nation' status –
held to exist in a liminal sovereign space of being neither American[77]
(and entitled to the constitutional benefits of such), nor foreign[78] (and
accorded the entitlements of an independent sovereign nation).[79]

As illustrated by this kind of legal history, race and sovereignty
were mutually constructed, with apparently neutral legal principles
devised in such a way as to effectively lock in racial hierarchies.
Cho and Gott proceed to show how this backdrop illuminates the
'imperialist-racial formation of enemy civilization peoples' in contemporary American national security law and policy discourse. They
conclude:

> In rethinking the questions of sovereignty, emergency, and legality, per-
> haps the fundamental question to ask ourselves is how our models of
> emergency constitutionalism relate to the ontology of order under empire.
> To perceive security interests as always already racialized and imperial
> moves us in another direction, one that problematizes the fascistic trap
> door in the foundation of modern imperial state power with its violence-
> legitimating discourses of security and exclusion.[80]

---

[74] *Ibid.*, 188–204.   [75] *Cherokee Nations v. Georgia* 30 U.S. 1 (5 Peters 1) (1831).
[76] Cho and Gott, 'The Racial Sovereign', 203.   [77] *Downes v. Bidwell* 182 U.S. 244 (1901).
[78] *DeLima v. Bidwell* 182 U.S. 1 (1901).
[79] It is worth noting that such doctrine is not a relic of nineteenth-century jurisprudence but
is replicated in contemporary situations of racial conflict and domination. Although
routinely incarcerated by Israeli authorities and prosecuted in Israeli courts, Palestinian
residents of the Gaza Strip, for example, are denied the protections of Israeli constitutional law, but simultaneously stripped of the rights of protected persons under the
Fourth Geneva Convention, with the Israeli state institutions insisting – contrary to
widespread consensus – that it is not in belligerent occupation of the Gaza Strip. See
Shane Darcy and John Reynolds, 'An Enduring Occupation: The Status of the Gaza Strip
from the Perspective of International Humanitarian Law' (2010) 15:2 *Journal of Conflict
and Security Law* 211.
[80] Cho and Gott, 'The Racial Sovereign', 227.

Where Cho and Gott zoom in on these dimensions of racialised sovereignty within the United States, Anghie provides a trenchant analysis of
the imperial origins of sovereignty doctrine in international law in the
broader context of the European colonial project.[81] His argument holds
that the colonial encounter was pivotal to the formation of international
law's foundational concept of sovereignty. Cultural subordination and
economic exploitation premised on racial discrimination were constitutive elements of sovereignty in the conquering and civilising missions.
As such, Anghie brings international lawyers back to our disciplinary
beginnings, where Vitoria was confronted with the problem of account-
ing legally for the Spanish conquest of the Americas in the sixteenth
century. Using the doctrinal and jurisprudential resources of natural law,
Vitoria first characterises the 'Indian' as primitive and therefore lacking
in full legal personality, before proceeding to outline a series of legal
principles that justify Spanish intervention for the purposes of civilising
the Indians.[82] Going against the grain of traditional appraisals of Vitoria
as having applied existing European inter-state juridical doctrines to
resolve the new situation arising from the 'discovery' of non-European
peoples and the need to determine their legal status,[83] Anghie demonstrates that 'while Vitoria's jurisprudence relies in many respects on
existing doctrines, he reconceptualizes these doctrines, or else invents
new ones, to deal with the novel problem of the Indians'.[84] Rather than
approaching the question of Spanish-Indian relations as the classical
international law conundrum of how best to create order among sovereign states, Vitoria sought to formulate a legal system to govern relations
between two very different cultural orders, each with their own specific
ideas of property and governance. His analysis does not proceed on the
basis that both parties are equally sovereign, but instead has at its root
what Anghie terms a 'dynamic of difference'[85] – entailing dichotomies
between private and public, civilised and uncivilised, sovereign and
non-sovereign – steeped in a sense of European cultural superiority.

---

[81] Anghie, *Imperialism, Sovereignty*.
[82] Francisco de Vitoria, *De Indis et de Ivre Belli Relectiones* (1532) (Ernest Nys ed., John
Pawley Bate trans., Washington, DC: Carnegie Institution of Washington, 1917).
[83] Anghie cites, by way of example, Pieter Hendrik Kooijmans, *The Doctrine of the Legal
Equality of States: An Inquiry into the Foundations of International Law* (Leiden: A.
W. Sijthoff, 1964).
[84] Anghie, *Imperialism, Sovereignty*, 15.
[85] *Ibid.*, 40. Anghie defines this dynamic of difference as 'the process by which a gap is
postulated between European and non-European peoples'.

This dynamic of difference thus illuminates how non-European societies were excluded from the realm of sovereignty at the outset of the colonial confrontation.

In order to sustain its politics of subordination, the British empire maintained a Victorian version of Vitoria's jurisprudential thought to describe and reify the rulers and the ruled. As the empire's tentacles extended ever wider, racialised difference remained the crucial yardstick that underpinned the institutionalisation and normalisation of imperial hegemony.[86] Race and cultural distinctions were the bases for establishing a legal right of occupation and abrogation of native sovereignty. In this regard, Stuart Hall defines purported biological difference and cultural difference and as racism's 'two logics', and notes the enduring constancy of British attitudes towards the empire's subordinated others: 'Britishness as a category has always been racialized through and through – when has it connoted anything but "whiteness"?'[87] This has persisted through to contemporary attitudes displayed towards people of colour in Britain, whether long-established communities and citizens, or recent migrants.[88] The malleable vision of the other in the context of security politics also reminds us that the boundaries of race are not fully secure or self-evident. As Stoler and Cooper observe: 'the otherness of colonized persons was neither inherent nor stable; his or her difference had to be defined and maintained'.[89]

We will see in later chapters the variegated ways in which racialised difference has been defined in the diverse settler colonial contexts (and maintained through the emergency legal frameworks) of Kenya, Palestine and Australia. The elasticity of racialised otherness is also evident

---

[86] Despite this, scholars such as Román point to race as the conspicuously 'missing variable' in discussions of colonialism. Although issues of race permeate the pervasive paternalism in traditional international discourse, race has been 'an all-too-often unspoken theme' in that context. Ediberto Román, 'Race as the Missing Variable in Both the Neocolonial and Self-Determination Discourses' (1999) 93 *Proceedings of the American Society of International Law* 226–228.

[87] Stuart Hall, 'Conclusion: The Multi-Cultural Question' in Barnor Hesse (ed.), *Un/settled Multiculturalisms: Diasporas, Entanglements, Transruptions* (London: Zed Books, 2000) 222–223.

[88] The 2016 'Brexit' referendum brought this to the surface in very visible and visceral ways. On the reconstruction of Britishness (and, more specifically, Englishness) as whiteness, see, for example, Akwugo Emejulu, 'On the Hideous Whiteness Of Brexit', *Verso Blog*, 28 June 2016.

[89] Frederick Cooper and Ann L. Stoler (eds.), *Tensions of Empire: Colonial Cultures in a Bourgeois World* (Berkeley: University of California Press, 1997) 7.

historically in two colonies that served as prominent incubators for the legislative germination of emergency powers in the British empire (as I will elaborate in Chapter 3) – India and Ireland. Given their apparent disparity in terms of racial formation, they merit some discussion here. India, in many ways, epitomised the racialised hierarchies created by empire. It is indisputable that law was complicit there in the racial stratification and segregation of the colonial space. Under British rule, a panoply of special exemptions and statuses divided the legal domain, primarily on the basis of racial distinctions between European settlers and natives (including separate courts with distinct jurisdictions[90]) and also on the basis of religion.[91] As one commentator put it: 'The goddess of British Justice, though blind, is able to distinguish unmistakably black from white.'[92] The delineation and construction of race by law was a fluid but permanent feature of the colonial regime: 'In India, the legal question of who counted as a European British subject was contested and reworked over time, offering evidence of how law participated in the determination and institutionalisation of racial difference.'[93]

Proponents of imperial rule offered the standard arguments as to the civilising and modernising benefits of injecting the spirit of English law into the colony, while glossing over the fact that, in the colonial context, such a system will invariably be applied selectively and with distinctions. Hussain offers us the self-evident but important reminder that 'not all the elements of a rule of law are so amenable to a colonial project of justifying rule through racial hierarchy'.[94] While James Fitzjames Stephen insisted on the need for all colonial authority to be rooted in appropriate forms of legal administration,[95] his belief – if we assume his argument was not presented in bad faith – in the efficacy and flexibility of law would prove misguided when confronted with insurgency and emergency.[96] The traditional narration of the state of exception suggests that the immediate needs or desires of the sovereign state are often not

---

[90] Company courts (jurisdiction over natives in the *mofussil*) and Crown courts (jurisdiction over all residents of the presidency town and only over British subjects in the *mofussil*).

[91] Hussain, *The Jurisprudence of Emergency*, 9.

[92] Bal Gangadhar Tilak, *Kesari*, 12 November 1907, IOR, L/PJ/6/848, File 453.

[93] Kolsky, *Colonial Justice in British India*, 12.

[94] Hussain, *The Jurisprudence of Emergency*, 134.

[95] James Fitzjames Stephen, *Minute on the Administration of Justice in British India* (1872) IOR V/23/19 Index 115.

[96] Hussain, *The Jurisprudence of Emergency*, 10.

possible to situate within a normative constitutional order. In a colonial setting such as British India, the glare of race simply functions to illuminate this chasm. The solution in India was to fill the gap between force and legality by inscribing the emergency powers needed within the statutory legal system.

Although very much peripheral to western Europe and possessing a distinct history, Britain's original colony of Ireland[97] – by virtue of its 'whiteness' – presented a problem for racial theorists and ethnologists wishing to invoke chromatism to justify colonialism.[98] The response to this anomaly, in the construction of 'those particularly unlikely Blacks, the Irish',[99] shows that racialising processes of differentiation and hierarchisation can occur even between apparently homologous groups. Theories of the Irish as a 'simianised' people were advanced in order to infuse an increased degree of difference, such as in prominent anthropologist John Beddoe's 'index of nigrescence' in his 1885 *Races of Britain* study.[100] On the back of such pseudo-science, popular discourse in nineteenth-century England was wont to describe the Irish as 'a kind of white negroes'.[101] Richard Ned Lebow's *White Britain and Black Ireland*, an examination of British perceptions of the Irish during the first half of the nineteenth century, draws on a range of historical sources to highlight prevailing stereotypes and their influence on colonial policy.[102] Pre-existing anti-Irish sentiment across the board of British society came to be increasingly couched in the language of racial differentiation during Victorian times. Caricatures of the Irish as primates were not uncommon in the popular media,[103] with the editorial outlook of *Punch* magazine

---

[97] Ceded to Henry II by Pope Adrian IV as a feudal province in 1155, subsumed into the English monarch's administrative jurisdiction by the Crown of Ireland Act 1542, formally annexed by the Act of Union in 1800 and governed by direct British rule from then until 1922.

[98] Peter Childs and Patrick Williams, *An Introduction to Post-Colonial Theory* (Hemel Hempstead: Prentice Hall, 1997) 67.

[99] Wolfe, *Traces of History*, 5.

[100] See Hugh A. MacDougall, *Racial Myth in English History* (New England: Harvest House, 1982) 123. This finds resonance in contemporary literature in the sardonic references to the Irish as 'the blacks of Europe' in Roddy Doyle's *The Commitments* (Dublin: King Farouk, 1987).

[101] Anne McClintock, *Imperial Leather: Race, Gender, and Sexuality in the Colonial Contest* (London: Routledge, 1995) 52–53.

[102] Richard Ned Lebow, *White Britain and Black Ireland: The Influence of Stereotypes on Colonial Policy* (Philadelphia: Institute for the Study of Human Issues, 1976).

[103] See also, for example, L.P. Curtis, Jr., *Apes and Angels: The Irishman in Victorian Caricature* (Newton Abbot: David & Charles, 1971).

unveiled by its characterisation of the Irish as 'the missing link between the gorilla and the Negro'.[104] Depictions of the Irish as ignorant, indolent and alcohol-dependent were not the preserve of a fringe element, but rather represented 'the dominant features of the British image of the Irish'.[105] This attitude can be traced to earlier British visitors to Ireland, as exemplified by the eighteenth-century travel writer who referred to the Irish as 'these beings who seem to form a different race'.[106] Descriptions of the 'filth and wretchedness almost exceeding what the greatest stretch of an Englishman's imagination can conceive',[107] in which Irish people were apparently perfectly content to live,[108] served to perpetuate 'the assumption that the Irish resembled insensitive animals more than they did human beings'.[109]

Beyond such racist projections, cultural and linguistic dynamics of difference were also used to highlight Irish incompatibilities with civilised Britain, and similarly served to underpin colonial policy. Routine English denunciations of the Irish centred around everything from the 'barbarism' of the Irish accent[110] to a projected predisposition to brutishness.[111] Native agrarian discontent at rack-renting and mass evictions by predominantly Protestant landowners in Ireland in the 1800s was portrayed by mainstream media and parliamentarians in Britain as rampant lawless and indiscriminate violence, belying the selective nature of the protest

[104] *Punch*, XIV (1849), 54; XXIV (1851), 26, 231.
[105] Ned Lebow, *White Britain and Black Ireland*, 40.
[106] Philip Luckombe, *A Tour Through Ireland* (London: T. Lowdnes, 1780) 19.
[107] James Page, *Ireland: Its Evils Traced to Their Source* (London: Seeley & Burnside, 1836) 10.
[108] *Blackwood's Magazine* went as far as to describe squalid filth and raggedness in Ireland as 'national tastes'. LIX *Blackwood's Magazine* (May 1846) 600, 602.
[109] Lebow, *White Britain and Black Ireland*, 40–41.
[110] Claire Wills, 'Language Politics, Narrative, Political Violence' (1991) 13 *Oxford Literary Review* 20.
[111] Thomas Macaulay (cited above for his pronouncements on the social and industrial value of Negro labour) explains Ireland's periodic rebellions through projections of an innate disposition towards anarchy and violence in Irish history, and a degraded 'Celtic' character. See, for example, Thomas B. Macaulay, *The History of England from the Accession of James II, vol. III* (Philadelphia: Porter & Coates, 1855). For a more measured understanding from British commentators and elected officials who were very much in the minority, see George Poulett Scrope, *How is Ireland to Be Governed?* (London: James Ridgway, 1846); statement of Sharman Crawford, *Hansard's Parliamentary Debates*, third series, LXIX (1843), 1010–1011 (where Crawford, a Protestant landlord himself, notes the selectivity of Irish agrarian outrage, and highlights the system of oppression by landlords in Ireland and the lack of any recourse to justice as the cause of such outrage).

and unrest. Common sentiment saw the Irish as even more savage than the savages themselves: 'The murders of this country would disgrace the most gloomy wilds of the most savage tribes that ever roamed in Asia, Africa or America.'[112] The perceived differences between the colonised and their coloniser were forcefully articulated in familiar imperial tropes by Benjamin Disraeli, who asserted that the Irish 'hate our free and fertile isle. They hate our order, our civilization, our enterprising industry, our sustained courage, our decorous liberty, our pure religion. This wild, reckless, indolent, uncertain, and superstitious race have no sympathy with the English character'.[113]

This broad construction of race – incorporating culture, language, religion and national identity – came to define both sides in opposition to one another.[114] Thus, in a certain setting in time and place at least, even a European nation constructed in other contexts as white (not least the context of colonising Irish migration to the United States during the same nineteenth-century period[115]) was not entirely exempt from the type of subordinating racialisation processes produced in starker forms and with more severe effects elsewhere under empire. And so when the British colonial authorities began legislating emergency measures to suppress agitation by the Irish peasantry in the 1800s, those measures were implemented according to a clearly institutionalised social hierarchy.

---

[112] James Johnson, *A Tour in Ireland: With Meditations and Reflections* (London: S. Highley, 1844) 144.

[113] Benjamin Disraeli, 'Letter XVI of the Runnymede Letters', *The Times*, 18 April 1836.

[114] Because of a protracted and painful colonial history, a derivative 'non-Britishness' has long been a defining feature of Irish identity. By way of illustration, we can recount Samuel Beckett's famous '*au contraire*' moment: when a Parisian inquired of the Irish playwright as to whether he was English, Beckett's reply was at once cryptic and telling: 'On the contrary'. Almost a hundred years after (partitioned) independence, Ireland is still coming to terms with the effect of this colonial history on its identity, remaining troubled by a form of postcolonial 'hybridity' in which typical colonial binaries are absent but a 'sameness-in-difference' paradox lingers. See, for example, Colin Graham, *Deconstructing Ireland: Identity, Theory, Culture* (Edinburgh: Edinburgh University Press, 2001); Luke Gibbons, *Transformations in Irish Culture* (Cork: Field Day, 1996). For a broad survey of race and racism in the Irish context, spanning the construction of the 'Irish race', from anti-Irish racism to Irish whiteness as racism, see Steve Garner, *Racism in the Irish Experience* (London: Pluto Press, 2004).

[115] Irish whiteness was of course reinforced in a range of other temporal and spatial settings. See, for example, Noel Ignatiev, *How the Irish Became White* (New York: Routledge, 1995).

The Racialisation of International Law

Concomitant to the discussions over the constitution of race and the role of law in the colonies in the nineteenth century were related debates in the realm of jurisprudential techniques of international law. A decisive realignment had taken place by the end of that century, whereby positivism had unseated naturalism as the discipline's principal method. The outcome was a reification of the view that law was not given, but was rather contingent on human societies and institutions for its creation.[116] This emphasis on institutions would underpin positivist understandings of the nature of the 'difference between civilized and uncivilized man', as articulated by John Westlake: 'it is just in the presence or absence of certain institutions or in their greater or less perfection, that that difference consists for the lawyer'.[117]

The connection between 'institutions' and civilisational hierarchies and the attention given to the character of such institutions by positivist jurisprudence in turn informed 'a shift which facilitated the racialization of law by delimiting the notion of law to very specific European institutions'.[118] This racialisation of international law formed part of a 'complex vocabulary of cultural and racial discrimination'[119] by which different standards could be applied to different categories of people and upon which determinations of sovereignty could be based. This is part of a centuries-long (and still continuing) process of international law serving to universalise European particularity. For TWAIL scholars, '[i]t is impossible to provide any other reading for the racialization of international by its chief authors' than that of it cementing Euroamerican domination of the globe.[120] Colonised non-European populations, although deemed sufficiently sovereign to legally contract to unequal treaties which expedited their dispossession at the hands of European powers, were barred by nineteenth-century international law from the realm of sovereignty. The acquisition of sovereignty by conquest over non-European territories was thereby vindicated as lawful by positivist jurisprudential thought and practice. Since colonised nations did not

---

[116] For an insightful analysis of the rise of positivist jurisprudence and its relation to the colonial civilising mission in the nineteenth century, see Anghie, *Imperialism, Sovereignty*, 32-114.

[117] John Westlake, *Chapters on the Principles of International Law* (Cambridge: Cambridge University Press, 1894) 137.

[118] Anghie, *Imperialism, Sovereignty*, 55.   [119] *Ibid.*, 100.

[120] Mutua, 'Critical Race Theory and International Law', 850.

enjoy equal legal personality, the imperial powers were not subject to the same legal constraints on the use of violence (to subjugate and pacify native populations) that bound them in their relationships with one another and their own metropolitan populations. In so far as the incompatibility of a conquest-based and racially stratified system of governance with the idea of a rule of law generated discomfort, particularly among some officials in Victorian Britain, one of the ways in which the quagmire was resolved was through the invocation of special powers under a state of emergency. Through this mandate, a legal smokescreen was provided, and consciences mollified.

With colonialism, race and sovereignty so entwined in the formation of international legal doctrine, and emergency doctrine itself rooted in the colonial context, the racial undertones of the state of emergency became, and remain, unavoidable. Twenty-first-century state policies in the form of globalised wars against non-state terror and militarised responses to migration have assumed a particularly racialised character, with much newfangled securitisation discourse effectively advocating an international legal configuration that harks back to a nineteenth-century colonial ordering of us and them. This is not to suggest a seamless continuity between colonial governance and the increasingly broad net being cast by the contemporary security state and border regimes, but the echoes are there. They are there in the racial underpinnings and discriminatory effects of states of emergency deployed in recent contexts in the USA, from the aftermath of Hurricane Katrina in New Orleans in 2005[121] to (often pre-emptive) governmental clampdowns on protests against racist police violence and impunity in Ferguson in 2014,[122] Baltimore in 2015[123] and Charlotte in 2016.[124] They are there in the 'migration emergencies'[125] (which international law itself constructs) and the 'immigration state of emergency' presented by Western citizenship

---

[121] Chester Hartman and Gregory D. Squires (eds.), *There is No Such Thing as a Natural Disaster: Race, Class, and Hurricane Katrina* (New York: Routledge, 2006); Mitchell F. Crusto, *Involuntary Heroes: Hurricane Katrina's Impact on Civil Liberties* (Durham, NC: Carolina Academic Press, 2015).

[122] Jon Swaine, 'Missouri Governor Declares State of Emergency as National Guard Called in to Ferguson', *The Guardian*, 17 November 2014.

[123] Jon Swaine, Ben Jacobs and Paul Lewis, 'Baltimore Protests Turn into Riots as Mayor Declares State of Emergency', *The Guardian*, 29 April 2015.

[124] Chris Graham, 'State of Emergency Declared after Protestor Shot in Second Night of Clashes over North Carolina Shooting', *The Daily Telegraph*, 22 September 2016.

[125] Jaya Ramji-Nogales, 'Migration Emergencies' (2017) 68:3 *Hastings Law Journal* 609.

and deportation regimes,[126] as well as in the deployment of armoured police and military troops to reinforce fortress Europe's borders under emergencies declared in the EU's peripheries.[127] And they are particularly resonant in states of emergency grounded in ongoing processes of occupation, settler coloniality, and structural discrimination in Palestine, Australia and elsewhere.

To first understand how we arrived at this point by the twenty-first century, a historical exploration of the doctrine of emergency is instructive. The next chapter chronicles, in greater detail, the regimes of emergency law that evolved as part of empire's polymorphous control techniques.

---

[126] Katie E. Oliviero, 'The Immigration State of Emergency: Racializing and Gendering National Vulnerability in Twenty-First-Century Citizenship and Deportation Regimes' (2013) 25:2 *Feminist Formations* 1.

[127] Fatos Bytyci, 'Macedonia Cracks Down on Flow of Migrants under Emergency Decree', *Reuters*, 20 August 2015; Human Rights Watch, 'Macedonia: Stop Police Violence Against Migrants', 22 August 2015; David Kearns, 'Hungary Takes Refugee Children Away from Parents as it Declares State of Emergency', *The Irish Independent*, 15 September 2015; Human Rights Watch, 'Hungary's New, Bigger Migrant Lockout', 9 March 2016.

3

Emergency Doctrine

A Colonial Account

The employment of extraordinary governmental measures as crisis management technique is not a modern invention. The genesis of the idea of emergency powers is often traced back to the regime of *aesymneteia*, a kind of 'elected tyrant' in whom the people of ancient Greece vested absolutist powers as a temporary exigency when their cities were under threat.[1] Analogy is similarly drawn to the institution of the Roman 'dictatorship' that spanned three centuries of the Republic,[2] as well as to the Roman law doctrine of *iustitium*.[3] Although there are commonalities between Roman law concepts and the notion of sovereign exception, however, the doctrine of emergency as we understand it today owes a heavier debt to more recent imperial systems. And while late French imperialism imposed *l'état d'urgence*[4] in

---

[1] Aristotle, *Politics* (Benjamin Jowett trans., Kitchener: Batoche Books, 1999) 73–74; Anna-Lena Svensson-McCarthy, *The International Law of Human Rights and States of Exception* (The Hague: Martinus Nijhoff, 1998) 9–11.

[2] Clinton L. Rossiter, *Constitutional Dictatorship: Crisis Government in the Modern Democracies* (Princeton: Princeton University Press, 1948) 15–28.

[3] Agamben, *State of Exception*, 41–51. Agamben (at 47–48) asserts that the *iustitium*, not the Roman dictatorship, is the appropriate parallel to be drawn with the modern state of exception.

[4] The French legal system takes in three incarnations of emergency doctrine. *L'état de siège* was spawned during the French Revolution, codified by a Constituent Assembly decree of 8 July 1791 and remains embedded in Article 36 of the 1958 Constitution, which enables the Council of Ministers to decree a state of siege under which the military assumes extensive governance powers. For historical analysis, see Théodore Reinach, *De l'état de siège: Étude historique et juridique* (Paris: F. Pichon, 1885). Article 16 of the 1958 Constitution mandates the President of the Republic to exercise such exceptional or emergency powers (*des pouvoirs exceptionnels*) as may be required when 'the institutions of the Republic, the independence of the Nation, the integrity of its territory or the fulfilment of its international commitments are under serious and immediate threat, and where the proper functioning of the constitutional public authorities is interrupted'. Both Article 16 and Article 36 exist in parallel to *Loi n° 55-385 du 3 avril 1955 relatif à l'état d'urgence*, which allows proclamation of a state of emergency (*l'état d'urgence*) by the Council of Ministers. This law was a product of empire, passed initially in the context of the Algerian war of independence, and later amended and applied in a number of France's Pacific

Algeria[5] and some of its Pacific territories,[6] an examination of European colonial history reveals the British empire as the site of the most established, sophisticated and pervasive system of emergency rule and legislation. Throughout that empire, the concept of emergency served as a medium through which Britain's colonial authorities sought to reconcile the unfettered sovereign power of imperial conquest with genuine concerns over the 'lawfulness' of their actions and policies vis-à-vis the natives. The relationship between the state of emergency and the rule of law in contemporary Western legalism and international law thus demands an understanding of British colonial legal history, and common law traditions of martial law and emergency legislative codes.

While martial law in its original form is distinct from the contemporary state of emergency, the production over time of special powers and security maxims has allowed the essence of martial law to be retained in a form more palatable to liberal taste buds. This refinement began with the enactment of emergency legislative codes in Ireland, India and beyond from the nineteenth century, and proliferated with the rise of national security doctrine through the twentieth century, as well as the crystallisation of economic-financial states of emergency. Meanwhile, a wholesale resort to emergency powers was evident in numerous British colonies during the 1940s and 1950s in a bid to stymie anti-colonial resistance in a

---

colonies. It was also applied in parts of metropolitan France in 2005 in response to unrest that followed the deaths of two Arab-French teenagers being pursued by police, and throughout France under the nation-wide emergency declared in 2015 (discussed at the beginning of Chapter 1).

[5] Emergencies were declared in Algeria under the 1955 law in 1955, 1958 and 1961, granting the colonial authorities powers of detention free from judicial oversight, imposing limitations on movement and expression, and crafting an emergency legal regime in which torture and other repressive practices proliferated. The 1961 emergency declared by the Council of Ministers also applied in mainland France and continued (after Algerian independence) until 1963, and for its first six months in 1961 was also accompanied by Article 16 powers invoked by the President. See further Sylvie Thénault, 'L'état d'urgence (1955–2005). De l'Algérie coloniale à la France contemporaine: destin d'une loi' (2007) no 218 *Le Mouvement Social* 63; Rita Maran, *Torture: The Role of Ideology in the French-Algerian War* (New York: Praeger, 1989); Raphaëlle Branche, 'Torture of terrorists? Use of Torture in a "War against Terrorism": Justification, Methods and Effects: The Case of France in Algeria, 1954–1962' (2007) 89 *International Review of the Red Cross* 543; Marnia Lazreg, *Torture and the Twilight of Empire: From Algiers to Baghdad* (Princeton: Princeton University Press, 2008).

[6] States of emergency were enforced, for example, in New Caledonia (1985), Wallis and Futuna (1986), and French Polynesia (1987). Svensson-McCarthy, *The International Law of Human Rights and States of Exception*, 222.

fragmenting empire. What emerges from this historical excavation is a picture of the state of emergency as an institutional and often racialised technique of governance, rather than a temporary response to an isolated crisis. The historiography further suggests a variation of forms within emergency doctrine, with progressions evident from the ad hoc invocation of martial law on one hand, to systems of governance in the modern security state – where the emergency becomes a normalised and productive process of managing populations – on the other. While some regimes have continued to invoke martial law in the sense of full transfer to military rule,[7] for the most part the transition from the lexicon and substance of martial law to that of emergency law was complete by the mid-twentieth century. As we will see in Chapter 4, the proliferation of states of emergency at this time formed the backdrop for the drafting of the foundational international human rights treaties, allowing the response to an imperial crisis of a particular historical moment to be ensconced in liberal human rights discourse.

This chapter first sketches the evolution of emergency doctrine in the British empire from martial law to legislative codification, and analyses the political economy aspects of emergency, all of which culminated in the state of emergency manifesting as a predominant mode of governance in the empire's last decades. In the context of this account of colonial legal history, there are two enduring models that illuminate how emergency governance continues to manifest itself today. One is a legislative model, whereby successive special measures are enacted as part of the 'ordinary' law-making process. In British colonies where more intricate legal systems had been implanted (Ireland and India are salient examples here), a cumulative legislative process emerged and continued throughout the 1800s. Emergency powers became embedded in 'normal' law, creating a permanent emergency legal framework that was evolved from the regime in which martial law operated as a more occasional and exceptional measure. This is a model that can be identified in contemporary Britain, where emergency measures have been normalised through parliamentary legislative procedures.[8]

---

[7] The Philippines, for example, placed Maguindanao province under martial law in December 2009. See Proclamation No. 1959: Proclaiming a State of Martial Law and Suspending the Privilege of the Writ of Habeas Corpus in the Province of Maguindanao, Except for Certain Areas. See also Asian Human Rights Commission, 'The State of Human Rights in the Philippines in 2009', AHRC-SPR-007–2009, 6.

[8] Many of the special powers provided for in the north of Ireland in the Emergency Powers Acts of the 1970s were repeatedly renewed and extended, and eventually made permanent

A second, distinct model involves the management of a population through executive decree. A (renewable) declaration of emergency or adoption of emergency law vests special powers in the executive (and/or the military) and involves at least partial suspension of the constitutional order and the regular judicial system (while at the same time often still requiring some form of parliamentary endorsement to maintain the emergency). Although distinct from martial law, this process can be seen as retaining closer ties to its martial law ancestry. This kind of emergency rule materialised in colonies where Britain did not have such an elaborate legislative or judicial system in place, leaving the colonial governor vested with a higher degree of executive discretion. The state of emergency that continued in Kenya throughout the 1950s (which I explore in further detail in Chapter 5) is illustrative, while aspects of this model continue to be seen in the emergency powers vested in Israel's military authorities in occupied Palestinian territory (which I will examine in Chapter 7).

Martial Law: 'Province and Purpose'

The official British reaction to the Jallianwala Bagh massacre in Amritsar in 1919 – in which 379 Indians were shot dead and thousands more wounded by British forces in a matter of less than fifteen minutes – was to stress the exceptionality of the event and the poor judgment of commanding officer General Dyer, whose actions, it was claimed, had gone 'beyond the province and purpose of martial law.'[9] This necessarily gives rise to the question of what is meant by martial law's 'province and purpose'. Implicit in the claims that Dyer went too far is an assumption that extraordinary powers such as those invoked under martial law are exercised for the common good of the population, are necessary to preserve legal order, and are therefore legitimate once kept in check and subject to oversight. In practice, however, the deployment of martial law in a context such as India was more commonly aimed at preserving imperial control, rather than the security and well-being of the general population. Here we must consider the fact that the 'threat' which

features of the legal system, not just in the northern Irish setting but throughout Britain itself by virtue of the Terrorism Act 2000 and subsequent wave of anti-terrorism legislation.
[9] Hussain, *The Jurisprudence of Emergency*, 100–101.

prompted General Dyer's response to general strikes in Amritsar was a threat to the political and economic interests of the colonial government. Such instances, widespread in the colonies, are testament to the underlying effects of conquest and racial subjugation in the constitution of martial law.

The concept of martial law has its roots in medieval England, where it originated as what is now more commonly referred to as 'military law' – a system of rules and regulations to maintain the order and discipline of the armed forces. From the fourteenth century, however, in addition to governing the behaviour of soldiers or sailors in active service, it was used to discipline and punish civilians: 'rebels and traitors, discharged soldiers and sailors, thieves, brigands, vagabonds, rioters, publishers and possessors of seditious books, even poachers, were condemned or threatened with the justice of martial law'.[10] Until the mid-sixteenth century, the invocation of martial law against civilians remained restricted for the most part to instances of war and open rebellion, albeit often as an offensive rather than defensive measure. During the 'Pilgrimage of Grace' rebellion in 1537, for example, Henry VIII instructed one of his commanding lieutenants to 'continue to proceed by martial law until the country was in such terror as to insure obedience'.[11] From the mid-1550s, the authorities gradually expanded the jurisdiction of martial law into spheres which had hitherto been the exclusive domain of regular criminal law. Martial law was invoked as a peacetime measure for the first time against the peasantry in Ireland in the 1550s, before being introduced in England to silence and intimidate those opposed to the Tudors' religious policies, and to prevent sedition.[12] Such a resort to martial law in times of peace continued under subsequent monarchs, most notably the Stuart kings who imposed the 'justice of martial law' as a means of punishing civilians, including by execution. Its widespread use under the Stuarts prompted vigorous debate, culminating in parliament outlawing the peacetime use of martial law – with Charles I asked to revoke and annul existing commissions of it – by virtue of the Petition of Right in 1628.[13]

Following this, the martial law transfer of power to military authorities over civilians in England fell into desuetude. As Britain subsequently

---

[10] J.V. Capua, 'The Early History of Martial Law in England from the Fourteenth Century to the Petition of Right' (1977) 36:1 *Cambridge Law Journal* 152, 153.

[11] *Letters and Papers Foreign and Domestic of the Reign of Henry VIII*, XII, i, 479.

[12] Capua, 'The Early History of Martial Law', 164–166.   [13] *Ibid.*, 171–172.

began to build up its colonial rule abroad, however, it was in the emerging tradition of European expansion that 'law followed behind, improvising by reference to facts on the ground',[14] and martial law became 'an essential part of the security apparatus of many parts of the empire'.[15] Abandoned at home because of its perceived violent and tyrannical character, the imposition of martial law against native populations in the colonies provoked considerably less reaction from the liberal English intelligentsia. Regimes of martial law came to be regularly imposed by the Crown's agents in India[16] and throughout the empire to protect British interests, consolidate imperial sovereignty and prevent native dissent against everything from colonial taxes and agrarian policies to the maltreatment of slaves. To such various ends, martial law was declared in numerous Caribbean and Asian colonies during the nineteenth century,[17] perhaps most infamously in 1865 'when a servile revolt in Jamaica was put down with the severity which one might expect from planter militia'.[18] A comparative approach – pitting martial law as it developed with colonialism through the eighteenth and nineteenth centuries against the domestic response to riots in England during the same time period, which the state purported to respond to within the rubric of ordinary law – illuminates the effect of racial difference on legal categorisations and classifications.[19]

As a 'summary form of criminal justice ... independent of the established processes of the common law courts',[20] martial law broadly entails a vast array of non-statutory, extraordinary powers for the state to deal with crisis and quell resistance. In certain iterations, 'the authority ordinarily vested in the civil power for the maintenance of order and police passes entirely to the army', but Dicey famously deemed martial

---

[14] Koskenniemi, 'Colonial Laws', 273.   [15] Kostal, *A Jurisprudence of Power*, 10.

[16] For a reflection on the Amritsar massacre of 1919, 'an incident which was neither the beginning nor the end of martial law' in India, see Nasser Hussain, 'Towards a Jurisprudence of Emergency: Colonialism and the Rule of Law' (1999) 10 *Law & Critique* 93 [quote at 94]. On the suppression of the Indian Mutiny in 1857–58, facilitated by martial law, see Saul David, *The Indian Mutiny, 1857* (London: Viking, 2002).

[17] Including Demerara (1823), Barbados (1805, 1816), Ceylon (1848), Cephalonia (1849), and St. Vincent (1863).

[18] Charles Fairman, 'The Law of Martial Rule and the National Emergency' (1942) 55 *Harvard Law Review* 1253, 1254.

[19] Hussain, *The Jurisprudence of Emergency*, 101.

[20] Joshua Bryant, *Account of the Insurrection of the Negro Slaves in the Colony of Demerara* (Georgetown: A. Stevenson, 1824) 152.

law in this sense to be 'unknown to the law of England'.[21] For him, under English law, governmental authority could never pass to the military – a restriction which provided 'unmistakable proof of the permanent supremacy of the law under our constitution'.[22] Dicey's scholarship in this regard is heavily relied upon by constitutional theorists to support arguments in favour of a full application of the rule of law and to reinforce the primacy of the judiciary above executive measures and military tribunals. While his claim that martial law in the sense of military rule was unknown to the English legal order may have held purchase during peacetime within England itself, the applicability of that assertion to colonised territories under the jurisdiction of the common law is controvertible. Dicey himself added what has remained a much overlooked proviso, clarifying that his assertion was intended to have 'no reference to the law of any other country than England, even though such country may form part of the British Empire'.[23] From this qualification a picture emerges of the colonial territories as distinct spaces under the British legal system, to which the supposed supremacy of the English rule of law does not extend. It can, in that respect, be understood as a tacit acknowledgment by Dicey of the racially contingent nature of the rule of law in an imperial context.

As we have seen, legalism in the colonies typically operated in the sense of encompassing the natives as objects of sovereign power while excluding them from certain benefits and protections of law. Legalism in that sense is bound up in the exercise of racialised hegemony. British rule operated within that paradigm, as starkly illustrated by the 'Jamaica affair', an uprising of Jamaican peasants that was met with the force of imperial troops empowered by a declaration of martial law. The conviction of a black Jamaican for trespassing on an abandoned plantation in October 1865 had triggered protests outside the courthouse in Morant Bay. Arrests of protestors then led to riots and attacks on colonial police. Driven on by white settler fears of a native conspiracy to expel them, the Governor proclaimed martial law throughout the county (bar Kingston). While the rebellion itself was small and quickly contained,

---

[21] A.V. Dicey, *Introduction to the Study of the Law of the Constitution* (London: Macmillan & Co., 8th edn., 1915) 283–284.

[22] *Ibid.*

[23] *Ibid.*, 283. This disclaimer is absent from earlier editions of Dicey's text [see, for example, A.V. Dicey, *Introduction to the Study of the Law of the Constitution* (London: Macmillan & Co., 5th edn., 1897) 270]; it was presumably added after the reality of the situation elsewhere in the empire had come to Dicey's attention.

its suppression was marked by sustained state-sanctioned violence, involving punitive reprisals and the use of heavy force. Under the martial law regime, British forces put 439 Jamaicans to death (some shot on the spot, some executed by court-martial), publicly flogged 600 more, and burnt down over 1,000 homes.[24] George William Gordon, a Jamaican parliamentarian, was sentenced to death for treason and complicity with the rebels for inflammatory remarks made before the protest, despite the fact that he had no direct involvement in the violence, was not in Morant Bay when it occurred, and had to be forcibly brought from Kingston into the territorial jurisdiction of the martial law regime.

Intense debate ensued in England over the legality and legitimacy of the actions of the Governor Eyre and the colonial troops, which Rande Kostal has narrated as revealing of the increasing centrality of law in the world-view of the English political classes of the time.[25] The justification of measures such as Gordon's hanging required a conceptualisation of necessity that inherently entailed a split between the legal identity of the metropole and that of the colony. The racialised nature of the events meant that any intended common constitutional identity was disrupted. The two unsuccessful attempts in England at indicting those involved in the Gordon case demonstrate this point. In *R vs. Nelson and Brand*,[26] it was argued that although the circumstances in Morant Bay may have initially warranted the invocation of extraordinary measures, the pro-longed continuation of martial law well after the swift subsidence of the rebellion could not be justified as legal. Since common law had been brought to Jamaica by white settlers, Alexander Cockburn argued in court, the crisis must be managed subject to the standards of English common law. In both this case and the *Eyre* case,[27] however, there were ultimately no indictments. The operation of martial law was granted a wide berth, with faith placed in the logic of sovereign prerogative. Jurists

---

[24] Jamaica Royal Commission, *Report of the Jamaica Royal Commission, Part I* (London: George Edward Eyre & William Spottiswoode, 1866).

[25] See generally Kostal, *A Jurisprudence of Power*.

[26] Alexander Cockburn, *Charge of the Lord Chief Justice of England to the Grand Jury at the Central Criminal Court, in the Case of the Queen v. Nelson and Brand* (London, 1867). Brigadier Nelson had established the military tribunal that tried Gordon; Lieutenant Brand sat as its president.

[27] *Report on the Case of The Queen v. Edward John Eyre on his Prosecution in the Court of Queen's Bench, for High Crimes and Misdemeanors Alleged to Have Been Committed by Him in His Office as Governor of Jamaica* (London: Stevens & Son, 1868). See further Bernard Semmel, *Jamaican Blood and the Victorian Conscience: The Governor Eyre Controversy* (Boston: Houghton Mifflin, 1962).

of the time, like William Finlason, presented arguments in defence of such a position, critiquing Cockburn for failing to see the situation in its racial context – including the grave threat to the settlers arising from the natives' numerical superiority – and for naively suggesting that English common law standards could be applied to a colonial conflict, where a different standard of necessity arises. Unlike the recalcitrant natives, according to Finlason, 'Englishmen never rise in rebellion.'[28] The implication of separate legal standards for subjects of the same sovereignty, based on racial difference, is clear.

Martial law was invoked similarly in other colonies – in Ceylon in 1848, and elsewhere – to crush revolts against colonial taxation and land confiscation policies. In this sense, the 'threat of martial law was an essential resource for the officials who maintained the British Empire, as they sought to defend imperial interests in the midst of an often very hostile local population'.[29] Although the Jamaica affair highlighted the concerns of the establishment in Britain with the legality of imperial activity and safeguarding the rule of law, the bounds of martial law continued to be stretched in the colonies, its scope of necessity broadened. The vindication of Governor Eyre's actions in the Jamaica affair signals an expansion of the temporal and substantive structure of martial law. The extraordinary powers invoked were not only approved despite their apparent disproportionality, but were allowed to outlive the disruption that triggered their initial deployment. It was in a similar vein that the Privy Council decision in the *Marais* case (stemming from the use of martial law during the Boer War) removed a major restriction on the exercise of martial law powers in holding that the trial of civilians by military tribunals was no longer barred by the fact that the ordinary courts remained open.[30] With this anchor uprooted, the net of special powers could be cast wider, with the legal conditions in the colonies further divorced from the domestic juridical framework. The malleability, temporal expansions and changing cognitive conditions of martial law in the colonies can be seen as creating the necessary underlying conditions for subsequent atrocities such as the Amritsar massacre in 1919 to occur.[31]

---

[28] W.F. Finlason, *The History of the Jamaica Case* (London: Chapman & Hall, 1868) 460.
[29] David Dyzenhaus, 'The Puzzle of Martial Law' (2009) 59 *University of Toronto Law Journal* 1.
[30] *Ex parte D.F. Marais* [1902] A.C. 109.
[31] For an excellent elucidation of this point, see Hussain, *The Jurisprudence of Emergency*, 118–131.

At the same time, a parallel process that may be described as the liberalisation of martial law powers was underway; that is, the 'generation of new concepts which permitted the key practices of martial law to be carried out under a conceptual form more easily defended on liberal terms'.[32] With the increasing excesses of martial law invariably came heightened criticism and opposition from liberal quarters. What was needed to subdue such criticism was a new language, 'less obviously violent and without the military overtones, that allowed the exercise of martial law powers, in other words, but in times of peace'.[33] And from this emerged the language and logic of emergency powers.

Legislative Normalisation: Codifying Emergency Powers

Justice Blackburn's opinion in the *Eyre* case emphasised 'the right of a colonial legislature to statutorily permit martial law'.[34] And while the tenor of British policy remained ostensibly committed to the belief that the violence of martial law could not be stipulated or legislated for in advance,[35] practice in certain colonies through the nineteenth century saw the inscription of the emergency framework into permanent legislation – to the extent that authorisation of special powers became more ubiquitous than ad hoc. While the form differed, the essence was similar; emergency laws created 'a form of statute-based martial law in which the will of the executive is supreme'.[36] This assimilation of emergency powers into written law can be read in parallel to a rise of positivism more generally at that time, disrupting traditional common law aversions to codification. The British authorities initially and steadily developed the portfolio of emergency legislation in the colonial territories

---

[32] Mark Neocleous, 'From Martial Law to the War on Terror' (2007) 10:4 *New Criminal Law Review* 490.

[33] Mark Neocleous, *Critique of Security* (Edinburgh: Edinburgh University Press, 2008) 50.

[34] Hussain, *The Jurisprudence of Emergency*, 115.

[35] See, for example, Lord Carnarvon (Secretary of State for the Colonies), 'Circular Despatch to Colonial Governors, Dated 30 January 1867, On the Subject of Martial Law', House of Commons, *Parliamentary Papers* [1867] Vol. 49, 395: 'legalizing in advance such measures as may be deemed conducive to the establishment of order by the military officer charged with the suppression of disturbances is ... entirely at variance with the spirit of English law'.

[36] A.W.B. Simpson, 'Round Up the Usual Suspects: The Legacy of British Colonialism and the European Convention on Human Rights' (1996) 41 *Loyola Law Review* 629, 640.

of Ireland[37] and India in particular, as a more refined and defined alternative to martial law, and more constant in its application.

Martial law was imposed by the King's viceroy in Ireland during the attempted rebellions of 1798 and 1803 in order to 'punish all persons acting, aiding, or in any manner assisting the said rebellion'.[38] After that, however, the use of martial law as a reactive measure was foregone in favour of a more constant and pervasive, less overtly violent, framework for dealing with 'disturbances' in Ireland. A steady stream of Insurrection Acts, Habeas Corpus Suspension Acts and Coercion Acts flowed across the water from the beginning of the nineteenth century, such that for the first three decades of that century 'the ordinary laws of a peaceful country were almost uninterruptedly superseded by a course of exceptional measures'[39] and by 1850 Ireland had been ruled under 'the ordinary course of the law' for only five of the preceding fifty years.[40] A letter from Engels to Marx in 1856 placed this in the larger Irish historical context of 'the English wars of conquest from 1100 to 1850', arguing that 'in reality both the wars and the state of siege lasted as long as that'.[41] Marx, for his part, reported in 1859 on how 'the world was startled by a proclamation of the Lord Lieutenant, placing Ireland (so to say) in a state of siege'.[42]

One of the statutes instituting the system of emergency law, the Act for the More Effective Suppression of Local Disturbances and Dangerous Associations in Ireland 1833,[43] is described by legal historian Brian Simpson as 'the ancestor of the modern code of emergency law'.[44] The Lord-Lieutenant, the King's viceroy in Ireland, was empowered to trigger the application of the law by declaring a county to be affected by local

---

[37] Ireland had been formally annexed by Britain through the Acts of Union in 1800 but continued to be governed thereafter as a colonial territory for all intents and purposes.
[38] 43 Geo. III c. 117; 39 Geo. III c. 11.
[39] Isaac S. Leadam, *Coercive Measures in Ireland, 1830–1880* (London: National Press Agency, 1886) 7.
[40] John L. Hammond, *Gladstone and the Irish Nation* (London: Longmans, 1938) 16.
[41] Friedrich Engels, Letter to Karl Marx, Manchester, 23 May 1856, reproduced in Karl Marx and Friedrich Engels, *On Colonies, Industrial Monopoly and Working Class Movement* (Copenhagen: Futura, 1972) 21–23. (In other translations of this passage of the letter, the term 'martial law' appears in place of 'state of siege'.)
[42] Karl Marx, 'The Excitement in Ireland', *New York Daily Tribune*, 11 January 1859. Reproduced in Karl Marx and Friedrich Engels, *Marx and Engels on Ireland* (Moscow: Progress Publishers, 1971).
[43] 3 Will. IV, c. 4.   [44] Simpson, *Human Rights and the End of Empire*, 79.

disturbances or 'dangerous' organisations to the extent that extraordinary powers not allowed for by the common law were required. In other words, the Lord-Lieutenant was essentially mandated to declare what is now understood as a state of emergency and given powers to prohibit gatherings and impose curfews, with offences under the Act to be tried by courts-martial. Nothing done under the Act could be questioned in any court of law. Ostensibly, the aim of the legislation was to stifle agitation from the Irish peasantry. There was a distinct divergence of opinion in Westminster, however, as to how much agitation or violence was actually occurring in Ireland at the time. John Key MP spoke of what was reported to him as a state of 'disgraceful insubordination'[45] prevailing in Ireland. Joseph Hume MP, on the other hand, relayed accounts that Ireland was in 'a state of perfect tranquillity'.[46] Such ambiguity naturally gives rises to suspicions that the degree of existing 'insubordination' may have been overplayed for a particular agenda. The comments of the Earl of Roden in the House of Lords debate shed much light. He spoke of the importance of 'suppressing agitation in Ireland' in order to preserve 'the integrity of the Empire'. The protection of the Protestant interest in Ireland by the British government was essential; otherwise 'it would be utterly impossible to prevent a Repeal of the Union, or, in other words, a dismemberment of the Empire'.[47] Viewed through a lens that recognises the primacy of the preservation and integrity of wider imperial sovereignty, the motivation behind the deprivation of rights that the 1833 Act heralded in Ireland comes into sharp focus. Such an analysis is consonant with the imperial outlook whereby every instance of disorder or opposition in a given colony was 'considered from an empire-wide perspective'.[48]

British rule continued to spin its web of emergency legislation throughout the nineteenth century. The Crime and Outrage Act 1847 was passed during the Great Famine in response to the 'system of terror' that George Grey claimed English landlords were being subjected to by the Irish peasantry.[49] This law empowered the Lord-Lieutenant to

---

[45] *Hansard*, vol. 16 c. 450, HC Deb 8 March 1833.

[46] *Hansard*, vol. 16 c. 406, HC Deb 8 March 1833.

[47] *Hansard*, vol. 16 c. 1312–1313, HL Deb 1 April 1833.

[48] Frank Füredi, *Colonial Wars and the Politics of Third World Nationalism* (London: I.B. Tauris, 1994) 156.

[49] *Hansard*, 20 November 1847, cited in Leadam, *Coercive Measures in Ireland, 1830–1880*, 20. It bears noting that this peasantry was then, according to the London *Times*, a populace that Britain and the landlords had exploited to the point of 'poverty,

proclaim districts 'disturbed', and to impose restrictions accordingly. Other notable additions included further Habeas Corpus Suspension Acts (1848–49, 1866–69), as well as the Protection of Life and Property (Ireland) Act 1871[50] and the Act for the Better Protection of Person and Property in Ireland 1881.[51] Both of the latter allowed for detention of suspects without charge or any form of judicial supervision. Detention was permitted by a Lord-Lieutenant's warrant, which was in itself considered conclusive evidence of what it stated and of the facts giving rise to the detention.

The role of emergency doctrine in curbing Fenian revolutionary activity was chronicled at the time by Jenny Marx-Longuet in the French socialist press. 'After the Fenian skirmish' [in 1867], she wrote, 'the English government declared a state of general emergency in Ireland. All guarantees of the freedom of the individual were suspended. Any person "being suspected of Fenianism" could be thrown into prison and kept there without being brought to court as long as it pleased the authorities.'[52] In 1870, Gladstone's Liberal government 'introduced a new Coercion Bill for Ireland, that is to say, the suppression of constitutional freedoms and the proclamation of a state of emergency.'[53] Marx-Longuet emphasises the longevity of the emergency paradigm in Ireland, and its nexus to both British land policy and the repression of anti-colonial dissent.

> Theoretical fiction has it that constitutional liberty is the rule and its suspension an exception, but the whole history of English rule in Ireland shows that a state of emergency is the rule and that the application of the constitution is the exception. Gladstone is making agrarian crimes the pretext for putting Ireland once more in a state of siege. His true motive is the desire to suppress the independent newspapers in Dublin. From henceforth the life or death of any Irish newspaper will depend on the goodwill of Mr. Gladstone. Moreover, this Coercion Bill is a necessary complement to the Land Bill recently introduced by Mr. Gladstone which consolidates landlordism in Ireland whilst appearing to come to the aid of the tenant farmers.[54]

---

disaffection, and degradation without a parallel in the world'. *The Times*, 24 March 1847, quoted in Christopher Morash & Richard Hayes (eds.), *Fearful Realities: New Perspectives on the Famine* (Dublin: Irish Academic Press, 1996) 61.
[50] 34 Vict. c. 25 (the 'Westmeath Act').   [51] 44 Vict c. 4.
[52] Jenny Marx-Longuet, 'On the Irish Question', *La Marseillaise*, 18 March 1870.
[53] *Ibid.*   [54] *Ibid.*

The Prevention of Crime (Ireland) Act 1883[55] conferred 'a variety of other repressive powers' on the colonial authorities in Ireland, including the abolition of jury trial for certain offences, the ability to prohibit meetings, ban or seize newspapers and pamphlets, and make arrests without warrant of suspects found outdoors at night time.[56] The trend continued through the turn of the century and amid rising cultural, political and socio-economic resistance to British rule. The last major act of legislation that allowed for emergency regulations before Irish independence was the Restoration of Order in Ireland Act 1920.[57] It marked an attempt to increase convictions of Irish nationalist leaders while averting the need to return to full martial law.[58] Ireland from 1800 until its partitioned independence in 1922 can therefore be seen as an embryo in which the institutionalisation of emergency powers and the notion of a permanent exception were fostered.

This legislative enshrinement of emergency powers in nineteenth-century Ireland was mirrored by parallel policies in British India. The Bengal State Prisoners Regulation 1818[59] was an early embodiment of one of the modalities of emergency rule – detention without trial – that was subsequently transferred from India to Ireland in the latter half of the nineteenth century.[60] With the regimes of emergency rule developing concomitantly in the two colonies, an imperial cross-pollination between the laws and policies of both is discernible, to the mutual benefit of colonial administrators in each.[61] From the late eighteenth century, the process of law-making as a manifestation of sovereign right was enthusiastically pursued in India under the British East India Company and subsequently under the colonial state. Lord Cornwallis' code of administrative regulations for Bengal in 1793 was followed by the substantial

---

[55] 46 Vict. c. 25.   [56] Simpson, *Human Rights and the End of Empire*, 80.

[57] 10 & 11 Geo. V c. 31.

[58] In the latter respect it was ultimately unsuccessful; the British authorities declared martial law in December 1920 as Irish resistance escalated.

[59] Bengal Regulation III of 1818: 'A Regulation for the Confinement of State Prisoners' (17 April 1818), 1 *Burma Code* 209.

[60] Simpson, 'Round Up the Usual Suspects', 639.

[61] This also extends well beyond the realm of emergency law itself; the extent of the parallels, affinities and connections between colonial Ireland and India across a wide socio-cultural and juridico-political spectrum is striking. See, for example, S. B. Cook, *Imperial Affinities: Nineteenth-Century Analogies between India and Ireland* (New Delhi: Sage, 1993); Michael Holmes & Denis Holmes (eds.), *Ireland and India: Connections, Comparisons, Contrasts* (Dublin: Folens, 1997); Tadhg Foley & Maureen O'Connor (eds.), *Ireland and India: Colonies, Culture and Empire* (Dublin: Irish Academic Press, 2006).

extension of the jurisdiction of the Bengal criminal courts, while annexed areas outside the Bengal administrative framework[62] were becoming 'a theatre for experiments of incipient legislation'.[63] T.B. Macauley would subsequently begin his project to formulate a comprehensive criminal code for India. The gift of justice and a rule of law was put forward as a central facet of the mission to civilise India, with British 'paramountcy' presented as a just and benevolent form of rule in the context of a humanitarian – indeed, *humanising* – colonialism.[64] As Elizabeth Kolsky's study of the justice system in colonial India demonstrates, however, ultimately 'law's paramount purpose was to maintain Britain's hold'.[65] Kolsky elaborates racial violence as an endemic rather than ephemeral part of imperial rule, exemplified as much by the quotidian acts of abuse, assault and murder by white planters and paupers as by the major military operations, mutinies and massacres that historians have tended to concentrate on.[66] According to James Fitzjames Stephen, the two pillars supporting the imperial bridge, 'by which India has passed from being a land of cruel wars, ghastly superstitions, and wasting plague and famine, to be at least a land of peace, order, and vast possibilities', were force and justice. By Fitzjames Stephen's reckoning, 'conquest [is] an essential factor in the building up of all nations ... Force without justice was the old scourge of India; but justice without force means the pursuit of unattainable ideals.'[67] Yet in light of the contrasting nature of these pulls, the question arises: '[h]ow could Britain forcibly cement its power in India while simultaneously ensuring justice?'[68]

Kolsky's interrogation of the justice system as it applied to natives and Europeans respectively confirms that, in one sense, it could not. The impunity afforded to the latter group reveals that 'the scales of colonial justice were imbalanced by the weight of race and the imperatives of

---

[62] Such as Delhi, annexed in 1803; Sagar and Narbada, annexed in 1818; Assam, Arakan and Tenasserim, annexed in 1824.

[63] F.j. Shore, Offg Commr, Sagar and Narbada territories to Secy, Sadar Board of Revenue, Allahabad, 7 May 1836, Home Misc. vol. 790, 422.

[64] Radhika Singha, *A Despotism of Law: Crime and Justice in Early Colonial India* (Delhi: Oxford University Press, 1998) 234. Singha highlights colonial campaigns to abolish sati and to eliminate thuggee in the context of British paramountcy, but points out that on other issues – such as that of capital punishment – the moral high ground of humanitarianism was not so easily claimed from the natives.

[65] Kolsky, *Colonial Justice in British India*, 4.   [66] *Ibid.*, 2.

[67] Leslie Stephen, *The Life of Sir James Fitzjames Stephen* (London: Smith, Elder, & Co., 1895) 395.

[68] Kolsky, *Colonial Justice in British India*, 3.

imperialism'.[69] In another sense, however, a solution to the apparent quagmire *was* developed by Fitzjames Stephen and the British legal apparatus in India. This came through the development of a doctrine of special powers and emergency measures as a means by which the expansive use of force by the military and police could be facilitated, yet kept within the orbit of a legal regime. The doctrine of emergency can thus be seen as a flying buttress linking Fitzjames Stephen's twin pillars of force and legality. In the same way that 'race provided an expedient resolution to the logical affront that colonialism presented to liberal-democratic ideology',[70] emergency doctrine provided a similar resolution to the seeming disjunct between physical conquest and liberal law. Emergency powers would become an integral element of the colonial rule of law and pivotal to the sustenance of British control in India. While 'British-Indian law became less a tool of liberty than an instrument of despotism'[71] and was rife with fundamental contradictions stemming from racial privilege – including conditions of forced labour and servitude[72] – such colonial despotism could nonetheless 'be extolled as superior to the arbitrary oriental variety'[73] precisely because it was rooted in and tempered by law. By consequence, Macauley could speak – without irony – of British government of India as 'an enlightened and paternal despotism'.[74] The doctrine of emergency is entwined in such a despotism of law – in the transition from a personalised sovereign despotism to a more diffuse system of bureaucratic-regulatory despotism. By the late eighteenth century, British involvement in India had evolved from the purely commercial interests of the Company to an all-encompassing regime of governmentality; the state charging itself with a comprehensive civilising mission. Confronted with certain levels of resistance to that regime, the colonial administration justified reliance on despotic practices on the basis of their appropriateness to India's socio-cultural environment – Britain merely 'embracing despotism as a cultural necessity'[75] – but claimed this was

---

[69] *Ibid.*, 4.   [70] Wolfe, *Traces of History*, 32.
[71] D. A. Washbrook, 'The Two Faces of Colonialism: India, 1818–1860' in Andrew Porter (ed.), *Oxford History of the British Empire, Volume III: The Nineteenth Century* (Oxford: Oxford University Press, 1999) 395, 407.
[72] See, for example, Ranajit Guha, 'Dominance without Hegemony and its Historiography' in Ranajit Guha (ed.), VI *Subaltern Studies* (Delhi: Oxford University Press, 1989).
[73] Singha, *A Despotism of Law*, 77.
[74] *Hansard*, 1833, quoted in Singha, *A Despotism of Law*, vii.
[75] Robert Travers, *Ideology and Empire in Eighteenth-Century India: The British in Bengal* (Cambridge: Cambridge University Press, 2007) 50.

nonetheless implemented in an enlightened form through the deployment of law-based emergency powers.

Despite this narrative, Britain's regime in India was ultimately one of conquest and the emergency regulations did entail force as much as law, highlighting perpetual tensions that pulled the colonial authorities between the two. The Janus-faced nature of British rule has prompted familiar descriptions of a 'rule by law', whereby 'while the state may make law for its subjects, it posits itself as above that law and unaccountable to it'.[76] The extent to which the jurisprudence of emergency distorts our understanding of the rule of law is highlighted by Hussain, who can neither conclude that the British failed to establish a rule of law in India, nor that they were entirely successful in doing so.[77] Although the elaborate British legal apparatus in India included a well-developed court system, the Bengal State Prisoners Regulation 1818 provided for the judiciary to be bypassed altogether in the case of pressing 'reasons of state'.[78] Echoing the primary motif of colonial martial law – the interests of the wider empire – the law invokes 'the security of British dominion from foreign hostility and internal commotion' as grounds upon which it is 'necessary to place under restraint individuals against whom there may not be sufficient ground to institute any judicial proceeding, or when such proceeding may not be adapted to the nature of the case, or may for other reason be unadvisable or improper'.[79] Thus, the machinery of internment without charge or trial, 'the most sought after emergency power',[80] was institutionalised. Such non-justiciable powers of detention went beyond what would have been permissible in Britain, demonstrating the effect of a supposed emergency context on the so-called 'non-repugnance' dictum, according to which locally enacted laws were not to conflict with the basic principles of English law.[81] Again, in this regard, the colony is rendered as a distinct emergency zone. Though enacting

---

[76] Washbrook, 'The Two Faces of Colonialism', 407.

[77] Hussain, *The Jurisprudence of Emergency*.

[78] Bengal Regulation III of 1818: A Regulation for the Confinement of State Prisoners (17 April 1818), 1 *Burma Code* 209, Article 1.

[79] *Ibid.*   [80] Simpson, *Human Rights and the End of Empire*, 55.

[81] English law was not transferred directly to the colony by the British parliamentary statutes relating to India. Instead, those statutory acts bestowed law-making power on the colonial government itself but always with a 'non-repugnance' clause. The Regulating Act 1773, for instance, authorised the Governor-General to enact ordinances and regulations within his jurisdiction, with the proviso that they could not be 'repugnant to the laws of the realm'. 13 Geo III, c. 63, s. 36.

extraordinary measures, the 1818 Regulation was not subject to temporal limitation or review, nor linked to a specific threat; it was enshrined as a permanent part of the Bengal legal system.

It is significant that a host of such regulations pre-date the Indian Revolt of 1857, typically presented as a definitive paradigm-shifting event in the imperial administration of India. While profound institutional changes were certainly effected in the aftermath of 1857, the practical consequences in the sphere of special powers entailed an expansion and consolidation of existing powers, rather than the initiation of an entirely new framework. Formal sovereignty was officially transferred from the East India Company to the Crown (where it had long resided *de facto*), and the Indian Councils Act 1861 enlarged the legislative and executive powers of both the Governor-General and Governing Council appointed by the Secretary of State for India.[82] This was not a radical departure from the thrust of earlier Regulating Acts, however. The State Prisoners Act 1858[83] simply extended the application of the 1818 Bengal State Prisoners Regulation throughout the whole of British India.[84] Significantly, it also overturned existing regulations prohibiting any detention that breached the procedures of arrest according to British law,[85] directly foreclosing the non-repugnance principle. A plethora of legislation had also been passed in 1857 which authorised various forms of emergency action and summary justice. The State Offences Act 1857[86] empowered local district executive governments to proclaim a state of rebellion, and respond accordingly. The Heinous Offences Act 1857[87] provided for trials by court martial, as did the Military and State Offences Act 1857.[88] This essentially rendered reliance on martial law 'in a strict sense unnecessary, though what was involved was a form of statutory martial law'.[89] Repressive emergency measures continued to be legislated for throughout the months

---

[82] 24 & 25 Vict., c. 67 s. 22.

[83] Act III of 1858 - State Prisoners Act (23 January 1858), I.O.R. V/8/36.

[84] The Regulation would remain in force until after Indian independence. In addition to Ireland, other colonial territories were subject to similar legislation later in the nineteenth century. See, for example, the Native Courts Regulations of East Africa 1897, which allowed for preventive detention or internment.

[85] Section 1 of the Act, for instance, repealed Regulation XXV of the Bombay Code which had provided for arrest and confinement in line with British legal principles.

[86] Act XI of 1857 - State Offences Act (30 May 1857).   [87] Act XVI of 1857.

[88] Act XIV of 1857.

[89] Simpson, *Human Rights and the End of Empire*, 78. See further J. Kaye, *Kaye and Malleson's History of the Indian Mutiny of 1857-8* (London: Longmans, Green & Co., 1907-11).

following the put-down of the revolt, including through the revealingly titled Act for Confiscation of Villages involved in Rebellion.[90]

Of the cases adjudicated in the period that followed, one of particular relevance for my analysis here is *In the Matter of Ameer Khan*.[91] Khan had been arrested and imprisoned without warrant and without details of any charges. The only information given to prison officials was that his detention was pursuant to special orders made under the 1818 Bengal State Prisoners Regulation. The case was a petition for a writ of habeas corpus. The suspension of the right of habeas corpus is generally indicative of an emergency law framework. In a racialised colonial setting, to consider the right of habeas corpus in the first place – that is, 'to examine the writ of liberty in a regime of conquest' – is something of an oxymoron.[92] From the perspective of colonialism, social and political conditions in the colony render habeas corpus impractical and inapplicable. At the same time, its ideological and institutional centrality to the role of judiciary and the law itself renders its arbitrary exclusion problematic. What is required, by consequence, is 'the maneuver of suspension'.[93]

In the context of British constitutional law, such suspension emanates from a temporary threat and accordingly must be temporary itself. Justice Norman's ingenuity in *Ameer Khan* was to frame the vulnerable colonial condition as subject to an indefinite threat by its very nature. An indefinite suspension is the logical upshot:

> ... if the danger to be apprehended ... is not temporary, but from the condition of the country must be permanent, it seems to me that the principles which justify the temporary suspension of the Habeas Corpus Act in England justify the Indian Legislature in entrusting to the Governor General in Council an exceptional power.[94]

While the necessity of suspending legal protections in the colony is equated with that which may occur in the metropole, the crucial temporal aspect of colonial emergency is revealed; it is intrinsically permanent. Highlighting this as a watershed moment in colonial jurisprudence, Hussain explains the decision as the logical conclusion, rather than abrogation, of the imperial rule of law.[95]

---

[90] Act X of 1858, An Act for Confiscation of Villages involved in Rebellion, I.O.R. V/8/36.
[91] *In the Matter of Ameer Khan* [1870] 6 *Bengal Law Reports* 392. For discussion see Hussain, *The Jurisprudence of Emergency*, 92–95.
[92] Hussain, *The Jurisprudence of Emergency*, 72.   [93] *Ibid.*, 92.
[94] *In the Matter of Ameer Khan* [1870] 6 *Bengal Law Reports* 392, 455.
[95] Hussain, *The Jurisprudence of Emergency*, 94.

In addition to this permanence of emergency powers, the roots of another prevalent feature of emergency discourse – the notion of the suspect community[96] – can be identified in the legal system of colonial India. The phenomenon of the 'criminal tribe' is among the most striking features of European imperial legal history. Born of encounters between British officers and peoples whom they profiled as 'born thieves'[97] in the expansive countryside of northern India in the late eighteenth and early nineteenth centuries, by the time of independence in 1947 India was home to 3.5 million individuals belonging to 128 tribes or castes ordained by the colonial state as collectively criminal.[98] That is, one in every hundred persons in the vast sub-continent was a criminal by birth.

The process by which this point was reached can be seen as imperial law's objectification of the colonised *in extremis*. Conquered and othered, the native is rendered unequal by law; the most wretched among them placed on the bottom rung of the civilisational ladder and cast as vagrants, vagabonds, thugs. Andrew Major explains the colonists' misconstructions of native identities, and points to the colonial politics underpinning hereditary criminal discourse:

> In the mistaken belief that these tribes were directly linked to the infamous confederacies of the Pindaris (marauder remnants of the Maratha armies) and the Thugs (dacoits, or highway robbers, who, the British believed, combined robbery with ritual murder in honour of the goddess Kali), the British quickly labelled them as the 'notorious tribes' and 'dangerous classes' whose threat to colonial authority had to be countered.[99]

While Simpson identifies the 1830s campaign to eradicate the Thugs as the 'starting-point'[100] from which the notion of criminal tribes sprung,

---

[96] See, for example, Paddy Hillyard, *Suspect Community: People's Experience of the Prevention of Terrorism Acts in Britain* (London: Pluto, 1993); Gil Gott, 'The Devil We Know: Racial Subordination and National Security Law' (2005) 50 *Villanova Law Review* 1073; Christina Pantazis and Simon Pemberton, 'From the "Old" to the "New" Suspect Community: Examining the Impacts of Recent UK Counter-Terrorist Legislation' (2009) 49:5 *British Journal of Criminology* 646.

[97] As one report put it: 'To be a Harnee, a Sansee, a Booriah – men whose ostensible livelihood is procured by hunting and bird-catching, who have no generally fixed abode, yet who nevertheless are often chosen as watchmen, to be one of *these* is to be known for many miles round as a born thief and vagabond.' *General Report on the Administration of the Punjab and its Dependencies for 1858–59* (Lahore, 1859) para. 14.

[98] Andrew J. Major, 'State and Criminal Tribes in Colonial Punjab: Surveillance, Control and Reclamation of the "Dangerous Classes"'(1999) 33 *Modern Asian Studies* 657, 657.

[99] *Ibid.*, 658.   [100] Simpson, *Human Rights and the End of Empire*, 83.

the beginnings of the phenomenon can in fact be detected as far back as 1772 legislation under Company rule. Collective punishment of those associated with a 'dacoit' was provided for: 'the village of which he is an inhabitant, shall be fined ... the family of the criminal shall become the slaves of the state; and be disposed of, for the general benefit and convenience of the people, according to the discretion of the Government.'[101] The Company courts justified the construction of hereditary and collective criminality on the basis that the dacoits of Bengal:

> are robbers by profession, and even by birth; they are formed into regular communities, and their families subsist by the spoils which they bring home to them; they are all, therefore, alike, criminal wretches, who have placed themselves in a declared war with our Government, and are therefore wholly excluded from every benefit of its laws.[102]

Singha is quick to grasp the mendacious nature of the legal discourse of Company officials, who routinely denounced Indian rulers for arbitrary extra-judicial interventions while themselves instituting a system that vitiated judicial process and deduced criminal intent 'from membership of a particular community, or a suspect way of life'.[103] This permeated more than a century's policing of criminal communities, simmering beneath a thin mask of cultural particularity invoked to justify pre-emptive measures against the felonious ethnicities. Nomadic lifestyles and inferior socio-economic standing would trigger not just social stereo-typing and associations with vagrancy and predatory crime; such associations would be enshrined in law, with incarceration not requiring the commission of any specific offence but instead flowing from affiliation with a group or class endowed with innate nefarious tendencies.[104] Law functions as propagator of the colonial racial schema, evoking Fanonian

---

[101] Article 35, General Regulations for the Administration of Justice, 21 August 1772.
[102] Committee of Circuit to Council at Fort Williams, 15 August 1772, J.E. Colebrooke, *Supplement to A digest of the regulations and laws* (1807) 13.
[103] Singha, *A Despotism of Law*, 27.
[104] *Ibid.*, 44. A quite extensive body of literature exists on the construction of criminal tribes in British India. See, for example, B. S. Bhargava, *The Criminal Tribes: A Socio-Economic Study of the Principal Criminal Tribes and Castes in Northern India* (Lucknow: Universal Publishers, 1949); Anand A. Yang, *Crime and Criminality in British India* (Tucson: University of Arizona Press, 1985); Sanjay Nigam, 'Disciplining and Policing the "Criminals by Birth", Part 1: The Making of a Colonial Stereotype – the Criminal Tribes and Castes of North India' (1990) 27:2 *Indian Economic Social History Review* 131; Sanjay Nigam, 'Disciplining and Policing the "Criminals by Birth", Part 2: The Development of a Disciplinary System, 1871–1900' (1990) 27:3 *Indian Economic Social History Review* 257; Meena Radhakrishna, *Dishonoured by History: "Criminal Tribes" and British*

imagery of the native, in the European imagination, as 'a sort of quintessence of evil'; the North African as a 'criminal by vocation'; the *fellaheen* as 'ambitious peasants, criminals'; the Algerians as 'born slackers, born liars, born robbers, and born criminals'.[105]

Codification continued with Regulation XXII of 1793[106] facilitating the coercion of suspect tribes into forced labour, and the sweeping Thuggee Act 1836,[107] which criminalised membership of 'any gang of Thugs' with retrospective ('either before or after the passage of this Act') and extraterritorial ('either within or without the Territories of the East India Company') effect with a punishment of mandatory life imprisonment with hard labour. On the basis of the legislation, communities were 'socialized into criminality' as part of the broader process of colonial management:

> The theme of criminal communities was also used to justify special executive powers or punitive drives of various sorts. The targets of such measures were supposed to have placed themselves outside the pale of society, thereby forfeiting their claim to the protection of regular procedure. In very general terms, such drives can be attributed to the wider process of colonial pacification, to the effort to make the subjects of empire both taxable and 'policeable'.[108]

For purposes of immobilising resistance to colonial government, it is of course far less burdensome to condemn people for membership of a vaguely-defined communal criminal enterprise than to prove individual culpability for particular offences. The case for special measures to target specific castes or tribes rested on the argument that such groups fell outside the pale of society and were inveterate reprobates. Suggestions that 'Pindaris were the "dregs" of society, the thugs originated from the parties of "vagrant" Muslims, the Badhaks were outcaste Hindus and Muslims' created impressions of an entrenched system of sedition 'which only the most rigorous measures could combat'.[109]

The Criminal Tribes Act 1871,[110] drafted by Fitzjames Stephen, served to collate and institutionalise earlier disparate measures of disciplining and controlling such supposedly delinquent communities. Local government

---

Colonial Policy (Hyderabad: Orient Longman, 2001); Henry Schwarz, *Constructing the Criminal Tribe in Colonial India: Acting Like a Thief* (London: Wiley-Blackwell, 2010).
[105] Fanon, *The Wretched of the Earth*, 32, 246, 232, 239.
[106] 'Regulations for the Police Collecterships of Bengal, Bihar and Orissa'.
[107] Act XXX of 1836.   [108] Singha, *A Despotism of Law*, 169–70.   [109] *Ibid.*, 189, 208.
[110] Act No. XXVII of 1871 ('An Act for the Registration of Criminal Tribes and Eunuchs').

authorities received powers, in conjunction with the Governor-General, to classify as criminal any tribe, gang or class of persons considered to be 'addicted to the systematic commission of non-bailable offences' and to publish notification of such classification in the Local Gazette, with the added proviso that such measures were immune from legal challenge: 'No Court of Justice shall question the validity of any such notification ... every such notification shall be conclusive proof that the provisions of the Act are applicable to the tribe, gang or class specified therein.'[111] On the basis of this racialised typecasting, designated groups were subject to a coercive architecture of measures controlling their registration, residence, movement, labour and family lives, with the Act also entailing a presumption of the guilt of individual tribe members for the commission of an offence under the Penal Code.[112] And so it continued. The 1911 Criminal Tribes Act delegated additional powers of classification and surveillance to local authorities. A similar legal path was followed in Burma, enabling the controlled residence or detention of entire 'crime-addicted' tribes.[113] In such measures racialised discourse is central. Where domination and colonial rule in general is justified by Eurocentric assumptions as to the superiority of Western socio-cultural values and the institutions of liberal democracy and capitalism, the moral justifications advanced by colonial agents for the criminalisation of certain native groups emanates from an orientalist appropriation of the caste system and other indigenous structures and practices. And while the brutality of empire and martial law in India is etched in our historical consciousness courtesy of particularly violent eruptions such as the 1857 Revolt or the Amritsar massacre in 1919, a more insidious politics of emergency was inscribed into the ongoing policing of society by pervasive emergency regulations and the exclusion of particularly 'uncivilised' tribes on the basis of a constant constructed threat to colonial interests.

With the onset of the First World War, the matrix of legislative emergency powers enacted in Ireland and India provided a ready-made template for the legal powers that the British government desired to summon. Based on the colonial model, a comprehensive code of emergency powers was enacted in the form of a series of Orders in Council under the aegis of the Defence of the Realm Act

---

[111] Sections 2, 5, 6.   [112] Sections 7, 8, 9, 13, 14, 17, 18, 20.

[113] See, for example, Kachin Hill Tribes Regulation 1895, 1 *Burma Code* 379, Regulation I of 1895; Burma Frontier Tribes Regulation 1896, 1 *Burma Code* 406, Regulation II of 1896; Criminal Tribes Act 1924, 1 *Burma Code* 410, India Act VI of 1924.

(DORA) 1914,[114] which fundamentally altered constitutional conditions during the emergency and channelled special powers to the military. In such an emergency code configuration, the enabling 'parent' legislation permits the executive to introduce new and unanticipated emergency regulations and to amend existing ones without the direct involvement of the legislature.[115] The granting of sweeping powers in this manner informs depictions of the Defence of the Realm Act as 'a hurriedly devised translation of martial rule and prerogative concepts into statutory provisions'[116] that gave rise to a 'delegated dictatorship'.[117] Under the procedures provided for, powers could be assumed, amended and enhanced by the executive without reversion to parliament. Executive detention – which had not been mentioned when the parent act went through parliament – was introduced through such means in 1915 by Order in Council, prompting Simpson to conclude that '[t]he structure of government under DORA closely resembled the situation in those colonial territories where the Governor and executive could force through any legislation desired.'[118]

Here we can see in action what Foucault describes (borrowing the phrase used by Aimé Césaire) as a 'boomerang effect' of colonial practice on juridical and political structures in the metropole: 'while colonization, with its techniques and its political and juridical weapons, obviously transported European models to other continents, it also had a considerable boomerang effect on the mechanisms of power in the West, and on the apparatuses, institutions, and techniques of power'.[119] As soon as difficult questions of national security, race and class struggle resurfaced in Britain, it became clear that emergency measures would not be limited to the colonial domain; the narrative and justifications of emergency would invariably rebound into the domestic realm. The system of delegated emergency rule initiated under the Defence of the Realm Acts was also quickly funnelled back to the colonial realm. An equivalent emergency code was implemented in India through the Defence of

---

[114] Defence of the Realm Acts 1914, 4 & 5 Geo. V c. 29; Defence of the Realm (Consolidation) Act 1914, 5 Geo. V. c. 8.
[115] Simpson, 'Round Up the Usual Suspects', 640.
[116] Cornelius P. Cotter, 'Constitutionalizing Emergency Powers: The British Experience' (1952–1953) 5 *Stanford Law Review* 382, 384.
[117] Rossiter, *Constitutional Dictatorship*, 230.
[118] Simpson, *Human Rights and the End of Empire*, 81.
[119] Foucault, *Society Must Be Defended*, 103.

India Act 1915,[120] under which the Governor-General was given free rein
to enact rules for 'the purpose of public safety and defence of British
India'.[121] The emergency powers grid in India continued to branch out
after the war through myriad legislative sprigs: the Anarchical and
Revolutionary Crimes Act 1919, the Criminal Tribes Act 1924, the
Bengal Criminal Law Amendment Acts 1925 and 1930, the Bengal
Emergency Powers Ordinance of 1931 and the Suppression of Terrorist
Outrages Act 1932; all with significant consequences in terms of the
controlled residence, forcible transfer and internment of the colonised.
A number of Indians acquitted at a trial of involvement in a raid on a
British armoury in 1930, for example, were nonetheless detained until
1938 under a Bengal Emergency Powers Ordinance.[122]

The state of emergency regime in India was fortified upon the outbreak of the Second World War by the Defence of India Act 1939. Under
this statute, an elaborate code of regulations, known as the Defence of
India Rules, was introduced. While the war created the conditions
conducive to the performance of an emergency internationally, it was
internally – against anti-colonial movements such as Quit India – that
the repressive powers were primarily discharged. Through 1942 and
1943, hundreds of Indians were killed by British police, thousands of
whipping sentences carried out under the revived Emergency Whipping
Act, and tens of thousands detained, including Mahatma Gandhi and
Jawaharlal Nehru.[123] Similar scenes were playing out across the empire,
where the Emergency Powers (Colonial Defence) Order in Council
1939 authorised the Governor (or equivalent) in numerous colonial
territories to 'make such Regulations as appear to him to be necessary
or expedient for securing the public safety, the defence of the territory,
the maintenance of public order and the suppression of mutiny, rebellion
and riot, and for maintaining supplies and services essential to the life of
the community'.[124] The breadth and scope of such a mandate is patent.

---

[120] Acts Passed by the Governor-General in Council, No. IV (1915).
[121] Simpson, 'Round up the Usual Suspects', 646.
[122] Charles Townshend, *Britain's Civil Wars: Counter Insurgency in the Twentieth Century* (London: Faber & Faber, 1986) 145–149. The Bengal Emergency Powers Ordinance was a successor of the 1818 Bengal State Prisoners Regulation.
[123] Simpson, *Human Rights and the End of Empire*, 87.
[124] Section 6(1), Emergency Powers (Colonial Defence) Order in Council, 1939. Under the Order in Council, a new code was introduced in Palestine in 1939, for example. This built upon prior emergency regulations that had no nexus to the war but rather had been aimed at stamping out Palestinian revolt during the 1930s. Under the Palestine

Through this history of colonial emergency rule and the wartime and inter-war periods, the scope of states of emergency also extended to encompass the economic realm.

The Political Economy of Emergency

Recourse by states to the paradigms of emergency and exception has never been limited solely to the sphere of 'national security'. It has been integral to economic law and policy in consolidating global finance structures, and has served to salvage late capitalism from its own crises. Analysis of states of emergency in international legal scholarship has, however, primarily revolved around the resort to special powers in the context of military engagement, ethnic conflict and securitisation; that is – to the extent that the two can be separated – in times of 'political' rather than 'economic' crisis. The typical approach acknowledges three distinct varieties of emergency – grave political crises, economic crises and natural disasters – before proceeding to focus on the first and dispense with the latter two.[125] In this regard, it is noted that 'liberal legal and political analysts have too often ignored the seriousness of the normative and institutional problems posed by the surprisingly pervasive reliance on emergency devices to grapple with the exigencies of economic affairs'.[126]

The premise of an economic state of emergency is analogous to that presented to justify the invocation and entrenchment of extraordinary powers in relation to national security threats and militarised conflict. It bears a similar relation to the concept of the purported common good; temporary abdication of the rights of some is necessary in the greater public interest, in order to stabilise and sustain a system seen as indispensable. In much the same way as such narratives of necessity underpin

(Defence) Orders in Council of 1931 and 1937, Britain's High Commissioner was empowered to declare a public emergency in Palestine. He did so during the Arab Revolt of 1936, whereupon collective punishment, property destruction, movement restrictions, censorship, detention, trial by military courts and deportation became par for the course for Palestinian nationalists.

[125] See, for example, Oren Gross and Fionnuala Ní Aoláin, *Law in Times of Crisis: Emergency Powers in Theory and Practice* (Cambridge: Cambridge University Press, 2006) 4.

[126] William E. Scheuerman, 'The Economic State of Emergency' (1999–2000) 21 *Cardozo Law Review* 1869, 1869–1870.

illiberal policies and consolidate security apparatuses in the civic sphere, however, in the socio-economic realm they pay undue deference to capitalist institutions and subvert the notion of the common good by reifying elitist misappropriations of the 'commons'. Indeed, concerns over the obfuscation of the common good in human rights discourse have deepened since the emergence of a pattern which 'reverses the notion that universal human rights are designed for the dignity and well being of human beings and insists, instead, upon the promotion and protection of the collective rights of global capital in ways that "justify" corporate well-being and dignity over that of human persons'.[127] Emergency economic measures feed into the contradictions of this emergent 'trade-related, market-friendly human rights paradigm',[128] insofar as they are couched in terms of promotion of the public interest, but in actuality function to protect global capital and dilute both the state's commitment to socio-economic equality and the global North's commitment to global redistribution. The language of emergency, premised on temporariness, is invoked to institute legislative and institutional changes whose effect will be felt far beyond the immediacy of a given crisis. Whilst the problems of normalised and entrenched 'exceptional' measures are endemic in the history and ongoing politics of national security emergencies, some commentators have plausibly argued that extra-constitutional responses to economic crises can ultimately degrade the interests of liberty as much as, or even more than, extra-constitutional responses to violent crises.[129]

The use of emergency measures as instruments of economic regulation and class subjugation must be understood against some important and related contextual backdrops: the intimate relationship that exists between capitalism and imperialism, the function of economic governance as an apparatus of security, and the susceptibility of capitalist economies to periodic 'crisis'. The story of emergency economic powers begins with their historical entwinement in colonial law and policy. From those foundations, the economic state of emergency evolved significantly through the inter-war period in Europe and North America. Emergency

---

[127] Upendra Baxi, 'Voices of Suffering and the Future of Human Rights' (1998) 8 *Transnational Law and Contemporary Problems* 125, 163-164.

[128] Upendra Baxi, *The Future of Human Rights* (Oxford: Oxford University Press, 2nd edn., 2006) 234–275.

[129] See, for example, Rebecca M. Kahan, 'Constitutional Stretch, Snap-Back, and Sag: Why Blaisdell was a Harsher Blow to Liberty than Korematsu' (2005) 99 *Northwestern University Law Review* 1279.

discourse has subsequently been relevant to the operation of the Bretton Woods institutions in the Third World, where the speculative mindset of 'opportunity in crisis' came to the fore, and emergency authority served as a vehicle for the implementation of neoliberal policy and an economic 'shock doctrine'.[130] Emergency modalities have played a similarly versatile role in preserving and sustaining prevalent global capitalist structures, in such diverse guises as declarations of states of emergency to target labour unions and suppress protest movements, the ambiguous role of security and economic emergency exceptions in international trade and investment law, and the utilisation of emergency discourse to justify austerity measures and bank 'bailouts' in the post-2008 financial environment. Even absent formal declarations of a state of emergency, the refrains and rhetoric of emergency, exception and necessity remain a constant echo.

The economic state of emergency cannot be chronicled without reference to capitalist expansion in the colonial context. As with the evolution to emergency powers more generally, this originates in martial law. I have noted above that martial law was invoked as a peacetime measure for the first time in the 1550s. This was a time of severe economic depression, and one of the purposes for which martial law was deployed was a means of class and political repression against 'those products of a depressed economy ... general undesirables with no apparent means of support'.[131] England's ruling establishment experimented with this primarily in Ireland at first. In 1556, Mary I authorised the Marshal of the army in Ireland to proceed against 'general undesirables' there by martial law.[132] In 1562, Thomas Radcliffe, 3rd Earl of Sussex, recommended to the Queen that an English-born ruler be appointed to govern the Irish province of Munster, with the 'authority to execute the martial law in times of necessity, but only against persons that have no possessions'.[133] As such, the class element of colonial martial law is evident from the outset. The ensuing history of the British empire is replete with the use of emergency measures to support and sustain expanding commercial interests – whether in the expropriation of land, the exploitation of resources, the quashing of peasant uprisings, the protection of settler plantation infrastructure, or the quelling of trade union activity.

---

[130] Naomi Klein, *The Shock Doctrine: The Rise of Disaster Capitalism* (New York: Metropolitan Books, 2007).
[131] Capua, 'The Early History of Martial Law', 164.
[132] *Calendar of State Papers, Ireland, 1509–1573*, 134.
[133] *Calendar of the Carew Manuscripts, 1515–1574*, 336.

Such usages of emergency law as a mode of class repression evolved in
concert with colonial expansion, in the context of the broader, mutually
interactive relationship between capitalism and colonialism. Marx and
Engels show this relationship to be an organic one, in which colonialism
is an outgrowth of the wider processes of capitalist transformation of
European society.[134] The divergences and internal contradictions within
the theorising of that relationship nothwithstanding, a wide spectrum of
thinkers from classic liberal political economy[135] to Marxist traditions[136]
and Third World approaches to international law[137] persuasively demonstrate the economic underpinnings of colonial expansion by capitalist
powers.[138] Put simply, '[e]conomization and colonization were syn-
onymous'.[139] Many of the key factors in this equation have been well
documented, particularly with reference to the intensification of imperial
conquest in the nineteenth century. In the context of population growth,
industrialisation, transport and technological advances, European capital
required access to raw materials, resources and markets such that economic expansion in both the temperate 'empty' lands of 'capitalist neo-

---

[134] The most comprehensive compendium of Marx and Engels' writings on colonialism can
be found in Karl Marx and Friedrich Engels, *On Colonialism* (Moscow: Foreign Languages Publishing House, 1960).

[135] See, for example, Adam Smith, *An Inquiry into the Nature and Causes of the Wealth of
Nations* (London: Ward, Lock & Co, 1776) vol. II, 25, affirming the economic benefits of
colonialism: 'By opening a new and inexhaustible market to all the commodities of
Europe, [colonial expansion] gave occasion to new divisions of labour and improve-
ments of art, which, in the narrow circle of the antient commerce, could never have
taken place.'

[136] Rudolf Hilferding, *Finance Capital: A Study of the Latest Phase of Capitalist Development*
(1910) (Tom Bottomore ed., Morris Watnick & Sam Gordon trans., London: Routledge,
1981); Rosa Luxemburg, *The Accumulation of Capital* (1913) (Kenneth J. Tarbuck ed.,
Rudolf Wichmann trans., London: Penguin, 1972); Nikolai Bukharin, *Imperialism and
World Economy* (1917) (London: The Merlin Press, 1972); V.I. Lenin, *Imperialism: The
Highest Stage of Capitalism: A Popular Outline* (1917) (New York: International Pub-
lishers, 1939). Lenin's work was heavily influenced by John A. Hobson, *Imperialism:
A Study* (London: James Nisbet, 1902).

[137] See, for example, B.S. Chimni, 'Third World Approaches to International Law:
A Manifesto' (2006) 8 *International Community Law Review* 3.

[138] As Chimni points out, however, more contemporary liberal thinkers (such as John
Rawls) and theorists of capitalism (such as Milton Friedman) manage to expunge the
history of colonialism entirely from their accounts of capitalism, and thus fail to
acknowledge the elemental relationship between imperialism and capitalism. B.S.
Chimni, 'Capitalism, Imperialism and International Law in the 21st Century' (2012)
14:1 *Oregon Review of International Law* 17, 25.

[139] Gustavo Esteva, 'Development' in Wolfgang Sachs (ed.), *The Development Dictionary:
A Guide to Knowledge as Power* (London: Zed, 2010) 14.

Europes' (the Americas, southern Africa and Australia) and the 'tropical periphery' (Asia, Africa and the Caribbean) was seen as necessary.[140] As such, appropriation is driven by capitalist social relations and structured by core-periphery bisections. What is also striking in this context is the role of economic emergency at home in the proliferation of conquest abroad. Europe's major economic depression of the nineteenth century came in the 1870s on the heels of entrenched free market and free trade policies. The work of Polanyi and others shows that by this time the formation of international economic structures were predicated on a deep-seated belief in the ability of the free market to organise life.[141] When currency fragility and falling profits threatened stability, unflinching faith in the market and conviction of the necessity of free trade meant that the only logical response was a drive for new markets and more resources. Hence the wave of major colonial expansion that encompassed the 'scramble' for Africa and the Berlin and Brussels Conferences of the mid-1880s.

What of the role of law and emergency in these developments? In the colonial domain, as elsewhere, legal relations and forms of state are moulded by the material conditions of social life, of which the economic structure of society is an integral component. Bedjaoui's quintessential dissection of classical international law characterised it as imbued with 'a geographical bias (it was a European law) ... [and] an economic motivation (it was a mercantilist law)'.[142] This reminds us that international legal structures were shaped in their origins by European economic exploitation of the colonies. The legal form of the colonial state itself encouraged and incentivised capitalist tendencies, by coupling a framework for commercial exploitation of colonial territories, resources and labour with protectionist policies for its own planters and industrialists. Emergency modalities were used in the enforcement of both. As the

---

[140] '"Empty" in the sense that the native peoples were ultimately unable to mount an effective resistance to capitalist colonization.' B.R. Tomlinson, 'Economics and Empire: The Periphery and the Imperial Economy' in Andrew Porter (ed.), *Oxford History of the British Empire, Volume III: The Nineteenth Century* (Oxford: Oxford University Press, 1999) 53, 55.

[141] For a TWAIL perspective of international political economy based on an insightful reading of Karl Polanyi's *The Great Transformation: The Political and Economic Origin of Our Time* (New York: Farrar & Rinehart, 1944), see Michael Fakhri, 'Law as the Interplay of Ideas, Institutions, and Interests: Using Polanyi (and Foucault) to ask TWAIL Questions' (2008) 10 *International Community Law Review* 455.

[142] Bedjaoui, 'Poverty of the International Order', 153.

model of colonial economic policy advanced towards a free trade template in the nineteenth century, so too did Western legal systems and, in turn, international legal norms and practice. Anghie brings us back to the British East India Company as the embryo in which commercial interests and colonial governance coalesced. In exercising sovereign powers over non-European territories, the company 'established systems of law and governance that were directed at furthering the commercial relations that were the very *sine qua non* of their existence. . . . The governance of non-European territories was assessed principally on the basis of whether it enabled Europeans to live and trade as they wished'.[143] This association between governance and commerce was augmented and refined under the direct governmental rule that succeeded the trading companies, culminating in the focus of the Berlin Conference on the efficient and orderly mercantile exploitation of Africa, with commercial development presented to the world as the means by which backward populations could enter the realm of civilisation. The role of capitalism in the civilising mission was elaborated through the colonial project's dual mandate of civilisation and commerce,[144] which would carry through to the League of Nations' missionary calling. During the League period, Anghie's 'dynamic of difference' could be seen clearly as not only a racial construct but one also infused with a class element, through characterisations of the non-European world as economically primitive. He shows that, irrespective of any rhetoric as to the humanism and well-being of colonised peoples, the commercial and trade interests of the West have remained paramount through the centuries.

In this colonial (as well as 'post-colonial') setting, the rule of liberal international law functions to reinforce capitalist agendas and expansions in several ways, including through a doctrine of emergency that operates in a manner that is not only racially contingent but is underpinned by

---

[143] Anghie, *Imperialism, Sovereignty*, 252. As Anghie points out, for positivists such as Westlake, the absence outside of Europe of a regulatory system for European commercial activity was justification in itself for the imposition of colonial rule and law: 'non-European states were uncivilized unless they could provide a system of government "under the protection of which . . . the former [Europeans] may carry on the complex life to which they have been accustomed in their homes." If such government was lacking, Westlake argued, "government should be furnished"'. Anghie, citing John Westlake, *Chapters on the Principles of International Law* (Cambridge: Cambridge University Press, 1894) 141–142.

[144] See Frederick Lugard, *The Dual Mandate in British Tropical Africa* (Hamden, CT: Archon Books, 1965).

class and commercial interests. In the colonies, capitalism, race and class intersect in particular ways through the doctrine of emergency. Capitalism is prone to crisis, and for the purposes of self-preservation, such crises must be mitigated. Marxists, Minskyians, Keynesians and other schools of heterodox economics may vary in their diagnoses of exactly how and why capitalist systems have an innate proclivity to instability, but all essentially agree on the fundamental point: that crisis is structurally endemic in capitalism.[145] Capitalism is also prone to challenges aimed at redistribution or reduction of inequalities; challenges which must similarly be managed, including through the disciplining of organised labour. In both regards, the versatility of emergency mechanisms in sustaining existing patterns of capital accumulation comes to the fore; whether in the justification of severe and austere economic measures as crisis management technique, or the containment of protest and industrial action. The emergency paradigm can surface regardless of the rationale underpinning a particular form or 'art' of government at a particular point in time. In this sense, reliance on emergency doctrine in the economic realm can be seen as symptomatic of a particularly Foucauldian idea of economic governance as itself as an apparatus of security.[146] In other words, economy remains inseparable from state security; 'the military and the monetary'[147] cannot be disentangled.

The flaws of Carl Schmitt's theoretical inquiries and the perniciousness of his ideological stance notwithstanding, William Scheuerman concludes that his work provides a useful insight into some of the real failings of capitalist liberal democracy,[148] particularly in relation to what Schmitt termed the 'economic-financial state of emergency'.[149] Schmitt

---

[145] For contemporary Marxist analyses, see, for example, David Harvey, *The Enigma of Capital and the Crises of Capitalism* (Oxford: Oxford University Press, 2010); John Bellamy Foster & Robert W. McChesney, 'Monopoly-Finance Capital and the Paradox of Accumulation' (2009) 61:5 *Monthly Review* 1. For Minsky's financial instability hypothesis, see Hyman P. Minsky, 'The Financial Instability Hypothesis', Levy Economics Institute of Bard College, Working Paper No. 74 (May 1992). For an outline of the structural Keynesian perspective as well as a succinct overview of the commonalities and divergences between the varying positions, see Thomas I. Palley, 'The Limits of Minsky's Financial Instability Hypothesis as an Explanation of the Crisis' (2010) 61:11 *Monthly Review* 28.

[146] Foucault, 'Governmentality', 87, 92.

[147] Gil Scott-Heron, 'Work for Peace', on his *Spirits* LP (New York: TVT Records, 1994).

[148] Scheuerman, 'The Economic State of Emergency'.

[149] Carl Schmitt, *Der Hüter der Verfassung* (Tübingen: J.C.B. Mohr, 1931) at 115–117, quoted in Ingeborg Maus, 'The 1933 "Break" in Carl Schmitt's Theory' (1997) 10 *Canadian Journal of Law & Jurisprudence* 125, 131.

accurately highlighted the tendency of liberal discourse to equate economic and financial crises with the threats posed by military attack or
armed rebellion. In this conflation, security of capital becomes entwined
with the state of emergency in a similar manner to national security.
Governmental assumption of emergency powers to pursue pervasive
economic measures is justified on the same premise of necessity. This
engenders the class component of the story of emergency. Where labour
and socialist agitation emerged as a challenge to the hegemony of capital,
constitutional emergency clauses were ready-made for legalised crackdowns. Marx describes the use of French Revolution 'state of siege'
emergency provisions as a weapon in the hands of the 'bourgeois dictatorship', invoked to buttress class privilege and sideline the interests of
workers and petty bourgeoisie.[150] Clinton Rossiter later observed that
such devices of constitutional dictatorship as the French *état de siege* – as
well as Article 48 of the Weimar Constitution and the Emergency Powers
Act 1920 in Britain – are 'ideally suited to be employed as a weapon of
reaction and class struggle'.[151]

   In the twentieth century inter-war period, the use of emergency
powers to regulate the economy was an integral element of the political
governance of major Western powers,[152] prompting depictions of 'economic dictatorship'.[153] Scheuerman describes a sequential pattern in the
story of emergency economic power, where emergency powers operated
in the economic realm initially to stifle organised labour, before being
invoked to manage the economy itself to the benefit of the capitalist
classes and later as an instrument to stave off or deflect the effects of the
next crisis.[154] Permeating this process is a fundamental conflation of
economy and security, evident in the capitalist West through perceptions
of workers as security threats and the construction of economic crises as
war-like situations. In Britain from the 1920s onwards, labour movements and industrial unrest were viewed and portrayed by business and
political elites as a form of civil insurrection, an intemperate uprising
against liberal conceptions of an ultimately flourishing and lucrative
market economy. These portrayals were in turn reflected in the

---

[150] Karl Marx, *The Eighteenth Brumaire of Louis Bonaparte* (1852) (Moscow: Progress
    Publishers, 1934) 26, 27, 42.
[151] Rossiter, *Constitutional Dictatorship*, 173.
[152] *Ibid.*, 41–53 (on Weimar Germany), 117–129 (on France), 171–183 (on Britain) and
    255–264 (on the United States).
[153] *Ibid.*, 51, 273.   [154] Scheuerman, 'The Economic State of Emergency', 1875.

emergency laws and powers deployed against such movements. Such practices followed the long-standing trend in the colonies, where strikes or protests by native workers were painted with the 'security threat' brush and colonial governors would declare a state of emergency to legitimise the use of force in their suppression.

The enabling legal framework emanated from the war-time codification of emergency powers in Britain, which, as we have seen, itself brought home the colonial experience. Although the Defence of the Realm Act 1914 lapsed in 1921, the sweeping authority that the cabinet had become accustomed to during the war years would continue to inform policy and extend to a range of economic issues in times of peace. With the 'power [that the Defence of the Realm Act] had brought them still fresh in their minds, the members of the Cabinet decided to ask Parliament for a direct grant of emergency competence, couched in terms of a permanent statute'.[155] Emergency powers were henceforth institutionalised in Britain in legislation that Rossiter describes as 'a revolution in English politics and government'.[156] The Emergency Powers Act 1920[157] allowed the Crown to proclaim a state of emergency under certain circumstances in relation to the supply and distribution of necessities (including food, water, fuel and light), granting special powers to the police in such regard, as well as effectively allowing for military intervention. Although presented by the government as discharging a longstanding commitment (simply rendered more urgent following the war experience) to such legislation in order to protect essential supplies, the social context in which the bill was passed is instructive. Rushed through parliament during strikes by miners and railway workers in October 1920, amidst a broader climate of escalating class conflict, it was 'abundantly clear to everyone that the new act was intended to be used against the strikers'.[158]

Scheuerman zooms in on the Act as a microcosm of the history of economic emergency power between the mid-nineteenth and mid-twentieth centuries:

> its proximity to the wartime context linked it to an earlier tradition in which emergency power chiefly functioned as a tool against violent uprisings and foreign invasions; its anti-strike thrust tied it closely to the widespread tendency to rely on emergency authority against the labor

---

[155] Rossiter, *Constitutional Dictatorship*, 174.   [156] *Ibid.*, 177.
[157] 10 & 11 Geo. V., C.55.
[158] Neocleous, 'From Martial Law to the War on Terror', 502.

movement; and finally, the Act's forthright concern with guaranteeing the 'supply and distribution of food, water, fuel, or light' clearly pointed the way towards the employment of emergency authority for peacetime economic coordination.[159]

While ostensibly confined to the category of essential supplies, the reach of the Act would in practice 'encompass a broader gamut of economic matters, industrial disputes and class conflict'.[160] Enacted as a permanent but dormant piece of law, it was quickly and consistently called into life: in 1921 in response to the coal strike; in 1924 for sectional transport workers' strikes; and in 1926 when the general strike throughout Britain was called.[161] In the last case, the strike itself lasted only a few days, while the state of emergency continued for eight months.[162] By this point, the pretence of a link to military conflict or armed insurrection as integral to the state of emergency had been dropped. Even outside formal declarations, the emergency continued as norm in Britain through the 1920s and 1930s, during which time 'drastic emergency laws were enacted in the normal manner'[163] (that is, through the regular parliamentary legislative process). Specific recourse to emergency executive authority in the form of enabling acts – delegating law-making power to the cabinet of Ramsay MacDonald's emergency 'national government' – was also made during the depression of 1931–1932.[164] This enactment of emergency doctrine persisted through and beyond the Second World War. While end of the war may have been assumed to herald a return to normalcy, the wartime emergency powers as set out in Britain by the Emergency Powers (Defence) Act 1939 were again retained by government to facilitate broad executive control in the economic sphere, including over industrial relations and

---

[159] Scheuerman, 'The Economic State of Emergency', 1878.
[160] Keith Jeffery and Peter Hennessy, States of Emergency: British Governments and Strikebreaking since 1919 (London: Routledge, 1983) 213.
[161] Cecil T. Carr, 'Crisis Legislation in Britain' (1940) 40 Columbia Law Review 1309, 1312–1313.
[162] Neocleous, 'From Martial Law to the War on Terror', 502, citing Gillian S. Morris, 'The Emergency Powers Act 1920' (1979) Public Law 317; Jane Morgan, Conflict and Order: The Police and Labour Disputes in England and Wales 1900–1939 (Oxford: Clarendon Press, 1987).
[163] Rossiter, Constitutional Dictatorship, 178.
[164] For analysis of the wide-ranging departures from accepted British constitutional practice in MacDonald's formation of the national government and management of the whole affair, see, for example, Harold Laski, The Crisis and the Constitution: 1931 and After (London: Hogarth Press, 1932).

the market price of supplies and services.[165] The Emergency Powers Act 1920 was consistently invoked during strikes from the late 1940s, with the Crown regularly declaring official states of emergency through the post-war decades.[166] Such routine exercise of emergency powers, essentially as an instrument of quotidian class struggle, illustrates the idea of emergency as banal but ideologically productive.

The colonies were also sites of regular engagement of emergency law as a mechanism of economic exploitation and a mode of subjugation that straddled class and race markers, particularly as Third World labour and liberation movements ramped up their resistance through the first half of the twentieth century. This was strikingly evident, for instance, in the state of emergency designed to crush native trade unionism in Malaya in 1948. Union membership and activism there had expanded rapidly in the 1940s, engendering a bolstered consciousness and assertion of workers' rights. This culminated in large-scale industrial conflict and repression by the British authorities, against a wider backdrop of anti-colonial agitation by the Malayan Communist Party. The counter-revolutionary reaction was strong: 'European plantation interests were vociferous in their demand for tough action' against organised labour, prompting colonial administrators to demand from London 'special powers for crushing trade unionism'.[167] At a meeting of colonial government officials in Malaya in May 1948 that initiated the process by which a state of emergency would be declared, it was decided that the emergency measures should include a 'a simultaneous raid on the headquarters of the PMFTU [Pan Malayan Federation of Trade Unions] in Kuala Lumpur and of the Federations in each of the states'.[168] The declaration of the

---

[165] See, for example, John Eaves, *Emergency Powers and the Parliamentary Watchdog: Parliament and the Executive in Great Britain, 1939-1951* (London: Hansard Society, 1957). Emergency powers were applied to an expansive range of fields through temporary regulations such as the Supplies and Services (Transitional Powers) Act 1945 (extending emergency economic powers from 1946-51) and through ordinary permanent legislation such as the Exchange Control Act 1947.

[166] House of Commons Library Research Division, Background Paper, No. 66: 'Emergency Powers' (January 1979). In 1973, for instance, on the basis of 'industrial disputes affecting persons employed in the coal mines and in the electricity supply industry ... Her Majesty ... deemed it proper ... to declare that a state of emergency exists'. 866 Parl. Deb., H.C. (5th ser.) (1973) 414-15. The Emergency Powers Act 1920 was amended during this period by the Emergency Powers Act 1964.

[167] Füredi, *Colonial Wars*, 160-161.

[168] Anthony Short, *The Communist Insurrection in Malaya, 1948-60* (London: Frederick Muller, 1975) 67. See also Michael Morgan, 'The Rise and Fall of Malayan Trade Unionism, 1945-50', in Mohamed Amin & Malcolm Caldwell (eds.), *Malaya, the*

state of emergency in June 1948 was indicative of broader developments in British imperial governance by that time.

Emergency as Governance

With the rise of anti-colonial liberation movements in Africa and Asia during the first half of the twentieth century, the empire's continuing cohesion was on the line. India was among the colonies at the forefront of such resistance. The emergency legislation there of the 1920s, 1930s and 1940s, which I have referred to above and by which Britain sought to construct and counter radical nationalism, prompted a 'terrorist threat' vernacular and a shift towards special courts that continues to echo in contemporary national security discourse. The colonial state's actions in this regard can be seen as exemplifying a mode of governance that understands, narrates and confronts a threat through an administrative rationale.[169] The British government resorted increasingly to emergency rule as it became embroiled in political and military struggles to maintain imperial sovereignty at the advent of the United Nations era. The wave of colonial wars during the late 1940s and 1950s were 'euphemistically self-styled as "emergencies"'[170] so that mass resistance could be dealt with by special powers enacted in the name of the restoration of 'normalcy' (rather than alternative narratives exposing the turn to violent force to sustain anti-democratic control). The post-war British political establishment 'had every intention of retaining the empire', but 'the use of force for the maintenance of the empire had become problematic . . . international and domestic opinion posed limits'.[171] A communication from Lord Killearn in the Cairo embassy back to London emphasised that 'the time has already gone in Egypt and in the Middle East as a whole when we can rely on force alone to maintain our position'.[172] What was required now was not just force, but the *force of law* to halt growing resistance throughout the

---

Making of a Neo Colony (Nottingham: Spokesman Books, 1977); Kumar Ramakrishna, *Emergency Propaganda: The Winning of Malayan Hearts and Minds, 1948–1958* (London: Routledge, 2002).

[169] Hussain, 'Hyperlegality', 521–523.

[170] Balakrishnan Rajagopal, *International Law from Below: Development, Social Movements and Third World Resistance* (Cambridge: Cambridge University Press, 2003).

[171] Füredi, *Colonial Wars*, 143.

[172] Public Record Office, FO 370/895, General Correspondence: Lord Killearn to Sir Maurice Peterson, 17 January 1944.

empire. As international organisations progressed towards binding human rights treaties, anxieties arose in government circles as to the compatibility of the special powers employed in the colonies with any new legal obligations towards colonised subjects. The Colonial Office expressed concern over the likely 'unwelcome criticism' were it to prove 'impossible to extend the [European Convention on Human Rights] to an appreciable number of colonial territories' because of such powers, and received advice from the Lord Chancellor and Law Officers who expressed serious misgivings over many such powers, indicating in particular that 'detention without trial was quite unacceptable except in declared states of emergency'.[173] The state of emergency was thus concocted as a legal antidote of sorts, by which the colonial state could mobilise counter-revolutionary force against liberation movements while at the same time extricating itself from human rights liability. This line of reasoning underpinned the performance of colonial emergencies, premised on the constructed avatars of native barbarism and communist subversion.

The 1948 'Panic in Whitehall',[174] generated by somewhat belated realisations of the empire's vulnerability, resulted in colonial officials looking 'to special powers to give them a breathing space in which they could reclaim the initiative. When the normal forms of political management failed to contain the nationalist challenge, the calling of an emergency was always a plausible option'.[175] To this end Britain sought to rely on legalised emergency in order to preserve perceptions of legitimacy. The state presented its use of force in the colonies as having little to do with imperialist domination; it related rather to upholding 'law and order' under the duress of emergency. Analyses of British policy during this time have concluded that 'every imperial response to anti-colonial protest contained elements of an informal emergency, while every formal emergency possessed a political dimension.'[176] A shroud of

---

[173] Simpson, *Human Rights and the End of Empire*, 831.
[174] Frank Füredi sketches a dividing line between British government policies in the colonies pre and post 1948: 'Whitehall's new attitude towards the problem of order in the colonies – expressed through a willingness to use special measures, emergencies and high-profile policing to manage political opposition – becomes apparent from early 1948. Until this period, especially up until mid-1947, Whitehall was comparatively relaxed about the problem of order in the colonies. Often it was the Colonial Office that tried to curb the enthusiasm of the local administration for enacting new special powers and emergencies.' Füredi, *Colonial Wars*, 94–95.
[175] *Ibid.*, 4.   [176] *Ibid.*, 5.

administrative legality was used to conceal underlying political objectives in colonies where Britain sought to target radical anti-colonial movements and to promote their more moderate counterparts.[177] In the late 1940s, in colonies like the Gold Coast and Malaya, the state of emergency was used as a technique of governance designed to re-establish control. Emergencies were declared by the respective colonial governors under the Emergency Powers (Colonial Defence) Order in Council 1939. Based on expansive interpretations of the 'necessary or expedient' mandate of the legislation, emergency powers were invoked not merely as a reactive mechanism to avert prevailing or imminent crises, but as calculated pre-emptive measures infused into the ongoing government of respective territories.[178]

Balakrishnan Rajagopal portrays the reality of emergency as a form of 'total rule' as prompted by a number of undergirding factors, including an infectious fear of the masses.[179] The political engagement of the peasant and working classes – in particular their increasing support for liberation movements by the 1940s – created cause for colonial concern. British authorities sought to distort the rationale of this emergent pattern by depicting the involvement of the masses in political activity as a dangerous manifestation of deluded tribal nationalism. Deployed and performed as part of the public relations machinery, fear of a carefully constructed native savage became a dominant theme in Eurocolonial discourse as it related to Third World resistance.[180] This fear dovetailed with the prevalent distrust of nationalism that fascism had provoked in

---

[177] Hence the 'Gold Coast experiment' attempt to mitigate the challenge to British rule in Ghana through the quasi-solution of 'semi-responsible government', as opposed to actual self-government or independence. Martin Meredith, *The State of Africa* (London: Free Press, 2005) 17–29. For the perspective of the colonial governor, see Charles Arden-Clarke, 'Gold Coast into Ghana: Some Problems of Transition' (1958) 34:1 *International Affairs* 49.

[178] See Füredi, *Colonial Wars*, 97, noting that: 'In this climate, even relatively liberal administrators were busy integrating emergency powers into their overall strategy. So Sir John Macpherson, governor of Nigeria, passed "legislation conferring emergency powers on the executive" in December 1948. Macpherson, like other governors, was planning ahead. Throughout the empire police forces and security arrangements were being reviewed and contingency plans drawn up.' See further Frank Füredi, 'Creating a Breathing Space: The Political Management of Colonial Emergencies', in Robert Holland (ed.), *Emergencies and Disorder in the European Empires After 1945* (Abingdon: Frank Cass, 1994) at 90, arguing that: 'Emergencies were as much pre-planned attempts at the political management of anti-colonial forces as belated responses to an unexpected challenge to the imperial order.'

[179] Rajagopal, *International Law from Below*, 178.   [180] *Ibid.*, 178–179.

Europe, and the pejorative connotation that the concept became loaded with as it gained traction in the colonies, particularly in Africa.[181] These two elements – fear of the barbaric indigene and concern over expressions of nationalism – are exemplified in the comments of Charles Arden-Clarke, British governor in the Gold Coast, describing Ghanaian political leader Kwame Nkrumah in a letter back to England in 1950 as 'our local Hitler'.[182] In this vein, the derision of native liberation agendas was a much adhered-to colonial tactic, plainly discernible in the manner that emergencies were implemented.

Fascism was just one brush with which opposition to colonial rule was tarred. With the spill-over of the Cold War into Africa and Asia by the 1950s, national liberation struggles in European colonies were cast as evidence of the steady encroachment of communism and the rising threat to 'Western values'. The catch-all slur of 'terrorism' was also projected onto any dissent or resistance, with similar broad strokes applied across the colonial canvas, from Latin America to Africa and East Asia. The spectre of a transnational conspiracy was summoned. One of the arguments used by a British constitutional commission to justify the suspension of the constitution in British Guiana in 1953 (an act characterised by the American consul at the time as a coup d'état), for instance, was that its minister for education had created an African and Colonial Affairs Committee which 'declared support for Mau Mau in Kenya and the Communist terrorists in Malaya'.[183] The use of emergency measures to repress the perceived communist threat went hand in hand with the economic objectives of colonialism that I have pointed to in the previous section. By consistently conjuring up images of savagery and Soviet subterfuge, and couching resistance in the colonies within the realms of criminality and public order – rather than self-determination or socio-economic justice – the colonial authorities sought to stage emergencies in which special powers were needed to counter subversive terrorist, communist threats. Emphasis on the need to restore 'order' allowed colonial agents to label and treat opponents as criminals and/or agitators oriented towards the wrong side of the iron curtain. Emergency

---

[181] For an insightful discussion of imperial attitudes towards Third World nationalism, see Füredi, *Colonial Wars*, 109–139.

[182] Quoted in Meredith, *The State of Africa*, 19.

[183] Robertson Commission, quoted in Füredi, *Colonial Wars*, 2. See also The Robertson Commission, 'Report of the British Guiana Constitutional Commission' (1954), presented by the Secretary of State for the Colonies to Parliament by Command of Her Majesty, September 1954.

regulations were rolled out to legitimise policies of detention, curfew and censorship. The prevalent states of emergency facilitated colonial governance and implementation of political and economic reforms free from constraint. Such moves are indicative of the more fundamental effects of imperial discourse, whereby the coloniser's world of law, state and civilisation is posited against the other's retrograde equivalents: custom, tribe and barbarism. Filtering colonial law through a Third World lens, it is clear that law is integral to governing non-European peoples and exploiting their territories and resources economically. The invocation of emergency can be understood as an extension of that purpose. It functioned as a method to contain the barbarism of the natives and to facilitate the continuance of the civilising mission. In the Jamaica case, for example, '[o]n the pretext of crushing a dangerous rebellion, British officials had indulged in a racially charged reign of terror.'[184] In this sense, the liberal rule of law is tainted by its own racial awareness. The state of emergency is revealed as a racialised component of colonial sovereignty; its historiography illuminates the political and legal context in which emergency came to be embedded in the legal condition of the modern state.

It was in this spirit of established colonial policy that states of emergency were proclaimed by British authorities in Jamaica in February 1946, Trinidad in January 1947 and March 1948, Aden in December 1947, the Gold Coast in March 1948 and January 1950, Malaya in June 1948, Singapore in July 1948, Zanzibar in September 1948, Uganda in April 1949, Nigeria in November 1949, and so on, as we will see in the next chapter. Emergency regulations imposed pursuant to the Emergency Powers (Colonial Defence) Order in Council 1939 or equivalent local legislation engendered wholesale powers of censorship, curfew, arrest, detention and deportation. These episodes were playing out concomitant to the drafting of the foundational charters of an emerging international human rights system. The positions adopted by Britain during that drafting process in the late 1940s and early 1950s, therefore, cannot be viewed in isolation from events in the colonies at the time. The historiography of colonial emergency is, in fact, very much relevant to the story of how the state of emergency came to be embedded in the international legal regime for the protection of human rights.

---

[184] Kostal, *A Jurisprudence of Power*, 461.

PART II

Empire's Law

. . . it seems all clear as daylight. The white man makes a rule or law. Through that rule or law or what you may call it, he takes away the land and then imposes many laws on the people concerning that land and many other things, all without people agreeing first as in the old days of the tribe. Now a man rises and opposes that law which made right the taking away of the land. Now that man is taken by the same people who made the laws against which that man was fighting. He is tried under those alien rules. Now tell me who is that man who can win even if the angels of God were his lawyers.

Ngũgĩ wa Thiong'o, Weep Not, Child, 75

4

Emergency Derogations and the International Human Rights Project

The liberal international human rights project, in its institutional form, was born into the lineage of an international law that was 'preoccupied with great crises, rather than the politics of everyday life'.[1] International human rights law is seen as a product of – and response to – the crisis and exceptionality that culminated in the Second World War. After the war, the Western-led juridical response to fascism and Axis atrocities took the form of select prosecutions in Nuremberg and Tokyo. This was followed up by the criminalisation of the most 'odious' manifestations of humanity's inhumanity in treaties such as the 1948 Genocide Convention.[2] The more 'everyday' politics of entrenched emergency governance and the constitutional structures of the state of emergency that had facilitated persecutory practices were, on the other hand, regulated – and thus to a certain degree condoned – in the derogations schema of the international human rights treaties that were developed.

Emergency rule continued in the British empire through the 1950s, and anchored France's war in Algeria. There was no suggestion of international criminal accountability attaching to normalised British and French violence in the colonies (or to the subjugation of native Americans and African Americans in the United States, for example) in the way that it had been meted out by the Allied powers.[3] The default position of imperial international lawyers and diplomats was that colonial policy would remain unaffected by any new international legal obligations that the colonial powers might ratify. From its inception in

---

[1] Hilary Charlesworth, 'International Law: A Discipline of Crisis' (2002) 65:3 *Modern Law Review* 383.

[2] Convention on the Prevention and Punishment of the Crime of Genocide, General Assembly Resolution 260 A (III), 9 December 1948.

[3] For further analysis of the legitimacy, selectivities and political economy of international law's criminal justice project from a TWAIL perspective, see, for example the symposium on 'Third World Approaches to International Criminal Law' in (2016) 14:4 *Journal of International Criminal Justice*.

the international human rights treaties developed at that time, the emergency derogations regime can be understood as foremost among the 'techniques of accommodation'[4] that international law provides in entrusting the state with ultimate discretion over the degree to which it binds itself by notions of human rights within and beyond its own territory. The fiction of the state of emergency – insofar as it purports to move beyond law in order to control a situation by law – can again be seen here. In spite of extensive evidence of abuse of state power, however, the presumption remains that allowances for emergency powers are legitimate; indeed, imperative. In the context of international human rights law, emergency derogations are typically accepted as a 'necessary evil'[5]; a 'realistic compromise'[6]; an essential 'safety valve'[7] for states. The inevitable consequence of bestowing universal applicability upon emergency doctrine, and separating it from its colonial and totalitarian pedigree, is the retention of the legal apparatus of emergency as an expedient utilitarian technique.

In the codification of international human rights, then, there is no definitive rupture, but rather a shift and consolidation of the paradigm of emergency within the very legal regime presented as a normative and institutional riposte to the most egregious consequences of fascism's emergency rule. While emergencies or crises are presented as the catalyst to which human rights continually respond, the ideas of emergency or crisis are themselves enshrined in international treaty law though provisions for legal derogation.[8] This chapter seeks to probe the historical

---

[4] Rosalyn Higgins, 'Derogation under Human Rights Treaties' (1976) 48 *British Yearbook of International Law* 281, 315.

[5] Sarah Joseph, Jenny Schultz and Melissa Castan, *The International Covenant on Civil and Political Rights: Cases, Materials, and Commentary* (Oxford: Oxford University Press, 2004) 824.

[6] Scott N. Carlson and Gregory Gisvold, *Practical Guide to the International Covenant on Civil and Political Rights* (Ardsley, NY: Transnational, 2003) 33.

[7] Emilie M. Hafner-Burton, Laurence R. Helfer and Christopher J. Fariss, 'Emergency and Escape: Explaining Derogations from Human Rights Treaties' (2011) 65:4 *International Organization* 673, 674.

[8] Authers and Charlesworth, 'The Crisis and the Quotidian', 20. While I take human rights law as my focus for illustrative purposes, it is not alone within the field of international law in its recognition and qualified accommodation of state 'necessity' arguments. The emergency derogation regime in human rights treaties is embroidered into a broader tapestry of necessity doctrines in public international law. As Vik Kanwar notes:

> In modern international law, there are four main contexts where doctrines of necessity are raised: (1) Doctrines of necessity as an excuse or exception in the law-governed relations between states (general law of treaties and

detail of how this came to pass, and the consequences that have ensued. The drafting histories of the European Convention on Human Rights and the International Covenant on Civil and Political Rights provide insight into the concerns of the European powers – Britain in particular – over the capacity of the emergent human rights project to restrict operations in the colonies, and into the tactics adopted to alleviate such concerns.

The Post-war Context

Extensive emergency legislation had been introduced for the duration of the Second World War in Britain, with significant numbers of people placed in detention without trial. This was justified on the basis of national security. The majority of those detained were refugees from Europe – defined as 'enemy aliens' for the purpose of their detention – but British citizens were also detained under Regulation 18B of the Defence Regulations, predominantly on the basis of perceived threats emanating from their racial or national origin. Churchill's administration made substantial recourse to this regulation in the early years of

state responsibility); (2) notions of self-defense based in customary law and the Charter of the United Nations; (3) standards of military necessity in the law of armed conflict; and (4) "Necessity" as a threshold for the derogation of treaty-based human rights obligations in states of emergency. And each of these is divided into more specialized branches and areas of application. In short, nearly every area of international law has, in its own development, attempted to provide doctrinal closure to unstable areas of "necessity".

Vik Kanwar, *The Politics of Necessity: Discourses and Doctrines of Exception in International Law* (unpublished dissertation, New York University, 2006). The old maxim that necessity knows no law notwithstanding, there is a certain inevitability to a state-centric international legal system making allowance for emergency governance through doctrines of necessity. Roberto Ago's 1980 study on necessity doctrines vis-à-vis state responsibility suggested that 'the concept of "state of necessity" is far too deeply rooted in the consciousness of the members of the international community and of individuals within States', such that even if it is 'driven out the door' it will inevitably 'return through a window'. Roberto Ago, Eighth report on State responsibility by Mr. Roberto Ago, Special Rapporteur—Addendum, A/CN.4/318/Add.5–7, 29 February 1980, para. 80. Varying doctrinal forms of necessity have by now established themselves in, for example, international trade and investment law (security exception regimes in the World Trade Organisation agreements and bilateral investment treaties, for instance). For further analysis of this see, for example, John Reynolds, 'The Political Economy of States of Emergency' (2012) 14:1 *Oregon Review of International Law* 85, 116–122. On necessity doctrines generally, see also Jens David Ohlin and Larry May, *Necessity in International Law* (Oxford: Oxford University Press, 2016).

the war.[9] As the war wore on, however, Churchill himself came to feel increasingly uncomfortable with the perception of civil liberties being vitiated in Britain. Anticipating opposition to the planned release from internment of Oswald Mosley, founder of the British Union of Fascists, Churchill told his Home Secretary in late 1943 that detention without charge or trial is itself 'the foundation of all totalitarian government':

> You might however consider whether you should not unfold as a background the great privilege of habeas corpus and trial by jury, which are the supreme protection invented by the English people for ordinary individuals against the state. The power of the Executive to cast a man in prison without formulating any charge known to the law, and particularly to deny him the judgment of his peers, is in the highest degree odious and is the foundation of all totalitarian government whether Nazi or Communist.[10]

The post-war movement for the international protection of human rights emerged ostensibly in response to totalitarianism; a liberal project conceived of in order to preclude the types of abuses perpetrated before and during the Second World War. International organisations such as the United Nations and the Council of Europe went about institutionalising legal mechanisms to serve such an end.[11] Major international human rights conventions formulated in response to the violence of exception and emergency ended up, however, granting signatories a pass to suspend or derogate from many of their newly-codified obligations in the event of a (self-diagnosed)

---

[9] For a detailed exploration of the use of Regulation 18B, see A.W.B. Simpson, *In the Highest Degree Odious: Detention without Trial in Wartime Britain* (Oxford: Oxford University Press, 1992).

[10] Telegram sent from Cairo by Prime Minister Winston Churchill to Home Secretary Herbert Morrison, 21 November 1943. Quoted in Simpson, *In the Highest Degree Odious*, 391.

[11] This notwithstanding, scholars such as Samuel Moyn argue that 'there was no widespread Holocaust consciousness in the postwar era, so human rights could not have been a response to it'. For Moyn, it was not until the 1970s, when other utopian ideologies – including socialism and revolutionary nationalism – had begun to recede, that human rights fully emerged as praxis. Samuel Moyn, *The Last Utopia: Human Rights in History* (Cambridge, MA: Harvard University Press, 2010) 7. Moyn's work forms part of a larger resurgence in debates around human rights histories. For critical engagement in such debates from Third World viewpoints, see, for example, José Manuel Barreto (ed.), *Human Rights from a Third World Perspective: Critique, History and International Law* (Newcastle: Cambridge Scholars Publishing, 2013).

emergency.[12] Churchill's sentiments on the iniquity of detention without trial appear to have been quickly forgotten following victory in the war.

The genesis of the emergency derogation clauses of the European Convention on Human Rights and the International Covenant on Civil and Political Rights[13] – whose drafting processes were underway by the late 1940s – demonstrate staunch British advocacy for states to reserve discretion to deploy extraordinary measures beyond the pale of the nascent human rights system. This naturally raises questions as to why Britain, in the context of developing safeguards for civil rights, was determined to provide for the suspension of those safeguards by virtue of emergency powers, including those that its wartime leader had described as fundamental to totalitarianism. Britain's historical reliance on martial law and emergency legislation in its overseas colonies, and the backdrop of the multiple states of emergency playing out at the time of the drafting of the conventions, indicate that the answer relates to the preservation of control in situations where government is maintained by force rather than consent. A statement made by the British representative during the drafting process of the European Convention on Human Rights that underlined the importance of deploying the Convention against threats to political stability 'from within *or without*'[14] is testament to the interrelation between the newly evolving international legal mechanisms and Britain's wartime and colonial emergency powers.

---

[12] Article 4 of the International Covenant on Civil and Political Rights; Article 15 of the Council of Europe Convention for the Protection of Human Rights and Fundamental Freedoms (commonly referred to as the European Convention on Human Rights); Article 27 of the American Convention on Human Rights.

[13] The other component of the International Bill of Rights, the International Covenant on Economic, Social and Cultural Rights (ICESCR), is not included here as it does not provide for states to derogate from its provisions in the event of a state of emergency. The rights set down in the ICESCR are subject to 'progressive realisation' according to the state's available resources. On that basis provision for emergency derogation may have been considered superfluous. For further discussion of the potential derogability of certain economic, social and cultural rights, see, for example, Amrei Müller, 'Limitations to and Derogations from Economic, Social and Cultural Rights' (2009) 9:4 *Human Rights Law Review* 557. The European Social Charter does provide for emergency derogations from its socio-economic rights obligations (in Part V, Article F), but no such derogation appears to have been invoked.

[14] Council of Europe, *Collected Edition of the Travaux Préparatoires of the European Convention on Human Rights* (The Hague: Martinus Nijhoff, 1975–1985) Vol. I, 30. Emphasis added.

Another particular aspect of the legal-historical context also merits note here. During the drafting process for the Universal Declaration of Human Rights, the question of the application of human rights to colonies – which had been absent entirely from initial deliberations and drafts – was raised in 1947 by the Soviet Union, self-proclaimed leader of the world's 'anti-imperialist camp'.[15] After that, 'the British and Soviet delegations clashed more than once over the implications of the Declaration for the peoples living in the colonies'.[16] Britain repeatedly moved to have the proposed article affirming the application of the Universal Declaration to non-self-governing-territories deleted. This would have been seen as running counter to the emerging if somewhat nebulous principles of universality, non-discrimination and self-determination. And so although the British government eventually succeeded in having the 'application to the colonies' provision demoted from its own separate article, a majority of states did decide to explicitly confirm – in the Preamble and as a part of Article 2 – that the Declaration *would* apply to the colonies.[17] A declaratory principle of the applicability of human rights law to all territories under a state's jurisdiction was thus established.

As a result, the British authorities entered the drafting process for the international treaties that would give 'binding' legal force to the principles of the Universal Declaration wary of the need to retain latitude for the forceful containment of anti-colonial revolts in the empire.[18] As the process got underway, the Colonial Office – having faced insurrection in Palestine that led to British withdrawal and by now encountering similar confrontations in Malaya and elsewhere – was pushing for additional

---

[15] Andrei Zhadanov, then chairman of the Soviet of the Union, quoted in Johannes Morsink, *The Universal Declaration of Human Rights: Origins, Drafting, and Intent* (Philadelphia: University of Pennsylvania Press, 1999) 97.

[16] Morsink, *The Universal Declaration of Human Rights*, 97.

[17] For a concise overview of the debate on this issue, see Morsink, *The Universal Declaration of Human Rights*, 96-101. The relevant line of the Preamble to the Universal Declaration makes reference to its rights applying 'both among the peoples of Member States themselves and among the peoples of territories under their jurisdiction', while Article 2 states that 'no distinction shall be made on the basis of the political, jurisdictional or international status of the country or territory to which a person belongs, whether it be independent, trust, non-self-governing or under any other limitation of sovereignty'.

[18] Initially, at least, Britain's view in relation to the European Convention was that it should be aspirational, rather than binding. The British position would remain resistant to the document being infused with binding force and, later, to the establishment of complaint mechanisms.

legislative powers to suppress native resistance even before any formal declaration of a state of emergency.[19]

From European Empire to European Convention on Human Rights

As multilateral international treaties go, the drafting process of the European Convention on Human Rights was relatively swift. Stemming from an initiative of the Consultative Assembly of the newly-established Council of Europe during its August–September 1949 sitting, an inter-governmental legal Committee of Experts was formed in early 1950 to work on a draft human rights convention. It floated a number of alternative drafts for consideration by a Conference of Senior Officials in June 1950, who amalgamated the drafts and prepared the ground for the political evaluation of the wording by the Council's Committee of Ministers. The Committee of Ministers adopted the text of a draft Convention for the Protection of Human Rights and Fundamental Freedoms in Strasbourg in August of that year; by November 1950 the Convention had been signed in Rome, entering into force in September 1953.[20]

The starting point for the Convention was a draft text included in a recommendation adopted in September 1949 by the Consultative Assembly on 'measures for the fulfilment of the declared aim of the Council of Europe, in accordance with Article 1 of the Statute in regard to the safeguarding and further relation of human rights and fundamental freedoms'.[21] This, the first working draft of the European Convention on Human Rights, contained no reference to, or provision for, derogation from human rights safeguards in times of emergency or crisis. It did, however, contain in draft Article 6 a general limitation clause that echoed Article 29(2) of the Universal Declaration of Human Rights in providing that:

> In the exercise of these rights, and in the enjoyment of the freedoms guaranteed by the Convention, no limitations shall be imposed except

[19] Simpson, *Human Rights and the End of Empire*, 513.
[20] The fullest available account of the drafting process and reproduction of published documents can be found in Council of Europe, *Collected Edition of the Travaux Préparatoires of the European Convention on Human Rights* (The Hague: Martinus Nijhoff, 1975–1985).
[21] European Commission of Human Rights, *Preparatory Work on Article 15 of the European Convention on Human Rights*, Council of Europe Doc. DH(56)4, 22 May 1956, 2.

those established by the law, with the sole object of ensuring the rights
and freedoms of others, or with the purpose of satisfying the just require-
ments of public morality, order and security in a democratic society.[22]

The drafting records indicate that such a limitation clause was at that
point considered sufficient to deal with any exceptional circumstances.
When the potential necessity of explicitly authorising states to take
'special measures' to deal with incitement to violence arose, the Committee on Legal and Administrative Questions determined this to be
unnecessary, with such situations already covered by the text of draft
Article 6.[23] The Rapporteur of that Committee, Pierre-Henri Teitgen,
asserted that this was 'quite simple', and that the permissible allowances
for states were 'stated clearly' in the limitation clause.[24] The records of
the Consultative Assembly's first session provide an early indication
of Britain's contrasting position. For the British government, the purpose
of enacting a human rights convention was not simply the protection of
individuals, it would also function to strengthen the legal armoury of the
state in suppressing opposition to its rule. The British representative,
Lord Layton, stressed to the Assembly the importance of operationalising
the proposed convention 'as a means of strengthening the resistance in
all our countries against insidious attempts to undermine our democratic
way of life from within or without, and thus to give to Western Europe as
a whole greater political stability'.[25]

It was with this in mind that Britain sought to introduce a provision at
the meetings of the Committee of Experts from 2–8 February
1950 allowing for derogation from the majority of the rights enumerated
in the Convention during times of public emergency. In advance of those
meetings, the Secretariat-General had drawn up a preparatory report on
a preliminary draft convention for the collective guarantee of human
rights. Part of that report was devoted to a comparison between the draft
International Covenant on Human Rights in progress at the time, and
the draft European Convention on Human Rights as recommended by
the Consultative Assembly. Regarding the state of emergency/derogation
provision being mooted for the International Covenant, the report found

---

[22] Council of Europe Doc. AS(1)108, 262.   [23] Council of Europe Doc. AS(1)77, 201.
[24] 'Report of the Consultative Assembly, sitting of 8 September 1949', Council of Europe,
Travaux Préparatoires of the European Convention on Human Rights, Vol. II, 32.
[25] 'Report of the Consultative Assembly, First Session, Part I, Fifth Sitting, 16 August 1949,
83–85; quoted in Council of Europe, *Travaux Préparatoires of the European Convention
on Human Rights*, Vol. I, 30.

that 'the inclusion of this provision in the European system appears to be unnecessary', having regard to the existing limitation clauses in the Consultative Assembly's draft.[26] Despite this, on 4 February 1950, Oscar Dowson submitted to the Committee of Experts on behalf of the British government an amendment to the Consultative Assembly draft to include an article allowing states to derogate from their obligations in 'time of war or other public emergency threatening the interests of the people'.[27] Such a right of derogation in exceptional circumstances was still deemed by other states, however, to be superfluous to the require-ments and aims of the Convention. Accordingly, the preliminary draft Convention developed by the Committee of Experts during its February 1950 session omitted any such clause.[28] Britain remained unyielding in its position, and at the second session of the Committee of Experts from 6–10 March tabled a new amendment, incorporating minor clarifications but imbued with the same general thrust as its previous proposal.[29]

Following lengthy discussion on a number of contentious issues, the Committee of Experts decided to submit alternative texts to the Com-mittee of Ministers without indicating a preference – one based predom-inantly 'on British proposals that provided detailed definitions of fundamental rights and the other based upon the Consultative Assembly draft that largely reflected the Universal Declaration of Human Rights'.[30] On its proposed amendment regarding emergency derogations, Britain was insistent. After successfully securing its inclusion in the first set of alternatives, the British representative rallied for it to also be included in the second set. In response, the French and Italian representatives opposed its insertion on the basis that the kinds of instances it would relate to were already covered by the general limitations clauses.[31] Ultimately, however, Britain persuaded other members of the Committee to come down on its side, on the basis of a belief that the procedure laid

---

[26] Council of Europe Doc. B22, 18.
[27] 'Report of the Meetings of the Committee of Experts, sitting of 4 February 1950', Council of Europe Doc. A782.
[28] Preliminary Draft Convention for the Maintenance and Further Realisation of Human Rights and Fundamental Freedoms, Council of Europe Doc. A833, 15 February 1950. This draft retained, with slightly different wording, the Article 6 general limitation clause of the original Consultative Assembly draft of September 1949.
[29] Council of Europe Doc. CM/WP 1(50)2, 1–2.
[30] William Schabas, *The European Convention on Human Rights: A Commentary* (Oxford: Oxford University Press, 2015) 590.
[31] Council of Europe Doc. CM/WP 1(50)2, 15, 20.

down in the derogation clause – and the bracketing of certain rights as non-derogable – 'could prove to be useful for the protection of Human Rights in exceptional circumstances'.[32] As a result, both sets of alternative drafts annexed to the Committee of Expert's Report to the Committee of Ministers ended up containing similar emergency derogation provisions.[33] Notably, that report draws attention to the importance attached by Britain to the imposition of clearly defined limitations on the rights enumerated in the Convention. While noting that all members of the Committee were in favour of drawing up a Convention aimed foremost at safeguarding human rights, the report observes that:

> Certain members, however – particularly the representatives of the United Kingdom and the Netherlands – considered that the fundamental rights to be safeguarded, and, *even more important*, the limitations of these rights, should be defined in this Convention in as detailed as manner as possible.[34]

A full reading of the *travaux préparatoires* of the European Convention indeed broadly supports this suggestion that British concerns were focused more on limitations on the rights prescribed in the Convention than the rights themselves.

With the derogations clause incorporated into both sets of alternatives proposed by the Committee of Experts, its inclusion in the final text of the Convention was all but secured. The Conference of Senior Officials in Strasbourg from 6–17 June 1950 amalgamated the alternatives into a single proposed text for consideration by the Committee of Ministers. Article 14 of the draft Convention annexed to the draft report of the Conference of Senior Officials read as follows:

1. In time of war or other public emergency threatening the interests of the people, a State may take measures derogating from its obligations under this Convention to the extent strictly limited by the exigencies of the situation, provided that such measures are not inconsistent with its other obligations under international law.
2. No derogation from Articles 2, except in respect of deaths occurring from lawful acts of war, 3, 4 (para. 1) or 7 can be made under this provision.

---

[32] *Ibid.*
[33] Council of Europe Doc. CM/WP1(50)15, Appendix, alternatives A and A/2, p. 4; alternatives B and B/2, 5–6.
[34] Council of Europe Doc. CM/WP 1(50)15; A924, 16 March 1950, reproduced in Council of Europe, *Travaux Préparatoires of the European Convention on Human Rights*, Vol. IV, 8. Emphasis added.

3. Any State party hereto availing itself of this right of derogation shall inform the Secretary-General of the Council of Europe fully of the measures which it has thus enacted and the reasons therefor. It shall also inform the Secretary-General of the Council of Europe when such measures have ceased to operate and the provisions of the Convention are again being fully executed.[35]

Article 14 of the draft Convention annexed to the final report of the Conference of Senior Officials is almost identical, save for one significant amendment: the term 'the interests of the people' was replaced with 'the life of the nation'.[36] No explanation for this last minute amendment is given in the report of the Conference Senior Officials. What can be surmised, however, is a preference by state delegates for an intervention rooted more in the interests of the state's governing apparatus, and less in those of its people; for a vertical conception over a horizontal one.[37]

The draft emergency derogation provision was adopted, without any special reference to it in the course of the Consultative Assembly's debate,[38] as Article 15 of the European Convention for the Protection of Human Rights and Fundamental Freedoms, to give it its full title. Minor formal linguistic changes and translation corrections[39] were made to Article 15 by the Committee of Legal Experts before the signing of the Convention on 4 November 1950. The final text of Article 15 reads as follows:

1. In time of war or other public emergency threatening the life of the nation any High Contracting Party may take measures derogating from its obligations under this Convention to the extent strictly required by the exigencies of the situation, provided that such measures are not inconsistent with its other obligations under international law.
2. No derogation from Article 2, except in respect of deaths resulting from lawful acts of war, or from Articles 3, 4 (paragraph 1) and 7 shall be made under this provision.[40]

---

[35] Council of Europe Doc. CM/WP 4(50)16, Appendix; A1445.
[36] Council of Europe Doc. CM/WP 4(50)19 annexe; CM/WP4(50)16rev.; A1452.
[37] A similar situation would also arise in relation to Article 4 of the International Covenant on Civil and Political Rights, discussed below.
[38] Council of Europe Doc. AS(2)104, 1035.
[39] Council of Europe Doc. CM/Adj.(50)3rev., para. 6.
[40] Article 2 relates to the right to life; Article 3 to the right to freedom from torture and inhuman or degrading treatment or punishment; Article 4(1) to freedom from slavery and servitude; Article 7 to the non-retroactivity of criminal law.

3. Any High Contracting Party availing itself of this right of derogation shall keep the Secretary-General of the Council of Europe fully informed of the measures which it has taken and the reasons therefore. It shall also inform the Secretary-General of the Council of Europe when such measures have ceased to operate and the provisions of the Convention are again being fully executed.

The individual limitation clauses for specific rights – that had been proposed originally as an *alternative* to full powers of derogation – were nonetheless also retained in the final Convention.[41] In ultimately accepting Britain's arguments for the inclusion of the full emergency derogation clause in the form of Article 15, the majority of the other members of the Council of Europe reasoned that 'it had the advantage of excluding, even in the case of war or threat to the life of the nation, any derogation of certain fundamental rights, and ... the procedure laid down in paragraph 3 could prove to be useful for the protection of Human Rights in exceptional circumstances'.[42] This interpretation presents the provision in its positive light in the sense that certain rights are excluded from derogation and some form of accountability is entailed by virtue of the procedure to be followed when emergency powers are introduced. The more critical read suggests that the institutionalisation of a framework under which derogations can take place during a self-proclaimed emergency may serve to cast a light of legitimacy on illiberal practices themselves. Though such an eventuality was foreseen during the drafting process, any lingering concerns were relegated as secondary. Questions remain over the extent to which this was due to a well-intended but somewhat naïve expectation on behalf of the drafters as to how states would henceforth conduct themselves in exceptional circumstances, or, conversely and as will be suggested by the analysis of the colonial derogations later in this chapter, the extent to which it was due to the realities of the enduring intrinsic structures of international law, whereby state power will ultimately legislate with self-preservation paramount.

---

[41] See European Convention on Human Rights, Articles 8–11. Limitations to the rights to respect for private and family life (Article 8), freedom of thought, conscience and religion (Article 9), freedom of expression (Article 10), and freedom of assembly and association (Article 11) are permissible on grounds including the interests of national security, territorial integrity or public safety, the prevention of disorder or crime, and the protection of health or morals.
[42] Council of Europe Doc. CM/WP1(50) 15, 20.

Universalising the State of Emergency

The European Commission of Human Rights has noted that '[a]s the preparatory work clearly shows, Article 15 of the European Convention on Human Rights closely followed, at the beginning, that of Article 4 of the United Nations draft Covenant'.[43] Indeed, at its initial introduction, Britain's proposed amendment to the draft European Convention 'appeared to be an almost textual reproduction'[44] of draft Article 4 of the Covenant.

The process that led to the adoption of the International Covenant on Civil and Political Rights began with the Drafting Committee of the UN Commission on Human Rights in 1947, mandated to prepare an international bill of human rights.[45] The proposal for an emergency clause came from a draft international bill of human rights submitted by Britain to the first session of the Drafting Committee. The Drafting Committee also had before it a number of draft outlines of an international bill of human rights prepared by the Division of Human Rights of the Secretariat, the USA and France respectively, none of which made any provision for derogation or emergency measures.[46] Article 4 of the British draft, on the other hand, stipulated that '[i]n time of war or other national emergency, a State may take measures derogating from its obligations under Article 2 above to the extent strictly limited by the exigencies of the situation'.[47] The sweeping nature of this proposed right of derogation is brought into sharp focus by the fact that Article 2 of Britain's draft Bill provided for states' obligations to secure and support *all* of the rights and fundamental freedoms set out in the Bill, as well as to provide effective remedy in cases of violation. The proposal, therefore, left every right enumerated exposed to derogation under a self-declared emergency,

---

[43] European Commission of Human Rights, *Preparatory Work on Article 15 of the European Convention on Human Rights*, Council of Europe Doc. DH(56)4, 22 May 1956, 10.

[44] *Ibid.*, 5.

[45] The International Bill of Human Rights would ultimately take the form of three documents: the Universal Declaration on Human Rights, adopted by the UN General Assembly in 1948, and two international treaties – the International Covenant on Civil and Political Rights, and the International Covenant on Economic, Social and Cultural Rights – both of which were adopted by the UN in 1966 and entered into force in 1976.

[46] 'Report of the Drafting Committee to the Commission on Human Rights', UN Doc. E/CN.4/21, annexes A, C, and D respectively.

[47] British Foreign Office, *United Kingdom Draft of an International Bill of Human Rights* (London: HMSO, 1947) 8. Reproduced in UN Doc. E/CN.4/21, 1 July 1947, annex B.

allowing no exemptions to define or protect non-derogable rights. The British draft Bill was passed on by the Drafting Committee to the Commission on Human Rights, where the proposed emergency derogation article was rejected by a vote at the Commission's second session in December 1947.[48]

Britain subsequently resubmitted an almost identical draft provision to the Commission[49] and this time successfully lobbied for its inclusion in the draft covenant, with the proposal accepted by four votes to three (with eight abstentions).[50] This draft derogation clause thus went back to the Drafting Committee, where it was criticised by a number of states, with the USA the most vocal among them. This opposition was based principally on the belief that a single, general limitation clause in the vein of Article 29(2) of the Universal Declaration of Human Rights was sufficient, and preferable.[51] Following the adoption of a number of special limitation clauses in relation to particular rights, the USA moved to strike off the entire derogation clause on the basis that it was rendered superfluous by the limitation clauses.[52] France proposed a compromise text, which amounted to a general limitation clause that would not apply to a wide range of non-limitable rights.[53] Britain maintained an unwavering position favouring derogation over limitation, however, and revised the French draft to include a derogation clause with a narrower range of non-derogable rights.[54] This was the version of Article 4 that was provisionally adopted by the Commission on Human Rights at its fifth session in June 1949.[55]

The British revision would serve as the basis for further revisions to the wording of Article 4. Despite continuing opposition from some quarters – particularly from Third World participants – the fundamental premise of the right of states to derogate during emergencies was not to be dislodged from the covenant. A Chilean proposal to delete Article 4 was rejected at the Commission's sixth session in 1950.[56] Interestingly, however, the *travaux préparatoires* show that the risk that Britain's proposal to permit rights suspensions during emergencies 'might produce complicated problems of interpretation

---

[48] UN Doc. E/CN.4/AC.3/SR.8, 11.   [49] UN Doc. E/CN.4/SR.423, 4.
[50] UN Doc. E/CN.4/SR.431, 5.
[51] The US representative submitted an alternative text accordingly. See UN Doc. E/800.
[52] UN Docs. E/CN.4/AC.1/SR.22; E/CN.4/SR.127; E/CN.4/170.Add.1.
[53] UN Doc. E/CN.4/187.   [54] UN Doc. E/CN.4/188.
[55] UN Docs. E/CN.4/187; E/1371, Article 4.   [56] UN Doc. E/CN.4/SR.195.

and give rise to considerable abuse'[57] was recognised at the time. Chile's opposition to the derogation provision was based on the belief that it was 'drafted in such indefinite terms that it would permit every kind of abuse'.[58] Other Third World delegations, such as those of the Philippines and Lebanon, were similarly opposed to the provision, with the Lebanese delegate asserting that it would be 'difficult to determine the case in which derogations were permissible on the basis of so elastic a term as "public emergency"', a 'very hazy' concept that 'might give rise to interpretations more far-reaching than . . . intended'.[59]

Ultimately, however, Britain did not have major problems in persuading enough members of the Commission that it was necessary to envisage possible conditions of emergency when derogations from the law of human rights 'would become essential'.[60] It strikes me as somewhat ironic that 'reference was made to the history of the past epoch during which emergency powers had been invoked to suppress human rights and to set up dictatorial régimes'[61] by those maintaining a position that emergency powers should be formally authorised and monitored, rather than precluded.

Throughout the 1950s and early 1960s, as the drafting process continued, debates arose with respect to various aspects of the wording of Article 4. Worth noting is the discussion on whether, in order for derogation to be justified, the 'public emergency' referred to in the article must pose a threat to 'the interests of the people' or, alternatively, 'the life of the nation'.

> It was thought that the reference to a public emergency 'which threatens the life of the nation' would avoid any doubt as to whether the intention was to refer to all or some of the people, although it was suggested that a reference to 'the interests of the people' was more appropriate in a covenant which dealt with the rights of individuals and that such a phrase would also prohibit Governments from acting contrary to the interests and welfare of their people.[62]

Again it was Britain that took the lead, replacing existing proposals that spoke of a 'public emergency gravely threatening the interests of the

---

[57] 'Annotations on the text of the draft International Covenants on Human Rights, prepared by the UN Secretary-General, UN Doc. A/2929', 1 July 1955, 23.
[58] UN Doc. E/CN.4/SR.195, para. 63.   [59] UN Doc. E/CN.4/SR.126, 6, 8.
[60] 'Annotations on the text of the draft International Covenants on Human Rights, prepared by the UN Secretary-General, UN Doc. A/2929', 1 July 1955', 23.
[61] *Ibid.*   [62] *Ibid.*

people'[63] with a revision that related to a 'public emergency threatening
the life of the nation'.[64] This more state-centric locution mirrored the
change of wording made in the drafting of the European Convention on
Human Rights, and was adopted in the UN process at the eighth session
of the Commission on Human Rights in 1952.[65] It remained unaltered in
Article 4 of the text that was eventually enacted as the International
Covenant on Civil and Political Rights in 1966.

Other issues that arose within the context of Article 4 included:
whether to make express reference to war as a particular category of
emergency; whether an emergency must be 'officially' proclaimed or
'legally' proclaimed; the extent of the measures which a state may take
in derogation of its obligations under the covenant; the rights that should
be listed as non-derogable; and the grounds upon which discrimination
ought to be prohibited in the exercise of emergency powers.[66] After much
debate on these points, the final text of Article 4 of the International
Covenant on Civil and Political Rights as adopted in 1966 reads as
follows:

1 In time of public emergency which threatens the life of the nation and
the existence of which is officially proclaimed, the States Parties to the
present Covenant may take measures derogating from their obligations
under the present Covenant to the extent strictly required by the
exigencies of the situation, provided that such measures are not inconsistent with their other obligations under international law and do not
involve discrimination solely on the ground of race, colour, sex,
language, religion or social origin.

2 No derogation from articles 6, 7, 8 (paragraphs I and 2), 11, 15, 16 and
18 may be made under this provision.[67]

3 Any State Party to the present Covenant availing itself of the right of
derogation shall immediately inform the other States Parties to the

---

[63] Proposals in UN Docs. E/CN.4/365 and E/CN.4/498.
[64] See UN Docs. E/CN.4/L.139 and E/CN.4/L.139/Rev.1.   [65] UN Doc. E/CN.4/SR.331, 5.
[66] For a useful overview of the debates on these issues, see Marc J. Bossuyt, *Guide to the Travaux Préparatoires of the International Covenant on Civil and Political Rights* (Dordrecht: Martinus Nijhoff, 1987) 85–99.
[67] These articles relate to the right to life; the right to freedom from torture and cruel, inhuman or degrading treatment or punishment; the right to freedom from slavery and servitude; the right to freedom from imprisonment merely on the ground of inability to fulfil a contractual obligation; the non-retroactivity of criminal law; the right to recognition before the law; and the right to freedom of thought, conscience and religion; respectively.

present Covenant, through the intermediary of the Secretary-General of the United Nations, of the provisions from which it has derogated and of the reasons by which it was actuated. A further communication shall be made, through the same intermediary, on the date on which it terminates such derogation.

There are small but not insignificant differences between the final wording of Article 4 of the Covenant and that of Article 15 of the European Convention – the omission of reference to 'war' in the Covenant, the narrower list of non-derogable rights in the European Convention, the lack of an explicit anti-discrimination clause in the European Convention – whose potential consequences have been considered in scholarship comparing the texts.[68] The broader general effect of the inclusion of Article 4 in the Covenant, however, was to render the emergent discourse of universal human rights as one in which rights themselves were left somewhat contingent, subject to universalised scope for derogations. The duality of the relationship between international law and emergency is manifested here. The human rights codification process came in response to the emergency and exceptionality of fascism and war. International law, in this sense, is a product of the state of emergency. At the same time, the notion of emergency operates through the derogations scheme to dilute the rights established in this codification process, in favour of competing interests of sovereignty and state preservation. International law, in this other sense, reifies the state of emergency. While the law places parameters on derogation, the emergency is constituted as a legitimate restriction on the reach and range of rights. The casting of such restriction as temporary and exceptional seeks to obscure the fact that international law itself attenuates the very rights that it creates, that the scope for derogation is rooted within the law – normalised and universalised. Rather than ensuring the exceptionality of derogation, 'international law in fact ensures that derogation is potentially repeatable'.[69] And in a manner somewhat analogous to the 'humanising' reforms of colonial law discussed in Chapter 2, international human rights law operates after the Second World War in the British imperial context to include colonial subjects – through the extension of

---

[68] See, for example, Marko Milanovic, 'Extraterritorial Derogations from Human Rights Treaties in Armed Conflict', in Nehal Bhuta (ed.), *The Frontiers of Human Rights: Extraterritoriality and its Challenges* (Oxford: Oxford Universty Press, 2015).

[69] Authers and Charlesworth, 'The Crisis and the Quotidian', 30.

rights; but in a way that is still ultimately repressive – through derogation and the lawful imposition of emergency powers.

The European Convention in the Colonies

The prefatory question to arise in the colonial context of the European Convention on Human Rights was the extent to which European signatories would be bound by its obligations in their overseas dominions. The rationale that had been set down in principle by the Universal Declaration of Human Rights espoused the full (extra-territorial) application of human rights law to all territories under a state's jurisdiction, including colonial territories. Having lost that battle in the drafting of the Universal Declaration, the European colonial powers were uneasy about the cementing of that declaratory principle in legally binding treaties. Article 63[70] of the European Convention, the 'colonial clause', was thus framed so as to waive the automatic application of the Convention to non-metropolitan territories. In addition, as we have seen, the inclusion of the emergency derogation clause in the Convention was secured at Britain's behest. European powers would thus have the choice of simply not extending the Convention to their colonial territories, or of extending it safe in the knowledge that they could fall back into the safety net of the Article 15 derogation regime whenever it would benefit them to do so. Belgium opted for the former approach and ratified the Convention but did not extend its application to the Congo. France – where the discrimination that was effectively allowed for by Article 63 was met with vehement opposition from the elected representatives of the French colonial territories – chose instead not to ratify the Convention until 1974, after the majority of its colonies had achieved independence. It did so with a reservation to Article 15 at that.[71] Portugal, similarly, did not become a member of the Council of Europe until 1976, after its major colonies had won their liberation.

In the British context, there was similar lack of enthusiasm in some Foreign Office and Colonial Office circles for the human rights project in general, as evidenced in this 1948 Foreign Office note:

---

[70] Now amended as Article 56.

[71] (1974) 27 *Yearbook of the European Convention on Human Rights* 4. Rita Maran, among others, comments on the irony of France, a central founding member of the Council of Europe, failing to ratify the Convention for so long. Rita Maran, *Torture: The Role of Ideology in the French-Algerian War* (New York: Praeger, 1989).

This submission of important problems concerning Human Rights to higher authority has evoked an expression of considerable misgivings. The misgivings centred round the dangers which might flow from the coming into force of the Covenant, despite any safeguards which it might be possible to have included in the Covenant. The Lord Chancellor, for instance, has stated that he regards the whole matter with grave misgiving. The Colonial Office, at a Ministerial Level, are known to view the whole question with even greater apprehension. It is also in line with these views, which anticipate considerable political difficulties if the Covenant ever comes into force, that the Secretary of State decided to instruct the U.K. delegate to adopt Fabian tactics when the question of individual petitions comes up for discussion. Viewed in light of the political considerations . . . therefore, there would be every advantage in delaying the coming into force of the Covenant and even greater in postponing this event *sine die.*[72]

Volumes of internal Colonial Office correspondence and communications with the Foreign Office and the British delegation at the UN reveal that so 'far as the Colonial Office was concerned the real belief of the officials was that British involvement in the whole human rights exercise had been regrettable and was potentially harmful to British interests'.[73] Britain was committed to the project in Europe, however, and signed and ratified the European Convention in 1951 ahead of its entry into force in 1953. The Colonial Office was thus forced to grapple with the question of how best to manage its impact on the colonies. While eschewing any universalist pretensions with claims that 'what may be a reasonable provision in Europe does not necessarily make sense here and now for Africa', Colonial Office officials had, by 1951, identified the 'propaganda value' of the European Convention and viewed it as the lesser of two evils when compared with the more ambiguous and precarious obligations provided for by the draft UN Covenant at that time.[74] Simpson observes that 'the primary motive was not to improve the lot of colonial subjects [but] to present British colonial policy and practice in a favourable light, by publicly committing colonial governments to respect for human rights and to furnish an argument for not accepting a UN Covenant if one was ever adopted'.[75] As we have seen, the European Convention's colonial clause gave state parties the discretion to choose whether or not to apply the Convention to territories over whose international relations it

---

[72] J. Hebblethwaite, Foreign Office Minute of 8 June 1948, FO 371/72808/UNE2273.
[73] Simpson, *Human Rights and the End of Empire*, 824.
[74] Edith Mercer, Colonial Office Minute of 18 January 1951, CO 936/157.
[75] Simpson, *Human Rights and the End of Empire*, 825.

exercises responsibility. British officials disclosed that the principal reason for such a compromise 'was to enable the United Kingdom to sign without immediately committing the dependent territories'.[76] Article 63(3) was also considered by Colonial Office officials to have 'provided a sufficient loophole for discrepancies we knew would arise between the practice in certain Colonies and what the Convention provided'.[77] And with the insurance clause of the emergency derogation procedure secured, European powers would be able extend the Convention to their colonial territories while falling back on the option of derogation under Article 15 if and whenever necessary.

Following consultation with the colonial authorities throughout the empire between 1951 and 1953,[78] this option of extension and derogation was the tack that Britain chose to take.[79] The context at the time was one in which the ripple of emergencies in the late 1940s from Jamaica to Malaya was continuing to fan out. British colonial authorities declared states of emergency, for instance, in Grenada in February 1951, Kenya in October 1952 and British Guiana in October 1953, straddling the coming into force of the Convention in September 1953. In October 1953, notice was given by the British government to the Council of Europe that the Convention would be extended to a large number of overseas territories. This broadened its jurisdictional reach to 68 million people in 42 British

[76] British Cabinet Steering Committee on International Relations, Working Party on Human Rights: Record of meeting held on 13 October 1953, FO 371/72808/UNE2273.

[77] E.C. Burr, Minute of 14 July 1958, CO 936/531.

[78] See Confidential Circular Despatch 25526/1/51 of 30 March 1951 from the Secretary of State for the Colonies to all colonial governors; replies from colonial governors in files CO 936/156 and CO 537/7157.

[79] As noted above, France, by contrast, did not ratify the Convention until after its empire had broken up. Denmark had been the first to act upon the provisions of Article 63, extending the Convention to Greenland. A similar process of consultation was embarked upon by the Colonial Office regarding the extension around the empire of the First Protocol to the European Convention relating to issues of property (Article 1), education (Article 2) and, most contentiously in the colonial context, elections (Article 3). Here, even the existence of a formal emergency suspending certain obligations was not considered ample insurance against liability. See, for example, Letter from Colonial Office official E.M. West to Foreign Office official E.R. Warner, 18 December 1953, in CO 936/155: 'I think you will agree that it would be injudicious to extend the Protocol to British Guiana, at least until the emergency has ceased to exist. Kenya has said that it does not propose to consider the extension of Protocol for the present, and we agree that Kenya should also be left out of account for the time being.' Ultimately, with the protocol presenting a number of potentially thorny issues in the colonies, the issue was shelved and the protocol was not extended to any British colonial or dependent territories until the 1990s.

territories (54 million of whom in Africa), more than the population of Britain itself at the time.[80] With the knots binding the empire beginning to unravel, intuitions that the inclusion of the emergency derogation provision would allow Britain to cast a light of lawfulness on illiberal policies in the colonies were borne out by practice in the early years of the Convention's application.

A number of the colonial governments did express concerns over the implications of coming under the Convention's jurisdiction in the first place, however, and it was not extended to all British colonies. The Aden Protectorate, Brunei, Hong Kong and Southern Rhodesia were among those to which the Convention was not extended, for varying reasons. The governor of Hong Kong informed the Secretary of State for the Colonies that he 'would greatly prefer that the Convention should not apply to Hong Kong for the present'.[81] This reluctance stemmed from a condition of emergency, which the governor argued prevailed in the colony due to a floating alien population and violence in 'Communist areas', and the potential burden involved in reviewing the special emergency measures in place and reporting to the Council of Europe under the Article 15 derogation procedure.[82] As detailed in a Colonial Office minute, the authorities in Hong Kong 'feel that they are faced with "a public emergency threatening the life of the nation" in which a "*complete negation* of human rights is the order of the day" and that it would not be practically reasonable to have the extension extended to them unless and until they can examine all their legislation.'[83] The archive files on this are revealing. Article 15 was viewed by the British authorities not as an oversight mechanism to regulate the use of emergency measures, but rather (and explicitly) as a 'loop-hole' which could be used to strip the Convention of the bulk of its operation in practice.[84] While concerns were raised internally over the disingenuousness of extending the Convention to a territory but then opting 'to send in a list of derogations which virtually nullify the whole thing',[85] this was not enough to sway the ultimate decision that, overall, the preferable course of action would be to extend the Convention to the colonies. This would allow Britain to gain

---

[80] Council of Europe, Directorate of Information, IP/643, 30 October 1953.
[81] Savingram No. 71 from the Governor, Hong Kong to from the Secretary of State for the Colonies, 12 January 1952, CO 936/156.
[82] *Ibid.*
[83] Note from E.C. Burr to Dr. Edith Mercer, 13 February 1952, CO 936/156. Emphasis added.
[84] *Ibid.*   [85] *Ibid.*

credit for doing so, and at the same time provide a shield from anti-imperialist critics should it choose not to accede to the UN Covenant.[86] Therefore, the decision not to extend the Convention to Hong Kong[87] was a deviation from the general policy pursued (taken essentially for fear of the undue reporting workload it would have created for colonial legal offices in Hong Kong), even in relation to colonies under states of emergency.

When the Convention was extended to the rest of the empire, it did encompass a number of territories where emergency legal regimes were already in force, including British Guiana, Kenya and the Federation of Malaya and Singapore. In those contexts, the colonial authorities were prepared to accept whatever accompanying baggage would be necessary to allow special powers to remain in place:

> In territories where the emergency was thought to be of a very temporary nature, as in lawyerless Sarawak, it raised no special problem. But where, as in the Federation of Malaya there was no immediate end in sight, there was going to have to be a derogation if the convention was extended. Kenya was in like case once the emergency had been declared in 1952.[88]

Within the first year of the European Convention's application, the British government had indeed submitted notice of derogations pursuant to the extant emergencies in Malaya and Singapore, British Guiana, Kenya and the Buganda province of Uganda.[89] The reasons given generally invoked some variation of a tersely worded formula pertaining to the attempted subversion of the 'lawfully constituted Government', or, in the Ugandan case, grounds as nebulous as the existence of 'a constitutional crisis'.[90] The general policy adopted by the British authorities was one of providing as little information as possible – both in respect of the reasons for the derogation itself, and in relation to the measures deployed under the derogation. Thus, virtually no information was transmitted to inform the Council of Europe in Strasbourg as to the scope and scale of emergency powers used, nor their legal form. From the outset, an approach

---

[86] Minute of Dr. Edith Mercer, 13 February 1952, CO 936/156.
[87] Minute of Mr. Hall, 20 February 1952, CO 936/156.
[88] Simpson, *Human Rights and the End of Empire*, 837.
[89] Note Verbale of 24 May 1954 (1958) 1 *Yearbook of the European Convention on Human Rights* 48–49.
[90] *Ibid.* Regarding the derogation for the Province of Buganda in the Protectorate of Uganda, Simpson notes that the state of emergency was 'of a somewhat fictitious nature' and had already ended by the time the notice of derogation was provided. Simpson, *Human Rights and the End of Empire*, 878, 881–884.

that avails of the derogations procedure without being overly burdened by its procedural requirements was discernible in Britain's engagement.[91] Article 15 was subsequently invoked by the British government to derogate from obligations in Cyprus,[92] Northern Rhodesia,[93] Nyasaland,[94] the Colony of Aden,[95] the Zanzibar Protectorate[96] and Mauritius.[97] Britain also notified the Council of Europe of further derogations in respect of Kenya,[98] Singapore,[99] Aden[100] and British Guiana.[101] An evident policy choice ordained emergency as the default setting by which to sideline the Convention in the colonies, particularly as it related to

[91] Indeed, in the first case adjudicated under the Convention to address Article 15, Britain was criticised by the European Commission of Human Rights for its inattentive and disparaging approach to the derogations procedure. See *Greece v. UK* ['the first *Cyprus* case'], Application No. 176/56, Report of the European Commission on Human Rights, 26 September 1958.

[92] Note Verbale of 7 October 1955 (1958) 1 *Yearbook of the European Convention on Human Rights* 49; Note Verbale of 13 April 1956 (1958) 1 *Yearbook of the European Convention on Human Rights* 49–50; Note Verbale of 21 January 1959 (1959) 2 *Yearbook of the European Convention on Human Rights* 78. For a full account of the emergency period in Cyprus, see, for example, Robert Holland, *Britain and the Revolt In Cyprus, 1954–1959* (Oxford: Oxford University Press, 1998). For background see Robert Holland, 'Never, Never Land: British Colonial Policy and the Roots of Violence in Cyprus, 1950–54', in Robert Holland (ed.), *Emergencies and Disorder in the European Empires After 1945* (Abingdon: Frank Cass, 1994).

[93] Note Verbale of 16 August 1957 (1958) 1 *Yearbook of the European Convention on Human Rights* 51.

[94] Note Verbale of 25 May 1959 (1959) 2 *Yearbook of the European Convention on Human Rights* 84; Note Verbale of 11 January 1961 (1961) 4 *Yearbook of the European Convention on Human Rights* 39.

[95] Note Verbale of 7 January 1960 (1960) 3 *Yearbook of the European Convention on Human Rights* 68.

[96] Note Verbale of 5 December 1961 (1961) 4 *Yearbook of the European Convention on Human Rights* 44. As Simpson points out, the election disturbances that prompted the state of emergency in Zanzibar 'would certainly have never been handled under emergency powers in mainland Britain'. Simpson, *Human Rights and the End of Empire*, 1071.

[97] Undated notice in (1965) 8 *Yearbook of the European Convention on Human Rights* 14–17.

[98] Note Verbale of 21 September 1960 (1960) 3 *Yearbook of the European Convention on Human Rights* 48.

[99] Note Verbale of 11 May 1960 (1960) 3 *Yearbook of the European Convention on Human Rights* 75. See also FO 371/154534/WUC1735/11.

[100] A state of emergency was formally declared in both the Aden colony and protectorate on 12 December 1963, while the relevant derogation notice was submitted to the Council of Europe on 30 August 1966.

[101] (1964) 6 *Yearbook of the European Convention on Human Rights* 28–29; (1965) 8 *Yearbook of the European Convention on Human Rights* 10–14.

central elements of colonial practice such as mass detention and the abrogation of liberty of person. A study by Denys Holland tallied twenty-nine separate British declarations of emergency between 1946 and 1960, in colonies from A(den) to Z(anzibar).[102] Some of these declarations had lapsed before the European Convention came in to force and not all were followed with formal derogations from the Convention.[103] That said, the number of derogations made by Britain in that first decade is greater than the total number derogations made by 45 other Council of Europe member states combined (that is, all other members apart from Turkey[104]) over the first six decades of the Convention's application.[105] This is obfuscated by statements such as those asserting that '[p]rior to 2015 there have been relatively few derogations – 8 altogether concerning Albania, Armenia, France, Georgia, Greece, Ireland, Turkey and the United Kingdom'.[106] The presentation of this list in such a manner implies no qualitative or quantitative differences of note between the single derogation entered by Armenia (covering one particular city for a period of just over two weeks in March 2008), for example, and the multiplicity of British derogations spread across time and space from African, Asian and South American colonies in the middle of the twentieth century, through decades of derogations relating to the north of Ireland, to the broader "war on terror" state of emergency

---

[102] Denys C. Holland, 'Emergency Legislation in the Commonwealth' (1960) 13 *Current Legal Problems* 148, 148.

[103] States of emergency enforced in Sarawak and North Borneo from December 1962, for example, were not subject to formal derogations as such a step was left 'altogether too late ... such derogation would be susceptible to serious misinformation if it became public knowledge at the present time'. See Simpson, *Human Rights and the End of Empire*, 1061, citing CO 936/853, 854.

[104] Turkey has derogated under Article 15 a number of times, including in 1963, 1974, 1978, 1979, 1980, and 1990. These derogations related for the most part to the situation in Turkish-occupied Cyprus and to the Turkish state's subjugation of its Kurdish population. In July 2016, following an attempted coup, the Turkish government declared a state of emergency under its constitution, and informed the Council of Europe that measures taken under this emergency 'may involve derogation from the obligations under the Convention'. Communication from the Government of Turkey to the Secretary-General of the Council of Europe, 21 July 2016, Annex to Note Verbale JJ8187C Tr./005–191, 22 July 2016.

[105] Derogations from the European Convention on Human Rights by state parties other than the United Kingdom and Turkey include those made by Greece (1967); Ireland (1957, 1976); France (1985 [in respect of New Caledonia], 2015); Albania (1997); Georgia (2006); Armenia (2008); Ukraine (2015).

[106] Michael O'Boyle, 'Emergency Government and Derogation under the ECHR', Lecture given to the Law Society, Dublin, 15 March 2016, accessible at www.lawsociety.ie, 5.

in the early twenty-first century. Similarly reductive representations can be seen in other recent studies. Emilie Hafner-Burton, Laurence Helfer and Christopher Fariss purport to offer 'the first systematic empirical evidence on derogations from human rights treaties in times of emergency'.[107] They take 1976 as their starting point, however, and leave the colonial foundations of derogations out of the picture in providing an apolitical and somewhat de-historicised analysis. The study deploys coding and statistical methods to theorise the likelihood of states derogating from human rights treaties, their reasons for doing so, and the probability of serial or prolonged derogations – all of which are presented as dependent on whether a given state has a stable democratic government with strong courts, or not. According to these authors' hypothesis, stable democracies such as Britain – with strong judiciaries and robust mechanisms to hold government accountable to civil society and the electorate – are 'unlikely to derogate for long periods, as our theory predicts'.[108] Yet even the study's own post-1976 data finds that the UK clocked up the most 'country-years' of derogations out of all 33 states that derogated from international human rights treaties in the 1976–2007 timeframe examined.[109] This is simply attributed by the authors to necessity in the face of political violence (although they do 'recognize, however, that our theory does not fully explain all serial derogations by these states'[110]), whereas Britain's imperial legal traditions and techniques of deploying emergency powers as well as its derogation policy from the outset of the European Convention's application are absent from the analysis.

Somewhat analogous elisions can be detected in debates over the extra-territorial applicability of (and interaction between) the European Convention and international humanitarian law norms in the context of more recent overseas military interventions by European states. A series of cases before the European Court centring around the actions of British forces in Iraq in 2003–2004[111] prompted renewed engagement in such debates. When human rights law scholars assert definitively that 'no state has ever derogated for an extraterritorial

---

[107] Hafner-Burton et al., 'Emergency and Escape', 703.   [108] *Ibid.*, 698.   [109] *Ibid.*, 679.
[110] *Ibid.*, 701.
[111] *Al-Skeini and Others v. the United Kingdom*, No. 55721/07, Grand Chamber Judgment, European Court of Human Rights, 7 July 2011; *Al-Jedda v. the United Kingdom*, No. 27021/08, Grand Chamber Judgment, European Court of Human Rights, 7 July 2011; *Hassan v. the United Kingdom*, No. 29750/09, Grand Chamber Judgment, European Court of Human Rights, 16 September 2014.

situation',[112] they are presumably following mainstream international law's reading of extra-territoriality which accepts a qualitative juridical difference between conquered colonial territory on one hand, and occupied territory or conflict zones in which state forces exercise effective control over protected persons on the other.[113] But in the ease with which the colonial derogations tend to be disregarded, it is difficult to shake the impression of international lawyers again edging the field's colonial backstory out of the picture. The European Court of Human Rights itself does acknowledge this history, but in the same single cursory sentence simultaneously dismisses its relevance:

> Leaving aside a number of declarations made by the United Kingdom between 1954 and 1966 in respect of powers put in place to quell uprisings in a number of its colonies, the derogations made by Contracting States under Article 15 of the Convention have all made reference to emergencies arising within the territory of the derogating State.[114]

In 'leaving aside' this formative period, we risk losing sight and memory of important contextual factors in the development of international legal doctrine. The assertion, for example, that states did not 'give any serious thought to the question of the extraterritorial application of human rights treaties generally until the mid-1990s'[115] is complicated by the discussions and dilemmas of the colonial powers in the 1950s. As we have seen, a particular form of 'extra-territorial' application of treaties such as the European Convention on Human Rights to the colonial territories is something that states did in fact give significant thought to in the drafting, ratification and implementation of those treaties. At the very least, engagement with those debates and developments can contribute to a fuller understanding of state practice and the intentions of the drafters

---

[112] Milanovic, 'Extraterritorial Derogations from Human Rights Treaties', 55.

[113] On the interaction between the European Convention's Article 1 jurisdiction clause and Article 56 "colonial clause", see Louise Moor and A.W.B. Simpson, 'Ghosts of Colonialism in the European Convention on Human Rights' (2005) 76:1 *British Yearbook of International Law* 121. See also Karen da Costa, *The Extraterritorial Application of Selected Human Rights Treaties* (Leiden: Martinus Nijhoff, 2013) 14. For the European Court's recent pronouncements in this area, see, for example, *Al-Skeini and Others v. the United Kingdom*, No. 55721/07, Grand Chamber Judgment, European Court of Human Rights, 7 July 2011, para. 140; *Chagos Islanders v. UK*, No. 35622/04, Admissibility Decision, European Court of Human Rights, 11 December 2012.

[114] *Hassan v. the United Kingdom*, No. 29750/09, Grand Chamber Judgment, European Court of Human Rights, 16 September 2014, para. 40.

[115] Milanovic, 'Extraterritorial Derogations from Human Rights Treaties', 57.

when we seek to address questions such as those posed by the 2014 judgment of *Hassan v. UK*[116] – questions as to the nature of human rights law's extra-territorial application, the reach of the European Convention's *espace juridique*, and whether extra-territorial derogations are possible under the Convention. The (vaguely formulated) plan announced by the British Conservative government in 2016 for the state to apply a blanket 'presumption to derogate' from the European Convention on Human Rights in all future military conflicts[117] illustrates the continuity of the imperial mindset and the propensity to exploit the emergency derogation regime. This only further reinforces the need to unpack the dynamics and legacy of Britain's mass overseas derogations in the early period of the European Convention's lifetime. One particularly illuminating example from that period – which offers insight into the interplay between colonial emergency and European human rights law, as well as into the temporal and racial politics that are often encoded in states of emergency – is the situation in Kenya in the 1950s.

---

[116] *Hassan v. the United Kingdom*, No. 29750/09, Grand Chamber Judgment, European Court of Human Rights, 16 September 2014.

[117] Michael Fallon, Defence Secretary, 2016 Conservative Party Conference speech, 4 October 2016, stating: 'I can announce today that in future conflicts we intend to derogate from the Convention.' See also Ministry of Defence press release, 'Government to protect Armed Forces from persistent legal claims in future overseas operations', 4 October 2016.

5

Kenya

A 'Purely Political' State of Emergency

In July 2012, the British government publicly acknowledged, for the first time, that its colonial authorities had perpetrated acts of torture during the state of emergency in Kenya some six decades earlier. Standing before the High Court of Justice of England and Wales, the state's legal counsel asserted that the government 'does not dispute that each of the claimants suffered torture and other ill-treatment at the hands of the colonial administration'.[1] The claimants in this instance were five former Kenyan detainees in British camps, survivors 'in our 70s and 80s who have travelled to London from our rural villages to tell the world of the torture and trauma we lived through at the hands of the British colonial regime'.[2] Leaving Kenya for the first time in their lives to file their tort claim against the British authorities in the High Court in London in 2009, they relayed a Kikuyu proverb that 'he who is defeated with unjust force will always come back, he who is dealt with justly will never come back'.[3]

Under the state of emergency that was declared in 1952 and the emergency measures that continued effectively until Kenyan independence in 1963, brutal treatment of detainees by British forces was widespread and institutionalised. Although it had been internalised as necessary and lawful in the context of emergency governance, colonial officials inevitably sought to bury this history when British rule was ousted by Kenyan resistance. Abuses during the emergency period comprising 'physical mistreatment of the most serious kind, including

---

[1] Jerome Taylor, 'Government admits Kenyans were tortured and sexually abused by colonial forces during Mau Mau uprising', *The Independent*, 17 July 2012. The statement was made in a High Court hearing in the case of *Mutua & others v. The Foreign and Commonwealth Office*.

[2] Letter from Ndiku Mutua, Paulo Nzili, Jane Muthoni Mara, Wambugu Wa Nyingi and Susan Ngondi to Gordon Brown, 24 June 2009, available at: www.leighday.co.uk/Leigh Day/media/LeighDay/documents/Mau%20Mau/Letter-to-Gordon-Brown-from-the-Mau-Mau-veterans.pdf.

[3] '*Muingatwo na kihoto dacokaga; muingatwo na njuguma niacokaga*'. *Ibid.*

torture, rape, castration and severe beatings'[4] have since been chronicled in much detail by historians, however, on the basis of primary documents and testimony of surviving perpetrators and victims.[5] The testimonies of the group of those surviving victims who brought the *Mutua* case are representative of this systematic violence of colonial emergency rule.

> We were moved from detention camp to detention camp, most of us were never charged or brought before a court of law and all of us were tortured. Two of our number were castrated, the two women suffered sexual and physical abuse. One of our number was beaten so badly that he was left for dead for three days at the Hola Camp in 1959. This was all done by, or under the direct supervision of, British officers.
>
> It is not an exaggeration to say that our lives have been devastated by what we have been through. Many of us live with injuries from that period and are unable to pay the medical bills for necessary treatment. Because of our injuries, many of us have not been able to have children or to marry, others have been unable to provide for or educate their families. The effects of the brutality we were subjected to are felt by our children and our children's children.
>
> Sadly, our experiences were not isolated incidents. Thousands of Kenyans were detained during the Kenyan Emergency and we know that thousands were tortured and treated inhumanely. We represent the forgotten people of Kenya whose story has finally emerged and whose cry for justice has become too deeply felt to remain unheard. And we have discovered now that this violence was known about and authorised at the highest levels of Government in London at the time. Our claim for justice is on behalf of all those who were abused and tortured at that time.[6]

In July 2011, the High Court issued a preliminary judgment ruling that the plaintiffs had arguable cases in law and that the case should proceed to trial.[7] The following year, as noted above, the British government

---

[4] *Mutua & others v. The Foreign and Commonwealth Office* [2011] EWHC 1913 (QB), 21 July 2011, para. 1.

[5] See, for example, Caroline Elkins, *Imperial Reckoning: The Untold Story of Britain's Gulag in Kenya* (London: Pimlico, 2005); David Anderson, *Histories of the Hanged: Britain's Dirty War in Kenya and the End of Empire* (London: Weidenfeld & Nicolson, 2005).

[6] Letter from Ndiku Mutua, Paulo Nzili, Jane Muthoni Mara, Wambugu Wa Nyingi and Susan Ngondi to Gordon Brown, 24 June 2009. See further High Court of Justice, Queen's Bench Division, Claim No. HQ09X02666: Witness Statement of Paulo Muoka Nzili, 3 November 2010; Witness Statement of Wambugu Wa Nyingi, 4 November 2010; Witness Statement of Jane Muthoni Mara, 4 November 2010.

[7] *Mutua & others v. The Foreign and Commonwealth Office* [2011] EWHC 1913 (QB), 21 July 2011. For discussion, see Devoka Hovell, 'The Gulf Between Tortious and Torturous: UK Responsibility for Mistreatment of the Mau Mau in Colonial Kenya' (2013) 11 *Journal of International Criminal Justice* 223. For background, see David

conceded the fact that torture and ill-treatment had indeed been meted out. Britain continues to deny its legal responsibility for such facts, however. Initially, this was on the basis that responsibility had passed to the successor state upon independence. The Court held that the British government could nonetheless be answerable for historic wrongs committed by its former colonial or military branches, under the principle of joint liability for torts. The government defence then shifted to a statute of limitations argument, claiming that too much time had elapsed for witness testimony to be reliable and that too many key witnesses and decision-makers had passed away for the full context and circumstances to be established. In October 2012, however, High Court presiding Justice McCombe, acting under the discretion permitted by section 33 of the Limitation Act 1980, ruled that there should be no time bar on the hearing of the case.

> the evidence on both sides remains significantly cogent for the Court to complete its task satisfactorily. The documentation is voluminous, as I have said already, and the governments and military commanders seem to have been meticulous record keepers. The Hanslope material has filled gaps in the parties' knowledge and understanding and that process is still continuing.[8]

The 'Hanslope material' here refers to colonial government files covering 37 former British colonial territories which were concealed from historians and the public for 50 years in a secret Foreign Office archive, before being handed over to the National Archives and made available to the public in 2012. The disclosure and phased release of upwards of 8,800 suppressed files between April 2012 and November 2013[9] came about by

---

Anderson, 'Mau Mau in the High Court and the 'Lost' British Empire Archives: Colonial Conspiracy or Bureaucratic Bungle?' (2011) 39:5 *Journal of Imperial and Commonwealth History* 699; Huw Bennett, 'Soldiers in the Court Room: The British Army's Part in the Kenya Emergency under the Legal Spotlight' (2011) 39:5 *Journal of Imperial and Commonwealth History* 717.

[8] *Mutua & others v. The Foreign and Commonwealth Office* [2012] EWHC 2678 (QB), 5 October 2012, para. 95.

[9] For an index of the Hanslope files (also referred to as the migrated archives), see The National Archives, 'Colonial Administration Records – Migrated Archives: Guides to the Records' (First Tranche, April 2012; Second Tranche, July 2012; Third Tranche, September 2012; Fourth Tranche, November 2012; Fifth Tranche, April 2013; Sixth Tranche, July 2013; Seventh Tranche, September 2013; Eighth Tranche, November 2013). For background, see Anthony Cary, 'Report on Migrated Archives', Foreign and Commonwealth Office, 24 February 2011; Statement of the Minister of State, Foreign and Commonwealth Office, 'Public Records: Colonial Documents', *Hansard*, Column WS133,

court order in the *Mutua* litigation, when it transpired that the government's disclosure of the documentation had been incomplete. Previous requests by the Kenyan government for the files' release had been refused, and the Foreign Office had continuously denied their existence. It turns out that thousands more files were destroyed or disposed of – burnt or dumped at sea – by colonial officials under instruction from London during the decolonisation period, in order to avoid embarrassment and incrimination.[10] Significantly, while uncovered in the context of the case based specifically on incarceration and physical violence during the emergency, the Hanslope files on Kenya also tell a wider story of the bureaucratic spatial-territorial and population control dynamics of colonial emergency legalities. The larger enterprise of colonial sovereignty in Kenya had deeper roots in territorial control established by conquest, settlement and dispossession. The state of emergency in the 1950s was aimed at reinforcing and stabilising that colonial sovereignty by managing and extinguishing

---

5 April 2011; David Anderson, 'Guilty Secrets: Deceit, Denial, and the Discovery of Kenya's "Migrated Archive"' (2015) 80:1 *History Workshop Journal* 142. Question marks remain over the transparency of the Foreign Office's approach in releasing the files; in April 2013 it emerged that many of the files were still being withheld without explanation under a catch-all exception clause in the Public Records Act 1958. Ian Cobain, 'Kenyan Mau Mau Promised Payout as UK Expresses Regret Over Abuse', *The Guardian*, 5 June 2013. See also Caroline Elkins, 'The Colonial Papers: FCO Transparency is a Carefully Cultivated Myth', *The Guardian*, 18 April 2012.

10 See Ian Cobain, Owen Bowcott & Richard Norton-Taylor, 'Britain Destroyed Records of Colonial Crimes', *The Guardian*, 18 April 2012, detailing documents contained in the Hanslope files which reveal 'the instructions for systematic destruction issued in 1961 after Iain Macleod, secretary of state for the colonies, directed that post-independence governments should not get any material that "might embarrass Her Majesty's government", that could "embarrass members of the police, military forces, public servants or others eg police informers", that might compromise intelligence sources, or that might "be used unethically by ministers in the successor government"'. On the methods of disposal of such material, colonial officials in Kenya were instructed that 'it is permissible, as an alternative to destruction by fire, for documents to be packed in weighted crates and dumped in very deep and current-free water at maximum practicable distance from the coast'. Caroline Elkins has said that 'the government itself was involved in a very highly choreographed, systematised process of destroying and removing documents so it could craft the official narrative that sits in these archives', while other historians such as Tony Badger suggest it may have been a more haphazard process. Marc Parry, 'A Historian's Day in Court' (2016) 62:38 *Chronicle of Higher Education*. For further reflections on the construction of a 'coherent decolonization process' through the 'carefully managed' archive, see Caroline Elkins, 'Looking Beyond Mau Mau: Archiving Violence in the Era of Decolonization' (2015) 120:3 *American Historical Review* 852.

native agitation. In concert with the scandal of physical atrocities perpetrated in the detention camps by British forces, the emergency in Kenya is also defined by the more quotidian policies of land expropriation and livestock confiscation. In the initial tranche of files released in April 2012, for example, there is less revelation than one might expect in terms of torture and ill-treatment in the internment camps in Kenya. The majority of the substantive files are catalogued under the heading of 'Collective Punishment under Emergency Regulations' and document the confiscation of property and sources of livelihood (land, crops, livestock) of natives suspected of supporting anti-colonial rebels.[11] One representative file contains a District Commissioner's 'Report of Collective Punishment ordered under Regulation 4B of the Emergency Regulations, 1952'. It certifies the seizure of 100 per cent of the livestock or property of seven Kenyan farmers in October 1954, with the 'reasons for punishment' given within the file as 'consorting with' and 'assisting terrorists' on grounds that an alleged rebel group's hide-out was located within a mile of their village. On the basis of the District Commissioner's report, a 'Forfeiture Order' transferring ownership of the property and livestock to the government was made by the Governor of Kenya, pursuant to powers conferred by the Emergency Regulations.[12] Such micro-level acts of appropriation were a constant, everyday feature of the emergency regulations at work. They are indicative of the banality of emergency in its relation to colonial sovereignty more broadly.

In this regard, it is notable that the witness statements in the *Mutua* case detailing the atrocities suffered under the emergency begin with the story of the alienation of land and the exploitation of labour under colonial rule.

> I was born on this white man's farm in Mulumini about 120 kilometres from Nairobi. He had a large cattle farm and the whole village of about 200 adults worked for him. The local population milked the cows and cleared the fields to create grazing land. Major Joyce was not a nice man. If anyone did anything wrong he would give the men six strokes of the cane. . . . There were several settlers in Makueni and most of the land was owned by the British in those days. The Kenyan population had very little land on which we could farm.[13]

---

[11] FCO 141/6086–6123.   [12] FCO 141/6089.
[13] High Court of Justice, Queen's Bench Division, Claim No. HQ09X02666: Witness Statement of Paulo Muoka Nzili, 3 November 2010.

The June 2011 and October 2012 preliminary High Court decisions in favour of the Kenyan victims' case being heard were landmark setbacks for the British government, but it appeared to remain adamant to contest that case on the merits. In June 2013, however, the government instead settled the case and announced its intention to provide compensation payments to the plaintiffs in the case, and to the remaining 5,228 survivors of abuse in Britain's internment camp complex in Kenya.[14] Before an almost-empty House of Commons, Foreign Secretary William Hague stated that 'the British government sincerely regrets that these abuses took place'.[15] When they initiated the case four years earlier, the survivors had made clear that above any financial reparation, '[f]irst and foremost, we seek recognition of the historic wrong which was done to us and apology from the British Government.'[16] While recognising the historic wrong in the same language as that used by the government lawyers in court a year earlier, Hague's statement emphasised wrongs committed on 'both sides', and stopped short of apology. It was, at best, 'an almost apology',[17] clearly calculated to evade culpability. The government remained resolute that the state bore no legal responsibility for this historic wrong: 'We continue to deny liability on behalf of the Government . . . for the actions of the colonial administration in respect of these claims. . . . And we do not believe that this settlement establishes a precedent in relation to any other former British colonial administration.'[18]

The reasons for this disclaimer are obvious. It was not only in Kenya that such atrocities had been perpetrated under the guise of emergency necessity. As we have seen, British actions in 36 other colonies were

[14] Ian Cobain, 'Kenyan Mau Mau Promised Payout as UK Expresses Regret over Abuse', *The Guardian*, 5 June 2013; 'Statement by Leigh Day on Kenyan Torture Victim Statement', 6 June 2013.

[15] Foreign & Commonwealth Office and William Hague, 'Statement to Parliament on Settlement of Mau Mau Claims', 6 June 2013.

[16] Letter from Ndiku Mutua, Paulo Nzili, Jane Muthoni Mara, Wambugu Wa Nyingi and Susan Ngondi to Gordon Brown, 24 June 2009.

[17] Daniel Howden and Kim Sengupta, '59 Years Late – but Mau Mau Accept an Almost Apology', *The Independent*, 7 June 2013.

[18] Foreign & Commonwealth Office and William Hague, 'Statement to Parliament on Settlement of Mau Mau Claims', 6 June 2013. In spite of this denial of precedent, more victims of the colonial emergency measures in Kenya have initiated claims seeking redress. In the summer of 2016, hearings commenced in a group action involving up to 40,000 Kenyans claiming compensation from the British state for torture, rape, wrongful detention and forced labour under the state of emergency. Owen Boycott, 'Mau Mau Lawsuit Due to Begin at High Court', *The Guardian*, 22 May 2016.

implicated in the Hanslope files. Against that wider backdrop, I examine the state of emergency in Kenya in this chapter as indicative of the normative-policy turn to emergency writ large at the decline of the British empire. It epitomises the colonial machinery's design and production run of a particular type of racialised emergency: rooted in the construction of a depraved and atavistic other, and deployed in pursuit of the consolidation and preservation of imperial sovereignty. Running concomitant to the drafting of the formative international human rights instruments, the Kenya emergency also demonstrates the 'long shadow'[19] cast by colonial legality, and the nature of the doctrine of emergency as an inbuilt 'Achilles' heel'[20] of the liberal human rights project from its inception.

Rehearsing the Emergency

The emergency in colonial Kenya manifested, in large part, as a war waged by British forces against a peasant revolt by the Kikuyu (Gĩkũyũ) people[21] of Kenya's central highlands.[22] While calling itself the Kenya

---

[19] John Reynolds, 'The Long Shadow of Colonialism: The Origins of the Doctrine of Emergency in International Human Rights Law' (2010) 6:5 *Osgoode Comparative Research in Law and Political Economy* 1.

[20] Balakrishnan Rajagopal, *International Law from Below: Development, Social Movements and Third World Resistance* (Cambridge: Cambridge University Press, 2003) 176.

[21] Neighbouring Emba, Kamba and Meru tribes were affected and involved, but to a much lesser degree.

[22] For further literature on the revolt and the state of emergency in Kenya from a range of perspectives, see, for example: Louis Leakey, *Defeating Mau Mau* (London: Methuen & Co, 1954); Peter Evans, *Law and Disorder: Scenes of Life in Kenya* (London: Secker & Warburg, 1956); Frank Corfield, *The Origins and Growth of Mau Mau: an Historical Survey* ("The Corfield Report") (Nairobi: Government of Kenya, 1960); Fred Majdalany, *State of Emergency: The Full Story of Mau Mau* (London: Longmans, 1962); Josiah Mwangi Kariuki, *'Mau Mau' Detainee* (Nairobi: Oxford University Press, 1963); Carl Rosberg and John Nottingham, *The Myth of 'Mau Mau': Nationalism in Kenya* (New York: Praeger, 1966); Donald Barnett and Karari Njama, *Mau Mau from Within: Autobiography and Analysis of Kenya's Peasant Revolt* (London: Macgibbon & Kee, 1966); Anthony Clayton, *Counter-Insurgency in Kenya 1952–60: A Study of the Military Operations against the Mau Mau* (Nairobi: Transafrica, 1976); Gucu G. Gikoyo, *We Fought for Freedom* (Nairobi: East African Publishing House, 1979); Frank Füredi, *The Mau Mau War in Perspective* (Nairobi: Heinemann, 1989); R.B. Egerton, *Mau Mau: An African Crucible* (New York: The Free Press, 1989); Bruce Berman & John Lonsdale, *Unhappy Valley: Conflict Kenya and Africa* (Nairobi: Heinemann, 1992); Wunyabari O. Maloba, *Mau Mau and Kenya: An Analysis of a Peasant Revolt* (Bloomington: Indiana University Press, 1993); Marshall Clough, *Mau Mau Memoirs: History, Memory, and*

Land and Freedom Army (or Land and Freedom Movement), the rebel-
ling group was and remains commonly referred to as 'Mau Mau'.[23] This
formation was the upshot of the emergence of more radical elements of
the mainstream nationalist Kenya African Union (KAU) and Kikuyu
Central Association (KCA) during the 1940s,[24] with its roots in the
Kikuyu 'Squatter Resistance' movement previously spawned by colonial
land policies. Agitation and unrest had been simmering for decades in a
context where a sizeable white settler population had occupied Kenya's
prime agricultural land, predominantly in Kikuyu territory.[25] With
Kenya experiencing the same rise of anti-imperial sentiment by the

Politics (Boulder, CO: Lynne Rienner, 1998); Kinuthia Macharia and Muigai Kanyua, The
Social Context of the Mau Mau Movement in Kenya (1952–1960) (Oxford: University
Press of America, 2006); S.M. Shamsul Alam, Rethinking Mau Mau in Colonial Kenya
(Basingstoke: Palgrave Macmillan, 2007); Daniel Branch, Defeating Mau Mau, Creating
Kenya (Cambridge, Cambridge University Press, 2009).

[23] The origins of the 'Mau Mau' label are uncertain. Fred Majdalany, writing contempor-
aneously from an unsympathetic European perspective, claims that it was a word without
meaning to the Kikuyu, but contends that it was most likely a code word or anagram; 'one
secret which the Kikuyu succeeded in keeping wholly to themselves'. Majdalany, State of
Emergency, 75–76. Simpson, on the other hand, asserts that Mau Mau was a tag conferred
by the colonists, although he provides no further explanation. Simpson, Human Rights
and the End of Empire, 835. There is likely an element of truth in both claims. Josiah
Kariuki, a detainee for most of the emergency period, explains that linguistic anagrams
were commonly used by Kikuyu children, including 'Mau, Mau' for 'Uma, Uma' (meaning 'Go, go' or 'Go out, go out'). 'Mau Mau' was the code adopted at some secret oathing
ceremonies to raise the alarm in the event of a British raid. From then, 'the oath of unity
was given the name "Mau Mau" [but] the members of the movement did not call the
movement "Mau Mau"'. Kariuki suggests that the British authorities embraced the Mau
Mau moniker for the movement as a whole so as to elide the 'land and freedom' elements
of the Kikuyu struggle. Kariuki, 'Mau Mau' Detainee, 23–24.

[24] Initial British assumptions of Jomo Kenyatta as the leader of Mau Mau were indicative of
the coloniser's lack of understanding of the socio-political dynamics of its colonised
subjects. S.M. Shamsul Alam intimates that the relationship between Kenyatta's mainstream (and, many would argue, bourgeois) nationalist movement and the Mau Mau
movement was 'one of ambivalence and suspicion, if not outright hostility'. Shamsul
Alam, Rethinking Mau Mau, 20, 101–121.

[25] For background on the politicisation of Kikuyu squatter communities going back at least
as far as the Master and Servants (Amendments) Ordinance 1924, see, for example,
Füredi, The Mau Mau War in Perspective, 22–109. David Anderson traces the line of
legalised dispossession to the Natives Removal Ordinance 1909, a 'catch-all piece of
colonial legislation'. Anderson, Histories of the Hanged, 16. On land issues, see also Frank
Füredi, 'The Social Composition of the Mau Mau Movement in the White Highlands'
(1974) 1 Journal of Peasant Studies 486; John Overton, 'The Origins of the Kikuyu Land
Problem: Land Alienation and Land Use in Kiambu, Kenya, 1895– 1920' (1988) 31
African Studies Review 109; Fiona Mackenzie, Land, Ecology and Resistance in Kenya,
1880-1952 (Edinburgh: Edinburgh University Press, 1998).

1940s as other parts of the colonised world, the Mau Mau revolt involved the coming together of specific local and national interests, and the blending of some of the traits of militant nationalism with those of an underground peasant movement. While exemplifying certain common characteristics of anti-colonial resistance, Mau Mau must be understood as possessing its own particular ideological, cultural and material thrust.

Britain's state of emergency in Kenya was formally declared by Governor Evelyn Baring in October 1952, but had been in the making for some time before that. The legal foundations were laid in 1948 by an Emergency Powers Ordinance empowering the Governor to proclaim a public emergency and to issue decrees as he deems necessary for the preservation of order and public safety.[26] This can be understood as a product of the 1948 'Panic in Whitehall', whereby increasing political opposition to British rule across numerous colonies unsettled the Colonial Office in London and prompted an empire-wide deployment of the emergency paradigm as a technique of containment: 'In this climate, even relatively liberal administrators were busy integrating emergency powers into their overall strategy. . . . Throughout the empire police forces and security arrangements were being reviewed and contingency plans drawn up.'[27] Colonial administrators and governors were planning ahead, prompted – in some instances – by vociferous settler populations. Parallel and somewhat naïve and tokenistic attempts by the British authorities to win over the hearts and minds of Kikuyu squatters were met with scorn and thus short-lived. Accordingly, as they saw it, 'the only option available was more repression'.[28]

An amendment to the Emergency Powers Ordinance two years later expanded the reach of the regulations to cover powers of search and arrest, detention, movement restriction (on top of the existing *kipande* pass laws[29]), curfew, censorship and restrictions on public meetings.[30] In 1950, security measures were intensified in preparation for a turn to a full-on emergency framework. An 'Emergency Scheme for Kenya Colony' was circulated by Britain's East Africa Command in March 1950 to make provision for the maintenance of law and order in Kenya

---

[26] Emergency Powers Ordinance, cap. 42 of 1948.   [27] Füredi, *Colonial Wars*, 97.
[28] Füredi, *The Mau Mau War in Perspective*, 115.
[29] The *kipande* was a registration certificate that all African adult males were required to carry at all times.
[30] Emergency Powers Ordinance, No. 5 of 8 February 1950.

'as *may become* necessary in the event of an emergency'.[31] The document details the factors that might trigger such an emergency, and provided for military resources and 'special funds' to be made available. It also created a Colony Emergency Committee ("EMCOM") comprised of members from across the spectrum of the Kenya administration, and provided for a procedure whereby local emergency organisations were to be set up in each of the colony's provinces and to report to the overarching Colony Emergency Committee twice daily. The Commissioner of Police was similarly instructed to furnish situation reports to the Committee every morning and evening.

This was, in effect, a contingency plan drawn up two and a half years in advance of the emergency being initiated by the British authorities. It preceded the large-scale proliferation of Mau Mau 'oathing'[32] campaigns and was developed before the colonial administration had any real understanding of what the Mau Mau movement was. The idea of pre-meditated measures inherent in such planning appears counter to the definitive elements of an 'emergency' as a sudden, unexpected, urgent, exceptional and temporary occurrence. In Kenya, as noted, British administrators were sketching the contours of an emergency that had yet to manifest. At a high level meeting in November 1950, senior colonial officers and leaders of the settler communities indicated their common support for 'far-reaching measures' and agreed upon the introduction of practices – communal penalties, summary evictions, new pass rules regulating movement – that created an 'increasingly harsh climate of law and order' and anticipated the emergency legislation of 1952.[33] The build-up of exceptional measures continued apace through 1951 and 1952. The Use of Collective Punishments Ordinance was put through in April 1952 and served as another precursor to the state of emergency. It was a blunt legal instrument that would be used with growing regularity over time.[34] The following month, district commissioners were given

[31] WO 276/106, 'Kenya – Emergency Scheme'. Emphasis added.
[32] A traditional Kikuyu practice. 'The Mau Mau movement used a campaign of ritualised oath-taking to gain the support and co-operation of the Gikuyu masses. . . . the oathing rituals are to be understood as part of the ideological apparatus of the movement, along with rallies and songs.' Maia Green, 'Mau Mau Oathing Rituals and Political Ideology in Kenya: A Re-analysis' (1990) 60:1 *Africa* 69.
[33] Füredi, *The Mau Mau War in Perspective*, 111–112, citing KNA, DC, NKU 2/386, Monthly Labour Reports No. 8, 27 November 1950, Mau Mau meeting, Provincial Commissioners' Offices.
[34] Anderson, *Histories of the Hanged*, 46.

further special powers, 'the equivalent of Supreme Court powers of punishment for certain offences which are commonly committed by adherents of the Mau Mau society'.[35]

Through these developments, white settlers continued to clamour for an institutionalisation of the use of force in the form of martial law or, at the least, formalised emergency powers. While Kikuyu resistance to the use of repressive measures ostensibly bolstered the case made by the settlers, the continuing absence of a clearly identifiable 'cause' for a state of emergency meant that the Colonial Office was less vehement:

> the pressure for a state of emergency emanated from the European settler community, who were able to gain the backing of the Nairobi administration for their project. Behind the scenes, there was considerable pressure to win the acquiescence of the Colonial Office for the implementation of the emergency. . . . The Colonial Office did not initiate but went along with the proposal to implement a state of emergency. There is a curiously passive tone to the deliberations in the Colonial Office on this subject.[36]

The assassination of prominent native collaborator, Chief Waruhiu, on 7 October 1952 is generally credited as the incident that united opinion around the need for drastic action, and sparked the emergency declaration.[37] As I have shown, however, the conditions of emergency were rooted in the increasingly severe policies that had been mounting over the preceding years. Archival histories of a variety of British colonial emergencies during this period reveal plans that were calculated to culminate in the declaration of states of emergency, rather than the declaration actually being – as presented – a reaction to a single incident or trigger. In the specific Kenyan context, a letter from the Acting Governor regarding the need for special powers had been sent to Whitehall on 17 August 1952, while on 2 September the Attorney-General in Nairobi sent draft copies of the proposed emergency laws for approval by the Colonial Office.[38] The killing of Waruhiu some weeks later simply provided the 'pretext' needed for this 'new offensive'.[39] It was ultimately launched with the Governor's declaration of

[35] Corfield Report Extracts from the Kenya Police Intelligence Summaries for 1952, quoted in Füredi, *The Mau Mau War in Perspective*, 116.
[36] Füredi, *Colonial Wars*, 163–164.
[37] See, for example, Rosberg and Nottingham, *The Myth of 'Mau Mau'*, 276.
[38] Füredi, *Colonial Wars*, 166–167.   [39] Füredi, *The Mau Mau War in Perspective*, 116.

the state of emergency on 20 October and the concomitant entry into force of a code of emergency regulations.[40]

Performing the Emergency

The bulk of historical and empirical work done on the Mau Mau revolt suggests that the direct effect of the proclamation of emergency was to aggravate conflict and resistance, and breed a spiral of violence. The emergency powers deployed by the British authorities provoked anti-colonial militancy at least as much as they curbed it.

From the formative 1950–52 period, it is clear that the political radicalisation of the Kikuyu squatter movement cannot be disentangled from the context of the laws and practices implemented by British rule.[41] The pre-emptive measures taken against the Kikuyu community in central Kenya marked, in effect, the onset of an informal emergency. This was ostensibly aimed at reining in subversive natives but ended up having the opposite effect, of fomenting revolt. In response to the crackdowns initiated by both colonial state and settlers in 1950, 'for the first time, squatter resistance went beyond civil disobedience to begin deploying force and sabotage against Europeans and Asians in the Highlands'.[42] The administration of oaths had been similarly negligible up until 1950. Mass arrest campaigns, preventive detention and increasingly indiscriminate and uncompromising police operations served only 'to exacerbate the tension and strengthen support for Mau Mau'.[43]

This was compounded by the declaration of the formal emergency and the arrival of British troops in 1952. Historians of the Mau Mau rebellion underline the point that armed revolt did not *precede* the calling of the emergency, but rather was the consequence of it. The emergency transformed dissent into revolt, pushing increasing numbers of Kikuyu into the forests where Mau Mau fighting units were organising.[44] The declaration of emergency can be understood as a catalyst which propelled the Mau Mau movement further towards armed resistance in response. In this sense, the state of emergency becomes self-fulfilling. Füredi notes that in Nakuru District, for instance, an area hitherto bereft of incident, violent confrontations escalated after October 1952.[45] Insofar as the

---

[40] (1952) 31 *Colony of Kenya Proclamations, Rules and Regulations* 490.
[41] Füredi, *The Mau Mau War in Perspective*, 112.   [42] *Ibid.*, 110.   [43] *Ibid.*, 116.
[44] Füredi, *Colonial Wars*, 154.   [45] Füredi, *The Mau Mau War in Perspective*, 118.

special measures were taken to shore up British authority, the policy was unsuccessful. The imposition of the state of emergency was received by the Kikuyu as a further incitement and affront, and precipitated a ground-swell of disorder and resistance to authority. Thus appear the hallmarks of the emergency as an aggravator of conflict. As David Anderson notes: '[i]t was not until October 1952 that the war properly got going, provoked by the British decision to declare a state of emergency and to move troops into the colony'.[46] Anderson shows that as the emergency began, Mau Mau was barely a fighting force at all. Over the following two months however, 'British hesitancy over how to target the Mau Mau leadership, combined with heavy-handed repression against ordinary Kikuyu, allowed the Muhimu time to gather their wits and drove many of the wavering Kikuyu majority into the rebel camp.'[47] Thus, the declaration of the state of emergency and the assumption of extraordinary powers by the colonial governor was performative, provoking a more direct conflict which reached a peak in intensity in 1954. Simpson explains the under-pinnings of the particularly severe dose of colonial violence that was meted out in response to Kikuyu demands for land and freedom: 'Notions of white racial superiority, allied to the belief that the uprising represented a return to "barbarism," added a special dimension to the ruthless nature of the government reaction to the uprising.'[48]

The emergency legal framework proliferated over the course of the 1950s in the form of a matrix of emergency regulations, special ordin-ances and 'exceptional' administrative decrees. Much of this was rooted in control over the native body, through the infliction of pain on one hand, and more mundane but insidious controls of movement and residence on the other. The implications of the emergency for native life and liberty were substantial, with mass internment of Kikuyu Kenyans in prison camps, and an execution of the death penalty on a scale unparal-leled elsewhere in the empire at that time. Capital punishment was not restricted to typically capital crimes such as murder, however. Under the emergency regulations, the death penalty could be imposed for lesser offences such as unlawful possession[49] or trading[50] of firearms.

---

[46] Anderson, *Histories of the Hanged*, 4.   [47] *Ibid.*, 69.
[48] Simpson, 'Round Up the Usual Suspects', 665.
[49] Amended Regulation 8A, 15 April 1953 (1953) 32 *Colony of Kenya Proclamations, Rules and Regulations* 339.
[50] Regulation 8AA, 14 May 1953 (1953) 32 *Colony of Kenya Proclamations, Rules and Regulations* 437.

Approximately 900 Kenyans were executed during the first two years of the state of emergency, at least a third of whom for crimes of arms possession or administration of unlawful oaths.[51] From June 1953 onwards, capital cases were heard by tailor-made Special Emergency Assize Courts[52] and by December 1956 the Courts had sentenced 1,574 Kikuyu to hang.[53] Additionally, official figures suggest that approximately 12,000 natives were killed by colonial security forces during the Mau Mau emergency, while independent research indicates that the actual figure was likely to have been over 20,000.[54]

In addition, Section 2 of the Emergency Regulations was broadly framed in respect of liberty of person, empowering the governor to make any order if 'satisfied that, for the purposes of maintaining public order, it is necessary to exercise control over any person'. This resulted in the customary panoply of restrictions on employment, movement and residence. Most significantly, extensive use was made of the paradigmatic emergency power of detention without charge or trial. Official records from the British authorities put the number of Kenyans interned under Section 2 by April 1957 at 73,106.[55] Simpson estimates the total for the 1950s at approximately 77,000,[56] while Josiah Kariuki, himself an inmate of fourteen of Kenya's detention camps between 1953 and 1960, ascertains that there were at least 80,000 detainees during the emergency.[57] These figures do not account for undocumented temporary detentions and evacuation orders. Anderson concludes that, all told, '150,000 or more Kikuyu spent time in detention camps during the rebellion', with the number incarcerated at any one time peaking at 71,346 (including some 8,000 women), the majority of whom administrative detainees incarcerated on the basis of mere suspicion.[58] Under 'screening' procedures deployed to identify Mau Mau supporters as part of large-scale military operations, thousands of natives would be interned en masse:

---

[51] Clayton, *Counter-Insurgency in Kenya 1952–60*, 15.

[52] Emergency (Emergency Assizes) Regulations 1953, *The Official Gazette of the Colony and Protectorate of Kenya, Supplement No. 45*, Government Notice 931 (16 June 1953) 523.

[53] Anderson, *Histories of the Hanged*, 6, and at 152–176 for further detail on the creation of the Special Emergency Assize Courts and the capital trials of Kenyan accused.

[54] *Ibid.*, 4.

[55] 72 Legislative Council Debates ch. 166 (GPO 1957) (Kenya), cited in Simpson, 'Round Up the Usual Suspects', 667.

[56] Simpson, 'Round Up the Usual Suspects', 667.   [57] Kariuki, *'Mau Mau' Detainee*, 1.

[58] Anderson, *Histories of the Hanged*, 5, 313–314.

in Operation Anvil in 1954 the authorities arrested something of the order
of 30,000 Africans, being practically the entire male population of Nairobi; they were held in reception centres under an evacuation order made
under the Emergency (Control of Nairobi) Regulations. The idea was to
identify Mau Mau supporters, and send them to work camps.[59]

Comparative research shows that Kenya had by far the greatest number
of detainees per target population of the British colonies of that era where
detention without trial was utilised as an emergency measure – roughly
ten times more than in Palestine, Malaya or Cyprus.[60] These extensive
detention measures were supplemented by additional powers stitched
into an emergency law fabric in which '[a]ny lack of a power was rapidly
remedied, either by way of a new regulation or amendment to an existing
law. . . . The governor could do whatever he liked.'[61] The upshot was a
pliable patchwork of collective punishment, land confiscation and property destruction. The decision to load indiscriminate punitive measures
into the emergency armoury was taken in advance of the formal declaration of emergency itself, and was often deployed to effect evictions of
entire communities. In one specific but indicative example, 4,324 Kikuyu
were evicted from their homes and land following the killing of a white
settler in Leshau in late 1952.[62] Through the emergency, arbitrary land
expropriation and population transfer continued to be effected via legislation such as the Forfeiture of Lands Bill 1953 and policies involving
compulsory resettlement in centralised, regulated villages that amounted
to 'little more than concentration camps to punish Mau Mau sympa-
thizers' – between June 1954 and October 1955 a total of 1,077,500
Kikuyu (from the population of approximately 1.4 million) were resettled
in 854 such villages.[63]

Communalised retribution of the type implemented in Leshau was
prescribed as policy, with the degree of punishment graded on the basis
of the gravity of the incident. In response to a serious incident such as a
murder, 'total evacuation of squatters and seizure of crops and stock' was
to be effected on the farm in question, and 50 per cent evacuation and
seizure on 'neighbouring farms within, say a 3 mile radius' (the 'say'

---

[59] Simpson, *Human Rights and the End of Empire*, 879.
[60] David French, *The British Way in Counter-Insurgency, 1945–1967* (Oxford: Oxford
University Press, 2012) 110–111.
[61] Simpson, 'Round Up the Usual Suspects', 665–666.
[62] Füredi, *The Mau Mau War in Perspective*, 119.
[63] Anderson, *Histories of the Hanged*, 271, 294.

betraying the entirely arbitrary nature of the delineation); for 'less serious incidents' – such as the holding of a Mau Mau meeting – the collective punishment scheme determined a reduced confiscation rate of 25 per cent.[64] Such normalised collective punishment is symptomatic of a punitive and often indiscriminate complexion to the abuse of power perpetrated by British forces throughout the emergency. It was not just members of the Mau Mau movement that were targeted; the Kikuyu racial group as a whole was collectively framed as suspect. 'From early November 1952', Füredi argues, 'the government had in effect declared war on the Kikuyu community'.[65] In Colonial Office files containing weekly police reports on 'Colony Appreciation of Crime and Subversion', the mindset and language of M.S. O'Rorke, Kenya's Commissioner of Police, is illustrative. Emboldened by the declaration of the state of emergency, the Commissioner's position hardened further from October 1952. At the end of November, he characterised the 90,000 Kikuyu males aged between 17 and 32 as 'really dangerous' and emphasised that there were 'almost the same number of young women who are showing themselves to be nearly as dangerous'. Thus, '[a]lmost 200,000 desperate potential criminals constitutes a most grave problem which requires such repressive measures as will produce a fear & respect for Government not yet fully felt.'[66] O'Rorke went on to itemise the punitive treatment meted out to the Kikuyu in the preceding week, but warns that it may not have been enough, and that 'constructive punishment must keep pace with repressive measures':

> the killing and wounding of over 40 in one affray alone, the arrest of 340 rioters, the breaking up of homes and the removal of nearly 3,000 back to desperation and poverty in their reserves, the seizing of large herds of their stock, the constant harassment by police and troops, the arrest of hundreds, are measures of the most repressive order which should make any people pause; whether they will do that and more than that, in the case of the Kikuyu, must remain to be seen.[67]

Systematised collective punishment ranging from the mundane to the brutal continued through the 1950s. The types of disciplinary and

---

[64] KNA, PC NKU 2/846, Provincial Commissioner, Rift Valley Province, to all District Commissioners, 23 December 1952.
[65] Füredi, *Colonial Wars*, 154.
[66] CO 822/447, 'Reports on the Mau Mau Situation by the Commissioner of Police, Kenya', 'Weekly Situation Appreciation: Week ending 27th Nov. 1952'.
[67] *Ibid.*

punitive violence that underpinned the *Mutua* litigation against the British authorities were exemplified in events such as the Hola Camp killings of 1959. There, eleven detainees were beaten and clubbed to death by British camp guards following their refusal to cooperate with uncompromising labour conditions designed to 'break' the prisoners. The incident is indicative of approaches sanctioned at the highest levels of colonial government regarding the treatment of Kikuyu detainees.

In this regard, the 'dilution technique', a 'systematic approach to brutalizing detainees and forcing them to confess',[68] had been pioneered earlier in the emergency in the detention camps on the Mwea plain in central Kenya. When the death toll of detainees began to rise, Governor Baring was careful to cover up the killings and became cautious for a time about the technique being used too widely. When a young officer named Terence Gavaghan was appointed to oversee 'rehabilitation' of 'hardcore' detainees in the six Mwea camps in 1957, however, he devised 'Operation Progress', 'a systematized and well-executed program of brutality' that would resurrect the dilution technique as central to detention policy.[69] As a means of complicating liberal rule of law standards, the emergency legal paradigm was central to this enterprise. Historian Caroline Elkins has chronicled the moves made by the administration in Kenya to satisfy Secretary of State for the Colonies, Alan Lennox-Boyd, of the need for what Baring described as 'a phase of violent shock':

> Baring and his attorney general, Eric Griffith-Jones, sent numerous secret memoranda to the Colonial Office, outlining the plan for systematic use of brute force and asking for official approval from the colonial secretary. . . . At first Lennox-Boyd balked when he learned of Gavaghan's methods. It was one thing to endorse unofficially the violence and torture that was ongoing in the camps and villages; it was another to make it officially sanctioned policy. . . . Griffith-Jones took charge, drafting a series of codes written in legal doublespeak, differentiating between something he termed legal *compelling force* from the otherwise illegal

---

[68] Elkins, *Imperial Reckoning*, 320.

[69] *Ibid.*, 321. As Chris McGreal notes, '"hard-core" did not mean the most egregious offenders, 'merely the most defiant'. Former inmate Epson Makanga recalls his experience of Gavaghan: 'He was a tall man with a thin face and we soon discovered his camp was about nothing more than being beaten and tortured. They beat us from the day we arrived, with sticks, with their fists, kicking us with their boots. They beat us to make us work. They beat us to force us to confess our Mau Mau oath. After a year I couldn't take it any longer. Gavaghan had won.' Chris McGreal, 'Shameful Legacy', *The Guardian*, 13 October 2006.

punitive force. Compelling force could be used "when immediately necessary to restrain or overpower a refractory detained person, or to compel
compliance with a lawful order to prevent disorder."[70]

The parallels with the legal acrobatics of Israel's state-sanctioned torture under the guise of 'moderate physical pressure' and the US
government's 'enhanced interrogation techniques'[71] programme under
the George W. Bush administration decades later are manifest. Griffith-
Jones' linguistic manoeuvres were enough to convince the Colonial
Secretary, who duly signed off on Regulation 17 of the Emergency
(Detained Persons) Regulations, authorising prison officers to use
discretionary on-the-spot violence against detainees.[72] Even if one were
to accept the pseudo-technical distinction between compelling and
punitive force, Gavaghan went on to acknowledge that '[p]unishment
was being meted out which clearly skirted the edges of the quasi-legal
concept of "compelling force"'; punishment which he admitted was
'visually "brutal and degrading," but was held to be both necessary
and effective.'[73] The legal cover constructed was a façade; according
to Gavaghan, no legal restraints were envisaged.[74] Griffith-Jones himself came to describe the treatment of detainees as 'distressingly

---

[70] Elkins, *Imperial Reckoning*, 323–324. Emphasis in original.
[71] For the 'torture memos' declaring the legality of certain forms of ill-treatment of detainees, see Jay S. Bybee, Assistant Attorney-General, 'Memorandum for Alberto R. Gonzales,
Counsel to the President, Re: Standards of Conduct for Interrogation under 18 U.S.C. §§
2340 – 2340A', 1 August 2002; Jay S. Bybee, Assistant Attorney-General, 'Memorandum
for John Rizzo, Acting General Counsel for the Central Intelligence Agency, Re: Interrogation of al Qaeda Operative', 1 August 2002; John Y. Coo, Deputy Assistant Attorney-
General, Letter to Alberto R. Gonzales, Counsel to the President, 1 August 2002. See also,
for example, Karen J. Greenberg and Joshua L. Dratel, *The Torture Papers: The Road to
Abu Ghraib* (Cambridge: Cambridge University Press, 2005); William E. Scheuerman,
'Carl Schmitt and the Road to Abu Ghraib' (2006) 13 *Constellations* 108; M. Cherif
Bassiouni, 'The Institutionalisation of Torture under the Bush Administration' (2006) 37
Case Western Reserve Journal of International Law 389; Philippe Sands, *Torture Team:
Rumsfeld's Memo and the Betrayal of American Values* (New York: Palgrave Macmillan,
2008).
[72] Elkins, *Imperial Reckoning*, 324, citing PRO, CO 822/1251/7, Telegram No. 53 from
Secretary of State for the Colonies for Baring, 16 July 1957; and PRO, CO 822/1251/8,
Telegram No. 597 from Baring to Secretary of State for the Colonies, 17 July 1957. For full
accounts of the background of systemic violence against Kenyan detainees, and of the
Hola Camp incident and its fallout, see Elkins, *Imperial Reckoning*, 311–353; Clayton,
Counter-Insurgency in Kenya 1952–60.
[73] Terence Gavaghan, *Corridors of Wire: A Saga of Colonial Power and Preventive Detention
in Kenya* (London: Terence Gavaghan, 1994) 90.
[74] *Ibid.*

reminiscent of conditions in Nazi Germany'.[75] The state of emergency was an effective mask, however. Despite a mounting campaign by opposition Labour MPs against such violence as the 1950s wore on, and even as more information about what was happening in the detention camps in Kenya came to light, it continued to be underwritten on the basis of an unspeakable savagery ascribed to the Mau Mau movement.

Mystifying Mau Mau: The Racialised Construction of a Diseased Mind

Branding any native political rebellion as both criminal connivance and communist conspiracy was standard operating procedure for a Western colonial power in the 1950s. It was only part of the story in Kenya, however. On top of a public relations campaign presenting Mau Mau as a criminal organisation in thrall to a global communist crusade, '[t]he colonial government went to great lengths to portray Mau Mau as an irrational force of evil, dominated by bestial influences'.[76] Attempts made to investigate and explain the possible socio-economic causes of the Mau Mau revolt were censored by authorities keen to sustain the (heavily racialised) narrative that the primary factor underlying Kikuyu resistance was not agrarian grievance but 'perverted tribalism'.[77] The mantra parroted in the Colonial Office, from press officer to Secretary of State, obviated any mention of 'Land and Freedom' and brandished Mau Mau with an image of irrationality and amorality. This fanned the flames of the imperial racist imagination:

> Like most wars, Mau Mau was as much about propaganda as it was about reality. From the start of the Emergency the colonial government was masterful in its public depiction of Mau Mau. ... The "horror of Mau Mau" stood in contrast to what the public relations officer called the "peaceful and progressive conditions" of Kenya prior to the Emergency. The "white" and "enlightened" forces of British colonialism were a stark contradistinction to the "dark," "evil," "foul," "secretive," and "degraded" Mau Mau. These descriptions spilled over into the Kenyan and British press, where sensationalist accounts juxtaposed white heroism with African, or Mau Mau, terrorism and savagery. ... It was the distinctive quality of Mau Mau oathing rituals, and methods of killing, that transformed the

---

[75] Quoted in Ian Cobain, *Cruel Britannia: A Secret History of Torture* (London: Portobello, 2012).
[76] Füredi, *The Mau Mau War in Perspective*, 3–4.
[77] *Ibid.*, 4, citing KNA, PO 3/129, No. 19, 21 October 1952.

virulent racism that had been the cornerstone of settler racial attitudes for over half a century into something even more lethal. ... in the settler imagination, Mau Mau adherents were scarcely part of humanity's continuum; they were indistinguishable in local thought and expression from the animals that roamed the colony.[78]

The likening of Mau Mau adherents not just to animals, but to deranged, bloodthirsty beasts at that, was common in the colonial parlance. According to one officer, most British soldiers in Kenya 'regarded the finding and disposing of the gang members in the same way as they would regard the hunting of a dangerous wild animal'.[79] Officials stationed in Kenya's Central Province described Mau Mau as a 'bestial', 'filthy', 'vile' and 'evil' movement.[80] Terence Gavaghan echoed these sentiments: 'Mau Mau was a seething mass of bestiality.'[81] In these characterisations, the line between Mau Mau as a movement and the broader Kikuyu community was blurred. Kenya's Commissioner of Police reported that: 'Kikuyu are showing themselves prone to insane frenzy ... added to the predilection of the Kikuyu for gangster crime, his savage cruelty, his cunning and ability to plan crime, makes him a most dangerous enemy.'[82] The 'brutality and blood lust' of Mau Mau, he asserted, were evidence of a 'return to the savage and primitive which there is good reason to believe is the heart of the whole movement'.[83]

Insofar as an emergency legal framework is seen as necessary to straitjacket this innate insanity and predisposition to sadism and criminality, law was co-opted into the pseudo-biological narratives of race that had become central to colonial discourse. In Kenya, the idea of the native rebels as both mentally diseased and possessed by evil was present

---

[78] Elkins, *Imperial Reckoning*, 46–48. Such setter imaginaries are neatly captured in Ngũgĩ wa Thiong'o's fiction: 'Who were black men and Mau Mau anyway, he asked for the thousandth time? Mere savages! A nice word – savages. Previously he had not thought of them as savages or otherwise, simply because he had not thought of them at all, except as part of the farm – the way one thought of donkeys or horses in his farm, except that in the case of donkeys and horses one had to think of their food and a place for them to sleep.' Ngũgĩ wa Thiong'o, *Weep Not, Child* (Nairobi: Heineman, 1964) 77.

[79] Frank Kitson, *Bunch of Five* (London: Faber & Faber, 1977) 13–14.

[80] Rhodes House, Mss. Brit. Emp. s. 527/528, *End of Empire, Kenya*, vol. 2, Sir Frank Loyd, interview. Cited in Elkins, *Imperial Reckoning*, 48.

[81] Terence Gavaghan, interview [with Caroline Elkins], London, England, 29 July 1998. Quoted in Elkins, *Imperial Reckoning*, 48.

[82] CO 822/447, 'Reports on the Mau Mau Situation by the Commissioner of Police, Kenya', 'Weekly Situation Appreciation: Week ending 27th Nov. 1952'.

[83] CO 822/447, 'Reports on the Mau Mau Situation by the Commissioner of Police, Kenya', 'Weekly Situation Appreciation: Week ending 8th April 1953'.

not only in security apparatus rhetoric. It permeated the work of medical and psychiatric officers, whose racialised 'ethno-psychiatry' theories both flowed from and complemented prevailing psychological and cultural postulations of the relationship between coloniser and colonised. Chief among European ethno-psychiatrists at this time was Dr. Colin Carothers. And chief among his contentions, informed by and further informing colonial ideology, was the notion that difference in physical characteristics connotes intrinsic behavioural and psychological difference.

Carothers was a district medical officer in Kenya who, in 1938, fell into the role of director of Mathari Mental Hospital in Nairobi (he had no special training in psychiatry), which he would end up occupying for more than a decade. Carothers was 'the right man in the right place', and became 'the most important author in the field of African Psychiatry' through the 1940s and 1950s.[84] He returned to England in 1950 and thereafter published his influential work on *The African Mind in Health and Disease*, courtesy of the World Health Organisation.[85] Carothers' delineation of a variety of African races on the basis of physical criteria including cranium shape, hair thickness and facial features fed in to a theory that correlated significant physical differences (skin colour, for instance) with disparities in mental and cognitive capacity. Due to what he presented as an idleness of the brain's frontal lobes in Africans,[86] Carothers suggested a relative underdevelopment of the African brain and a biologically fixed cognitive inferiority therein. This was based on 'classical conceptions' of the African mentality as observed by European neuropsychiatrists – conceptions which Carothers found to 'represent the truth', namely that an 'immaturity' of the mental faculty 'prevents complexity and integration in the emotional life' of the African and gives rise to her/his inherently primitive mindset and violent 'impulsivity'.[87]

---

[84] Raymond H. Prince, 'John Colin D. Carothers (1903–1989) and African Colonial Psychiatry' (1996) 33 *Transcultural Psychiatry* 226, 236.

[85] J.C. Carothers, *The African Mind in Health and Disease* (Geneva: World Health Organization, 1953).

[86] J.C. Carothers, 'Frontal Lobe Function and the African' (1951) 97 *Journal of Mental Science* 12.

[87] Carothers, *The African Mind*, 85–87, with reference to the work of, inter alia, Diedrich Westermann, P. Gallais & L. Planques, and R. Barbé. Carothers' frontal lobe hypothesis echoed the work of fellow colonial psychiatrists, most notably Antonin Porot of the University of Algiers, who had advanced similar findings of brain deficiency in respect of north African Muslims.

This, in turn, provided scientific basis for the notion of Africans as intrinsically psychologically imbalanced and fuelled the tanks of colonial stereotyping. Carothers also argued that 'detribalised' rural Africans became more susceptible to mental illness upon relocation from their native habitat to an urbanised setting.

Thus, when the British administration in Kenya took the telling step in 1954 of eliciting a psychological assessment of the Mau Mau rebellion and advice on potential 'cures' for its proponents (the clear implication being that the movement was 'a form of Kikuyu madness which could best be understood and described by a specialist in mental disorders'[88]), Carothers was the natural choice. Through this manoeuvre, ethno-psychiatry was 'commandeered to clothe the political interests of the colonists in the pseudo-scientific language of psychiatry to legitimize European suzerainty'.[89] Carothers duly obliged.[90] Jock McCulloch provides a succinct summation of Carothers' projection of prejudicial cultural assumptions and racialised conceptions of mental illness onto Kikuyu resistance:

> In his account of the reasons for Mau-Mau, Carothers dismisses any suggestion that there were social, political or economic grounds motivating the Kikuyu's protest. The Mau-Mau arose because of the inability of the African personality to adapt to change and because of the "neurotic" predisposition of the Kikuyu when faced with stress and insecurity. The violence of the Mau-Mau and their radical rejection of European authority must be traced ultimately to the childlike quality of the African personality rather than to the influence of socioeconomic conditions. The onus for the rebellion rests with the deficiencies characteristic of the native Kenyans and not with the policies of the British colonial government.[91]

The 'cure' implied for such native mental debility is one of pacification, subjugation and rehabilitation. In the coloniser's outlook, as Fanon puts it, 'seeking to "cure" a native properly [entails] seeking to make him thoroughly a part of a social background of the colonial type'.[92]

---

[88] Prince, 'John Colin D. Carothers (1903–1989) and African Colonial Psychiatry', 230.
[89] Ibid.
[90] J.C. Carothers, *The Psychology of Mau Mau* (Nairobi: Government Printer, 1954). See also Anderson, *Histories of the Hanged*, 279–288; John Lonsdale, 'Mau Maus of the Mind: Making Mau Mau and Remaking Kenya' (1990) 31:3 *Journal of African History* 393.
[91] Jock McCulloch, *Black Soul White Artifact: Fanon's Clinical Psychology and Social Theory* (Cambridge: Cambridge University Press, 1983) 21.
[92] Fanon, *The Wretched of the Earth*, 250.

This requires stringent disciplinary policy vis-à-vis 'the African who, like the European adolescent, needs firm guidance'.[93] Disciplinary policy, that is, that a framework of emergency law and detention camps can facilitate. It is in that context that the idea of the 'rehabilitative' nature of severe practices such as the dilution technique gains traction.

The narratives of mental disease and evil suffused up to the top echelons of colonial government, in both Nairobi and London. Governor Baring, while more moderate in his views compared to the fervour of much of his settler constituency, nonetheless saw Mau Mau as an 'atavistic savage sort of affair' that needed to be eliminated.[94] Oathing ceremonies were constructed in the European imagination as the incarnation of psychopathic depravity. Alan Lennox-Boyd's predecessor as Secretary of State for the Colonies, Oliver Lyttelton, wrote that:

> The Mau Mau oath is the most bestial, filthy and nauseating incantation which perverted minds can ever have brewed. . . . [I have never felt] the forces of evil to be so near and so strong as in Mau Mau. . . . As I wrote memoranda or instruction . . . I would suddenly see a shadow fall across the page — the horned shadow of the Devil himself.[95]

All of this is marked by a wilful absence of socio-cultural awareness. Notwithstanding the aggressive and coercive nature of the Mau Mau 'oathing' campaigns, standard colonial characterisations fail to offer even tokenistic pretences at contextualisation.

As Füredi reminds us, the oppression, economic discrimination and hostility that the Kikuyu population had been subjected to since the First World War forced them 'into a permanent state of semi-secrecy and underground organization. This was necessary even for simple operations like the movement of livestock and the disposal of produce. It was inevitable that the much more dangerous endeavour of political resistance would develop along similar lines. Like peasant movements throughout the world the Kikuyu squatters turned to mass oathing and secret organization'.[96] As a counterpoint to the narrative of a subversive

---

[93] McCulloch, *Black Soul White Artifact*, 21, citing Carothers, *The Psychology of Mau Mau*, 19.

[94] Rhodes House, Mss. Afr. S. 1574, Lord Howick (Sir Evelyn Baring) and Dame Margery Perham, interview, 19 November 1969. Quoted in Elkins, *Imperial Reckoning*, 50.

[95] Oliver Lyttelton [Lord Chandos], *The Memoirs of Lord Chandos: An Unexpected View from the Summit* (New York: New American Library, 1963) 380. Quoted in Elkins, *Imperial Reckoning*, 50.

[96] Füredi, *The Mau Mau War in Perspective*, 98–99.

sorcery at play, Ngotho, father of Ngũgĩ's protagonist in *Weep Not, Child*, explains that 'oath-taking as a means of binding a person to a promise was a normal feature of tribal life'.[97]

The oath is, however, a convenient brush with which to paint the Mau Mau movement in a seditious and necromantic light. To justify their own positions, '[t]he British administration and its moderate African allies had a common interest in mystifying the Mau Mau revolt'.[98] Even relatively empathetic British figures in the Kenyan story perpetuated a narrative whereby the 'bestiality' of the Mau Mau oaths meant that 'those who used such methods ceased to be normal human beings'.[99] The language of emergency is invoked to obscure the structural nature of colonial violence and explain it away as 'random' and 'unsanctioned' cruelties perpetrated by renegade officers in the mitigating circumstances of 'exceptional fear and crisis'.[100] More broadly, the demonisation of Mau Mau serves to justify the deployment of emergency powers against the Kikuyu population.

Purely Political International Law

The obvious value of the emergency legal framework, in Kenya as elsewhere, was that for as much as it may be considered a deviation from the core spirit of the 'rule of law', it carries the gravitas and legitimacy of 'law' nonetheless. The use of legal fronts provided the basis for arguments alluding to a benevolent imperial rule with 'standards of law, justice and humanity to which [Kenyans] could appeal'.[101]

While perhaps appealing to certain liberal and lawyerly inclinations, simplistic binaries distinguishing law from the political did not and do not sustain.[102] In the Kenyan context, decisions on the state of emergency – ostensibly technical legal questions pertaining to the declaration, implementation and retention of the emergency – were approached and

---

[97] Ngũgĩ wa Thiong'o, *Weep Not, Child*, 74.
[98] Füredi, *The Mau Mau War in Perspective*, 3.
[99] Margery Perham, 'Foreword' to Josiah Mwangi Kariuki, *'Mau Mau' Detainee* (Nairobi: Oxford University Press, 1963) xiv, xix.
[100] *Ibid.*, xx.   [101] *Ibid.*, xvi.
[102] In the context of international law and the political, for example, see Martti Koskenniemi, *From Apology to Utopia: The Structure of International Legal Argument* (Helsinki: Lakimiesliiton Kustannus, 1989); Martti Koskenniemi, *The Politics of International Law* (Oxford: Hart, 2011).

determined by political actors on political terms, with the express intention of complicating particular rights and obligations under international law.

In a shifting global context in which it was becoming more difficult both militarily and politically to hold a colony through force alone, the declaration of emergency in the first place can be seen as the calculated use of force 'designed to establish new terms on which colonial relations could be negotiated'; it was the absence of room for manoeuvre, more than the conditions requiring special powers, that necessitated the calling of states of emergency.[103] In 1954, Arthur Young, one of Britain's most senior colonial policemen, advocated the maintenance of the emergency as a strategic asset in the political process in Kenya, writing of the need 'to hold the emergency until political reforms and development can take place'.[104]

Internal debates within the colonial administration regarding the legality of the emergency in its implementation surfaced regularly. In the context of policies of screening, arrest and 'evacuation' to work camps[105] under the Emergency (Control of Nairobi) Regulations during Operation Anvil in 1954, for instance, concerns were raised that the compulsory work involved may be in violation of the European Convention on Human Rights (and the 1930 Forced Labour Convention) and that Britain's notice of derogation indicating a right for detainees to appeal to a judicial committee had been plainly misleading. The Colonial Office deflected such arguments by adopting the position that so long as the forced labour could be presented as in some way geared towards ending the emergency, suggestions of violations would be mitigated. The tactic pursued vis-à-vis the Council of Europe was to provide as little information as possible to the Strasbourg institutions.[106]

---

[103] Füredi, *Colonial Wars*, 144.

[104] Sir Arthur Young Papers, Young to Newson 1954, quoted in Füredi, *Colonial Wars*, 144.

[105] Walter Rodney's magisterial study of how colonial exploitation 'underdeveloped' Africa (with minimal investment of capital and massive extraction of labour) refers to the role of such work camps in the Kenyan context. Rodney highlights the example of the construction of Nairobi's Embakasi airport from 1953 onwards: 'Embakasi, which initially covered seven square miles and had four runways, was described as "the world's first handmade international airport." Mau Mau suspects numbering several thousand were to be found there "laboring under armed guard at a million-ton excavation job, filling in craters, laying a half million tons of stone with nothing but shovels, stone hammers and their bare hands"'. Walter Rodney, *How Europe Underdeveloped Africa* (London: Bogle-L'Ouverture, 1972) 210.

[106] Simpson, *Human Rights and the End of Empire*, 879–880.

One notable chain of internal correspondence preceding a visit of the Secretary of State for the Colonies to Kenya in 1957 highlights consensus among British officials that 'normalcy' had returned to Kenya by that point. It also reveals the authorities' explicit decision to nevertheless retain the legal state of emergency in order to facilitate continued reliance on emergency powers, free from concerns over human rights obligations. A brief prepared by the Colonial Office's East African Department in October 1957, tellingly entitled 'The Continuation of the Emergency', is particularly instructive, and merits attention. Consistent with a prior 'Note on the History of the Emergency in Kenya' submitted to Minister of Defence Duncan Sandys in advance of his trip to East Africa in May 1957,[107] the brief begins with a description of the 'return to normal' in Kenya. It notes that since the Secretary of State's previous visit in October 1954, there was 'a vast improvement in the restoration of public order', citing a drop from 'some 8,250 active terrorists still at large' in 1954 to 'fewer than 160 known terrorists unaccounted for, none of whom has been responsible for organised violence for a considerable time'. From 47,500 held in internment in November 1954 plus 17,500 Mau Mau convicts, the respective figures three years later had fallen to less than 20,000 'administrative' detainees and 4,900 convicted prisoners.[108]

> The people of the colony do not, therefore, need much telling that things are back to normal as far as everyday life is concerned. . . . The Emergency is lucky if it gets a mention on the back pages. . . . It is therefore likely, especially if the Secretary of State's visit coincides with the fifth anniversary of the declaration of the Emergency on 20th October, that such pressure as will develop will be for the termination of the legal Emergency, or at least a reduction in emergency measures.[109]

Notwithstanding the awareness of such pressure and the return to the 'normalcy' of colonial suppression, the brief proceeds in its next section to examine the possibilities of the 'retention of the legal Emergency'. It is highlighted that any official termination of the state of emergency would entail the automatic withdrawal of the torrent of emergency regulations adopted and emergency powers assumed over the preceding five years. From a Colonial Office perspective, this 'would create both immediate and more distant difficulties', including the release of administrative detainees on a large scale and the disappearance of emergency checks

---

[107] CO 822/1220, 'The History of the Emergency in Kenya'.
[108] CO 822/1229, 'The Continuation of the Emergency in Kenya', para. 1.
[109] Ibid., paras. 2–3.

on African political life, potentially entailing a deterioration of the security situation.[110]

The brief then considers the quandary of how special powers and colonial policy on 'irreconcilable detainees' could be sustained if the state of emergency were to formally come to an end. The assumption was that the powers wielded by emergency regulation in the colony would need to be transposed into permanent law to allow the government to continue 'to forestall would-be subversive movements, including political movements' and 'to detain trouble-makers without trial'.[111] While this may have amounted to a straightforward solution in terms of internal constitutional and security law in Kenya, it was complicated by its relation to Britain's international legal commitments. Repealing the state of emergency would connote withdrawal of the derogation submitted in respect of Kenya under the European Convention, thus dissolving the buffer created by the Article 15 derogations regime. Colonial officials were acutely aware of this:

> The main difficulty about assuming non-Emergency powers for the purposes [of detention without trial] is the adherence of Her Majesty's Govt to international Conventions, and particularly the European Human Rights Convention and the I.L.O. Forced Labour Convention of 1930. . . . Although a good deal will depend on the precise wording of any non-Emergency legislation, it looks very much as though it will be impossible to introduce such powers, even for the retention of existing detainees, without having to declare, and justify to the world, a breach of these international obligations. For as long as a legal State of Emergency continues, however, it looks as though the maintenance of these powers can be sustained despite increasing criticisms; they might, however be attenuated in scope and geography, stage by stage, to meet that criticism. In the last resort we must be prepared to sustain existing practices deemed essential for the maintenance of peace in Kenya even if we have to stand frankly in default of international obligations.
>
> The conclusion must be that for as long as possible the Emergency should be kept alive and that attempts for its revocation should be resisted. In the meantime examination will continue in London to see whether there are any ways through the legal difficulties of maintaining Emergency powers without an Emergency. It is likely, however, that the ultimate decision will have to be a purely political one whether or not to declare and justify a breach of the Conventions.[112]

At this juncture, then, the admittedly 'purely political' decision was taken to retain the legal state of emergency. The express objective was to benefit

---

[110] *Ibid.*, paras. 4–5.   [111] *Ibid.*, paras. 6–7.   [112] *Ibid.*, paras. 8–9.

from the leeway allowed by international law in times of a threat to the life of the nation, despite that such times – even in government eyes – had abated in Kenya.

The dilemma over how to retain emergency powers in a 'post-emergency' situation was to continue through the final years of the 1950s. It had been asserted in the 1957 Colonial Office brief that '[i]f the Emergency comes legally to an end, therefore, powers will have to be taken to enable their continued detention and also to compel them to work where necessary.'[113] The thrust of this point is replicated in a Cabinet memo in late 1959:

> [The British Government's] main concern was now to secure special powers within the framework of normalcy. In its discussion of Kenya, a Cabinet paper suggested that the problem was one of how to end the 'Emergency' which had existed for seven years and yet enable the governor: (1) to continue to detain the hardcore of Mau Mau; and (2) to assume certain other powers considered immediately necessary, such as controlling the size of meetings and the formation of societies.[114]

Through the 1950s, the British authorities felt unduly exposed by the lack of muddy waters between the instability of a state of emergency on one side, and the legal checks and balances of a state of normalcy on the other. Their preference was for a murky middle ground in which both special powers and the aura of stability could be retained.

The idea of a 'twilight emergency' situation had matured with British policy in Cyprus, where the Detention of Persons Law of 1955 was enacted to give the Governor what were, in essence, emergency powers in the hope of rendering a formal declaration of emergency unnecessary.[115] It was argued in policy circles that in the twilight zones that book-end a state of emergency, there is typically 'a period in which it is not desirable to have a proclaimed state of emergency but in which there is a public emergency in fact for which special powers, including the power to detain without trial, may have to be exercised'.[116] Yet it was actually the opposite for much of the duration of the Kenyan emergency. There was no grave emergency in fact for the colonial institutions, but in

---

[113] *Ibid.*, para. 6.
[114] Füredi, *Colonial Wars*, 270, citing PREM 11/2618, 'Memo to Prime Minister: Security Powers of Colonial Governors (C.P.C. (59)18) by J.B'., 4 November 1959.
[115] Simpson, *Human Rights and the End of Empire*, 1065.
[116] Draft Paper for the Colonial Policy Committee, FO 371/146286/WUC 1733/26 (June 1959). See also FO 371/146288/WUC 1733/45.

spite of this the proclaimed state of emergency was retained. By the latter part of the 1950s, the governing authorities were fixated with finding a way to end the formal emergency but to keep their special powers for an indefinite twilight period, particularly as far as detention policy was concerned. In the reappraisal of the situation in a number of African territories undertaken by the Colonial Office in 1958 and 1959, 'it came to be agreed that the real problem in applying the [European] Convention to African colonies was that the convention made no proper provision for the twilight periods'.[117]

The plan devised in response, for extraordinary powers to be absorbed into 'ordinary' law in a number of colonies, originated with then Kenyan Attorney-General, E.N. Griffith-Jones. By late 1958, it had assumed the form of a draft Colonial Office ordinance 'under which it would be a normal part of the law in Kenya (and other colonies) for the Governor to be able to assume emergency powers ... without the need for any declaration of an emergency'.[118] A June 1959 brief for the Foreign minister explained that '[t]he object of the proposal is to enable us to give the impression in Kenya that the emergency is over, whilst retaining room to argue in Strasbourg (if necessary) that it still continues'.[119] The advice suggested that colonial governors, when revoking a state of emergency, should add a disclaimer to the effect that: 'None the less there is a *situation* threatening the life of the nation'.[120] Such contrivances seek to capitalise on the existence of the doctrine of emergency in the Council of Europe system by stretching the concept of the emergency itself. The Foreign Office was happy to go along with the Colonial Office scheme. Britain's Attorney-General, Reginald Manningham-Buller, although opposed in general to 'the premature recourse to extra legal devices' by governors, was sympathetic in the Kenyan instance to hyperlegally enshrining emergency powers in permanent law given the 'subhuman level' to which the Mau Mau had descended.[121]

This was not enough, however, to convince the Attorney-General and the Lord Chancellor to sign off on the Colonial Office scheme to embed exceptional powers as a feature of regular law throughout the empire. The compromise that was arrived at was a two-tier system dependent on the gravity of the emergency. A first tier of emergency powers could be invoked by a governor where considered necessary for the preservation of

---

[117] Simpson, *Human Rights and the End of Empire*, 1066.
[118] *Ibid.* The draft ordinance can be found in FO 371/146286/WUC 1733/26.
[119] FO 371/146286/WUC 1733/26.   [120] *Ibid.*   [121] FO 371/146288/WUC 1733/47.

public security, but would exclude regulations for detention without trial and the direction of labour. The governor, however, was left with discretion to utilise internment and forced labour if the first tier powers were deemed inadequate.[122] To put this scheme into law in Kenya, the Preservation of Public Security Ordinance[123] was brought into force there in January 1960, the same month that the state of emergency was formally ended.[124]

This instrument provided for measures in response to future threats to 'public security' – defined expansively by the ordinance – but required an official declaration of emergency. The repeal of Kenya's state of emergency proved problematic as the Governor was reluctant to release the so-called 'hard-core' Mau Mau detainees that remained. In place of being made a permanent legal feature, the agreed solution was that twilight emergency powers, for the purposes of legalising prolonged detention, would be enacted through temporary ad hoc legislation. In Kenya this took the form of the Detained and Restricted Persons (Special Provisions) Ordinance. The notice of derogation at the Council of Europe was withdrawn, but Colonial Office officials remained cognisant of the fact that were Britain to find itself arraigned before the European Commission on Human Rights, 'there is considerable doubt whether our arguments on the legitimacy of our actions would be accepted . . . among these doubtful topics are post-emergency detention in Kenya and Nyasaland'.[125]

*

In the final years of British rule in Kenya, against a historical backdrop of dispossession and alienation, and of politics of a particularly racial complexion, an increasingly totalitarian condition emerged, in which power and law were intimately bound up. Violence was legally institutionalised through the emergency juridical order. The decision on the emergency was an ideological one, framed in legal nomenclature. The retention of the state of emergency – even when, by the colonial authorities' own admissions, no actual public security threat existed – is illustrative of an approach that has been repeated elsewhere, whereby state actors are loathe to have their policy hands tied by rights protections. The doctrine of emergency has proved itself particularly malleable in this respect.

---

[122] Simpson, *Human Rights and the End of Empire*, 1070.
[123] No. 2 of 1960. The ordinance adopted a very expansive definition of "public security".
[124] (1960) 39 *Colony of Kenya Proclamations, Rules and Regulations* 83.
[125] CO 936/657, Henry Steel, Minute of 3 October 1960.

The preeminent theory of law adhered to by thinkers and practitioners of the late British empire is one that exalts legality, but a very pliable legality that can be shaped to shield state counter-insurgency forces from liability. This standpoint is embodied in the reflections of Frank Kitson, who joined the British army as an emergency commission second lieutentant in 1948, before being promoted to captain as he went from colony to colony through the 1950s and 1960s. Having worked as an officer with the intelligence branch of the Kenya Police from 1953–1955, Kitson subsequently served in Malaya, Oman and Cyprus (being awarded various honours for his role in suppressing native resistance and eradicating communist organisations) before rising through the ranks in Northern Ireland in the 1970s and eventually being appointed Commander-in-Chief of the Land Forces in the 1982. He wrote an influential book on counter-insurgency tactics in 'low-intensity conflict',[126] and in his military memoir set out an approach to law very much representative of liberal imperial discourse:

> No country which relies on the law of the land to regulate the lives of its citizens can afford to see that law flouted by its own government, even in an insurgency situation. In other words everything done by a government and its agents in combating insurgency must be legal. But this does not mean that the government must work within exactly the same set of laws during an insurgency as existed beforehand, because it is a function of government to make new laws when necessary. ... It is therefore perfectly normal for governments not only to introduce Emergency Regulations as an insurgency progresses, but also to ... [alter] the way in which law is administered. Ways by which the legal system can be amended range from changing rules governing the giving of evidence to dispensing with juries altogether, or even to introducing some form of internment without proper trial.[127]

What emerges from the Kenyan experience, as from similar instances of state practice continuing to the present day, is a picture of law as subject to capture by hegemonic forces, and of the doctrine of emergency as a cavernous chink in the armour of rights protection, diluting as it does the already limited counter-hegemonic tendencies in international human rights law. In the illumination of the colonial shadows from which it emerged, the state of emergency is revealed as a vehicle for instrumental

---

[126] Frank Kitson, *Low Intensity Operations: Subversion, Insurgency and Peacekeeping* (London: Faber & Faber, 1971).
[127] Kitson, *Bunch of Five*, 289.

violence, grounded in dynamics of dispossession and domination. It operates as a vanishing point at which rights are eclipsed by executive prerogative. This is not something temporary or unique to any one particular apparition of emergency legality, but has long been the case, borne out in colonial laws and their post-colonial or neo-colonial successors. This normative phenomenon has also found an international institutional home at the European Court of Human Rights, manifest in its approach to emergency derogations for purposes of state security.

6

The Margin of Appreciation Doctrine

Colonial Origins

The particular technique of accommodation that was fashioned by the European human rights machinery in response to complaints against expansive states of emergency is the margin of appreciation doctrine. Characterised as the room for manoeuvre that the Council of Europe's human rights organs are willing to grant to member state national authorities, the margin of appreciation is, by now, well-established as a prominent and permanent feature of the Court's jurisprudence. The term 'margin of appreciation' itself does not appear in the text of the European Convention on Human Rights, nor in its preparatory work. It is a court-created doctrine in the European human rights system, which finds certain analogy in doctrines of administrative discretion in civil law jurisdictions.[1] The use of the doctrine has become most prevalent in cases that relate to social issues on which competing religious, cultural or moral value systems engender a lack of consensus across the Council of Europe's jurisdictional domain. In such instances – matters relating to reproductive rights, religious expression, sexual orientation, privacy, assisted suicide, and so on – the Strasbourg Court will often impose a form of self-restraint on its judicial review powers and grant varying degrees of latitude (sometimes wide, sometimes narrow) to the domestic authorities concerned, on the basis that they are best placed to determine the appropriate approach in the given socio-cultural context.[2]

The origins of the margin of appreciation in the European regional human rights system, however, are rooted in its state of emergency jurisprudence. The margin of appreciation has been extensively discussed in the legal literature, and critical scholars have provided cogent analysis on the width of

---

[1] See, for example, Yutaka Arai-Takahashi, 'Administrative Discretion in German Law: Doctrinal Discourse Revisited' (2000) 6 *European Public Law* 69.

[2] For an overview of relevant case law, see, for example, Steven Greer, 'The Margin of Appreciation: Interpretation and Discretion under the European Convention on Human Rights' (Strasbourg: Council of Europe, 2000). Greer notes that from 1958 to 1998, the margin of appreciation was adopted in over 700 judgments of the European Court of Human Rights.

the margin granted by the Court to states on matters of national security.[3] My simple aim in this chapter is to supplement the existing scholarship by placing emphasis on the margin of appreciation's colonial origins.

The Cyprus Case

While the 1976 freedom of expression case of *Handyside*[4] is regularly cited as the original[5] or canonical[6] use of the margin of appreciation doctrine, its earliest traces can be located in the inter-state *Cyprus* dispute.[7] This was a case lodged by Greece against the British government in May 1956 on foot of diplomatic tensions between the two parties over Britain's increasingly heavy-handed repression of the Greek Cypriot self-determination movement. The *Cyprus* dispute was a preview to many of the issues that would be central to national security and derogations cases before the European Court of Human Rights over the ensuing decades. The story of the margin of appreciation's evolution during that time maps on to a distinctly British genealogy that encompasses insurgents in colonial Cyprus, republicans in the north of Ireland, and Muslim detainees in the transnational 'war' against non-state terrorism.[8] The approach of the European Commission of Human Rights[9] to Article

---

[3] See, for example, Susan Marks, 'Civil Liberties at the Margin: the UK Derogation and the European Court of Human Rights' (1995) 15 *Oxford Journal of Legal Studies* 69; Kathleen A. Cavanaugh, 'Policing the Margins: Rights Protection and the European Court of Human Rights' (2006) 4 *European Human Rights Law Review* 422.

[4] *Handyside v. the United Kingdom*, No. 5493/72, Judgment, European Court of Human Rights, 7 December 1976.

[5] See, for example, Nina-Louisa Arold, *The Legal Culture of the European Court of Human Rights* (Leiden: Martinus Nijhoff, 2007) 38.

[6] Jan Kratochvíl, 'The Inflation of the Margin of Appreciation by the European Court of Human Rights' (2011) 29:3 *Netherlands Quarterly of Human Rights* 329.

[7] *Greece v. the United Kingdom*, No. 176/56 (the first *Cyprus* case).

[8] The role that the margin of appreciation has played in facilitating security politics also cannot be disentangled from the colonial context within which the emergency derogation regime more broadly was inserted into the Convention.

[9] The first port of call for complaints filed under the European Convention on Human Rights from 1954 to 1998. Between 1954 and 1959, the Commission was the only dispute settlement body under the Convention. The European Court of Human Rights was established in 1959, but applicants did not have direct access to it – they would instead submit their petitions to the Commission, which determined the admissibility of claims and functioned as a filter for the Court. Protocol No. 11 to the European Convention on Human Rights abolished the Commission in 1998, enlarged the Court, and allowed petitions to be submitted directly to the Court.

172   EMPIRE'S LAW

15 and its reasoning in formulating the margin of appreciation concept in the *Cyprus* case was formative, and would end up shaping the Court's jurisprudence in a profound way. Amidst lengthy analyses of the margin of appreciation, however, the *Cyprus* case often receives no more than a passing reference or cursory footnote as the site of inception of the doctrine.[10]

As it had done in so many other colonies, the British government employed emergency modalities in Cyprus to facilitate its militarised policing and prevention of political dissent. In the summer of 1955, existing special powers were bolstered by the passing of legislation such as the Curfews Law 1955 and the Detention of Persons Law 1955. Britain submitted accompanying notices of derogation from the European Convention on Human Rights on 7 October 1955 and 13 April 1956.[11] A formal state of emergency was declared in the colony in November 1955, and Emergency Powers Regulations were issued pursuant to that declaration. The British colonial authorities promptly made extensive use of the regulations' seventy-six clauses, particularly that granting expansive detention powers. For the Greek government, the tipping point was reached following the deportation of Archbishop Makarios in March 1956 and the execution in May 1956 of two young Cypriots (Michael Karaolis and Andreas Demetriou) under the emergency regulations.

[10] See, for example, Howard Charles Yourow, *The Margin of Appreciation Doctrine in the Dynamics of European Human Rights Jurisprudence* (Dordrecht: Martinus Nijhoff, 1996) 15–16; Yutaka Arai-Takahashi, *The Margin of Appreciation Doctrine and the Principle of Proportionality in the Jurisprudence of the ECHR* (Antwerp: Intersentia, 2002) 5; Andrew Legg, *The Margin of Appreciation in International Human Rights Law: Deference and Proportionality* (Oxford: Oxford University Press, 2012); Oren Gross and Fionnuala Ní Aoláin, 'From Discretion to Scrutiny: Revisiting the Application of the Margin of Appreciation Doctrine in the Context of Article 15 of the European Convention on Human Rights' (2001) 23 *Human Rights Quarterly* 625, 631; Murat Tümay, 'The "Margin of Appreciation Doctrine" Developed by the European Court of Human Rights' (2008) 5:2 *Ankara Law Review* 201, 209. Brian Simpson's work, as so often is the case when it comes to the context in which the European Convention system was born and evolved, is a notable exception. See Simpson, *Human Rights and the End of Empire*, 924-1052 (providing extensive detail of the background to the case, the institution and unfolding of proceedings, and the opinion issued by the Commission); A.W.B. Simpson, 'Emergency Powers and Their Abuse: Lessons from the End of the British Empire' (2004) 33 *Israel Yearbook of Human Rights* 219.

[11] The Secretary of State for the Colonies told the House of Commons that such derogation '*fully* discharged Her Majesty's Government's obligations under the Convention'. House of Commons Debates, vol. 552, col. 375, 2 May 1956. Emphasis added.

Greece's complaint to the Council of Europe alleged rights violations arising from British emergency policies including: torture, whipping and other forms of ill-treatment; arbitrary arrest, detention and deportation; collective punishment in the forms of fines and movement restrictions; restrictions on privacy, expression and assembly. For the many British officials who had harboured fears over the extension to the colonies of human rights obligations under the European Convention, the Greek complaint was proof of the folly of that decision:

> Thought has not yet ranged beyond Cyprus to the question whether the whole Convention is not an embarrassing nonsense if we can be put on trial over any of our colonial territories (except Hong Kong, Aden Protectorate and Brunei) by any other signatory wishing to pursue a quarrel. France and Belgium had their feet sufficiently on the ground to avoid extending the Convention to their overseas territories, indeed France has never ratified at all.[12]

Appraisals of derogations jurisprudence under the European Convention tend to bifurcate Article 15 into the two primary branches upon which its application turns: (i) whether there exists a state of emergency that warrants derogation, in the form of a threat to the life of the nation; (ii) whether the emergency measures taken within the context of such derogation are proportionate to the exigencies of the situation. As we will see in relation to the first limb in particular, the European Court has for the most part been consistent in its deference to the state concerned in determining that the threshold of emergency has been passed. The two constitutive elements of Article 15 were, in any event, front and centre to the derogation aspects of the *Cyprus* case. Before the British government had even submitted a written reply or decided whether it would oppose the admissibility of the Greek claim, its counsel made one thing clear: that 'when a state relied upon a derogation under Article 15 the Commission ought not to entertain any enquiry whatever into the necessity for the measures taken'.[13] That is, the decision to resort to a state of emergency in the first instance essentially comes within the exclusive purview of the government concerned – in this case the British government in Cyprus – and should not be subject to external judicial review.

Having held the application admissible, the European Commission of Human Rights appointed a Sub-Commission with a mandate to try to

---

[12] A.S. Aldridge, quoted in Simpson, *Human Rights and the End of Empire*, 986.
[13] *Ibid.*, 938.

secure a friendly resolution of the dispute between the two parties. The efforts of the Sub-Commission hinged on hope that a settlement could be brought about if the British authorities 'would re-examine the emergency legislation in force with a view to making the greatest possible relaxation of that legislation'.[14] The British government saw the Sub-Commission's requests for information regarding the need to maintain the state of emergency, and its calls to dilute the emergency measures, as unreasonable. The proposals for a resolution were thus rejected by Britain, whose position remained clear: whatever about the compatibility of certain incidents with the Convention, 'some of the conditions specified in Article 15 were for the British government alone to decide, in particular the necessity of the measures which had been taken'.[15] In this view, the governing authorities were best placed to determine the overarching state of emergency and its legislative framework, free from interference: 'a decision of this kind is at least prima facie one with the sovereign powers of the Government of the territory in which the emergency arises'.[16] It was submitted by Britain that there was 'at least a strong presumption in favour of the determination by the Government'.[17] Given that the colonial government in Cyprus had at its disposal the full information concerning the security situation in the colony, some of it sensitive information which could not be revealed, it alone was qualified to judge. The British representative, F.A. Vallat, developed this line of argument during the proceedings, and concluded 'that the Commission should not examine too critically what a Government has considered necessary to meet an emergency'.[18]

That argument, tendered by a self-(pre)serving colonial government in the 1950s and endorsed by the Commission, has remained for all intents and purposes the position of the European Court of Human Rights into the twenty-first century. The British submission to the Commission cited Elihu Lauterpacht's writings arguing in favour of discretion: 'it is arguable that the determination of the British Government that the situation in Cyprus was one of "public emergency threatening the life of the nation" ... is a matter within their sole

---

[14] *Greece v. the United Kingdom*, No. 176/56, Report of the European Commission of Human Rights, 26 September 1958, para. 85.

[15] Simpson, *Human Rights and the End of Empire*, 999.

[16] *Greece v. the United Kingdom*, No. 176/56, Report of the European Commission of Human Rights, 26 September 1958, para. 116.

[17] *Ibid.*, para. 118.   [18] *Ibid.*

discretion'.[19] Assuming an inquisitorial form, the Commission allowed itself an expansive mandate in adopting the margin of appreciation (*marge d'appréciation*) approach:

> Having been set up, in accordance with Article 19 of the Convention, to ensure observance of the engagements undertaken by the Contracting Parties, the Commission cannot merely restrict itself to the legal conclusions reached by the latter: it is its duty to submit *ex officio*, wherever necessary, such arguments as will conduce to the formation of its opinion.[20]

The margin of appreciation concept found analogy, at the time, in established doctrine in the German legal system as it related to judicial review of decisions by administrative bodies.[21] In relation to Britain's emergency measures in Cyprus, the German member of the Commission, Adolf Süsterhenn, 'had expressed the view that the Government had a certain margin of appreciation'; when another member later summarised the prevailing consensus that Britain's deduction of a threat to the life of the nation ought not to be contested by the Commission, Süsterhenn intervened to say that it would be preferable to couch it in the terms that the state 'had not gone beyond the limit of appreciation'.[22] This framing would duly underpin the majority opinion.

> The Commission of Human Rights is authorised by the Convention to express a critical opinion on derogations under Article 15, but the Government concerned retains, within certain limits, its discretion in appreciating the threat to the life of the nation.[23]

It was held that, in the case at hand, the colonial government in Cyprus had 'not gone beyond these limits of appreciation'.[24]

---

[19] Elihu Lauterpacht, 'The Contemporary Practice of the United Kingdom in the Field of International Law—Survey and Comment' (1956) 5:3 *International Law Quarterly* 405, 433–434.

[20] *Greece v. the United Kingdom*, No. 176/56, Report of the European Commission of Human Rights, 26 September 1958, para. 89.

[21] The German concept of administrative discretion was, however, somewhat narrower than the margin of appreciation as it has developed in the law of the European Convention. See, for example, Georg Nolte, 'General Principles of German and European Administrative Law – A Comparison in Historical Perspective' (1994) 57:2 *Modern Law Review* 191–212.

[22] Simpson, *Human Rights and the End of Empire*, 1002.

[23] *Greece v. the United Kingdom*, No. 176/56, Report of the European Commission of Human Rights, 26 September 1958, para. 136.

[24] *Ibid.*

In the heel of the judicial hunt, a number of important issues arose as regards the existence of an emergency under Article 15. Foremost among them was the question of what is meant by 'the nation', whose existential threat is required under Article 15 for emergency measures to be justified. Whilst not explicitly framing 'the nation' in this context as metropole Britain or as the British empire writ large,[25] the Commission's understanding did privilege the colonial authorities and institutions in Cyprus.

> As to the understanding of the word "nation", the Commission finds that the Convention is based on the notion of the State as defined by international law. It must therefore be accepted that the term "nation" means the people and its institutions, even in a non-self-governing territory, or in other words, the organised society, including the authorities responsible both under domestic and international law for the maintenance of law and order.[26]

To the extent that any 'nation' can be said to exist, the nation in Cyprus might seem to most naturally be understood as comprising those who identify as belonging to some form of collective Cypriot socio-political community, regardless of which state's jurisdictional umbrella they fall under at a given time. That the European Commission of Human Rights instead located 'the nation' in the institutions of the governing state, its status as a foreign power notwithstanding, appears merely to corroborate international law's embedded structural configuration. Reflecting international law's innate state-centrism, the Commission found it 'inconceivable' that the High Contracting Parties to the Convention could have intended or agreed to apply the Convention to colonial territories were the colonial state unable to invoke Article 15 against anti-colonial insurrection challenging 'the established Government of the territory'.[27] This is of course almost certainly true in terms of the intentions of the Convention's founding state parties, several of whom were colonial powers. Through conquest and the extension of sovereignty, colonialism, in essence, usurps the nation. The Commission majority assumed no role for itself in challenging this position.[28]

---

[25] The Greek government, however, did raise valid arguments around the interconnected nature of Britain's colonial emergency politics. If the nation connotes only the colony concerned, counsel for Greece asked, then how could the governor of the Seychelles derogate from the European Convention on the basis of a security threat not in the colony of the Seychelles but in the colony of Cyprus? *Ibid.*, para. 115.

[26] *Ibid.*, para. 130.B.   [27] *Ibid.*

[28] Commissioner Eustathiades offered the sole voice of reasoned dissent on this issue, noting that 'the peculiarity of [the] régime cannot be invoked to justify an interpretation of Article

Typically entangled in ideological altercations over colonialism are derivative contestations over the framing of anti-colonial resistance. What the British authorities described as Cypriot 'terrorism', the Greek government categorised as 'counter-terrorism' against the violence of the coloniser. What is important to note here, from the perspective of whether Britain was justified in invoking the emergency legal regime, is that while strong evidence was presented to the Commission to suggest that – as was the case in Kenya – the declaration of emergency was pre-emptive rather than responsive and that the emergency measures deployed served to aggravate the conflict, the margin of discretion again favoured the colonial authorities' position.

With regard to the second branch of the Article 15 appraisal – whether measures taken under the state of emergency were justified – the Commission opted not to engage directly the language of Article 15 that requires a state of emergency to be 'strictly required by the exigencies of the situation'. It again left a margin of discretion to the colonial authorities:

> In general, the Commission takes the same view as it did with regard to the question of a "public emergency threatening the life of the nation", namely that the Government of Cyprus should be able to exercise a certain measure of discretion in assessing the "extent strictly required by the exigencies of the situation". The question whether that discretion has or has not been exceeded is a question of substance which will be dealt with as each individual measure is examined.[29]

From the outset of the proceedings, and during the Commission's investigative mission to Cyprus, the British Foreign Office and local government officials had mined as much information as possible from their staff and sources regarding the personal and professional backgrounds of the members of the Commission, speculating over the potentially anti-imperial politics of certain members. Iceland's Jonasson: 'We fear he will vote for Human Rights.' Germany's Süsterhenn: 'emotional and likely to dislike British policy on the island'. Ireland's Crosbie: 'found it difficult to disentangle emotions from facts'. Belgium's Janssen-Pevtschin: 'known

---

15 as meaning that under a colonial system such as that in Cyprus the Government authorities are part of the nation and that a threat to these authorities is therefore a threat to the nation as a whole. That would be an unreal approach. ... to adopt the fictitious premises accepted by the majority is tantamount to conferring on the colonial authorities the means of inordinately consolidating their powers'. *Ibid.*, para. 139.

[29] *Ibid.*, para. 143.

to be strongly anti-British'.[30] In the end, however, the majority decision
of the Commission to allow a margin of appreciation to the colonial state
in determining a threat to the life of the nation was carried by a
resounding ten votes to one, with only the Greek member Eustathiades
dissenting. The Commission was unanimous in affording discretion to
the state in assessing whether particular measures taken within the
context of the self-determined emergency were strictly justified. Ultimately, it appeared to boil down to the fact that the 'majority of the
Commission seem to have principally been concerned over unease at
being cast in a role which might require them to pass judgment on the
decisions taken by the government'.[31]

The Cyprus case set the tone for the general lack of judicial oversight
and deference to state sovereign authority that would (with one significant exception,[32] discussed below) come to define the Council of Europe's approach to declarations of national emergency. The Commission
also did not reject the position held by the British Foreign Office and
Colonial Office at the time that the limitations clauses in Articles 8–11 of
the Convention could justify emergency powers being exercised even
without the derogation regime being triggered. By such logic, the qualitative distinction between disruption of public order/security and an
existential threat to the nation is collapsed. The effect, as Simpson notes,
was that 'after the Cyprus case many forms of emergency measure did
not require the submission of a notice of derogation. A great deal of
repressive activity was possible'.[33]

This was evidenced in Malaya and numerous African colonies until
independence. In one colonial conflict situated geographically and politically beyond the orbit of Third World decolonisation, the British government would continue to rely on the formal state of emergency regime
as a legal technique to facilitate dominion.

The Troubles

The north of Ireland was subject to derogations under Article 15 of the
European Convention that continued from the 1950s until 2001, with

---

[30] Simpson, Human Rights and the End of Empire, 941, 993–994.   [31] Ibid., 1002.
[32] Denmark, Norway, Sweden & the Netherlands v. Greece, No. 3321/67; 3322/67; 3323/67;
    3324/67 (the Greek case), Report of the European Commission of Human Rights, 5
    November 1969.
[33] Simpson, Human Rights and the End of Empire, 1061.

only brief interruption. While new emergency powers had been introduced in 1954, Britain's derogation was not submitted until June 1957,
applicable specifically to the six counties of Ireland that had been
retained under British rule following Ireland's war of independence and
partition in the 1920s.

> Owing to a recurrence in Northern Ireland of organized terrorism, certain
> emergency powers have been brought into operation at various dates
> between June 16, 1954, and January 11, 1957, in order to preserve the
> peace and prevent outbreaks of violence, loss of life and damage to
> property.[34]

The derogation was not limited to special powers of detention; the British
submission informed the Council of Europe that it had also reserved
powers of arbitrary search and seizure, as well as a broad censorship
remit 'to prohibit the publication and distribution of certain printed
matter'.[35] When the Irish Republican Army's 'border campaign' against
British targets began skirting Ireland's partition line in late 1956, the Irish
state implemented special powers of detention without trial[36] and itself
submitted a derogation to the Council of Europe in July 1957. The case of
Lawless v. Ireland followed, and was the first complaint to be referred by
the Commission to the European Court of Human Rights. In upholding
Ireland's detention of an alleged IRA member under emergency powers,
the Strasbourg bodies followed the 'measure of discretion' rationale of the
Cyprus case, now cementing the moniker of the decisive doctrine as that
of the 'margin of appreciation':

> it is evident that a certain discretion – a certain margin of appreciation –
> must be left to the Government in determining whether there exists a
> public emergency which threatens the life of the nation and which must
> be dealt with by exceptional measures derogating from its normal obliga-
> tions under the Convention.[37]

By any reasonable understanding, the idea that sporadic low-intensity
operations against British targets in border areas posed an existential
threat to the life of the Irish nation appears implausible; no less so by the
understanding of a state of emergency articulated by the Court itself in

---

[34] Letter of 27 June 1957 (1958) 1 *Yearbook of the European Convention on Human
Rights* 50.
[35] *Ibid.*   [36] Under the Offences against the State (Amendment) Act 1940.
[37] *Lawless v. Ireland*, No. 332/1957, Report of the European Commission of Human Rights,
19 December 1959, para. 90.

Lawless, denoting 'an exceptional situation of crisis or emergency which affects the whole population and constitutes a threat to the organised life of the community of which the State is composed'.[38] The expectation of states that Article 15 ought essentially to be beyond the purview of the Court, however, is reflected in the Irish government's submission which argued it to be 'inconceivable that a Government acting in good faith should be held to be in breach of their obligations under the Convention merely because their appreciation of the circumstances which constitute an emergency, or of the measures necessary to deal with the emergency, should differ from the views of the Court'.[39] The implication of this argument being accepted by the Commission and the Court is articulated by Simpson:

> The fact that Ireland won the case could be read as indicating that governments had little to fear from Strasbourg over the handling of emergencies, more particularly since the claim that there was at the time, in the Republic of Ireland, an emergency threatening the life of the nation was utterly ludicrous; the majority decision in the Commission and that of the court reflected a determination to back the authorities, come what may, as over Cyprus in the earlier case. . . . The doctrine of the margin of appreciation, the legacy of the first Cyprus case . . . enabled the majority to cover the decision with a cloak of legality.[40]

The British authorities, long paranoid about the possibility of a challenge under the European Convention to military and security policy in the north of Ireland, were thus reassured by the scope given to the state authorities in the *Cyprus* and *Lawless* cases vis-à-vis derogation. Elsewhere in Europe, Greece's military dictatorship received no such grace from Strasbourg in 1969.[41] Instead, the supposition was inverted and the margin of appreciation reined in on the basis of the regime's presumed antipathy towards civil liberties. The emergency derogation submitted by the Greek junta was, therefore, adjudged to be invalid; the Commission felt equipped to determine that there was no emergency threatening the 'the organised life of the community' and that situation could have been

---

[38] *Lawless v. Ireland*, No. 332/1957, Judgment (No.3), European Court of Human Rights, 1 July 1961, para. 28.
[39] *Lawless v. Ireland*, No. 332/1957, Counter-memorial submitted by the Government of Ireland, 27 August 1960.
[40] Simpson, *Human Rights and the End of Empire*, 1088.
[41] *Denmark, Norway, Sweden & the Netherlands v. Greece*, No. 3321/67; 3322/67; 3323/67; 3324/67, Report of the European Commission of Human Rights, 5 November 1969.

governed by 'normal measures'.[42] This is the only time that such a finding has been returned under the law of the European Convention on Human Rights. And while it was certainly not an unwarranted decision, it also certainly was a far easier decision politically to remove the margin of appreciation from a pariah authoritarian Greek regime than from liberal democratic Britain (undemocratic British colonial regime on Greece's neighbouring island notwithstanding). This reflects a form of cultural relativism that can be seen at play in some of the jurisprudence under the Convention more broadly – in the sense of perceived 'human rights cultures' impacting upon decisions, something which the Commission and the Court have not attempted to mask. As a liberal democracy, Britain benefits from the assumptions of international institutions that it will generally act in good faith to uphold its international legal obligations. Hence, it has been granted wide remit in derogating from obligations. Similar patterns can be detected in relation to the leeway afforded to Britain vis-à-vis the proportionality of emergency measures under the second limb of Article 15. When, for example, the Court's 1993 decision in *Brannigan & McBride v. the United Kingdom* (discussed below) is juxtaposed with its 1996 ruling in *Aksoy v. Turkey*, it is seen that the Court was 'clearly more confident that the United Kingdom would apply appropriate human rights safeguards' than its purportedly less liberal Turkish counterpart.[43]

The Commission and the Court in the *Cyprus* and *Lawless* cases had, at least, proclaimed 'certain' limits on the state's discretion, and asserted a competence and duty to examine a government's pronunciation of a public emergency threatening the life of the nation under Article 15. The leeway given to Britain was subsequently to be rendered even more broadly; a *certain* margin of appreciation was stretched to a *wide* margin of appreciation. When the Irish government brought an inter-state complaint challenging the legality of internment, detention and interrogation in the north between 1971 and 1975, Britain's defence relied on its Article 15 derogation. The European Court again displayed a reluctance to critically examine the existence of an existential public emergency or to investigate the necessity of the derogation. According to the judgment, '[t]he limits on the Court's powers of review ... are particularly apparent where Article 15 is concerned'.[44] Indeed, the decision in *Ireland v. UK*

---

[42] Ibid., §.143–144.   [43] Cavanaugh, 'Policing the Margins', 441.
[44] *Ireland v. the United Kingdom*, No. 5310/71, Judgment, European Court of Human Rights, 18 January 1978, para. 207.

expanded the margin of appreciation, both in relation to the existence of an emergency in the first place, and the appropriate measures to be taken in deviation from the Convention.

> It falls in the first place to each Contracting State, with its responsibility for "the life of [its] nation", to determine whether that life is threatened by a "public emergency" and, if so, how far it is necessary to go in attempting to overcome the emergency. By reason of their direct and continuous contact with the pressing needs of the moment, the national authorities are in principle in a better position than the international judge to decide both on the presence of such an emergency and on the nature and scope of derogations necessary to avert it. In this matter Article 15 para. 1 leaves those authorities a wide margin of appreciation.[45]

The benefits afforded by this reasoning to the state are self-evident. Civil rights issues arising from Britain's emergency legal structures have come before the European Court of Human Rights several more times since *Ireland v. UK*. The validity of its derogations, however, has not been placed under the microscope by the Court in any sense of seriously questioning the existence of the self-ordained states of emergency. One chain of events in this regard is particularly telling. The *Brogan* case[46] related to special powers promulgated under the Prevention of Terrorism Act 1984 that allowed persons suspected to have been involved in acts of 'terrorism' to be detained for seven days without charge or judicial approval. The Court found such measures to constitute a violation of Article 5 of the Convention. Britain's previous derogation from the European Convention had been withdrawn in 1984, so in this instance the violation in law could not be mitigated by the existence of a lodged state of emergency. The Court's decision in *Brogan* 'undoubtedly came as a surprise to the British government, and it quickly had to decide how to react'.[47] Two alternative courses of action were identified and considered: to reformulate procedures such that judicial authorisation would be necessary for extensions of detention; or to reinstate the derogation under Article 15 in order to exempt the seven-day executive detention power from compliance with the Convention.[48] Within weeks of the

---

[45] *Ibid.*
[46] *Brogan & Others v. the United Kingdom*, No. 11209/84; 11234/84; 11266/84; 11386/85, Judgment, European Court of Human Rights, 29 November 1988.
[47] Brice Dickson, 'The Detention of Suspected Terrorists in Northern Ireland and Great Britain' (2009) 43 *University of Richmond Law Review* 927, 948.
[48] Marks, 'Civil Liberties at the Margin', 71.

Court's judgment, a new derogation was lodged under Article 15.[49] The British argument in this regard was not that there was no emergency continuing in fact, but that it had believed itself to be operating within the boundaries of Article 5. When the contrary was established by the Court, the government was forced to revert to derogation so that the doctrine of emergency and its ancillary margin of appreciation would provide sufficient insulation from the reach of the Court.

In response to a subsequent petition that challenged the validity of the new derogation, the European Court came down on the state's side. This decision in *Brannigan & McBride v. UK*[50] was seen as confirmation of 'an exceptionally undemanding standard of review by the organs where derogations are concerned'.[51] On the basis of the margin of appreciation doctrine, the Court upheld the derogation without any substantive inquiry into the facts on the ground at the time. Submissions to the Court by human rights organisations had argued that even if there had previously been a crisis in the north of Ireland threatening the life of the nation, this had dissipated by 1988.[52] Without engaging directly or offering rebuttals to these arguments, the Court's majority simply said it was not persuaded. Had the Court effectively supervised and 'undertaken a review of the changing security situation in Northern Ireland in the decade that followed *Ireland v. UK*, it would have discovered a significant decline in the record of violence'.[53] The Court, however, 'exhibited greater deference to government judgment than organs applying other treaties would be likely to exhibit'.[54] The same wide margin of appreciation was granted as had been done in the *Ireland v. UK* case, with the language of the judgment lifted almost verbatim:

> The Court recalls that it falls to each Contracting State, with its responsi-
> bility for "the life of [its] nation", to determine whether that life is

---

[49] Note verbale of 23 December 1988 (1988) 31 *Yearbook of the European Convention on Human Rights* 15–16.

[50] *Brannigan & McBride v. the United Kingdom*, No. 14553/89; 14554/89, Judgment, European Court of Human Rights, 25 May 1993.

[51] Marks, 'Civil Liberties at the Margin', 70.

[52] *Brannigan & McBride v. the United Kingdom*, No. 14553/89; 14554/89, Third Party Intervention of Liberty, Interights & the Committee on the Administration of Justice.

[53] Cavanaugh, 'Policing the Margins', 438.

[54] Marks, 'Civil Liberties at the Margin', 76. The jurisprudence of the Human Rights Committee (see, for example, *Landinelli Silva v. Uruguay*, UN Doc. A/36/40, 130, para. 8.3) and the Inter-American Court is somewhat more restrictive in the width of margin of appreciation allowed.

threatened by a "public emergency" and, if so, how far it is necessary to go in attempting to overcome the emergency. By reason of their direct and continuous contact with the pressing needs of the moment, the national authorities are in principle in a better position than the international judge to decide both on the presence of such an emergency and on the nature and scope of derogations necessary to avert it. Accordingly, in this matter a wide margin of appreciation should be left to the national authorities.[55]

The use of the state of emergency as a governmental tool of choice in contemporary politics, and the continued coalescence of exception and norm is starkly illustrated by the fact that arguably the most draconian piece of British emergency or national security legislation – the Terrorism Act 2000 – was enacted after the 1998 Good Friday Agreement heralded the tapering of overt conflict in the north of Ireland, and before the events of 11 September 2001 and 7 July 2005 had transpired. The last of the derogations from the European Convention in respect of Britain and the north of Ireland was withdrawn in early 2001.[56] With the Irish republican threat superseded by newly perceived 'Islamic' threats in the wake of September 2001, however, a state of emergency was swiftly re-activated by the British government at the end of that year, based on a generalised (and racialised) suspicion of a security threat from foreign nationals.[57]

The Belmarsh Case

In its 2009 decision in *A v. UK* – relating to Muslims 'preventatively' detained in Belmarsh prison under anti-terrorism legal provisions specifically aimed at foreign nationals – the European Court of Human

[55] *Brannigan & McBride v. the United Kingdom*, No. 14553/89; 14554/89, Judgment, European Court of Human Rights, 25 May 1993, para. 43.
[56] Letter from the Permanent Representative of the United Kingdom to the Secretary-General of the Council of Europe, 19 February 2001. Derogation continued in respect of Jersey, Guernsey and the Isle of Man until 2006.
[57] On 11 November 2001, the Secretary of State made a Derogation Order under section 14 of the Human Rights Act 1998. Human Rights Act 1998 (Designated Derogation) Order 2001 (SI 2001/3644). On 18 December 2001, the British government lodged its derogation under the European Convention with the Secretary-General of the Council of Europe, asserting that a public emergency within the meaning of Article 15 existed throughout the state by virtue of 'foreign nationals present in the United Kingdom who are suspected of being concerned in the commission, preparation or instigation of acts of international terrorism, of being members of organisations or groups which are so concerned or of having links with members of such organisations or groups'. The derogation remained in effect until March 2005.

Rights adjudged that although certain measures implemented pursuant to Britain's 'war against terrorism' derogation were discriminatory and disproportionate to the threat posed to the life of the nation, the declaration of emergency and the derogation itself were justified.[58] In so doing, the decision upheld the earlier ruling of the House of Lords, where eight of the nine judges accepted the claim of the Secretary of State for the Home Department that the question of the existence of an emergency is 'pre-eminently one within the discretionary area of judgment reserved to the Secretary of State and his colleagues, exercising their judgment with the benefit of official advice, and to Parliament'.[59] Citing with approval 'the unintrusive approach of the European Court to such a question',[60] the House of Lords had thus refrained from challenging the government's emergency derogation from the European Convention.

In his dissent, Lord Hoffman, while acknowledging that 'the necessity of draconian powers in moments of national crisis is recognised in our constitutional history',[61] had argued that the threshold for such a necessity had not been met in this case. In deconstructing the meaning of a 'threat to the life of the nation', Hoffman accepted that there was credible evidence of a risk of subversive activity in Britain, but considered it fundamentally incapable of endangering 'our institutions of government or our existence as a civil community'.[62] He concluded that '[t]he real threat to the life of the nation, in the sense of a people living in accordance with its traditional laws and political values, comes not from terrorism but from laws such as these.'[63] This was a lone voice of dissent in a House of Lords otherwise unanimous in its deference to the executive and the legislature. Hoffman's threshold for the existence of an emergency was likewise seen as unduly onerous by the European Court's Grand Chamber:

> the Court has in previous cases been prepared to take into account a much broader range of factors in determining the nature and degree of the actual or imminent threat to the "nation" and has in the past concluded that emergency situations have existed even though the institutions of the State did not appear to be imperilled to the extent envisaged by Lord Hoffman.[64]

---

[58] *A. and Others v. the United Kingdom*, No. 3455/05, Grand Chamber Judgment, European Court of Human Rights, 19 February 2009.

[59] *A (FC) and others (FC) v. Secretary of State for the Home Department* [2004] UKHL 56, para. 25.

[60] *Ibid.*, para. 29.   [61] *Ibid.*, para. 89.   [62] *Ibid.*, para. 96.   [63] *Ibid.*, para. 97.

[64] *A. and Others v. the United Kingdom*, No. 3455/05, Grand Chamber Judgment, European Court of Human Rights, 19 February 2009, para. 179.

Fifty years after the prevailing interpretation of a 'threat to the life of the nation' in a manner that privileged colonial rule in Cyprus had been questioned by Eustathiades, Hoffman's concerns were similarly side-lined by the granting of a wide margin of appreciation to the state in its conduct of anti-terrorism policy.

> As previously stated, the national authorities enjoy a wide margin of appreciation under Article 15 in assessing whether the life of their nation is threatened by a public emergency. While it is striking that the United Kingdom was the only Convention State to have lodged a derogation in response to the danger from al'Qaeda, although other States were also the subject of threats, the Court accepts that it was for each Government, as the guardian of their own people's safety, to make their own assessment on the basis of the facts known to them. Weight must, therefore, attach to the judgment of the United Kingdom's executive and Parliament on this question. In addition, significant weight must be accorded to the views of the national courts, who were better placed to assess the evidence relating to the existence of an emergency.[65]

The Court's position in 2009 had thus not departed or progressed in any fundamental way from the position presented to the Commission by the British government in 1958:

> the Government of the territory is in the best position to judge whether an emergency threatening the life of the nation has arisen. That is a question on which governments always tend to reserve their own discretion, and ... it would be very, very risky if the Commission were not at least to lean very favourably toward the opinion of the Government, because the Government has in its possession all the relevant information, much of which must, in the nature of things, be subject to security classifications.[66]

The decision in *A v. UK* echoes the permissive thrust of the Cyprus and north of Ireland jurisprudence, and demonstrates that the breadth of the margin of appreciation with respect to the first limb of Article 15 – the determination of an existential threat warranting a state of emergency derogation – extends to the point that jurisdiction over the merits of

---

[65] *Ibid.*, para. 180. The fact that other European states subject to a similar general increased risk of non-state terrorist activity did not issue derogations from the Convention was also highlighted by the Committee of Privy Counsellors established pursuant to Britain's Anti-terrorism, Crime and Security Act of 2001. See 'Anti-terrorism, Crime and Security Act 2001 Review: Report', HC 100, 18 December 2003, para. 189.

[66] *Greece v. the United Kingdom*, No. 176/56, Report of the European Commission of Human Rights, 26 September 1958, para. 118.

derogation is all but abdicated. The requirement of the 'imminence' of the threat, so central to the reasoning by which the Court held the Greek fascist regime's emergency declaration to be invalid,[67] has been incrementally relegated in the context of the British cases. The Court also explicitly discarded the standard refrain of liberal human rights institutions that, to be permissible, emergency measures must be temporary. No such temporal limit had ever been required by the Court itself, the judges remind us.[68] And this is true. In *Marshall v. UK*, another case involving an Irish prisoner, the applicant was arrested and detained in Belfast in 1998 for seven days without at any stage being brought before any judicial authority. The British government invoked its (post-*Brogan*) 1988 and 1989 notices of derogation from the European Convention in defence against the claim that the applicant's liberty and due process rights had been violated. Marshall argued that over the nine years that had passed since derogation – a period that encompassed the implementation of paramilitary cease-fire, a much improved security situation, and successful peace negotiations – 'any public emergency which might have existed in Northern Ireland was effectively over by the time of his unlawful detention'.[69] He asserted that the retention of the emergency legal framework in this context amounted to an indefinite or permanent emergency, and submitted that 'the Government should not be permitted under the Convention to impose a permanent state of emergency on the province with the pernicious consequences which that would entail'.[70] The European Court effectively rejected the argument that an Article 15 emergency must be temporary. Although noting 'the fact that almost nine years separate the prolonged administrative detention of the applicants Brannigan and McBride from that of the applicant in the case before it', the Court found nothing in international law conflicting with the continuation of an emergency for such a period – nor any qualitative change in the security situation in the north of Ireland during that time – to warrant a departure from the margin of appreciation afforded to the state in *Brannigan & McBride*. By dispelling the myth of the temporariness of emergency in cases such

---

[67] *Denmark, Norway, Sweden & the Netherlands v. Greece*, No. 3321/67; 3322/67; 3323/67; 3324/67, Report of the European Commission of Human Rights, 5 November 1969.

[68] *A. and Others v. the United Kingdom*, No. 3455/05, Grand Chamber Judgment, European Court of Human Rights, 19 February 2009, para. 178.

[69] *Marshall v. the United Kingdom*, No. 41571/98, Admissibility Decision, European Court of Human Rights, 10 July 2001.

[70] *Ibid.*

as *Marshall* and *A v. UK*, the European Court of Human Rights essentially underlines the fiction of the norm/emergency binary.

Without in any way intending to belittle prevailing human security issues, it must be noted that it can be misleading to conflate the habitual maintenance of public order with the preservation of the very existence of the state as a social and political entity. The story of Britain's colonial and racialised counter-terrorism emergencies demonstrates that the state of emergency (and its constitutive language: threat, the nation, temporariness, imminence) as grounds for the lawful escalation of state violence was always sufficiently malleable and indeterminate to function as a utilitarian technology of control. Calls for preservation of the separation of emergency and normalcy miss the crucial point that the two are deeply structurally entwined, particularly in the contexts of colonial governance and anti-terrorism law.

On the second limb of Article 15, the Court did rule that the Belmarsh detention policies were not justified by the exigencies of the particular existential threat being faced by Britain. The discriminatory aspect of the legislation rendered the actions of the British authorities beyond the margin of appreciation permitted to them. The Court essentially felt it unreasonable for the emergency measures to discriminate between 'British Muslims' and 'foreign Muslims'.[71] It appeared, however, to have no issue with the unavoidable implication of that particular binary: a presumption that those subjected to the emergency measures would naturally be Muslims. The anti-discrimination position expounded by the Court explicitly denounced Britain's detention measures on the basis of the distinction between British and foreign nationals, while implicitly condoning derogation from the Convention on the basis of a framing of the Muslim community as a whole as suspect. The Court thus failed to draw the logical conclusion that the emergency itself was discriminatory – both in law, where the derogation was specifically linked to acts of perceived 'Islamic' terrorism; and in practice, through the tendency of the British security services 'to assume that any devout Muslim who believed that the way of life practised by the Taliban in Afghanistan was the true way to follow must be suspect'.[72] Here, the

---

[71] *Ibid.*, para. 188.
[72] Special Immigration Appeals Commission, Judgment of 29 October 2003, quoted in *A. and Others v. the United Kingdom*, No. 3455/05, Grand Chamber Judgment, European Court of Human Rights, 19 February 2009, para. 31.

Court's articulation of its reasoning on the second limb of Article 15 helps us to understand its decision on the first limb.

A Third World Alternative?

The legacy of colonial emergency rule on the African continent cannot be disregarded when reflecting on the fact that, in contrast to other regional and international human rights instruments, the African Charter on Human and Peoples' Rights makes no allowance for emergency derogations from any of its provisions. Following the formulation of the Charter and its entry into force in 1986, it was argued by jurists in the global North that, despite the absence of any emergency derogation clause, the Charter did not prevent states parties from invoking established state of necessity or emergency doctrines under international law.[73] It has also been asserted that the exclusion of a derogation regime in the African system is simply a reflection of a differing conception of sovereignty to that in, for example, Europe;[74] one not bracketed by a common political project comparable to Europe's post-war rallying against (internal) totalitarianism. Provision for emergency derogation is absent, it is argued, not to preclude states imposing emergency measures, but rather to avert any external oversight or regulation. This oppositional thinking belies the drafting and applied experience of the European Convention on Human Rights, however, where the staunchest advocates of the emergency derogations regime were concerned primarily with the preservation of sovereign emergency prerogative, rather than its limitation. The jurisprudence of the African Commission on Human and Peoples' Rights has held, in contrast, that a state of national emergency cannot be invoked under any circumstances to allow the suspension of state obligations. As such, 'limitations on the rights and freedoms enshrined in the Charter cannot be justified by emergencies and special circumstances'.[75] Even situations

---

[73] Theodor Meron, *Human Rights and Humanitarian Norms as Customary Law* (Oxford: Clarendon, 1989) 218–219. Meron was conscious, however, that were emergency derogations to be precluded, that would 'undoubtedly serve the effective protection of human rights'.

[74] Frederick Cowell, 'Sovereignty and the Question of Derogation: An Analysis of Article 15 of the ECHR and the Absence of a Derogation Clause in the ACHPR' (2013) 1 *Birkbeck Law Review* 135.

[75] *Media Rights Agenda and others v Nigeria*, Communications 105/93, 128/94,130/94 & 152/96 (joined), ACHPR 24th ordinary session, October 1998, 12th Annual Activity Report, para. 67.

of civil war 'cannot be used as an excuse by the State violating or permitting violations of rights in the African Charter'.[76] Emergency doctrine does not apply to allow for derogations, whether from rights that are traditionally non-derogable (such as freedom from torture) or derogable (fair trial, freedom from arbitrary detention) in other systems. The African Charter does attach some standard limitation or 'clawback' clauses to certain rights (such as freedom of assembly and freedom of movement) for the purposes of protecting 'national security, law and order, public health or morality'.[77] On foot of this, Mutua suggests that a (higher threshold) general state of emergency derogation clause is unnecessary because the limitation clauses allow for the effective suspension of the particular rights to which they pertain.[78] The Commission explicitly distinguishes the African human rights system in this regard, however, emphasising that the 'African Charter, unlike other human rights instruments, does not allow for states parties to derogate from their treaty obligations during emergency situations'.[79] The extent to which this is a direct product of African experiences of European colonial states of emergency is unclear from the *travaux préparatoires* of the Charter. With the conceptualisation of the African Charter originating in the first Congress of African Jurists in 1961, and the drafting process concluding in 1981, however, it cannot be easily decontextualised from the recent history of colonial emergency rule across the continent, and the contemporaneous impact of, and resistance to, emergency law in apartheid South Africa.

Whether the elimination of emergency derogations from African regional human rights instruments is viewed as a progressive normative international legal development that departs from the influence of colonial legal doctrine or not, recourse to repressive state of emergency measures has, in any event, not been eliminated in 'the modern African state, which in many respects is colonial to its core'.[80]

---

[76] *Commission Nationale des Droits de l'Homme et des Libertés v. Chad*, Communication No. 74/92, ACHPR 18th Ordinary session, October 1995, 9th Annual Activity Report, para. 21.

[77] Article 12, African Charter on Human and Peoples' Rights.

[78] Makau Mutua, 'The African Human Rights Court: A Two-Legged Stool?' (1999) 21 *Human Rights Quarterly* 343, 358.

[79] *Commission Nationale des Droits de l'Homme et des Libertés v. Chad*, Communication No. 74/92, ACHPR 18th Ordinary session, October 1995, 9th Annual Activity Report, para. 21.

[80] Mutua, 'The African Human Rights Court', 343. 'Although the African Charter makes a significant contribution to the human rights corpus', the postcolonial state in Africa has

As such, struggles from below continue against emergency governmentality in Africa and throughout the global South.[81]

Imperialism Redux

In its use of torture and mass internment during the emergency in Kenya, as well as the more banal methods of collective punishment, the British state employed customary techniques of colonial violence in furtherance of its extended sovereignty. Sovereign actors – whether in the form of governor, administrator, solider or policeman – deployed their own form of terror against the colonised population. This was nothing extraordinary; along the arc of imperial history, the violence of colonisation was increasingly codified (and sanitised) by positive law. When certain elements of the native population sought to resist, the community at large was branded as suspect, an existential threat to the law and order of empire.

Contemporary wars against non-state terrorism – whether linked directly to ongoing settlement colonisation processes, or to other modes of state power – can be seen as similarly constitutive of sovereignty. Law, through the racial formation of emergency legislation and security powers, is ubiquitous in that arrangement. Conventional counter-terrorism discourses around appropriate 'balancing' – of security and liberty, legality and necessity, norm and exception – tend to miss certain crucial points: that security, in an imperial context, is intrinsically premised on the very denial of liberty; that necessity becomes legality through emergency doctrine; that the norm/exception binary has long been collapsed. The state of emergency is typically characterised by the deference or subordination of the legislative and judicial branches to an executive vested with increased powers. Any such transfer, however, is generally defined by legal decree; legal powers may be reconfigured but law itself does not recede. Significantly, the emergency is not constrained

---

been 'such an egregious human rights violator that skepticism about its ability to create an effective regional human rights system is appropriate'.

[81] Social movements and Indigenous peoples in Latin American continue to be at the vanguard of resistance to states of emergency in the context of large-scale extractive industry projects. A 2013 study of protests around the world in the preceding seven years highlights a number of movements that were explicitly confronting state of emergency laws in contexts as diverse as lawyers' dissent against mass dismissal of judges in Pakistan, and student actions against university corruption in Bangladesh. Isabel Ortiz, Sara Burke, Mohamed Barrada and Hernán Cortés, 'Working Paper: World Protests, 2006–2013' (Initiative for Policy Dialogue & Friedrich-Ebert-Stiftung, September 2013).

by temporal limitations. Thus, a war against the very concept of non-state terrorism, conceived in such an amorphous way – particularly in the transnational context – raises the spectre of a permanent situation of emergency, in much the same way as colonial policy was founded on an assumption of the indefinite continuation of empire. And with similar constructions of emergency doctrine as the bridge between force and legality, it has been shown that 'in the particular case of the war on terror and all it has entailed, the invocation of emergency has a peculiarly colonial character'.[82] The coloniality of legal discourse in the post-2001 Western counter-terrorism context is evident not only in the parallels raised by emergency doctrine, but in multifarious ways: the construction of the terrorist as a barbarian force, who, like the savage tribe, lacks respect for the law of armed conflict and is in turn excluded from its protection; the forfeiture or absence of sovereignty in 'uncivilised' nations ('rogue' states); the justification of aggression and occupation with reference to self-defence, and so on.[83] In this context, the normalisation of emergency measures can been seen as a feature of the colonial past that retains a contemporary resonance in post-colonial conflict settings, as well as in a 'colonial present'.

---

[82] Anghie, 'Rethinking Sovereignty in International Law', 306.
[83] See, for example, Anghie, *Imperialism, Sovereignty*, 273–309; cf. Elbridge Colby, 'How to Fight Savage Tribes' (1927) 21 *American Journal of International Law* 279.

PART III

The Colonial Present

While they may be displaced, distorted and (most often) denied, the capacities that inhere within the colonial past are routinely reaffirmed and reactivated in the colonial present.

Derek Gregory, *The Colonial Present*, 7

7

Palestine

'A Scattered, Shattered Space of Exception'?

Clear skies. Calm blue sea. Northerly winds. Good visibility. But the autumn clouds – the symbolic name for killing – wipe out an entire family, made up of seventeen lives. The news searches for their names under the rubble. Apart from that, abnormal life appears to be running its normal course.[1]

Israel is a normal country that is not normal.[2]

In his study of the intersecting cartographies of modern imperial violence, political geographer Derek Gregory uses the events of 11 September 2001 as a fulcrum around which to map the barbed boundaries of the 'colonial present'.[3] Referring to an intrinsically colonial modernity and its performative force, Gregory relates Edward Said's 'imaginative geographies' – which fold distances into differences by amplifying spatial partitions that divide 'us' from 'them'[4] – to Western representations of Islam and 'the Orient'. While making it clear that his analysis does not imply that we remain confined within nineteenth century paradigms, Gregory shows that some of the particulars of colonial history have been projected into a colonial present and continue to pervade our social and legal systems.

This argument is advanced through a narration of the global 'war on terror' as a continuum of spatial stories set in Afghanistan, Iraq and Palestine. By exploiting the 'conditions of possibility for regarding others as threats or antagonists'[5] and mobilising imaginative geographies

---

[1] Mahmoud Darwish, 'Routine', in *A River Dies of Thirst* [*Athar al-Farâsha*] (2008) (Catherine Cobham trans., Brooklyn, NY: Archipelago Books, 2009) 40.
[2] Supreme Court of Israel, *The Association for Civil Rights in Israel (ACRI) v. The Knesset and the Government of Israel*, HCJ 3091/99, judgment, 8 May 2012, para. 19. Extracts quoted from this judgment are based on an unofficial professional translation; on file with the author.
[3] Derek Gregory, *The Colonial Present* (Malden, MA: Blackwell, 2004).
[4] See Edward W. Said, *Orientalism* (London: Penguin, 1978) 44–73.
[5] Michael J. Shapiro, *Violent Cartographies: Mapping Cultures of War* (Minneapolis: University of Minnesota Press, 1997) xi.

constructed into an 'architecture of enmity', the USA justified its wars in Afghanistan and Iraq (and, since the time of Gregory's analysis, its interventions – 'humanitarian' or otherwise – in Libya and Syria[6]). This architecture operates to 'mark people as irredeemably "Other" and [to] license the unleashing of exemplary violence against them'.[7] A distinctly colonial milieu crystallises through such wars, Gregory argues, by virtue of an integrated machinery of geopolitics and geoeconomics. Applying the lens of the colonial present to the USA's exercise of global hegemony relies on a somewhat expansive construction of 'colonial', however – one that is severed from the element of expansionary *settlement* inherent in its etymology. In the traditional gradations of colonialism and imperialism, '"colonialism" denotes the actual conquest, occupation and settlement of a country, whereas "imperialism" suggests a broader set of practices, including those by which a great power in essence governs the world according to its own vision, using a variety of means that may or may not include actual conquest or settlement'.[8] While the USA's twenty-first century foreign policy certainly lays down infrastructures extra-territorially through its military interventions and global 'counter-terrorism' crusades, and through the perpetuation of aid dependency and surrogate governance apparatuses (as well as by proxy through the reach of its multinational corporations), its dominion is more accurately framed in the broad terms of imperialism than the specific colonisation process of conquering and settling territory.

The paradigm of an explicitly colonial present, however, does remain prominent within settler colonial societies and colonial-ethnic conflicts that continue to chip away the edges of supposedly smooth 'post-colonial' temporal and territorial parameters. The dynamics in

---

[6] See, for example, Vijay Prashad, *The Death of the Nation and the Future of the Arab Revolution* (Oakland: University of California Press, 2016).

[7] Gregory, *The Colonial Present*, 16. As one commentator observed in the context of the American decision to go to war in Afghanistan, '[m]ore than a rational calculation of interests takes us to war. People go to war because of how they see, perceive, picture, imagine and speak of others: that is, how they construct the difference of others as well as the sameness of themselves through representation.' James der Derian, 'The War of Networks' (2001) 5:4 *Theory & Event* §.21.

[8] Anghie, *Imperialism, Sovereignty*, 273. Within the spectrum of colonialism, of course, settler colonialism may be distinguished from extractive colonialism or exploitative colonialism on the basis of a primary purpose of human settlement of the territory beyond simply resource extraction or labour exploitation, but some degree of physical colonisation and imposition of rule from the metropole is common to the pursuit of all such forms of colonialism.

Palestine/Israel today continue to entail conquest, militarised hegemony and exploitation of resources by the Israeli state, in the context of racialised discourse and ordering. They also entail civilian settlement and plantation of occupied territory, and the imposition of direct political and legal administration. As such, the conceptual framework of the colonial present is perhaps most fitting in the Palestine segments of Gregory's work.[9] While the ideological, legal and technological parallels between Israel's state security policies and the post-2001 'international state of emergency'[10] are pronounced, Israel's relationship with the Palestinians remains distinct, evoking archetypal coloniser-colonised dynamics that are planted firmly in a struggle for control of the land. The categories and framings that were widely presented as new on the international plane after 2001 have long resided in Israel's legal landscape. The settler colonial and colonising Israeli state has, indeed, operated in a self-declared state of emergency since the first week of its formal existence in May 1948, spawning a complex matrix of emergency modalities that continues to burgeon. This is an emergency very much marked by both its longevity and its racialised anatomy. Palestine remains subject to colonial technologies of surveillance and securitisation that encage the colonised and foment a deep-rooted siege mentality in the coloniser. Israel's displacement of Palestine's people and violation of its places and spaces has, for Gregory, splintered it into 'a scattered, shattered space of the exception'.[11] I present this 'shattered space' as a space heavily populated by law, however, rather than the legal vacuum that the idea of exception evokes for some. In the construction of a supposedly exceptional nomos in Palestine, law remains integral. It has spun a convoluted web of emergency powers, regulations, statutes, military orders and courts. Every micro aspect of Palestinian life is enveloped by the suffocating hold of racialised emergency management. The emergency does not produce something novel or exceptional, but rather reproduces colonial nodes of governance through proliferation of law and legal stratification.

---

[9] In addition to chapters 5–6 of *The Colonial Present*, see Derek Gregory, 'Palestine and the "War on Terror"' (2004) 24:1 *Comparative Studies of South Asia, Africa and the Middle East* 183.

[10] Kanishka Jayasuriya, 'Struggle over Legality in the Midnight Hour: Governing the International State of Emergency' in Victor V. Ramraj (ed.), *Emergencies and the Limits of Legality* (Cambridge: Cambridge University Press, 2008).

[11] Gregory, *The Colonial Present*, 136.

At the same time, the image of a spatial zone at the bounds of law (most clearly manifested through the discharge of mechanised violence against the Gaza Strip) that Gregory's framing evokes is apposite to aspects of Israel's relationship with the Palestinians. It is notable that Israel's representatives and apologists present the state as simultaneously normal and exceptional – a normal Western liberal democracy, but one which is subject to unique threats to its state security. Critical analysis of Israel can mirror this imagery of parallel exemplarity and exceptionality from a different vantage point, however: Israel is in one sense exceptional as a state in which racialised privilege is legally encoded in a manner that undercuts democracy; in another sense it is an archetypal enactment of settler colonialism. This dyadic structure shapes 'the oscillating relation between norm and exception that [in turn] constitutes the paradoxes of the Israeli-Palestinian relation'.[12] Inherent in Israel's exemplary coloniality is the sense that racialised emergency rule is itself exemplary of settler colonialism.[13] The first section of this chapter thus reflects on state of exception discourse as it relates to Palestine, before the sections that follow examine the suffocating hold of racialised emergency legal structures on Palestinian life.

Palestine as Space of Exception

The imperial-racial formations of contemporary 'counter-terrorism' narratives evoke Said's imaginative geographies. Internally and externally, spaces are created between the 'homeland' and a perceived enemy population. The resulting self/other projections and dynamics are reminiscent of Victorian-era Britain's engagement with its empire. The colonialist tendency to respond to perceived threats with the creation of an identifiable and targetable 'native' suspect illustrates an extension of racialised states of emergency from former empire to colonial present. Such forces are well established in Israeli security politics, capturing – to varying degrees – all of the spatial zones and personal status layers into which Palestine and its people have been fragmented (citizens of Israel; residents of East Jerusalem; inhabitants of the remainder of the West Bank; besieged populace of the Gaza Strip; refugees excluded from the space of historic Palestine). The customary depiction of the Palestinians as a 'terrorist' nation stems from the imaginative geographies that separate

[12] Lloyd, 'Settler Colonialism', 60.   [13] *Ibid.*, 71.

the Jewish-Israeli population from its Arab-Palestinian counterpart.[14] This is the underpinning of the architecture of enmity that pervades much of mainstream Israeli society, playing out in multiple ways. From above, it is evidenced in calls by Israeli political leaders to block supplies to Gaza in order to 'put the Palestinians on a diet'[15] and decrees by prominent religious authorities approving[16] and inciting[17] attacks by the Israeli army on Palestinian civilians. From below, it comes in the form of units of soldiers printing t-shirts adorned with images (a pregnant Palestinian woman in the crosshairs of a sniper rifle, for example) and slogans ('One shot, two kills')[18] that betray a view of Palestinian life as subordinate. The pervasiveness of such attitudes is encapsulated in their ubiquity in contemporary social media: photographs of Palestinian children taken through the viewfinder of a rifle and flippantly uploaded for global consumption with the touch of a single vintage camera icon; grandstanding statements relaying past or planned acts of racialised military violence in 140 characters or less.[19] Violence against Palestinians is normalised in the banality of a daily 'status update'.

Such predilections go some way to explaining the scholarly trend of applying Agamben's thinking to Palestine. While Palestine carries the burden of its own particular history and circumstances, the notion of

---

[14] This is mirrored in different contexts in Israel's 'othering' of the native Bedouin and nomadic peoples, as well as of African migrant and asylum-seeking communities, for example.

[15] Dov Weisglass, advisor to then Israeli Prime Minister Ehud Olmert, quoted in Conal Urquhart, 'Gaza on brink of implosion as aid cut-off starts to bite', *The Observer*, 16 April 2006.

[16] During 'Operation Cast Lead', four leading Israeli rabbis issued a *Halakhic* [Jewish legal] ruling stating: 'When a population living near a Jewish town sends bombs at the Jewish town with the purpose of killing and destroying Jewish existence there, it is permitted, according to Jewish Law, to fire shells and bombs at the firing sites, even if they are populated by civilians.' See Hillel Fendel, 'Top Rabbis: Morally OK to Fire at Civilian Rocket Source', *Arutz Sheva/Israel National News*, 30 December 2008.

[17] See, for example, Amos Harel, 'IDF rabbinate publication during Gaza war: We will show no mercy on the cruel', *Ha'aretz*, 26 January 2009; Chaim Levinson, 'Police release rabbi arrested for inciting to kill non-Jews', *Ha'aretz*, 27 July 2010.

[18] See Uri Blau, 'Dead Palestinian babies and bombed mosques – IDF fashion 2009', *Ha'aretz*, 20 March 2009.

[19] See, for example, Phoebe Greenwood, 'Israeli soldier posts Instagram image of Palestinian child in crosshairs of rifle', *The Guardian*, 18 February 2013; Ali Abunimah, 'Stoned, Naked, Armed and Dangerous: More Disturbing Images from an Israeli Soldier's Instagram', *The Electronic Intifada*, 20 February 2013. See further Max Blumenthal, 'For Israeli Soldiers, Social Media has become a Showcase of Horrors', *Salon*, 13 October 2013, excerpted from Max Blumenthal, *Goliath: Life and Loathing in Greater Israel* (New York: Nation Books, 2013).

bare life resonates, particularly in the Gaza Strip where the Israeli policy of keeping the population penned inside the besieged strip of land has led to the 'open-air prison' analogy becoming a common refrain.[20] Within the enclosed and densely populated space, the consequences of Israeli military offensives are severe. Hermetic closure of the borders means that the default refuge of a population under bombardment – the ability to flee to neighbouring territories – is erased. The killing of civilians in Gaza is, as Mahmoud Darwish's poem has it, 'routine',[21] with no question of meaningful accountability arising to date.[22] With the possibility of becoming refugees elsewhere precluded, Gaza's population is also perhaps unique in the sense that its majority are already refugees. More than 70 per cent of its inhabitants are UN-registered refugees,[23] approximately half of whom continue to live in refugee camps seven decades years after being forcibly displaced and legally barred from returning to their ancestral homes by the racialised residency and citizenship regime instated by Israel's 1950 Law of Return and 1952 Citizenship Law.[24] The precarious existence of Gaza's population is further highlighted by its economic

---

[20] This refrain has been sounded not only by NGOs, journalists and activists, but by authorities such as the UN Under-Secretary-General for Humanitarian Affairs. See, for example, 'UN humanitarian chief warns of disaster if Gaza siege continues', Ha'aretz, 12 March 2010.

[21] Darwish, 'Routine'.

[22] 3,253 Palestinians classified as civilians were killed by Israeli forces in the Gaza Strip between 29 September 2000 and 5 January 2010. Palestinian Centre for Human Rights, 'Statistics related to the Al Aqsa (Second) Intifada', 5 January 2010, at www.pchrgaza.org/alaqsaintifada.html. According to the United Nations, a further 1,906 Gazan civilians were killed in Israeli offensives between from the start of 2012 to the end of 2015. United Office for the Coordination of Humanitarian Affairs, 'Conflict-related Casualties and Violence: Monthly Figures', 1 February 2016, at www.ochaopt.org/content/monthly-figures.

[23] As of 1 July 2014, 1,258,559 of Gaza's estimated population of 1,760,000 are refugees registered with the United Nations Relief and Works Agency for Palestine Refugees in the Near East (UNRWA). See www.unrwa.org/where-we-work/gaza-strip.

[24] The 1950 Law of Return constructs Israel as the state of the 'Jewish nation' and entitles every Jewish person to immigrate to Israel (and, since 1967, to the occupied Palestinian territory) under an *oleh* visa. The 1952 Citizenship Law then grants such immigrants the right to gain immediate citizenship, while explicitly excluding (under Article 3) from its purview those who were residents and citizens of Palestine before the creation of the state of Israel if they were not 'in Israel, or in an area which became Israeli territory after the establishment of the State, from the day of the establishment of the State [May 1948] to the day of the coming into force of this Law [April 1952]'. The calculated implication was that long-time Palestinian residents who were forcibly displaced during the war of 1948 were legally barred from taking up citizenship in the newly created state and returning to their homes. Palestinians who had managed to stay in 1948 were able to

suppression. Since the victory of Hamas in the 2006 parliamentary elections throughout the occupied territories, the near comprehensive siege and blockade of the Gaza Strip as retaliatory collective punishment by Israel has obstructed movement of goods and services, and limited supplies of fuel, electricity, water and medical equipment. An impoverished society continues to be subject to 'de-development'.[25]

For Gregory, Gaza is an exemplar of the space of the exception; a zone of indistinction established by Israel's sovereign power that asserts 'a monopoly of legitimate violence even as it suspends the law and abandons any responsibility for civil society'.[26] Under such circumstances, Israel the occupier is an unrestrained sovereign, and the 'temporary' nature of its occupation provides the boundless licence of the state of emergency.[27] Even the Israel government's competing claim that it no longer occupies the Gaza Strip[28] feeds into the notion that Palestinian life is rendered bare, amounting as it does to an attempt to exclude civil society in Gaza from Israeli responsibility while simultaneously preventing the Palestinians from exercising their own sovereignty. This arguably produces 'a zone of anomie, in which a violence without any juridical form acts'.[29] In Gaza we can see the very tangible effects of this which, in Judith Butler's critique, Agamben's general claims on sovereign power and bare life fail to show:

> how this power functions differentially, to target and manage certain populations, to derealize the humanity of subjects who might potentially belong to a community bound by commonly recognized laws; ... how sovereignty, understood as state sovereignty in this instance, works by differentiating populations on the basis of ethnicity and race, how the systematic management and derealisation of populations function to

claim (Israeli) citizenship [*ezrahūt*] but are excluded from the (Jewish) nationality (*le'om*) that confers crucial substantive rights under Israeli constitutional law.

[25] Sara Roy, *The Gaza Strip: The Political Economy of De-development* (Beirut: Institute for Palestine Studies, 3rd edn., 2016).

[26] Gregory, 'Palestine and the "War on Terror"', 189.

[27] Adi Ophir, 'A Time of Occupation' in Roane Carey and Jonathan Shainin (eds.), *The Other Israel* (New York: The New Press, 2002) 51, 60.

[28] See, for example, the government position as upheld by the Israeli Supreme Court in *Bassiouni Ahmed et al* v. *Prime* Minister, HCJ 9132/07, Judgment of 30 January 2008, para. 12. For discussion, see Darcy and Reynolds, 'An Enduring Occupation'. The legal philosophy underpinning Israel's position on the status of Gaza is reminiscent of that which prevailed during colonial encounter to enable the European powers to rule over non-Europeans without the administrative burdens or political accountability of formal sovereignty.

[29] Agamben, *State of Exception*, 59.

support and extend the claims of a sovereignty accountable to no law; how sovereignty extends its own power precisely through the tactical and permanent deferral of the law itself.[30]

The violence exacted during, for example, 'Operation Rainbow' (2004), 'Operation Days of Penitence' (2004), 'Operation Summer Rains' (2006), Operation 'Autumn Clouds' (2006), 'Operation Hot Winter' (2008), 'Operation Cast Lead' (2008–9), 'Operation Pillar of Cloud' (2012) and 'Operation Protective Edge' (2014) suggests that in the institutional psyche of the Israeli military, all Gazans (political leaders, police cadets, partisans and peasants; civilians and combatants alike) are stripped of the protections and safeguards of 'normal' law (whether understood as Israeli constitutional law, international law, or some other abstracted conception of law). This reading is supported by the documentation of UN fact-finding missions such the 'Goldstone Report'[31] (which includes the testimonies of Israeli soldiers themselves), and more broadly from the repeated executive decisions to launch wholesale attacks on a crowded, impoverished and already besieged territory. Gazans are reduced to targets, subject not only to lethal fire and home raids by troops on the ground, but to white phosphorous raining from the skies, and to surveillance and attack from above by unmanned drones. Here, Said's portrayal of the war on Iraq as 'imperial arrogance unschooled in worldliness . . . undeterred by history or human complexity, unrepentant in its violence and the cruelty of its technology'[32] appears similarly resonant. For Gregory, Israeli violence against the Palestinians, much like that of the USA in Afghanistan and Iraq, can be understood as a war of perceived 'civilisation' against 'barbarism' (this colonial trope evoking Zionist 'visionary' Theodor Herzl's characterisation of a Jewish state in Palestine as 'a rampart of Europe against Asia, an outpost of civilization as opposed to barbarism'[33]), within a space of the exception.

This paradigm of exception is a circular schematic in the Palestinian context. The Israeli state was born into a 'national' emergency bound up in colonisation, war and dispossession. It builds a matrix of control, surveillance and fear, which underpins narratives of the necessity of emergency powers. As heightened repression leads to mobilisation and

---

[30] Judith Butler, *Precarious Life* (London: Verso, 2004) 68.
[31] Report of the United Nations Fact-Finding Mission on the Gaza Conflict, UN Doc. A/ HRC/12.48, 25 September 2009.
[32] Edward W. Said, 'The Academy of Lagado', *London Review of Books*, 17 April 2003.
[33] Theodor Herzl, *The Jewish State* (1896) (Raleigh: Hayes Barton Press, 2006) 18.

resistance on the Palestinian side, the cycle is set in motion. The spatial developments of Israel's control system in the occupied territories since 1967 – the construction of settlements, walls, fences, roads, tunnels, watchtowers and checkpoints involved in the cantonisation of Palestinian territory into a 'carceral archipelago' – are, for Gregory, the visceral physical embodiment of the exception. Bare life 'is constituted through the production and performance of the space of exception, but in Palestine this process assumes an ever more physical form'.[34] In this reading, the West Bank and Gaza emerge as zones of indistinction where, in the words of Israeli military reservists who refuse to serve in those occupied territories, 'the legal and the lawful can no longer be distinguished from the illegal and unlawful'.[35]

Gregory's theorisation of this vista in Palestine is echoed by other prominent voices. Palestinian feminist scholar Nadera Shalhoub-Kevorkian presents Israeli state violence as an intersection of biopolitics and 'security theology' which produces an economy of life and death and determines who should live and who should die, and how.[36] In Palestine, China Miéville writes, '[u]ndesirable life is ended, and unauthorized death is banned'.[37] Agamben himself has asserted that '[t]he state of Israel is a good example of how when the state of exception is prolonged in such a situation then all democratic institutions collapse'.[38] For Ronit Lentin, 'Israel is arguably a textbook example of Agamben's state of exception.'[39] This association is elaborated by a number of theorists offering varying and intricate accounts of the spatial and juridical optics of Israel's state of exception. Neve Gordon, for example, focuses on events following the outbreak of the second intifada. He argues that despite its redeployment of troops in all major Palestinian cities

---

[34] Gregory, *The Colonial Present*, 122. For a compelling account of the colonial control mechanisms and physical transformation of Palestinian territorial spaces under occupation, from subterranean realm to militarised airspace, see Eyal Weizman, *Hollow Land: Israel's Architecture of Occupation* (London: Verso, 2007). On the "besieging cartography" of Israel's convoluted surveillance apparatus, see Camille Mansour, 'Israel's Colonial Impasse' (2001) 30:4 *Journal of Palestine Studies* 83, 87.

[35] Refuser Solidarity Network, quoted in Gregory, *The Colonial Present*, 125.

[36] Nadera Shalhoub-Kevorkian, *Security Theology, Surveillance and the Politics of Fear* (Cambridge: Cambridge University Press, 2015).

[37] China Miéville, 'Exit Strategy', *Guernica*, 1 November 2013.

[38] Giorgio Agamben, 'The State of Exception - Der Ausnahmezustand', lecture at the European Graduate School, August 2003, transcribed by Anton Pulverenti.

[39] Ronit Lentin, 'Palestine/Israel and State Criminality: Exception, Settler Colonialism and Racialization' (2016) 5:1 *State Crime* 32, 33.

throughout 'Area A'[40] of the West Bank and its effective disabling of the
Palestinian Authority,

> Israel did not reinstate any disciplinary forms of control and refused to
> reassume the role of managing the population's lives. Instead, Israel
> emphasized a series of controlling practices informed by a type of sover-
> eign power, which have functioned less through the instatement of the law
> and more through the law's suspension. Israel now operates primarily by
> destroying the most vital social securities and by reducing members of
> Palestinian society to what Giorgio Agamben has called *homo sacer*,
> people whose lives can be taken with impunity. This helps explain, for
> example, Israel's widespread use of extrajudicial executions and the use of
> Palestinians as human shields. These extralegal actions stand in sharp
> contrast to the approach Israel adopted during the first intifada, which
> was in many ways characterized by a proliferation of trials and legal
> interventions.[41]

Here, then, a disjunct is constructed between the juridically-based nature
of Israel's interventions in the first intifada, and the eclipse of the
juridical order through the exceptionality of its second intifada violence.
While Israel's use of force during 'Operation Defensive Shield' was on
a scale not witnessed during the first intifada, it appears an overly
neat distinction. The issuing of military orders to underwrite home
demolitions, internment and curfews, and the prosecutions of demon-
strators, stone-throwers and youths were as relevant in 2002 as they were
in 1989.

A disjunct of a different type can be found in Sari Hanafi's positing of
the 'imposed form' of the Palestinian refugee camp as itself a particular
'territory of exception' in which not only the Israeli state, but the
Palestinian authorities and UN agencies 'involved in the different
modes of governance have been contributing to the suspension of law

---

[40] Under the 1995 Israeli-Palestinian Interim Agreement on the West Bank and the Gaza
Strip (the Oslo II Accord), the West Bank was divided into three distinct temporary
administrative divisions, pending a final status agreement: Area A, to be administered
under full Palestinian civil and security control (comprising 2 per cent of the territory of
the West Bank); Area B, placed under Palestinian civil administration and Israeli security
control (26 per cent); and Area C, under full Israeli civil and security control (72 per
cent). The boundaries were to be gradually redrawn but have been frozen since the
1999 Sharm el Sheikh Memorandum on Implementation Timeline of Outstanding
Commitments of Agreements Signed and the Resumption of Permanent Status Negotiations at 17, 24 and 59 per cent, respectively.

[41] Neve Gordon, *Israel's Occupation* (Berkeley: University of California Press, 2008) 21.

in this space'.[42] Interestingly, Hanafi presents the camps not – as one might have expected – as a microcosmic exceptional space within Israel's larger state of exception, but rather as *the* extra-legal exception (in which laws and planning regulations vanish) from the 'normal' legal order of the West Bank and Gaza:

> While the PNA and the Israeli authorities generally have exercised their presence in the Occupied Palestinian Territories by the rule of law, they have abandoned the camps and allowed them to become spaces devoid of laws and regulations.[43]

As well as state of exception analyses, invocations of bare life and arguments around the aspirations and capacity of Israeli occupation to dehumanise are similarly prevalent in scholarly discourse. In her reading of the gendered meanings of *homo sacer* – something upon which Agamben dwells only momentarily – Lentin presents the female Palestinian figure as *femina sacra*. Using the example of Jawaher Abu Rahma, killed by Israeli forces at a demonstration in the West Bank village of Bil'in, Lentin relates the experiences of Palestinian women to Agamben's theory of bare life as that of the excluded being, devoid of value.[44] At the same time, however, both Lentin and Hanafi emphasise an important disclaimer regarding the agency of the Palestinians and the (in)ability of conditions of emergency or exception to dehumanise. As an agent of resistance against the colonial and racial state, the Palestinian female must not be viewed as disempowered despite Israel's best efforts to do so, argues Lentin. Similarly, for Hanafi, 'Agamben fails to account for the agency of the actors resisting the "total institution" of the camp'; so while Palestinian refugees are constituted as bare life and placed at the limits of law, 'by revolting and resisting these conditions, they express their agency and transgress the role assigned to them by their oppressors'.[45]

---

[42] Sari Hanafi, 'Palestinian Refugee Camps in the Palestinian Territory: Territory of Exception and Locus of Resistance' in Adi Ophir, Michal Givoni and Sari Hanafi (eds.), *The Power of Inclusive Exclusion: Anatomy of Israeli Rule in the Occupied Palestinian Territories* (New York: Zone Books, 2009) 495–496.

[43] *Ibid.*, 506.

[44] Ronit Lentin, 'Palestinian Women: From *Femina Sacra* to Agents of Active Resistance' (2011) 34:2 *Women's Studies International Forum* 165. See also Ronit Lentin, '*Femina sacra*: Gendered Memory and Political Violence' (2006) 29:5 *Women's Studies International Forum* 463–473; Cristina Masters, '*Femina Sacra*: The "War on/of Terror", Women and the Feminine' (2009) 40:1 *Security Dialogue* 29–49.

[45] Hanafi, 'Palestinian Refugee Camps', 508, 511.

As I have alluded to in Chapter 2, Achille Mbembe's formulation of necropower builds on and surpasses Agamben's enunciation of sovereign control over life and death. And as with Agamben citing Israel as exemplary of the state of exception, Mbembe explicitly invokes the contemporary colonial occupation of the West Bank and Gaza as the 'most accomplished form' of necropower.[46] This late-modern occupation differs from earlier forms of colonial occupation and is, for him, in many ways more severe, combining as it does the disciplinary, the biopolitical, and the necropolitical. This combination 'allocates to the colonial power an absolute domination over the inhabitants of the occupied territory' in which the sovereign prerogative to kill chosen targets is not only unrestrained by law, but entire populations are the target of the sovereign.[47]

The Israeli colonial state, Mbembe reminds us, bases its foundational claims of sovereignty and legitimacy on its own weighted narrative of history and identity. Particular versions of history, geography, cartography and archaeology are invoked to reinforce the political-theological claim of divine right to the land of Palestine, and to exclude any competing claims to the same space. Identity and topology are thus welded together. The result is that 'colonial violence and occupation are profoundly underwritten by the sacred terror of truth and exclusivity (mass expulsions, resettlement of "stateless" people in refugee camps, settlement of new colonies)'.[48] Here, Mbembe channels Fanon's analysis of the spatial features of colonial occupation to Palestine's occupied territories. For Fanon, colonialism involves a process of spatial division and compartmentalisation. The colonial world 'is a world divided into compartments ... a world cut in two': native quarters and settler quarters; native schools and settler schools; opposed zones segregated by the frontiers of military barracks and police stations.[49] This segregation follows a logic of racialised mutual exclusivity:

> This world divided into compartments, this world cut in two is inhabited by two different species. ... When you examine at close quarters the colonial context, it is evident that what parcels out the world is to begin with the fact of belonging to or not belonging to a given race.[50]

In the Palestinian context, racialised segregation plays out most obviously in the fragmentation of the occupied territories that comes with Israeli settlement construction and its supporting infrastructure. This is very

[46] Mbembe, 'Necropolitics', 30.   [47] Ibid.   [48] Ibid., 27.
[49] Fanon, Wretched of the Earth, 37–38.   [50] Ibid., 39–40.

much three-dimensional in its topography, with communities separated not only 'horizontally' across the territory, but also across a y-axis as settlement control of hilltops and the elevation of settler roads over Palestinian tunnels and underpasses reinforce the 'politics of verticality'[51] and the 'symbolics of the *top*'.[52] On top of (and beneath) the surface spatialities, Israel's control extends to the additional layers of the subterranean and the skies. Occupation of the airspace has become particularly central to Israel's policing of the Palestinian population, and the set-piece killing of targets below.[53] Such 'high-tech tools of late-modern terror'[54] are, for Mbembe, indicative of the form of necropower that stems from the racial demarcation of conqueror and native and that resides in a state of exception. This creates the conditions in which the coloniser seeks to dehumanise the colonised. The characterisation of the Palestinian as a form of savage or animal life that is common to public discourse in Israel also finds expression in the legal-institutional sphere. Of four Palestinians prosecuted for the killing of six Israeli settlers in an attack in occupied Hebron, for example, the Israeli military court declared: 'the defendants are beasts, bereft of all humanity.'[55] The military judge, as such, claims an authority to pronounce who is human and who is not, much as the military commander exercises discretion as to when and whom to shoot.

Along with the infrastructural and technological violence of occupation, Mbembe includes within his framing of necropolitics the quotidian restrictions on Palestinian movement, administration and livelihoods that constitute the smaller cogs in a larger machine: 'Movement between the territorial cells requires formal permits. Local civil institutions are systematically destroyed. The besieged population is deprived of their means of income. Invisible killing is added to outright executions'.[56] The emphasis on movement restrictions, specifically, is echoed in Yehouda Shenhav and Yael Berda's analysis of Israel's closure policy in the occupied territories:

> in 1993, Israel declared the first closure of the borders between the OPT and Israel. It took the form of a state of exception without declaring an end date for the closure. . . . The state of exception in the form of military

[51] Eyal Weizman, 'The Politics of Verticality', *Open Democracy*, 23 April – 1 May 2002.
[52] Mbembe, 'Necropolitics', 29. Emphasis in original.
[53] See, for example, Markus Gunneflo, *Targeted Killing: A Legal and Political History* (Cambridge: Cambridge University Press, 2016).
[54] Mbembe, 'Necropolitics', 29.
[55] *Military Prosecutor* v. *Adnan Jaber et al.* Translation quoted in Ra'anan Alexandrowicz, *The Law in These Parts* (2011).
[56] Mbembe, 'Necropolitics', 30.

closures took two forms: closures that brought to a halt the entrance of
Palestinians to Israel and internal closures that restricted the movement of
Palestinians within the West Bank itself.[57]

The focus here is not on colonialism's overt physical violence but instead
on its more mundane bureaucratic violence. The permit regime that
controls Palestinian movement and access to livelihood is situated at
the heart of Israel's occupation. Shenhav and Berda present the permit
regime as the state of exception in itself. In adopting this line, they offer a
somewhat expansive interpretation of the state of exception. They suggest that it is not necessarily defined by a liminal space at the margin of
juridicality, let alone an absence or suspension of law, but can simply
entail a selective or discriminatory use of law. The application of separate
laws and different procedural standards to Arabs and Jews in the occupied territories are said to constitute a state of exception. The exception
crystallises through 'a legal and administrative patchwork'; 'selective use
of the law, an infinite number of decrees, and an abruptly changing set of
rules and regulations about movement in the region'.[58] This state of
exception as legal patchwork or selective enforcement of law is contrasted
with 'the unified liberal rule of law'.[59] Such a dialectic perhaps places
undue faith in the liberal rule of law, suggesting that an entirely neutral,
consistent and non-selective application of law is not only possible, but
prevalent elsewhere. At the same time, however, Shenhav and Berda hold
the law responsible for its own suspension and maintain that the state of
exception is not a form of violence beyond the pale of law, but rather a
'violence embedded in the law'.[60] The state of exception is invoked as 'a
space in which the rule of law is suspended under the cover of law'[61] –
echoing Hanafi and many others who refer to 'the suspension of law in
this space under the cover of laws and regulations themselves' and to
both the 'flexible use of law *and* its suspension' at the same time.[62] The
sense of law's ambiguous role is heightened by Shenhav and Berda's

---

[57] Yehouda Shenhav and Yael Berda, 'The Colonial Foundations of the State of Exception:
Juxtaposing the Israeli Occupation of the Palestinian Territories with Colonial Bureaucratic History' in Ophir, Givoni and Hanafi (eds.), *The Power of Inclusive Exclusion*,
338–339. See also Yehouda Shenhav, 'The Imperial History of "State of Exception"'
(2006) 29 *Theory and Criticism* 205.

[58] Shenhav and Berda, 'The Colonial Foundations', 347, 350.   [59] *Ibid.*, 347.

[60] *Ibid.*, 344. Shenhav and Berda also remind us that the founding violence of law is as
relevant to law in the metropole as it is in the colony, which negates the idea of the colony
as an exceptional space in that particular regard.

[61] *Ibid.*   [62] Hanafi, 'Palestinian Refugee Camps', 495–496, 507. Emphasis added.

oscillation between the language of the state of exception on the one hand, and, on the other, that of 'the state of emergency [that] has become the rule rather than the exception'.[63] Shenhav and Berda's central conclusion is that colonial bureaucracy is not the dysfunctional model that it is typically presented as, but is rather a form of organised chaos that intentionally departs from Max Weber's 'rational model' of bureaucracy: 'this seeming patchwork of arbitrary policies is in fact based on a coherent and well-articulated approach to the implementation of a colonial bureaucracy . . . rendering it functional and effective for the exacerbation of control and domination over the colonized.'[64]

The disparities between the classic liberal rational model of bureaucracy and the actual model in Palestine and other colonies should be understood, according to Shenhav and Berda, not as exceptions to the rule but as the rule itself. This appears to somewhat problematise their own argument of colonial bureaucracy as the state of exception. What they describe, ultimately, is a control system built on a labyrinth of legal regulation. This operationalises what Shlomo Gazit, the first head of Israel's Civil Administration in the occupied territories, argued was its primary aim: to 'provide law', in contrast to unregulated military discretion.[65]

These disparities and ambiguities again raise the spectre of the perennial exclusion/inclusion binary. To a certain point, as the episodic bombardments of Gaza show, Palestinians can be seen as utterly excluded from protection by law and subjected to indiscriminate violence:

> colonisation and separation both presuppose the exclusion of the Occupied Palestinian Territories and their inhabitants from the pale of law and the normalisation of a state of exception in which the Palestinian population as a whole and individuals within in are exposed to arbitrary violence and coercive regulation of daily life.[66]

Such exclusion is qualified by Adi Ophir, Michal Givoni and Sari Hanafi as a 'series of inclusive exclusions' that cuts the occupied Palestinian population off from its increasingly segmented and appropriated territory and envelops it within the Israeli ruling apparatus.[67] The formulation of inclusive exclusion again harks back to questions of the

---

[63] Shenhav and Berda, 'The Colonial Foundations', 346.   [64] *Ibid.*, 340, 366.
[65] Shlomo Gazit, quoted in Shenhav and Berda, 'The Colonial Foundations', 337.
[66] Adi Ophir, Michal Givoni and Sari Hanafi, 'Introduction' in Ophir, Givoni and Hanafi (eds.), *The Power of Inclusive Exclusion*, 23.
[67] *Ibid.*

conceptual relationship between law and exception. Agamben's state of exception is 'an *inclusive exclusion* (which thus serves to include what is excluded)'.[68] Sovereign violence, however, is founded 'on the *exclusive inclusion* of bare life in the state'.[69]

In the Palestinian context, Stephen Morton speaks of both 'the logic of *inclusive exclusion*' behind Zionist settler colonial ideology and, 'the potential logic of *exclusive inclusion*' of Israel's state of exception.[70] There is no explicit reference to Agamben here, and it is unclear whether the term is reversed unwittingly (considered interchangeable) or intentionally (on the basis of two distinct, albeit unelaborated, meanings). The *inclusive exclusion* articulated by Ophir, Givoni and Hanafi, for their part, involves a severing or exclusion of West Bank and Gazan Palestinians from their own territories for the purpose of encompassing them within the Israeli control system. This is, in short, *excluding to include*. It is not clear exactly how this ties in with the exclusion from the pale of law that the same authors speak of.

There is much valuable insight in the notion of the colonised's inclusion within the colonial juridical order remaining somewhat contingent and exclusionary, and of their humanity being ostensibly acknowledged but perpetually deferred pending ever-further levels of 'development'. This risks being lost, however, in what are at times muddy theoretical waters around concepts of inclusive exclusion and exclusive inclusion. To try and clarify things somewhat, I articulate the dynamics of legality, emergency and sovereignty in this context in terms of *repressive inclusion*. This framing suggests – perhaps in subtle contrast to

---

[68] Agamben, *Homo Sacer*, 21. Emphasis added. This notion of including what is excluded is applied by Michelle Farrell in her exploration of torture in Coetzee's *Waiting for the Barbarians*. The barbarian (the excluded) is civilised (included) through subjection to torture. The act of torture 'signifies nothing other than the Empire's ability to render life bare and to inscribe the meaning of humanity upon the excluded body'. It is thus, for Farrell, 'an act of "inclusive exclusion" enabled through a process of dehumanisation and facilitated by a distorted construction of justice and morality'. Michelle Farrell, *The Prohibition of Torture in Exceptional Circumstances* (Cambridge: Cambridge University Press, 2013) 249–251.

[69] Agamben, *Homo Sacer*, 107. Emphasis added. For Agamben, the exception is an *inclusive exclusion*, whereas the example functions as an *exclusive inclusion*. He distinguishes between the two as such: 'While the example is excluded from the set is so far as it belongs to it, the exception is included in the normal case precisely because it does not belong to it. … exception and example are correlative concepts that are ultimately indistinguishable.' *Ibid.*, 22.

[70] Stephen Morton, *States of Emergency: Colonialism, Literature and Law* (Liverpool: Liverpool University Press, 2013) 174. Emphasis added.

usages of inclusive exclusion – a process whereby Palestinians are included within the Israeli juridical order but in a manner in which they are legally differentiated and discriminated against. They are denied the privileges afforded to Jewish nationals, while Israel's policies of segregation and apartheid are given institutional and legal grounding.[71] The 'provision' of law by Israel's civil authorities, and the extensive use of legal discourse and institutions – even if in decisionistic form – by the military authorities, speak to a form of inclusion within the juridical order. Here, the net effect is that of a discriminating and repressive inclusion, and one that is racially contingent.

This conceptualisation arguably provides a fuller explanation than that of exclusion. Intermittent crises and moments of exception are bridged and transcended by mundane everyday legal techniques of control and oppression. It also applies (in different ways through different legal statuses and techniques, but with a common logic) to Palestinian citizens of Israel as well as to Palestinians living under occupation in the West Bank and Gaza. As such, it allows for a more holistic approach to Israel's control system throughout historic (Mandate) Palestine than Ophir, Givoni and Hanafi's analyses, which are rooted specifically in the Palestinian territories occupied by Israel since 1967. The effect of such compartmentalisation, as Morton notes, is to 'separate the occupation as an object of inquiry from the contested colonial genealogy of Zionism, and the disputed ethnic cleansing of Palestine in 1948'.[72] This is an important point in relation to state of exception discourse on Palestine. Mbembe, Shenhav and Berda are also representative of the body of scholars that base their state of exception analysis on the West Bank and Gaza. By side-lining the socio-political situation inside Israel and the foundational aspects of Israeli constitutional, immigration and citizenship law, this approach can be implicated somewhat in the legal and geographical masks that obfuscate the underlying roots and realities of the situation. The broader limitations of spatial compartmentalisation in the Palestinian context – where all Palestinians are subjected to a single totalising regime of Israeli domination regardless of any artificial lines drawn between them – are equally pertinent to the specifics of emergency law. Focusing only on the 1967 occupied territories obscures the emergency legal regimes that applied in a heavily racialised manner within Israel

---

[71] See further John Dugard and John Reynolds, 'Apartheid, International Law, and the Occupied Palestinian Territory' (2013) 24:3 *European Journal of International Law* 867.
[72] Morton, *States of Emergency*, 174. Footnote omitted.

from 1948, as well as Palestine's particular colonial history of emergency that preceded the state of Israel. It may also feed the illusory construction of the occupation as a temporary and exceptional situation grounded in defensive necessities of state security.

Against this backdrop, Ilan Pappé warns against bracketing Israel within the same 'war on terror' frame as the north Atlantic liberal democracies, which, he argues, have degenerated from a point to which they, by contrast, can potentially return (this itself, of course, remains debatable, and occludes the founding oppression on which many such liberal democratic states were built). While the traits of Agamben's state of exception paradigm are present in Israel's relationship with the Palestinians, Pappé argues, it is not the appropriate analytic lens as it fails to encapsulate the inherent oppression built into the concept of the Jewish state. Due to its colonial and discriminatory essence, Zionism, for Pappé, entails a state of oppression rather than a state of exception.[73]

The state of exception lens in Palestine does, as noted, materialise most tangibly in the major assaults on the Gaza Strip. It is in the longer 'calms' between such fitful seasonal storms ('Summer Rains', 'Autumn Clouds' and 'Hot Winter', in the Israeli military's operational nomenclature) that the more mundane state of emergency trundles steadily along in support of the colonial order, defined by a proliferation of law, rather than its absence. While the hot violence of Israel's periodic wars on Gaza dominates our news feeds at sporadic intervals, the slow, cold violence of the state's legal armoury serves to entrench other particular forms of control in Israel and the West Bank.[74] Emergency modalities are central to this regime. Amidst the array of emergency regulations promulgated by Israel's executive, legislature and military, the Palestinian space emerges as a realm saturated by legal regulation and control. The discourse of exception, with its implication of strands of extralegality, does not tell the full story. It is necessary, then, in the Palestinian case as much as broader colonial contexts, to explore the extent to which the state of emergency and related mechanisms are pivotal to the construction of a juridical order that itself inscribes conquest, occupation and settlement.

---

[73] Ilan Pappé, 'The *Mukhabarat* State of Israel: A State of Oppression is not a State of Exception' in Ronit Lentin (ed.), *Thinking Palestine* (London: Zed, 2008) 148, 149.

[74] Teju Cole, 'Bad Laws' in Vijay Prashad (ed.), *Letters to Palestine: Writers Respond to War and Occupation* (London: Verso, 2014).

The Law in These Parts: Settlement, Sovereignty, Emergency

The routine, everydayness of the violence – physical, psychological and administrative – of segregation and occupation reveals 'the *banality* of the colonial present'.[75] The filtering of this violence through (normalised colonial emergency) law aims to legitimise its performance for both external and internal audiences. Israeli actions are justified in regulations, statutes, commissions of inquiry and judgments. International lawyers may argue as to whether those actions and legal regimes actually uphold the 'rule of law', or comply with the strictures of the Geneva Conventions, or are permissible derogations from international human rights covenants, but they remain within the space of some form of juridical order.

In many ways, law is itself the connective tissue binding the twin colonial logic of fear and dispossession that haunts the Palestinian national and social condition. Law and legal narratives are indeed central to the story of the colonisation of Palestine. Early Zionist settlement was facilitated by particular instruments of international law. This settlement then became the basis for the assertion of sovereignty through the establishment of the Israeli state and, subsequently, that state's annexationist policies in the West Bank – most notably and legalistically in respect of East Jerusalem. To preserve this expanding sovereignty, the international legal doctrine of self-defence has routinely been invoked by Israel.[76] Conquest, that is, by self-defence. Emergency laws and powers are intimately connected to this offensive defence. Emergency doctrine is an integral weapon in the arsenal with which occupation is waged. It is instrumentalised to foment and sustain fear so as to underwrite the measured tightening of the grip on Palestinian land, movement and thought. Settler colonial policy in Israel is, as it has been elsewhere, performed through law.

The settler colonial analytic is, as Brenna Bhandar and Rafeef Ziadah put it, 'an essential lens to understand the myriad forms of dispossession experienced by Palestinians from the late nineteenth century',[77] and one

75 Gregory, *The Colonial Present*, 16. Emphasis in original.
76 On such invocation of self-defence (and the acquiescence of large parts of the international community) as justification for its "Operation Cast Lead" offensive on the Gaza Strip, for example, see John Reynolds, 'The Use of Force in a Colonial Present, and the Goldstone Report's Blind Spot' (2010) 16 *Palestine Yearbook of International Law* 55.
77 Brenna Bhandar and Rafeef Ziadah, 'Acts and Omissions: Framing Settler Colonialism in Palestine Studies', *Jadaliyya*, 14 January 2016. For a sample of the (renewed) engagement

that allows us to historicize the colonization of Palestine as a process that began long before 1948. Jewish migration to Palestine, as it began on a collective scale in the early 1880s following the establishment of the first colony in 1878, was quickly followed by the escalation of Zionist discourse aimed at the creating the ideological framework of a Jewish state in Palestine. By the time of the 'Second Aliyah' of 1904–1914, it was clearly constituted as a settler colonial movement whose constituents sought no part in the existing polity in Palestine, but rather aimed to establish their own sovereignty.[78] In the idiom of Zionist ideology, the term 'settlement' (*yishuv*) carries a powerful resonance. Its roots lie in the phrase *Yishuv Eretz Yisrael* ('settlement of the land of Israel'), and the pre-state Jewish community in Palestine is still referred to in Hebrew as the *Yishuv*. For the Zionist movement, settlement is inextricably linked to the procurement of sovereignty, an essential precursor to the attainment of statehood and title to territory. This epitomises settler colonial ideology, and illuminates the rationale underpinning Israel's continuing 'settlement' of the West Bank.

While anchored by certain cardinal features, every colonial encounter and every settler colonial process has its own defining idiosyncrasies. Zionist settler colonialism is somewhat distinct that it did not have one specific 'mother' nation-state in Europe from which the settler population and other forms of logistical and political support were drawn. It was based, instead, on the 'more diffuse but no less potent "Western civilization" of which Zionism has believed itself representative since the earliest days of the colonisation of Palestine'.[79] In the context of the Balfour Declaration and the League of Nations Mandate for Palestine (which resolved to 'facilitate Jewish immigration' and 'encourage, in cooperation with the Jewish Agency . . . close settlement by Jews of the land'), settler sovereignty developed under the protective guard of British administration. The emergence of the Israeli state from that imperial sanctuary was a markedly less anti-colonial moment than other decolonisations throughout Africa and Asia that came soon afterwards.

Instead, a spiral of colonialisms curls through the Israeli self-determination project, connecting early Zionist settlement with British

<hr/>

of Palestine scholarship with settler colonial studies, see the special issue on 'Past is Present: Settler Colonialism in Palestine' in (2012) 2:1 *Settler Colonial Studies* 1–272.
[78] See, for example, Gershon Shafir, *Land, Labor and the Origins of the Israeli-Palestinian Conflict, 1882–1914* (Cambridge: Cambridge University Press, 1989).
[79] Lloyd, 'Settler Colonialism', 68.

colonial foreign policy, the League of Nations Mandate, the role of the United Nations in legitimising Zionist claims to sovereignty via settlement (in the 1947 partition plan and subsequent recognition of Israel's independence), and Israel's continued colonisation of the West Bank today. These connections are woven deep into the fabric of political and legal discourse in Palestine, and suggest that international law and institutions, far from remaining above the political fray, are profoundly compromised by their engagement in the whole affair. Palestine emerges as a victim of the coloniality in which international law's heritage is rooted. There is a readily identifiable 'train of legal instruments which sweeps through the last century from the Balfour Declaration onwards through the League of Nations Mandate, the UK's Order-in-Council, the United Nations Partition Resolution, Security Council Resolution 242, the Oslo Agreements and the Quartet Road Map', from which it becomes clear that international law 'has constructed the Palestinians as peripheral' and that '[l]aw has played a major role in pushing Palestine and the Palestinians to the political and territorial margins'.[80]

The language of the early twentieth century international legal instruments – the 'Jewish national home' promised in the Balfour Declaration; the commitments made in the League of Nations Mandate to 'facilitate Jewish immigration' and 'encourage, in cooperation with the Jewish Agency... close settlement by Jews of the land'; the reduction in that same text of Palestine's 90 per cent Arab majority to 'other sections of the population' and 'existing non-Jewish communities' – set the tone for the marginalisation of the Palestinians. The elision of Palestinian identity by the League of Nations and the British Mandate in particular contributed to the fostering of conditions in which the dispossession of Palestinian land would occur.[81] From a pre-Mandate articulation of the 'determination of the Jewish people to live with the Arab people on terms of unity and mutual respect and together with them to make a common home

---

[80] John Strawson, 'British (and International) Legal Foundations for the Israeli Wall: International Law and Multi-Colonialism' (2004–2005) 13 *Palestine Yearbook of International Law* 1, 2.

[81] 'The Mandate marginalized the identity of the Palestinians, enshrining this in law. Whereas the Jewish population ... has a clear identity, the Palestinians (90% of the population) were merely "non-Jewish" or "other". In this way, international legal discourse dispossessed a people of their identity which opened the way for others to dispossess them of their land.' John Strawson, 'Reflections on Edward Said and the Legal Narratives of Palestine: Israeli Settlements and Palestinian Self-Determination' (2002) 20:2 *Penn State International Law Review* 363, 369.

into a flourishing community',[82] Zionism was able to evolve into an increasingly exclusionary form of Jewish nationalism under the British protectorate. Zionist settlement in Palestine proliferated during the League of Nations era, with the Jewish population rising from 80,000 in 1917 to 390,000 in 1939; 'the context of the Mandate created the framework in which Jewish political and legal identity developed. It was the Mandate that gave Jews the first quasi-national political institution with legal powers – the Jewish Agency',[83] which would subsequently form the nucleus of the Israeli state.[84] The UN's 1947 partition plan and recognition of Israeli sovereignty amounted to a legitimation of settler colonial policy and an acceptance of the idea that the territory of Mandate Palestine was legally disputed.

Since then, international law has shown itself sufficiently indeterminate[85] to have been harnessed and sculpted by Israel's military legal advisors and Supreme Court judges. Law is invoked in Israel to endorse colonial policies and, among other things: to deny the existence of any sovereign claims to the West Bank and Gaza concomitant or subsequent to their status as British colonial territory and prior to their colonisation by Israel; to discard the 'non-humanitarian aspects' of humanitarian law; to afford privileges and protections to settlers; to legitimise the construction of the Wall and its associated colonising infrastructure in the West Bank; to sanction targeted killing policies; to legislatively categorise Palestinian fighters as 'unlawful combatants' and deprive them of the

---

[82] Resolution of the Zionist Congress, September 1921.

[83] Strawson, 'Reflections on Edward Said', 376.

[84] The Jewish Agency, along with the World Zionist Organisation and other 'para-state' institutions, remains central to the continuing colonisation of Palestinian land.

[85] '[E]ven where there is no semantic ambivalence whatsoever, international law remains indeterminate because it is based on contradictory premises and seeks to regulate a future in regard to which even single actors' preferences remain unsettled. To say this is not to say much more than that international law emerges from a political process whose participants have contradictory priorities and rarely know with clarity how such priorities should be turned into directives to deal with an uncertain future. ... It follows that it is possible to defend any course of action – including deviation from a clear rule – by professionally impeccable legal arguments that look from rules to their underlying reasons, make choices between several rules as well as rules and exceptions, and interpret rules in the context of evaluative standards. The important point I wish to make ... is not that all of this should be thought of as a scandal or (even less) a structural "deficiency" but that indeterminacy is an absolutely central aspect of international law's acceptability.' Martti Koskenniemi, *From Apology to Utopia: The Structure of International Legal Argument* (Reissue with a New Epilogue, Cambridge: Cambridge University Press, 2005) 590–591.

protections afforded to either civilians or combatants; and to legitimise the siege of Gaza and the launching of aerial bombardments and ground incursions in 'self-defence'. As has been noted, 'the historical record shows that it can be convenient for the hegemon to have a body of law to work with, provided that it is suitably adapted'.[86] The attention paid to both domestic and international law by the Israeli military is politically significant.

Ra'anan Alexandrowicz's 2011 documentary on the Israeli legal apparatus as it relates to the occupied territories, *The Law in These Parts*, provides lucid insight into the role of Supreme Court and military court judges in the administration of the occupation, and into the function of law as an instrument for settler colonial ends. Alexandrowicz presents 'law as an issue of language; its inefficacy and its arbitrariness, its brutality'. It is a language that most people do not understand, but also one whose meaning is contingent on its speaker. In the Israeli-occupied territories, law serves as an alibi for power rather than a constraint on it, and as such has been emptied of any meaningful relation to concepts of justice. One particularly revealing passage in the film relates to legal justifications for the seizure of Palestinian land in the West Bank for the purposes of settlement construction. Former military judge and legal advisor to the West Bank military command, Alexander Ramat, recounts how Ariel Sharon (Minister for Agriculture and head of the government's settlement committee at the time) summonsed the Israeli military lawyers for a meeting within minutes of the *Elon Moreh* judgment[87] being handed down by the Supreme Court in October 1979. In that case, Palestinian land-owners Azat Muhamed and Mustafa Dweikat had argued that the military seizure of their and their neighbours' privately owned land[88] – occupied in June 1979 by a settler group in an operation

---

[86] Detlev F. Vagts, 'Hegemonic International Law' (2001) 95 *American Journal of International Law* 843, 845.

[87] *Dweikat v. Government of Israel*, HCJ 390/79, judgment, 22 October 1979.

[88] The fact that – going back to the Ottoman Land Law of 1858 – much of the land in Palestine was marked as state land (*miri*) as opposed to privately owned land (*mulk*) had already been exploited by Israel, through the construction of an argument that state land in occupied territory is open to civilian settlement by the occupier (the purported temporariness of belligerent occupation notwithstanding). The British Mandate authorities had, for their part, modified the Ottoman laws to extend the reach of state land, effectively liberalising the land expropriation process, as well as making it easy for the military to seize any category of land for self-prescribed 'security measures'. See further Raja Shehadeh, *The Law of the Land: Settlement and Land Issues under Israeli Military Occupation* (Jerusalem: PASSIA, 1993); John Strawson, 'Britain's Shadows: Post-colonialism and

directed by Sharon[89] – for the purposes of Israeli civilian settlement had
been illegal. Preceding Supreme Court jurisprudence had upheld similar
requisitions of private land as permissible under the laws of occupation,
on the grounds that the civilian settlements and infrastructure concerned
performed valid and essential military and security functions.[90] As Eyal
Weizman explains:

> Between 1967 and 1979, on the basis of the exceptions of "temporariness"
> and "security" the government issued dozens of orders for the requisition
> of private land in the West Bank. When called upon to do so, the
> government and the military demonstrated their claim for the pressing
> security needs by inviting expert witnesses, usually high-ranking military
> officers or the Chief of Staff himself, to testify that a particular settlement
> dominated a major artery, or another strategic location, that it could
> participate in the general effort of "regional defence", or in the supervision
> and control of a hostile population. As long as this claim was maintained,
> the High Court of Justice rejected all petitions of Palestinian landowners
> and accepted the government's interpretation of the term "temporary
> military necessity".[91]

The concepts of temporariness and security are embedded in the idea of
the state of emergency, as well as that of occupation. In the *Elon Moreh*
case, such defences against the claim of unlawful expropriation were less
than coherently presented by the state. Then Israeli military Chief of
Staff, Refael Eitan, couched the necessity of the settlement in terms of
'regional defence' in the hypothetical event of an inter-state war in the
region, rather than any specific or immediate security threats within the
West Bank. At the same time, the Gush Emunim movement involved
in settling the land around Dweikat's village of Rujeib – supported
by elements of the Likud government that had come to power in

---

Palestine' in Tareq Y. Ismael (ed.), *The International Relations of the Middle East in the Twenty-First Century* (Aldershot: Ashgate, 2000) 203–225. In this case, the Israeli authorities had now moved to settling privately owned land in addition.

[89] Weizman, *Hollow Land*, 100.

[90] See, for example, *Abu Hilo v. Government of Israel* [Rafah], HCJ 302/72, with Justice Vitkon explaining that although the seized land was designated for civilian settlement rather than military installations, the settlements 'are in themselves, in this case, a security measure'. See also *Abu Hilo v. Government of Israel* [Beit El], HCJ 258/79, with Justice Vitkon again: 'In terms of purely security-based considerations, there can be no doubt that the presence in the administered territory of settlements - even "civilian" ones - of the citizens of the administering power makes a significant contribution to the security situation in that territory, and facilitates the army's performance of its tasks.'

[91] Weizman, *Hollow Land*, 105.

1977 – was unreserved about the permanence of their intentions. They made no claims to the settlement serving mere temporary or security purposes. One of the settlers, Menachem Felix, made the point clear in his testimony to the Court:

> Basing the requisition orders on security grounds in their narrow, technical meaning rather than their basic and comprehensive meaning as explained above can be construed only in one way: the settlement is temporary and replaceable. We reject this frightening conclusion outright. It is also inconsistent with the government's decision on our settling on this site. In all our contacts and from the many promises we received from government ministers, and most importantly from the prime minister himself – and the said seizure order was issued in accordance with the personal intervention of the prime minister – all see Elon Moreh to be a permanent Jewish settlement no less than Deganya or Netanya.[92]

Presented with such overtly contradictory positions to the discourse of 'temporary' security needs, the Supreme Court ordered the authorities to return the land in Rujeib to its owners, prompting Sharon to immediately set about devising an alternative legal premise for the project of seizing and settling Palestinian land.[93] At the meeting called by Sharon in the wake of the judgment, Ramat offered the idea of reviving the concept of *mawat* land ('dead' or 'unused' land) from nineteenth century Ottoman agrarian land law. According to this doctrine, land lying a certain distance outside a given village, even if belonging to someone, is only owned temporarily as long as that owner cultivates it. If it is not cultivated for three consecutive years, it is considered "dead land" belonging to no one, and reverts to the empire. Satisfied that this could serve the settlement project's purpose, Sharon gathered a team of lawyers and geographers and set about identifying, mapping and registering uncultivated land using aerial photometry. Elon Moreh was established on an alternative site on this basis, and throughout the West Bank swathes of land were declared state land by the regional military command. A number of techniques were then constructed around this policy, such as the reduction of water quotas to Palestinian farmers to curtail their capacity to

---

[92] Cited in B'Tselem, 'Land Grab: Israel's Settlement Policy in the West Bank' (Jerusalem: B'Tselem, 2002) 49.

[93] It must be noted here that the *Elon Moreh* ruling did not have any bearing on the continued settlement of "state land" in the occupied territories, nor on prior requisition orders of private Palestinian land, which remained valid as far as Israeli law was concerned.

cultivate land.[94] The expropriation through re-categorisaton was upheld by the Supreme Court, and the scale and pace of settlement construction proliferated from the late 1970s. As Weizman notes, therefore:

> Although the liberal press celebrated the Elon Moreh ruling as a victory over the Likud government, it later became clear that this ruling was nothing but a Pyrrhic victory. Not only was Elon Moreh established on an alternative site; indeed, for whoever wished to read it, the ruling's wording itself indicated alternative methods of access to land. The court confirmed that future access to land in the Occupied Territories for the construction of settlements would be permitted on public land entrusted to the custo-dianship of the military power, and added that if the state adheres to this principle, the court would no longer interfere in its future settlement efforts.[95]

The Supreme Court did this through accepting the seizure of huge quantities of state land, including private Palestinian land recast as state land,[96] as well as by holding that the legality of the settlements them-selves was a 'political' question and as such not justiciable before the courts.[97] Former Chief Justice Meir Shamgar claims that the develop-ments initiated by the Israeli military legal professionals and the deci-sions taken by the Supreme Court had no bearing on the manner in which Israel's land and settlement policies proceeded in the occupied territories, arguing there was 'no indication that the steps taken by the Court are connected to this phenomenon. ... This is a political phenom-enon, not connected to the Court'.[98] Alexandrowicz plainly exposes this constructed law/politics binary as a false and implausible separation.

Law was very much part of the political discourse and dynamic of settlement. The 'dead land' concept finds obvious analogy in the

---

[94] In just six years from 1979 to 1985, the cultivated land in the West Bank was reduced by 40 per cent. Weizman, *Hollow Land*, 120.

[95] *Ibid.*, 108.

[96] According to Israeli organisation Peace Now's Settlement Watch team, by 2006, 38.76 per cent of the land on which settlements and settler industrial zones in the West Bank are located was privately owned Palestinian property. Dror Etkes and Hagit Ofran, *Breaking the Law in the West Bank: Israeli Settlement Building on Private Palestinian Property* (Jerusalem: Peace Now, 2006) 15. In February 2017, the Israeli legislature enacted the Settlements Regularisation Law (or Validation Law) to explicitly allow the state to expropriate private Palestinian lands in occupied territory for the purposes of settlement construction. Under the legislation, settlements built on private Palestinian land in the OPT can be 'legalised' and 'regularised' through retroactive expropriation, planning and zoning regulations.

[97] See, for example, *Bargil* v. *Government of Israel*, HCJ 4481/91, judgment, 25 August 1993.

[98] Quoted in Ra'anan Alexandrowicz, *The Law in These Parts* (2011).

common law doctrine of *terra nullius*, used to great effect in the colonisation of Australia and North America through the acquisition of land marked not by emptiness per se, but by an absence of 'civilised' society capable of exercising sovereignty. It also evokes a liberal imperial theory of property rights, which justified the non-consensual nature of colonial dominion and the dispossession of Indigenous peoples who were not cultivating the land in question. Settlers who did mix their labour with the land to 'improve' it gained rights to the land. Once such rights had been established, any native attempts to regain the land could be put down with force. As Alexandrowicz's narration highlights, with Israel's military occupation now succeeding Ottoman and British rule, 'what the IDF [Israeli military] says goes ... the regional commander is now the empire'.

Within the broader legal discourse in Israel, the direct and concrete legacy of British colonial emergency measures occupies a central position. Israel remains in a perpetual state of national emergency and continues to apply the British Defence (Emergency) Regulations 1945 as part of the legal basis for policy as it relates to the Palestinians. In the construction of a supposedly exceptional *nomos* in Palestine, law remains integral. The state of emergency serves to frame the situation for both domestic and international consumption as one of defensive security rather than aggressive conquest. The deeper reality of institutionalised domination, however, reinforces the notion of racialisation as a prominent component of the invocation of sovereign emergency power. As has typically been the case in colonial spaces, emergency powers are necessary to the preservation of sovereignty, serving as a bridge between the twinned pillars of liberal empire: conquest by force, and rule of law. The line connecting settlement and emergency powers can also be mapped. Settlement and cultivation act, for Zionism, as a precursor to the establishment of sovereignty. Emergency powers are subsequently discharged as an element of that acquired sovereignty in order to consolidate its supremacy over any competing claims. An array of emergency legal mechanisms converge to inscribe a form of control over the body, mind and territory of the colonised, and to suppress resistance to such control.

Israel's Emergency Modalities

The Mandate-era Defence (Emergency) Regulations constitute one element of Israel's broader, multifarious emergency legal regime. Within a region noted for prolonged use of emergency law as a governmental structure of authoritarian rule,[99] Israel stands out as an exemplar of permanent emergency. In addition to retention of the British emergency regulations, a state of emergency was proclaimed by the Provisional State Council on 19 May 1948 – in the first few days of the state's existence – and has persisted without interruption since then. This enables the executive branch to alter or suspend laws passed by the legislature. Some but not all elements of Israel's emergency modalities are dependent on this declared emergency. The Israeli legal system includes several mechanisms of emergency law that overlap, but exist independently of each other. The emergency jurisprudential situation is complex to the point of being described as 'incoherent' and 'convoluted'.[100] Contrary to conceptions of this situation as the inadvertent accumulation of necessary threat-specific responses enacted at particular points in time, however, it is more revealingly understood as a concerted tool of governance whose structural ambiguity offers a convenient flexibility.

Emergency modalities in the Israeli legal order assume three principal legal forms. The Defence (Emergency) Regulations, as noted, remain on the law books of the land long after the departure of their original British authors. While framed in the lineage of colonial emergency doctrine, their subsequent application by Israel is not tied to the declaration of a state of emergency.[101] Israel has itself constructed two further bases in law for extraordinary measures. Specific administrative emergency orders or regulations can be promulgated by the executive branch of government, and are dependent upon a declared state of emergency. Primary emergency legislation enacted by the Knesset (Israel's parliament) can similarly be made contingent on the existence of a declared emergency, but may alternatively be worded to apply independently.[102]

---

[99] See, for example: Syria 1963–2011; Egypt 1981–2012; Algeria 1992–2011.

[100] Yoav Mehozay, 'The Fluid Jurisprudence of Israel's Emergency Powers: Legal Patchwork as a Governing Norm' (2012) 46:1 *Law & Society Review* 137, 137–138.

[101] Simon Shetreet, 'A Contemporary Model of Emergency Detention Law: An Assessment of the Israeli Law' (1984) 14 *Israel Yearbook on Human Rights* 182, 183–184, cited in Emanuel Gross, 'Human Rights, Terrorism and the Problem of Administrative Detention in Israel: Does a Democracy Have the Right to Hold Terrorists as Bargaining Chips?' (2001) 18:3 *Arizona Journal of International and Comparative Law* 721, 754: 'The Courts held that neither the provisions of the Mandate nor the language of, nor the qualifications contained in Section 11 excluded the reception of the Defense Regulations, including Regulation 11 dealing with administrative detention. The application of the Defense Regulations does not depend upon a proclamation of a state of emergency under Section 9 of the Law and Administration Ordinance 1948.'

[102] Mehozay, 'The Fluid Jurisprudence', 140–141.

The Defence (Emergency) Regulations

The Defence (Emergency) Regulations 1945 was the last version of the emergency code deployed by Britain in its administration of Palestine. It followed on from previous instruments that had been used suppress Arab revolt against foreign rule from the early 1930s: the Palestine (Defence) Order in Council 1931; the Palestine Martial Law (Defence) Order in Council 1936; the Emergency Regulations 1936; the Palestine (Defence) Order in Council 1937; the Defence (Military Courts) Regulation 1937; the Defence (Military Commanders) Regulations 1938; and the Defence Regulations 1939. Such texts had, between them, offered the typical panoply of emergency powers – censorship, curfew, closure, house demolition, movement restriction, detention without trial, deportation and land requisition – to the executive and military authorities. The Defence (Emergency) Regulations 1945 integrated much of what had been included in these instruments in a consolidated and more comprehensive form. The Regulations were used against both Palestinian Arabs and Jews in the post-war years before Britain abdicated its Mandate. They were condemned by Zionist leaders of the time as undemocratic and racist laws, to the point of being compared unfavourably to Nazi legal regimes.[103]

Following the establishment of the Israeli state, the Defence (Emergency) Regulations were adopted by Israel under Section 11 of the Law and Administration Ordinance 1948 (the first piece of legislation enacted by Israel's Provisional State Council).[104] Proposals for the revocation of the Regulations (or their replacement by permanent legislation) were made in the Knesset in 1949, and on a number of occasions in the 1950s.

[103] See, for example, the speech of Yacob Shimshon Shapira (later Israeli Attorney-General and Minister for Justice), Jewish Bar Association, Tel Aviv, 7 February 1946, quoted in *Ha Praklit* (February 1946): 'The regime established in Palestine with the publication of the Emergency Regulations is quite unique for enlightened countries. Even Nazi Germany didn't have such laws, and acts such as those perpetrated at Maidanek actually ran against the letter of German law.' The Regulations were also condemned by the Jewish community in Palestine as indicative of a 'police state'. Bernard Joseph, *British Rule in Palestine* (Washington: Public Affairs Press, 1948) 222.

[104] On Britain's repeal of the Defence (Emergency) Regulations before relinquishing the Mandate in May 1948, and the subsequent legislative manoeuvring of the Knesset to profess that the regulations had not in fact been validly repealed, see, for example, John Quigley, *The Case for Palestine: An International Law Perspective* (Durham: Duke University Press, 2nd edn., 2005) 103. Only Regulations 102 (which reinforced Britain's Immigration Ordinance 1941) and 107c dealing with illegal immigration were dropped so as to allow Jews who entered Palestine illegally under the British Mandate to remain in the new state.

Criticism voiced by Jewish-Israeli judges, legislators and religious figures routinely characterised the regulations as fascist and authoritarian. The context of this opposition was a small number of high-profile instances of administrative detention of members of Zionist paramilitary groups. In a 1951 Knesset debate over whether the provisions of the Regulations providing for detention without trial ought to be extirpated from the Israeli legal system, then opposition leader Menachem Begin challenged Foreign Minister (and, at the time, acting Prime Minister) Moshe Sharett's defence of administrative detention and his contention that 'law is law':

> Not so! There are tyrannical laws, there are unethical laws ... And an unethical law is also an illegal law. The detention is therefore illegal, and your order is arbitrary.[105]

Notably, however, the Regulations had also emerged by 1950 as the legal basis for the system of military government imposed on the predominantly Palestinian Arab regions within Israel. As the threat of Jewish attacks against the state dissipated, the racialising impact of the Regulations intensified through their use against Palestinian citizens of Israel. By the end of 1948, the main Arab population centres inside what had materialised as Israel's de facto borders – most of which had been mapped outside of Israel's designated borders under the UN partition plan – were effectively under military rule. Five military governorates were created: Jaffa, Ramle-Lod, Nazareth, the Western Galilee and the Negev. Throughout 1949, these areas were classified as occupied territories, before an integrated system of military government was established in 1950 under the direction and coordination of the Ministry of Defence. This form of military rule of Palestinians within Israel continued until 1966, with the Defence (Emergency) Regulations as its primary legal framework. As such, a territorial zone of emergency was carved out within Israel in a racially contingent manner, based on the demographic make-up of the region concerned. For Edward Said, the implications were clear:

> These laws were openly racist in that they were never used in Israel against Jews. When Israel retained them after 1948 for use in controlling the Arab minority, they forbade Arabs the right of movement, the right of

---

[105] 9 *Knesset Debates* 1807, 12 May 1951, quoted in B'Tselem, 'Detained Without Trial: Administrative Detention in the Occupied Territories Since the Beginning of the Intifada' (Jerusalem: B'Tselem, 1992) 24. See also, for example, Don Peretz, 'Early State Policy towards the Arab Population, 1948–1955' in Laurence J. Silberstein (ed.), *New Perspectives on Israeli History: The Early Years of the State* (New York: New York University Press, 1991) 92.

purchase of land, the right of settlement, and so forth. Under the mandate the regulations were regularly denounced by the Jews as colonial and racist. Yet as soon as Israel became a state, those same laws were used against the Arabs. . . . Until 1966, the Arab citizens of Israel were ruled by a military government exclusively in existence to control, bend, manipulate, terrorize, tamper with every facet of Arab life from birth virtually to death.[106]

Israeli scholars acknowledge that the regulations were used almost exclusively against Arabs,[107] and at the time the state comptroller held there to be 'something improper' about a law like this being enforced against one particular group of the population.[108] Said asserts that the purpose underlying the application of stringent emergency powers was 'to pay that wretched [Palestinian population] for its temerity in staying where it did not belong', seeing it as entwined with the 'Judaisation' of those parts of Israel that retained an Arab majority.[109] The discourse of Israeli leaders during this period offers little to dispute that claim, with a racialised vision of the state very much to the fore. David Ben-Gurion's 1960 speech to the World Zionist Congress is a case in point, eliding the binational character of the country's population:

In Israel there are not two spheres. . . . Here everybody is both Jewish and universal: the soil we walk upon, the trees whose fruit we eat, the roads on which we travel, the houses we live in, the factories where we work, the schools where our children are educated, the army in which they are trained, the ships we sail in and the planes in which we fly, the language we speak and the air we breath, the landscape we see and the vegetation that surrounds us – all of it is Jewish.[110]

While military rule and the Defence (Emergency) Regulations are most commonly associated with the security provisions mandating restrictions on liberty through powers of arrest, detention and curfew, other aspects of the Regulations that have had a more profound structural impact on relations with the Palestinians. Ben-Gurion was frank about the primary function of the internal military government over Israel's Palestinian population: 'the military regime came into existence to protect the right

---

[106] Edward W. Said, *The Question of Palestine* (New York: Times Books, 1979) 36, 105.
[107] David Kretzmer, *The Legal Status of the Arabs in Israel* (Boulder: Westview Press, 1990) 116, 128.
[108] State Comptroller's Report no. 9 (1957/58) 78, quoted in Quigley, *The Case for Palestine*, 104.
[109] Said, *The Question of Palestine*, 103.
[110] 'Address by Prime Minister Ben Gurion', *New York Times* 52–53, 8 January 1961.

of Jewish settlement in all parts of the state'.[111] The Defence (Emergency) Regulations were central to land and planning policies in Israel's formative years, underpinning an ideology of pioneering settlement that was as central within the new state as it had been in Mandate Palestine and would be in the post-1967 occupied territories. The regulations were used to expropriate large parcels of Palestinian land inside Israel through the creation of 'closed' security zones. Under Regulation 125:

> A Military Commander may by order declare any area or place to be a closed area for the purposes of these Regulations. Any person who, during any period in which any such order is in force in relation to any area or place, enters or leaves that area or place without a permit in writing issued by or on behalf of the Military Commander shall be guilty of an offense against these Regulations.[112]

From 1948, all of the Arab-Palestinian villages and towns in Israel, whether still inhabited or not, were declared by the military authorities as separate closed areas. This encompassed approximately 85 per cent of the Palestinians on the Israeli side of the armistice line, with only those living in predominantly Jewish urban areas not directly affected.[113] Large tracts of land were closed by the military, with their inhabitants expelled or their owners denied access, and the land in turn confiscated by the state. Under Regulation 125, Palestinians were prevented from leaving their own village or town without a permit from the Israeli military authorities, even for the purposes of cultivating and harvesting their own lands, or of travelling to market towns to sell their produce. The Galilee area alone was divided into fifty-eight sectors for travel permit purposes. Applying for permits was a burdensome process, with requests often rejected. Palestinians residing or travelling without a permit – or with an expired permit, or a permit for a different route – were summarily fined or imprisoned, with recourse only to military courts. The Regulations thus operated to prevent Palestinian farmers from accessing and cultivating their own land. In a similar fashion to later developments in the occupied territories, the Minister of Agriculture was in turn mandated to classify closed-off Palestinian land as 'uncultivated' and

---

[111] 36 *Knesset Debates* 1217, 20 February 1963, quoted in Quigley, *The Case for Palestine*, 109.
[112] Government of Palestine, The Defence (Emergency) Regulations, 1945, *Palestine Gazette* no. 1442, Supplement no. 2, 27 September 1945, Regulation 125.
[113] Quigley, *The Case for Palestine*, 106.

thus unprotected from expropriation.[114] Shimon Peres made it clear that the fundamental value of the Defence (Emergency) Regulations was rooted not in immediate security concerns, but in facilitating Zionism's overarching goals: 'By making use of Article 125, on which the Military Government is to a great extent based, we can directly continue the struggle for Jewish settlement and Jewish immigration.'[115] Regulation 125 was used in tandem with other mechanisms developed in the state's legal apparatus for the purposes of expropriating and acquiring Palestinian land, including the Abandoned Areas Ordinance 1948 and the Land Acquisition (Validation of Acts and Compensation) Law 1953.

Dispossession of Palestinians under this emergency infrastructure was sustained even where it was not condoned by the Israeli Supreme Court. Don Peretz chronicles one example relating to the Arab-Palestinian population of the northern border village of Iqrit:

> After surrendering to the [Israeli military] on 31 October 1948, the villagers were asked to leave for fifteen days because of "security reasons." Most left with only enough personal belongings for two weeks, but five years later the army still gave no indication that it would permit them to return. When the case was brought to the High Court of Justice in 1953, the court did not dispute the army's right to evacuate a population in times of emergency. However, questioning the procedures followed to prevent the return of the villagers after termination of the emergency, it ordered the army to permit the inhabitants to go home. The [Israeli military] responded by destroying most of the village and refusing to obey the court.[116]

The Defence (Emergency) Regulations were used to extend the closure order in 1963 and again in 1972. Iqrit's expelled villagers went back to the Supreme Court with another petition in 1981, where it was this time held that their continued displacement was justified.[117] The displaced Palestinians continued their campaign to return to their village. A Ministerial Committee appointed in 1993 found that there was no security imperative for the ongoing expulsion of those evacuated in 1948, and recommended a 'compromise' solution whereby approximately ten per cent of

[114] Hanna Dib Nakkara, 'Israeli Land Seizure under Various Defense and Emergency Regulations' (1985) 14:2 *Journal of Palestine Studies* 13, 15–16.
[115] Shimon Peres, 'Military Law is the Fruit of Military Governance', *Davar*, 26 January 1962. Peres was Director-General of Israel's Ministry of Defence in 1962.
[116] Peretz, 'Early State Policy', 90.
[117] *Committee of Displaced Persons from Iqrit, Rama and Others* v. *Government of Israel*, HCJ 141/81.

their original land would be restored to the villagers, on which each family would be entitled to build one house. In 2001, however, the Israeli cabinet issued a decision asserting that the same security concerns which had informed the 1972 closure under the Defence (Emergency) Regulations remained relevant, and the villagers were therefore prevented from returning. The Supreme Court deferred to this position and proposed that compensation be paid instead, a solution that was unacceptable to the displaced residents.[118]

As the Iqrit case demonstrates, the Defence (Emergency) Regulations were retained inside Israel after the dissolution of military rule in 1966 and the transfer of government functions for the country's Arab areas to the state's civil authorities. Since then, the Regulations have continued to be used inside Israel, particularly in relation to land issues arising in border areas. Provisions of the Defence (Emergency) Regulations providing for the banning of 'unlawful associations' (Regulations 84 and 85) and censorship (Regulations 86–101) continue to be invoked in recent years to close Arabic-language newspapers, to ban Palestinian political parties and associations, and to disqualify their candidates from Knesset elections.[119]

The use of the Defence (Emergency) Regulations inside Israel was most pronounced, however, during the crucial period of military rule up to 1966, as the state went about consolidating its demographic and territorial dominance. As Said reminds us, 'the best introduction to what has been taking place in the Occupied Territories is the testimony of Israeli Arabs who suffered through Israeli legal brutality before 1967'.[120] The legal tools were certainly carried across, with the Defence (Emergency) Regulations assuming a significant role in the legal architecture of the occupation. The racialised use of the Regulations continues to this day in the occupied territories through almost exclusive application to Palestinian residents. They provide the basis for a profusion of military orders covering administrative detention, home demolition, land seizure, curfew, deportation, and censorship. Defenders of Israeli security policy in this regard argue that the discriminatory application of the

---

[118] Hussein Abu Hussein and Fiona McKay, *Access Denied: Palestinian Land Rights in Israel* (London: Zed Books, 2003) 85.

[119] For a number of examples, see Quigley, *The Case for Palestine*, 133–134.

[120] Said, *The Question of Palestine*, 106. Here, Said refers us to Sabri Jiryis, *The Arabs in Israel* (New York: Monthly Review Press, 1976), Fouzi al-Asmar, *To Be an Arab in Israel* (Beirut: Institute for Palestine Studies, 1978), and Elia T. Zurayk's *The Palestinians in Israel: A Study in Internal Colonialism* (London: Routledge, 1979).

emergency regulations is between Israelis and non-Israelis purely on grounds of citizenship, not between Jewish-Israeli settlers and Arab-Palestinians on grounds of national or ethnic origin. Israel's prior targeted application of the emergency regulations towards its Arab citizens in the internal military government period, however, undermines this claim. The Defence (Emergency) Regulations have now been retained in the Israeli legal system for seven decades, playing on the licence granted by a supposed temporariness, but deeply entangled with the state's brand of racial sovereignty.

Emergency Measures under the Declared State of Emergency

Pursuant to Section 9 of the Law and Administration Ordinance 1948, Israel was ushered into a declared and temporally indeterminate state of emergency from the first week of the state's formal existence. After more than forty years of the emergency as status quo, the governing legal framework was given a slight procedural makeover, with the authority to declare an emergency reconstituted in the 1992 Basic Law: Government,[121] and subjected to a condition that the declaration 'may not exceed one year'. With the Basic Law proceeding to allow for unlimited renewals by parliament, however, the temporality of the emergency in effect remained indefinite. The Knesset has renewed the state of emergency every year thereafter without fail, meaning that Israel's national emergency has continued since May 1948 without respite.

A number of mechanisms are triggered by a declared state of emergency. The government is authorised to enact discrete administrative emergency regulations to circumvent 'normal' constitutional guarantees. As such, while the legislature is responsible for declaring and renewing (normalising) the state of emergency, under Section 9 of the Law and Administration Ordinance the executive has full discretion as to the nature of exceptional measures to be taken: 'Government may authorise the Prime Minister or any other Minister to make such emergency regulations as may seem to him expedient in the interests of the defence of the State, public security and the maintenance of supplies and essential services.' Emergency regulations propagated under this authority can and do take supremacy over ordinary parliamentary legislation, prompting human rights organisations to decry the fact that bestowing such a mandate to the executive serves to

---

[121] Originally Article 49; now Article 38.

'violate the principles of the rule of law and the separation of powers'.[122] Executive emergency regulations have been imposed consistently from 1948. Many of them have supplemented Israel's land appropriation mechanisms under the Defence (Emergency) Regulations.

The Emergency Regulations (Absentees' Property) Law 1948 marks the genesis of Israel's 'absentee property' doctrine. Under this doctrine, the land of an individual deemed an 'absentee' can be confiscated by the state. This concept was moulded for the confiscation of property belonging to Palestinians that had been killed or forced to flee to neighbouring countries in 1948, but was applied even if, as 'in many cases, the absentees were present – a legal fiction of Kafkaesque subtlety'.[123] Internally displaced Palestinians who were barred from returning to their homes, although still in Israel, were constructed as "present absentees". Significantly, in terms of racialisation, even if Jewish individuals could have ostensibly fallen within the definition,[124] the Absentee Property doctrine has been implemented only against Arabs. An 'absentee' is defined as any person owning land in Israel who is a citizen, national or resident of Lebanon, Egypt, Syria, Saudi Arabia, Jordan, Iraq, Yemen, the West Bank or Gaza, or who was a citizen of British Palestine but left the area that became Israel in 1948. These particular emergency regulations set the tone for the permanent legislation that superseded them in the form of the Absentees' Property Law 1950. Beyond the particular case of the 'absent' Palestinian population – whether refugees outside the Green Line or internally displaced within – substantial tracts of land still remained in the possession of Palestinians who managed to stay and become citizens in Israel. The Israeli authorities thus devised additional emergency regulations aimed at accumulating further land. As early as the summer of 1948, a series of emergency orders were introduced to underwrite large-scale land transfers on purported state security grounds.[125] The Emergency Regulations (Requisition of Property) Law 1948, for instance, was promulgated by decree to allow the provisional government to seize property. This was replaced and cemented by legislation enacted by the Knesset the following year. Significantly, the

---

[122] Adalah, 'Information Sheet #1: State of Emergency', submitted to the UN Human Rights Committee, 22 July 2003.
[123] Said, *The Question of Palestine*, 105. The Absentees' Property Law was enacted in 1950.
[124] Kretzmer, *The Legal Status of the Arabs in Israel* 102, 115.
[125] Amichai Cohen and Stuart Cohen, *Israel's National Security Law: Political Dynamics and Historical Development* (London: Routledge, 2011) 56.

Emergency Land Requisition (Regulation) Law 1949 authorises land and housing requisition orders by the Israeli authorities not only for 'the defense of the State, public security, the maintenance of essential supplies or essential public services' but also to facilitate 'the absorption of immigrants or the rehabilitation of ex-soldiers or war invalids'.[126] As such, the legislation's thrust transcends security and defence necessities, and is explicitly linked to immigration and citizenship policies aimed at consolidating settler colonial domination. It is also important to note that land seizure under these orders was initially defined as a temporary requisition subject to certain time limitations which were eliminated in subsequent amendments, 'effectively transforming the initial requisition into permanent expropriation'.[127]

In a similar vein, a series of instruments relating to 'waste' land put in train a process whereby Israel's Minister of Agriculture could assume control of 'uncultivated' Palestinian land. This originated in the Emergency Regulations (Cultivation of Waste Lands) 1948, which was amended by the Emergency Regulations (Cultivation of Waste Lands) (Extension of Validity) Ordinance 1949 and the Emergency Regulations (Cultivation of Waste [Uncultivated] Lands) Law 1949, culminating in the Emergency Regulations (Cultivation of Waste Lands) Law 1951. In addition to being empowered to confiscate uncultivated land, the Minister of Agriculture is also mandated to assume control 'of water resources and water installations which in his opinion are not sufficiently utilised'.[128] These measures have typically been used in conjunction with the Defence (Emergency) Regulations, whereby areas closed by the military authorities are subsequently confiscated by the Minister of Agriculture on the basis that they are no longer being cultivated.[129]

---

[126] Emergency Land Requisition (Regulation) Law 1949, Article 3(a).
[127] George Bisharat, 'Land, Law, and Legitimacy in Israel and the Occupied Territories' (1994) 43 *The American University Law Review* 467, 517.
[128] Emergency Regulations (Cultivation of Waste Lands) (Extension of Validity) Ordinance 1949, Schedule: Emergency Regulations Concerning the Cultivation of Waste Lands and the Use of Unexploited Water Resources, Article 17(a).
[129] See further, for example, Ian Lustick, *Arabs in a Jewish State: Israel's Control of a National Minority* (Austin: University of Texas Press, 1980) 178: 'Typically the process works in the following way: An area encompassing Arab-owned agricultural lands is declared a "closed area." The owners of the lands are then denied permission by the security authorities to enter the area for any purpose whatsoever, including cultivation. After three years pass, the Ministry of Agriculture issues certificates which classify the lands as uncultivated. The owners are notified that unless cultivation is renewed immediately the lands will be subject to expropriation. The owners, still barred by the

The Emergency Regulations (Security Zones) Law 1949 gives the Minister of Defence discretion to categorise areas (within ten kilometres of Israel's northern borders, and twenty-five kilometres of the borders in the south) as security zones that must be evacuated. This policy has been applied particularly in the Galilee region, the areas towards the Lebanese and Syrian borders, and around the Gaza Strip. Land acquired under this order has typically been sold or transferred to the Jewish National Fund, a para-state institution mandated to 'acquire and develop lands in Palestine for the exclusive benefit of the Jewish people'.[130] Such measures, framed in a security discourse, function to feed into the deeper structural and demographic aspects of Israel's land policies.

The extensive grid of related emergency laws and regulations that are used in parallel and in mutually reinforcing ways is indicative of the state of emergency paradigm as a surface upon which settler colonial policies were legally inscribed from the outset in Israel. The torrent of emergency measures enacted for the purposes of land expropriation so soon after the state's foundation implies a degree of premeditation, and a continuity of pre-state Zionist policies and plans aimed at the conquest of Palestinian land.[131] To reify that conquest, and Jewish-Israeli domination of state institutions, a range of emergency mechanisms also operate to obstruct Palestinian participation in the political and social life of Israel and the region. The Emergency Regulations (Foreign Travel) 1948 [an instrument authorising the Minister of Interior to prevent Israeli citizens from

---

security authorities from entering the 'closed area' within which their lands are located, cannot resume cultivation. The lands are then expropriated and become part of the general land reserve for Jewish settlement.

[130] Souad R. Dajani, *Ruling Palestine: A History of the Legally Sanctioned Jewish-Israeli Seizure of Land and Housing in Palestine* (Geneva and Bethlehem: Centre on Housing Rights and Evictions (COHRE) & BADIL Resource Center for Palestinian Residency & Refugee Rights, 2005) 18, 40.

[131] A series of plans and guidelines were drawn up from 1944 by the Haganah, the pre-state Zionist militia in Palestine, designed to take control of territory for the Jewish state. This process culminated in Plan Dalet in early 1948, described as a 'master plan for the conquest of Palestine' by Palestinian historian Walid Khalidi, and a 'blueprint for ethnic cleansing' by Israeli historian Ilan Pappé. Walid Khalidi, 'Plan Dalet: Master Plan for the Conquest of Palestine' (1988) 18:1 *Journal of Palestine Studies* 4; Ilan Pappé, *The Ethnic Cleansing of Palestine* (Oxford: Oneworld, 2006) 86. In contrast, Israeli military historian David Tal argues that while the plan did provide for the deportation of Palestinian residents and the destruction of their villages, this was not its raison d'être – rather, the primary purpose of establishing Jewish-Israeli territorial control was as a defensive safeguard in the event of invasion. See David Tal, *War in Palestine, 1948: Strategy and Diplomacy* (London: Routledge, 2004) 87.

travelling abroad 'as he sees fit', and on the basis of secret evidence] and the Prevention of Infiltration (Offences and Jurisdiction) Law 1954 [an emergency law prohibiting travel, or assistance others in travelling, to a number of Arab states designated as 'enemy states'] continue to be used to prosecute or impose travel bans on Palestinians. In 2002, for example, Palestinian member of the Knesset Azmi Bishara was indicted under these laws for helping Palestinian citizens of Israel to visit relatives in Syria. While his case was pending, the Knesset passed Amendment 7 to the Emergency Regulations (Foreign Travel) 1948, to remove diplomatic travel immunity from parliament members. From 2002, similarly, Sheikh Ra'ed Salah, a Muslim Palestinian religious leader in Israel, was prevented from travelling for annual pilgrimage by an emergency travel ban order issued by the Minister of Interior and upheld on security grounds by the Supreme Court.[132]

Although ostensibly tied to national security matters, Israel's emergency legal regime infiltrates a diversity of areas, often, as noted, without any discernible connection to perceived threats to the existence or security of the state. In addition to underwriting land expropriation and colonisation processes, dozens of sets of emergency regulations have been enacted in spheres spanning economic regulation, labour relations, civil registration, family unification and residency, trade and monetary issues, health care procedures, shipping practices, fire-fighting services and regulation of taxi meters. It has been noted that emergency regulatory powers under Section 9 of the Law and Administration Ordinance 1948 have been invoked, for instance, in 'an almost routine fashion' since the Yom Kippur war in 1973 to bypass burdensome industrial dispute resolution processes 'in situations where no special urgency was present or when other, less drastic means had been available'.[133]

In addition to executive emergency decrees or regulations, statutory legislation – while enacted and amended by the Knesset in the same fashion as ordinary statutes – can also be framed in such a way that applicability is contingent upon the existence of a state of emergency. The Emergency Powers (Detention) Law 1979, for example, which enables administrative detention of residents of Israel, residents of

---

[132] Sheikh Ra'ed Salah v. Minister of Interior, HCJ 4706/02, judgment, 17 July 2002.
[133] Gross and Ní Aoláin, Law in Times of Crisis, 232–233, citing Menachem Hofnung, Democracy, Law and National Security in Israel (Brookfield, VT: Dartmouth, 1996) 55–60, and Mordechai Mironi, Back-to-Work Emergency Orders: Government Intervention in Labor Disputes in Essential Services (1986) 15 Mishpatim 350, 380–386.

territory occupied by Israel, and residents of other states, was framed so that it 'shall only apply in a period in which a state of emergency exists in the State by virtue of a declaration under section 9 of the Law and Administration Ordinance'. This succeeded Regulations 108 and 111 of the Defence (Emergency) Regulations and grants discretion to the Minister of Defence to issue (and renew indefinitely) administrative detention orders where he or she 'has reasonable cause to believe that reasons of state security or public security require that a particular person be detained'. In the context of a perpetually renewed state of emergency, this ordinance effectively functions as an ordinary piece of permanent legislation, thus normalising the exceptional powers of detention without trial in the legal system. The fact that (leaving aside the continuing use of the law against Palestinian citizens of Israel) more than 800,000 Palestinians in the occupied territories – encompassing 40 per cent of the total male population – have been detained since 1967 under military order is testament to this normalisation.[134]

Such deprivation of liberty en masse is ostensibly inimical to international human rights and fair trial standards. Upon ratifying the International Covenant on Civil and Political Rights in 1991, however, Israel submitted a formal notification stating that (since 1948) its security situation has constituted a public emergency within the meaning of the Covenant's derogation provision in Article 4 – that is, an existential 'threat to the life of the nation'. On this basis, Israel declared that it was suspending certain obligations under the Covenant and derogating from Article 9 (right to liberty).[135] While expressing 'concern' at Israel's reliance on the state of emergency in its periodic reviews of the state, the UN Human Rights Committee acknowledges Israel's security concerns and accepts that international law entitles states to derogate at their own discretion.[136] As such, international law shows itself to be implicated in the perpetuation of Israel's emergency modalities. Characterisations of

---

[134] Addameer, 'Palestinian Political Prisoners in Israeli Prisons' (Ramallah: Addameer, 2012) 4.

[135] 'Multilateral Treaties Deposited with the Secretary-General: Status as at 31 December 1991' UN Doc. ST/LEG/SER.E/10 (1992) 149.

[136] See, for example, UN Human Rights Committee, 'Concluding Observations: Israel', UN Doc. CCPR/C/79/Add.93, 18 August 1998, §.4,11. Some international lawyers, such as John Quigley, however, do question the procedural and substantive validity of Israel's derogation. John Quigley, 'Israel's Forty-Five Year Emergency: Are There Time Limits to Derogations from Human Rights Obligations?' (1994) 15 Michigan Journal of International Law 491.

Israel's state of emergency as oppositional to international law thus present a somewhat simplified and idealised vision of the international legal system – a vision divorced from the field's own colonial legacy and its facilitation of emergency powers.

In its first review of Israel in 1998, the Human Rights Committee recommended that Israel reassess what was by then a fifty-year-old state of emergency 'with a view to limiting as far as possible its scope'.[137] In its subsequent periodic review in 2003, the Committee remained concerned about the scope of Israel's emergency, while 'welcoming the State party's decision to review the need to maintain the declared state of emergency and to prolong it on a yearly rather than an indefinite basis'.[138] As I have noted above, however, it had been clear from quite soon after the introduction of this change in the 1990s that it was essentially a cosmetic procedural reform that allowed for unlimited renewals and, as such, did not qualitatively affect the emergency's indefinite status. Israel has repeatedly told the Committee since this time that it 'has been inclined to refrain from extending the state of emergency any further [but that] the actual termination of the state of emergency could not be executed immediately, as certain fundamental laws, orders and regulations legally depend upon the existence of a state of emergency'.[139] In its 2010 and 2014 reviews of Israel, the Committee reiterated its concern at the continuing state of emergency and detention without trial of Palestinians, while continuing to acknowledge at face value 'the ongoing legislative process regarding the future cancellation of the state of emergency'.[140] Far from taking collective action or imposing sanctions on Israel, the international community of states – particularly its Western powers – continues to covet and purchase the techniques and military technologies by which Israel maintains its colonial emergency rule.[141]

On the domestic legal register in Israel, judicial challenges to both the Defence (Emergency) Regulations and the declared state of emergency

---

[137] UN Human Rights Committee, 'Concluding Observations: Israel', UN Doc. CCPR/C/79/Add.93, 18 August 1998, §.11.

[138] UN Human Rights Committee, 'Concluding Observations: Israel', UN Doc. CCPR/CO/78/ISR, 21 August 2003, §.12.

[139] Government of Israel, 'Second Periodic Report to the Human Rights Committee', 20 November 2001, Addendum to UN Doc. CCPR/C/ISR/2011/2, 4 December 2001.

[140] UN Human Rights Committee, 'Concluding Observations: Israel', UN Doc. CCPR/C/ISR/CO/4, 21 November 2014, §.10; UN Human Rights Committee, 'Concluding Observations: Israel', UN Doc. CCPR/C/ISR/CO/3, 29 July 2010, §.5,7.

[141] Lloyd, 'Settler Colonialism', 77.

have been brought at various points since 1948, resulting in the Israeli Supreme Court repeatedly stamping its imprimatur on the government and military authorities' use of emergency doctrine, thereby facilitating its normalisation.

'Intent to Regularise': Emergency on Trial

One of the first cases brought before Israel's Supreme Court in 1948, arising from a request for revocation of an administrative detention order under the Defence (Emergency) Regulations 1945, involved a challenge to the validity of the British Regulations themselves in the nascent state's legal order. A minority dissenting opinion in the case was expressed by Justice Shalom Kassan. Justice Kassan argued that the regulations granting broad emergency powers to the executive and military authorities were undemocratic and inapplicable:

> I cannot act and pass judgment in accordance with the defense regulations which are still on the statute book. Believing as I do that these laws are essentially invalid, I should not be asked to act against my conscience merely because the present government has not yet officially repealed them, though its members declared them illegal as soon as they were passed. . . . If the courts of the British Mandate did not cross these laws off the statute book, this court is honorbound to do so and to utterly eradicate them.[142]

The positivist majority decision of the Court, however, although expressing similar misgivings about the nature of the emergency regulations, held that the judiciary 'must accept the regulations as they are, that is as valid, legal regulations'. The outcome notwithstanding, a clear assumption that the government would annul the regulations in due course ran through the judgment. In a subsequent case of administrative detention of a Palestinian resident of Jaffa, the Defence (Emergency) Regulations were reaffirmed, although in this instance the detention order was annulled on procedural grounds.[143] Petitions challenging the validity of the Defence Regulations 1939 in the early days of Israel's existence were similarly rejected in formalistic terms by the Supreme Court, which refused to accept that the earlier Regulations had been implicitly repealed

---

[142] Dr. Herzl Cook v. Defense Minister of the Provisional Government of the State of Israel, et al.; Ziborah Wienerski v. The Minister of Defense, et al., HCJ 1/48; 2/48, HaMishpat vol. 3, 1948; quoted in Jiryis, The Arabs in Israel, 13–14.
[143] Al-Karbutli v. Minister of Defence et al., HCJ 7/48, judgment of 3 January 1949.

by the Law and Administration Ordinance 1948, or were inconsistent with the Declaration of the Establishment of the State of Israel.[144] In essence, these judgments held that the promise of a new legal order based on equality, contained in Israel's declaration of independence, was not legally binding in character and did not invalidate arbitrary British colonial rules.[145]

With the precedent asserted as to the Defence (Emergency) Regulations' standing, subsequent legal challenges sought instead to contest specific orders issued under the Regulations. In the *El-Ard* case in 1964, permission for the publication of an Arabic-language magazine in northern Israel was denied by the authorities on security grounds under Regulation 94. The association seeking to publish the magazine petitioned the Supreme Court, claiming the decision was unfounded and discriminatory. The Court indicated its tendency to defer to the executive and military on security matters and dismissed the petition, holding that Regulation 94 does not permit the Supreme Court to conduct an investigation of the facts and that its judicial review mandate is very limited under the Regulations.[146] In the 1979 *Al-Assad* case, again arising from denial of a publication permit under Regulation 94, a Supreme Court majority this time rule that the Ministry of Interior should issue the permit. While not required to disclose evidence revealing the security concerns on which the denial had been based, the authorities in this instance had failed to fulfil their procedural obligations to provide other specified information to the Court.[147] In a 1980s case arising from very similar facts, the Supreme Court upheld the decision to withhold the permit on security grounds, as no such procedural mistakes on the part of the state arose.[148]

When the inherent problems in the doctrine of emergency are left to one side, two normative legal questions arise and remain in relation to Israel's declared state of emergency. The first is whether Israel's situation has, since 1948, continued to surpass the threshold constructed of an

[144] *Zeev* v. *The Acting District Commissioner of the Urban Area of Tel Aviv (Gubernik)*, HCJ 10/48; *Leon* v. *Acting District Commissioner of Tel Aviv*, HCJ 5/48.
[145] Hassan Jabareen, 'Why "Jewish and Democratic" Values Negate Palestinian Equal Rights', *The Nakba Files*, 8 September 2016. See further Mazen Masri, *The Dynamics of Exclusionary Constitutionalism: Israel as a Jewish and Democratic State* (Oxford: Hart, 2017).
[146] *El-Ard* v. *Commissioner of the Northern District*, HCJ 39/64.
[147] *Al-Assad* v. *Minister of Interior*, HCJ 2/1979.
[148] *Makhoul* v. *Jerusalem District Commissioner*, HCJ 322/81.

impending threat to the life of the nation that is sufficiently grave to warrant the imposition of an emergency legal framework. The second, given that successive Israeli governments have argued that the state of emergency has reached the necessary threshold, is whether the measures enacted in the state of emergency paradigm are a necessary and proportionate response to the perceived threat. These are legal issues that continue to plague a number of states, often marked by deficits of judicial supervision, and have preoccupied the case law and commentary of international human rights bodies. It was concerns over both of these questions that prompted legal activists to seek judicial review of Israel's declared state of emergency.

In 1999, the Association for Civil Rights in Israel (ACRI) submitted a petition to the Supreme Court against the legislature, challenging the constitutionality of the continued state of emergency and seeking its annulment. The petition argued that the Knesset's persistent renewal and extension of a state of emergency has transgressed Israeli constitutional law and international legal norms, on the basis that Israel's security circumstances are not of such extraordinary status as to justify an extraordinary regime that subverts liberal understandings of rule of law and separation of powers. It was put forward that, in contrast to the purported intentions of the doctrine of emergency (here construed in a favourable light, detached from its own imperial history) to enable the implementation of urgent and necessary measures for a limited duration, Israel's state of emergency was permanent in time and unlimited in scope – and thus unlawful. ACRI further submitted that the declared emergency enabled the imposition of legislation and regulations that violate property rights, that unduly hamper free expression, association and assembly, and that contravene Israel's own Basic Laws.

As hearings proceeded following the outbreak of the second Palestinian intifada in 2000, the Supreme Court under former Chief Justice Aharon Barak suggested that the petition should be withdrawn given the exacerbated security situation. ACRI submitted an amended petition in 2003, which argued that even in a context of heightened threats to security the use of emergency powers should be minimal in time and scope, and that Israel's state of emergency declaration was still unfounded. The state's response (with the government of Israel now added to the Knesset as a respondent) claimed that repeal of the emergency would create a legal vacuum and deprive the authorities of the necessary means of suppressing threats to security. The government did emphasise its intention to move away from the (declared) state of emergency, and told the Court that it would continue to take steps to amend or replace legislation that is contingent on the existence of a formal emergency.

The Ministry of Justice provided the Court with ongoing notifications regarding the revocation and replacement of certain pieces of emergency legislation. The authorities presented the seemingly contradictory position that although a state of emergency continues to exist in fact, the state of emergency in law should be gradually phased out. What can be inferred from this is both a tacit acknowledgment that the factual situation does not justify the application of exceptional emergency legalities and, at the same time, a conflicting assumption that those exceptional legalities should be subsumed into the 'normal' legal order over time.

The Supreme Court essentially agreed that while the continuing state of emergency is not ideal, it is a necessary 'transitional' measure. Although acknowledging in regard to the legal framework that 'the present situation must not remain unchanged', the Court has consistently framed the issue as a 'complex and sensitive' one in which the authorities must be left with a generous margin of flexibility.[149] In an interim decision of August 2006, the Court rejected ACRI's claim that Israel's situation was not in fact one of an ongoing state of emergency: 'the war with terror is raging at full force, and it is impossible to disregard this'.[150] At the same time, the Court noted that 'the state of emergency has been exploited for statutory matters regarding which balanced legislation could have been enacted long ago'.[151] The Court gave the respondents time to institute changes to civil legislation that was tied to the state of emergency, and by 2011 was satisfied that:

> Progress has been made in the legislative processes. Part of the legislation that was contingent on the state of emergency was altered and amended, another part is in various stages of the legislative process, and there is an intent to regularise the remainder.[152]

Accordingly, in May 2012, after twelve hearings over the course of twelve years, the Court issued a twelve-page judgment (half of which comprises background information and summaries of the arguments) concluding that the petition had 'run its course' and should be dismissed.[153] Israel,

---

[149] *The Association for Civil Rights in Israel (ACRI)* v. *The Knesset and the Government of Israel*, HCJ 3091/99, judgment, 8 May 2012, paras. 7, 9, 11.
[150] *ACRI* v. *Israel*, interim decision, 1 August 2006.   [151] *Ibid.*
[152] *ACRI* v. *Israel*, interim decision, 7 December 2011.
[153] *ACRI* v. *Israel*, judgment, 8 May 2012, para. 11.

according to the Court, continued to face a state of emergency, with the judgment asserting that 'the winds of war have never ceased to blow, and unfortunately the situation remains relatively unchanged'.[154] Justice Rubinstein's opinion, on behalf of the Court, evokes Israel's siege mentality with lengthy descriptions of 'the unending threats of our enemies from near and far'. He quotes an extract from a ruling of the Court in the early 1980s – roughly the half-way point of Israel's state of emergency to date – from which it becomes clear that little had changed in the Court's approach over the intervening thirty years:

> As known, the state of emergency has lasted for over 30 years, and who knows how much longer it will continue. The fact that the state of emergency persists does, on the one hand, mandate the reduction of the emergency means the state employs to defend its existence so that, as much as possible, these means will not violate civil rights, but on the other hand, the continuing state of emergency, owing to well-known reasons and circumstances, points to the fact that it is difficult to compare the situation the State of Israel has been in since its foundation to that of any other state.[155]

Rubinstein maintains this narrative of Israeli exceptionalism in his depiction of a normal country (in that it is an 'active democracy in which fundamental rights ... are safeguarded') that is not normal (in that it is subject to threats of a gravity faced by no other 'normal' democratic country).[156] The gauntlet thrown down by this 'unique' situation thus challenges Israel to construct a juridical order that can respond to the exceptional threat without compromising the state's 'normality'. Rubinstein commends the state for its work to date in phasing out and replacing some emergency legislation, and highlights the need to continue extricating relevant security and anti-terrorism measures from a declared state of emergency; that is, to embed them instead within the 'normal' legal system. Before and until this process is complete, it is not the place of the judiciary, the argument goes, to obstruct executive or legislative renewals of the state of emergency, nor to restrict the use of necessary powers that remain dependent on the declared state of emergency. Here, the Supreme Court's accustomed deference to the security agencies is apparent: 'this court is not a substitute for the discretion of the authorised agencies'.[157]

---

[154] Ibid., para. 11. [155] Kahana v. The Minister of Defence, HCJ 1/80, PD 35(2), 253, 257.
[156] ACRI v. Israel, 8 May 2012, para. 19. [157] Ibid., para. 17.

A similar methodology to that deployed in British counter-terrorism law since the late 1990s (which I alluded to earlier in the book in the context of Hussain's diagnosis of 'hyperlegality' in the modern security state) can be detected in the process endorsed by Israel's Supreme Court. This seeks to construct a framework of permanent extraordinary measures in order to preserve the control system over the Palestinians, as opposed to properly disentangling the web of emergency powers spun over the last six decades. The concept of hyperlegality is echoed here in descriptions of 'Israel's military hyperregulation of everyday life [which] has been catastrophic for the Palestinians'.[158] The normalcy/emergency binary cedes part of the space of exception to a complementary paradigm in which the state of emergency is normalised in ordinary legislation[159] and bolstered by 'super-emergency' measures during large-scale hostilities.[160] The non-contingent emergency laws will of course remain in place even if the state does follow through on its promise to phase out the official state of emergency, and the fluidity of Israel's disparate emergency legal mechanisms will continue to offer a vehicle for the execution of sovereign prerogative.

This process of incorporating emergency powers into the ordinary legal system is underway and ongoing. In the summer of 2016, Israel's Knesset enacted the Anti-Terror Law 2016, an extensive piece of counterterrorism legislation that had been roundly criticised by human rights organisations from its early inception as a 'draconian' move designed 'to legally anchor the "state of emergency" regulations ... and turn them into permanent legislation'.[161] The law was advanced by Minister for Justice Ayelet Shaked, of the far-right Jewish Home party, as the enactment of her assertion that acts of – and support for – Palestinian violence 'can only be vanquished through appropriate punishment and deter-

---

[158] Saree Makdisi, *Palestine Inside Out: An Everyday Occupation* (New York: W.W. Norton & Co., 2008) 6.

[159] For example, parts of Israel's 1973 emergency regulations relating to naval vessels were simply renamed and consolidated in permanent legislation in the form of the Shipping Law (Foreign Naval Vessel Under Israeli Control) 2005 and the Shipping Law (Violations Against the Security of International Sailing and Maritime Facilities) 2008.

[160] Yuval Shany and Ido Rosenzweig, 'High Court of Justice Rejects Petition to End Israel's State of Emergency', 41 *Terrorism & Democracy* (May 2012), citing the 2008 Incarceration of Unlawful Combatants Law (Temporary Order and Amendment) enacted in anticipation of Operation Cast Lead.

[161] The Association for Civil Rights in Israel, 'Counter-Terrorism Bill: Undemocratic Emergency Regulations Could Become Permanent Law', 4 August 2011.

rence'.[162] This legislation applies specifically to Israel and occupied East Jerusalem, rather than the rest of the West Bank (where Palestinians remain governed by the separate military law system). It is an omnibus law that replaces a number of existing ordinances on terrorism and effectively re-imports a raft of provisions from the British Defence (Emergency) Regulations (which, as we have seen above, still apply in the occupied territories), as well as other temporary Israeli emergency/security regulations, into permanent Israeli criminal law. The legislation also introduces new crimes, including offences relating to public expressions of support or sympathy for groups designated as 'terrorist' organisations, and expands the definition of 'incitement' such that a link to any likely or actual act of violence is no longer necessary. Emergency style powers assigned to state authorities under the law include: sweeping arrest powers, detention without trial, use of secret evidence, suspension of habeas corpus, significantly increased criminal sentences, travel bans, control orders and computerised surveillance, as well as powers vested personally in the Minister of Defence to expropriate the homes and property of alleged members of banned organisations without requiring approval by the courts.

The law allows for a broad interpretation of what constitutes a 'terrorist' organisation (it bears noting that most Palestinian political movements are already designated as such by Israel), and expands the definition of indictable membership of such organisations to include 'passive members' who play no direct role in the organisation's activities. It casts the political activities and expression of Palestinians in Israel – including those of a social, humanitarian and charitable nature, particularly where they assist Palestinians in the occupied territories – as suspect and susceptible to prosecution. As such, the Anti-Terror Law appears designed to persecute Palestinian citizens – marking them out as suspect 'simply because they are Arab'[163] – and to suppress their political activities in support of Palestinians living under occupation.[164] The racial

---

[162] Quoted in Jonathan Lis, 'Knesset Passes Sweeping Anti-terrorism Law', *Ha'aretz*, 15 June 2016.

[163] Adalah, 'Israel's New Anti-Terror Law Violates Arab Citizens' Human Rights', 19 June 2016.

[164] Within 24 hours of the legislation passing parliamentary approval, Israel's Minister for Public Security, Strategic Affairs and Information, Gilad Erdan, stated that 'a price must be paid' by activists who support the Palestinian civil society call for boycott, divestment and sanctions (BDS) against Israel. Erdan said he has put together 'a legal team that is working with the Israeli Justice Ministry to ensure that there is a price for boycott',

overtones of the legislation are clear – both in itself, and within the context of the broader matrix of discriminatory law-making[165] of which it forms part. It is criticised on this basis by Palestinian and left-wing Israeli members of the Knesset as 'racist and totalitarian',[166] with Ayman Odeh (head of the 'Joint List', the alliance of the four predominantly Arab-Palestinian political parties in Israel) reading the law in its imperial context: 'I see panic, the panic of the final stage of all colonialism worldwide. The panic of the French at the end of the occupation of Algeria. I see the panic of the Americans in the final phase of the occupation of Vietnam'.[167]

Thus we return to the framing of the colonial present. Emergency modalities, as we have seen, have occupied a central place in the legal system of the colonised Palestinian space. Emergency doctrine's malleability and constructed exceptionality facilitates the forcible imposition of settler sovereignty, while its legality provides the necessary authorisation and veneer of legitimacy. It was, and is, an expression of law as a conduit for racialised hegemony, as the stage upon which scenes of dispossession are performed. The separate opinion of Chief Justice Beinisch in the Israeli Supreme Court decision on the state of emergency is candid in this regard: 'The state of emergency declared by law is, to a large extent, the result of a political outlook'.[168]

---

implying that this team would seek to find connections between BDS activism and support for terrorism. Michael Schaeffer Omer-Man, 'Senior Israeli Minister: Make BDS Activists in Israel "pay a price"', +972 Magazine, 16 June 2016.

[165] Following the 2009 elections in Israel and the formation of a series of increasingly right-wing coalition governments under Benjamin Netanyahu – spanning the 18th Knesset from 2009–2013, the 19th Knesset from 2013–2015, and the 20th Knesset from 2015 on – 'a flood of discriminatory legislation' was initiated which seek to dispossess and discriminate in various ways against Palestinian citizens of Israel. See Adalah's 'Discriminatory Law Database' at www.adalah.org/en/law/index, which by July 2016 had documented 76 pieces of Israeli legislation already in force or at different stages in the legislative process.

[166] Lahav Harkov, 'Terror Bill Passes into Law', The Jerusalem Post, 15 June 2016.

[167] 'Israel's Knesset Passes "Draconian" Anti-terrorism Law', Ma'an News, 15 June 2016.

[168] ACRI v. Israel, judgment, 8 May 2012, separate opinion of Chief Justice (Retired) D. Beinisch.

8

Australia

Racialised Emergency Intervention

In 1982, the Commonwealth Games – that sporting remnant of British empire – were held in Brisbane. The games were staged against a backdrop of ongoing Australian federal government and Queensland state suppression of Indigenous struggles for land rights, cultural preservation, and political and economic self-determination. Aboriginal and Torres Strait Islander peoples planned to use the spotlight of the event to expose discriminatory policy and legislation that denied them civil liberties and access to their native lands. In the build-up, they called for a boycott of the games – particularly by African nations – and sought to connect their movement to the sporting boycott of apartheid South Africa.[1] In advance of the games, the Queensland state government set out pre-emptive emergency measures, enacting specific statutory law to introduce new and extraordinary security powers. This legislation, the Commonwealth Games Act 1982,[2] was passed in May 1982 to come into effect in September 1982, a fortnight before the games commenced. It effectively instituted a state of emergency for a four-week period prior to and during the games, and was marked by 'its threats of severe punishment and its purpose to silence Aboriginal dissent during the period of the Games'.[3] The legislation endowed police officers with the authority to declare localised situations of emergency, and granted special powers of search, arrest and detention to the police. For the duration of the designated period of the games, protest was effectively prohibited, a restrictive permit system for demonstrations imposed, and the

---

[1] 'Renewed Attempts for Ban on Games', *Townsville Bulletin*, 24 February 1982; 'Aborigines Call for Boycott Support', *Townsville Bulletin*, 21 April 1982. Threats of such a boycott were ultimately averted by concessions granted by the Commonwealth Games Federation to its anti-apartheid caucus membership.

[2] Commonwealth Games Act, No. 27 of 1982, 'An Act to Facilitate the Holding of the XIIth Commonwealth Games and to Provide for the Orderly Conduct of Persons and for the Security of Per Security of Persons and Property During Those Games'.

[3] Ciaron O'Reilly, *The Revolution Will not be Televised!: A Campaign for Free Expression in Queensland (1982–1983)* (Sydney: Jura Books, 1986).

dissemination of political materials banned. Land was rezoned and access to certain areas was restricted.

A Black Protest Committee representing various delegations of Indigenous communities planned and coordinated non-violent actions around and inside the event stadium. Demonstrations and sit-ins featured placards and banners articulating demands for 'Black Control of Black Affairs' and 'Land Rights Now', and insisting that 'Racist Acts Must Go'. Posters asked spectators in Brisbane: 'If you knew about land rights, would you still enjoy the games?' Indigenous people from around Australia arrived to join the demonstrations, as well as international solidarity delegations including representatives from the Pan Africanist Congress. The directives from the protest coordinating committee were clear – for demonstrations to be peaceful and unified. Numerous marches and actions were held by Indigenous groups and their allies during the games. While non-violent, the demonstrations were staged without permits and culminated in a major protest towards the end of the games that was 'illegal' by dint of the emergency law rubric.[4] The police response under the emergency legislation was predictably heavy-handed, resulting in mass arrests of hundreds of people.[5] Earlier predictions that special security legislation for the Commonwealth Games would produce a 'police state' scenario in Queensland were said to have been borne out,[6] while Indigenous activists claimed some success in garnering international attention for their resistance to the continuing effects of settler colonialism on their lives and land.

While temporally contained to the period around the hosting of the Commonwealth Games, this episode gives an insight into the deployment of emergency measures as a technique of governmentality in the context of Australian racial sovereignty. It is an illustrative precursor to the deeper emergency that would be instituted 25 years later, with far more pervasive consequences for Indigenous communities.

The 'Intervention' in the Northern Territory

On 21 June 2007, Australia's federal government declared a state of emergency emanating from the country's Northern Territory, and

---

[4] Ross Peake, 'Land Rights Campaign has Emotional Finale', *The Australian* 8 October 1982.
[5] '400 Police Mop up a March', *Daily Sun*, 8 October 1982; '370 Charges Over March', *Townsville Bulletin*, 9 October 1982.
[6] '"Police State" Games Act', *Courier Mail*, 21 September 1981.

launched the Northern Territory Emergency Response intervention against Indigenous communities in that region. This came on the back of the publication of a local government-commissioned board of inquiry report into child abuse and issues of health, education and welfare, which the report situated in the context of a broader milieu of social disadvantage, deprivation and discrimination in the territory.[7] A cluster of legislation was tabled in the federal parliament and adopted with bipartisan support within weeks of the executive proclamation of the national emergency.[8] The stated purpose of 'the intervention', as it has come to be commonly described, was to address sexual abuse of children within Aboriginal communities. The Australian media had 'feasted on claims of "paedophile rings" and the assertion that traditional Indigenous culture actually condoned the rape of children under the guise of "customary law"'.[9]

The emergency was premised on an objective of 'normalising' Indigenous communities through exceptional treatment. It encompassed 73 prescribed areas of the Northern Territory – all of which comprise Indigenous people as the sole or predominant inhabitants – and all land subject to the Aboriginal Land Rights Act (Northern Territory) 1976. This affected approximately 45,500 Indigenous people in up to 500 communities, covering areas amounting to over 600,000 km^2 altogether.[10] The staging of the intervention included: the mobilisation and deployment of military troops into those communities; the displacement of parts of the population; the compulsory acquisition of land by the federal government through imposed rent-free leases over Aboriginal land and community living areas; the denial of compensation equivalent to that which non-Indigenous landholders would be

---

[7] Rex Wild and Patricia Anderson, *Ampe Akelyernemane Meke Mekarle: Little Children are Sacred*, Report of the Northern Territory Board of Inquiry into the Protection of Aboriginal Children from Sexual Abuse (June 2007).

[8] Northern Territory National Emergency Response Act 2007; Social Security and Other Legislation Amendment (Welfare Payment Reform) Act 2007; Families, Community Services and Indigenous Affairs and Other Legislation Amendment (Northern Territory National Emergency Response and Other Measures) Act 2007; Appropriation (Northern Territory National Emergency Response) Act (No. 1, 2007–2008) 2007; Appropriation (Northern Territory National Emergency Response) Act (No. 2, 2007–2008) 2007. These five statutes, amounting to 480 pages of complex legislation, were tabled and passed without amendment by the House of Representatives in a single day.

[9] Carmen Lawrence, 'The "Emergency Intervention" in Northern Territory Indigenous Communities' (2008) 7 *The New Critic*.

[10] Northern Territory Emergency Response Review Board Report, October 2008.

entitled for compulsory acquisition; the suspension of the permit system regulating external access to Indigenous territory; the quarantine of welfare payments to Indigenous recipients for designated 'essential' expenses only; and the dismantling of community development employment schemes.[11] It also involved the creation of ministerial prerogative to 'suspend all the members of a community government council'.[12] Thalia Anthony explains how the emergency intervention amounted to a mechanism for the federal and regional governments to tap into an 'anxiety about unfinished colonialism' in the Northern Territory and to deepen external control over Indigenous communities there by installing 'Government Business Managers' and 'Government Shires' to replace the local community councils.[13] In addition, the intervention exemplifies state governance and disciplining of Indigenous Australians though criminalisation and increasing levels of incarceration. It involved a series of measures aimed at preventing Aboriginal indulgence in 'excess', including 'a total ban on the possession and consumption of alcohol, compulsory income management for all welfare recipients (ration cards), compulsory installation of anti-pornography filters on all public computers as well as obligatory record-keeping of all computer users [and] the federal government takeover of local services and community stores'.[14] The emergency legislation also banned courts in the Northern Territory from taking 'any form of customary law or cultural practice into account' on certain questions,[15] on the basis of a perception that sexual abuse was being systematically whitewashed by customary law norms or defences. This was notwithstanding the fact that the board of inquiry report itself had debunked such a perception as baseless: 'The Inquiry was unable to find any case where Aboriginal law has been used and accepted as a

[11] Chloe Cameron, 'Recognising Human Rights in Australia's Third World: A Critical Analysis of the Displacement and Dispossession Caused by the Federal Government's Northern Territory Emergency Response' (2011) 4:2 *Queensland Law Student Review* 71.
[12] Northern Territory National Emergency Response Act 2007, No. 129 of 2007, s.78.
[13] Thalia Anthony, *Indigenous People, Crime and Punishment* (Abingdon: Routledge, 2013) 108.
[14] Sarah Keenan, 'Australian Government Asked to Leave Aboriginal Community', *Critical Legal Thinking*, 5 September 2012. See further Families, Community Services and Indigenous Affairs and Other Legislation Amendment (Northern Territory National Emergency Response and Other Measures) Act 2007, No. 128 of 2007; Northern Territory National Emergency Response Act 2007, No. 129 of 2007.
[15] Northern Territory National Emergency Response Act 2007, No. 129 of 2007, s.90–91.

defence (in that it would exonerate an accused from any criminal responsibility) for an offence of violence against a woman or a child.'[16]

This is revealing of the broader disconnect between the report's findings and the emergency legislation professing to flow from them by way of legal response and policy action. The declaration of a national emergency itself and the imposition of federal intervention measures were in direct conflict with the approach advocated by the report – one of coordinated federal and provincial government action undertaken through dialogue with the affected communities. The board of inquiry report in no way suggested that an intervention involving military forces might be appropriate. While the report did make a total of 97 recommendations, and while the Chief Minister of the Northern Territory had stated that the territorial government was committed to implementing each and every one of those recommendations,[17] 'one of the first things that became apparent was that the intervention strategy made no reference to the *Little Children are Sacred* report on which it purported to rely. It has followed none of its recommendations'.[18] The authors of the report themselves publicly criticised the intervention from very early in its implementation, saying they felt '"betrayed, disappointed, hurt, appalled, angry, all at the same time" as the intervention unfolded in a manner completely at odds with the report's 97 carefully wrought recommendations'.[19] Chief among these recommendations was the primacy of consultation, and the participation of Indigenous communities themselves in responding to prevailing social problems. No such consultation was undertaken. The emergency intervention instead assumed a distinctly vertical form. A statement by Aboriginal elders emphasised this clearly: 'As people in our own land, we are shocked by the failure of democratic processes, of the failure to consult with us and of the total disregard for us as

---

[16] Wild and Anderson, *Ampe Akelyernemane Meke Mekarle*, 58. The inquiry report also debunked a number of other related 'myths' around Aboriginal law and culture, at 57–59.

[17] Clare Martin, Press Statement (untitled) of the Northern Territory Chief Minister, 15 June 2007.

[18] Larissa Behrendt, 'The Emergency We Had to Have', in Jon Altman and Melinda Hinkson (eds.), *Coercive Reconciliation: Stabilise, Normalise, Exit Aboriginal Australia* (Melbourne: Arena, 2007) 15.

[19] Rebecca Stringer, 'A Nightmare of the Neocolonial Kind: Politics of Suffering in Howard's Northern Territory Intervention' (2007) 6:2 *Borderlands*, para. 5, quoting Pat Anderson in Murray McLaughlin, 'Intervention Plan meets Hostility from Indigenous Leaders', *Australian Broadcasting Corporation*, 6 August 2007).

human beings.'[20] Others portrayed the role of white Australians working on Indigenous policy affairs in similarly stark terms: 'They fly in, squawk a lot, shit on you and then fly out again'.[21]

The board of inquiry report had made clear that there was 'nothing new or extraordinary in the allegations of sexual abuse of Aboriginal children in the Northern Territory'.[22] To emphasise this is not to undermine or belittle the gravity of the issues in this context, but rather to highlight the Australian state's failure to engage with them as structural problems. In place of such engagement, Aboriginal communities are portrayed as 'generically (and, by inference, "genetically") "dysfunctional" spaces where rampant and out-of-control bestial sexual transgression was the norm rather than an exception, despite statistical evidence ... to the contrary'.[23] The increased powers of surveillance and arrest under the emergency failed to unearth any concrete evidence that rates of child sex abuse in the Northern Territory were much different to elsewhere in Australia.[24] Invasive disciplining and corrective emergency measures did not lead to the expected raft of convictions. Analysis conducted by the federal government's own Department of Health during the intervention returned statistics which showed that of a total of 7,433 Indigenous children examined by government doctors and health workers in the Northern Territory, just 39 were found to be at risk of neglect or abuse, of whom a maximum of four were suspected sexual abuse victims.[25]

With regard to the much-touted 'paedophile rings', the Australian Crime Commission concluded an 18-month investigation with the finding that there was no organised paedophilia in Indigenous communities.[26] In contrast to government representations of culturally endemic sexual abuse of minors in Aboriginal society, a series of policing and intelligence taskforces returned no evidence of such practice; the upshot instead under the emergency measures was an increase in the prosecution of consensual relationships involving Indigenous teenagers

[20] Rosalie Kunoth-Monks et al., 'To the People of Australia', 7 February 2011.
[21] Quoted in Hanna Sandgren, 'White People in Indigenous Affairs: A Conservator's Perspective', *Demos Journal*, 21 June 2016.
[22] Wild and Anderson, *Ampe Akelyernemane Meke Mekarle*, 5.
[23] Deirdre Tedmanson and Dinesh Wadiwel, 'Neoptolemus: The Governmentality of New Race/Pleasure Wars' (2010) 16:1 *Culture and Organization* 7, 15.
[24] Keenan, 'Australian Government Asked to Leave Aboriginal Community'.
[25] 'Indigenous Child Abuse in New Light', *The Courier-Mail*, 25 May 2008.
[26] Nick McKenzie, 'Pedophile Ring Claims Unfounded', *The Age*, 5 July 2009.

and young adults (stemming from a form of settler moral panic over under-age sex in customary marriage).[27] It is also apparent that the Australian government fundamentally failed to grasp and contextualise the nature of abuse and neglect in their implementation of the intervention.[28] The impact of the emergency measures was socially regressive. Government statistics three years into the intervention showed Indigenous incarceration rates to have risen by 30 per cent,[29] employment programmes closed down, higher unemployment, school attendance rates dropping, and increases in suicide and self-harm.[30]

In 2012, the 'emergency response' was succeeded, in name at least, by a 'stronger futures' policy. On the same day that the five-year sunset clause of the 2007 legislation kicked in, the Stronger Futures in the Northern Territory Act 2012 came into force.[31] In the face of strong popular resistance and grass-roots campaigns against the Stronger Futures legislation, both the main government and opposition parties in parliament voted to adopt it into law for a designated period of ten years. This legislation, although rhetorically framed as less drastic, retains key elements of the Northern Territory Emergency Response Act and 'ensures the continuation of most of the measures begun under the 2007 Act'[32] through to at least 2022. It also reinforced the proscription on courts taking cultural practice or customary law into consideration, removed a respondent's right to silence, extended the restrictions on internet usage, heightened the penalties on social security payments to include 13-week deduction periods for parents and carers whose children fail to fulfil school attendance criteria, and introduced harsher punishments for alcohol offences (including up to 6 months in prison for unlawful possession of a single can of beer, along with a relatively discounted term

---

[27] Anthony, *Indigenous People, Crime and Punishment*, 109, citing by way of example *The Queen v. Aiden Kelly* [2010]; *A v. The Queen* [2010]; *The Queen v. Tewedy Maxwell* [2011].

[28] Kyllie Cripps, 'Indigenous Family Violence: From Emergency Measures to Committed Long-Term Action' (2007) 11:2 *Australian Indigenous Law Review* 6.

[29] *Northern Territory Quarterly Crime and Justice Statistics*, Issue 21 (September 2007) and Issue 32 (June 2010).

[30] Australian Government Department of Social Services, 'Closing the Gap in the Northern Territory: Monitoring Report', June 2010; Stop the Intervention, 'Rebuilding from the Ground Up: An Alternative to the Northern Territory Intervention'.

[31] Along with two other pieces of legislation in the Stronger Futures package: the Social Security Legislation Amendment Act 2012, and the Stronger Futures in the Northern Territory (Consequential and Transitional Provisions) Act 2012.

[32] Keenan, 'Australian Government Asked to Leave Aboriginal Community'.

of 18 months for six cans). In light of this, it is claimed that the Stronger Futures avatar of the intervention retains its racial effects and amounts to 'covert assimilation reinvigorating historical traumas of paternalistic control, dispossession and attempted cultural genocide'.[33] In elongating and consolidating the application of the original emergency measures, the Stronger Futures legislation is also in many respects exemplary of the type of 'hyperlegality' that we see reproduced in so many extended emergency or post-emergency contexts.

Traces of Racial History

I refer to the Northern Territory emergency – whose introduction in 2007 failed to register prominently on the radar of international discourse at a time when Bush and Blair's security crusade continued to preoccupy the space of critical analysis – as demonstrative of the continued centrality of race to states of emergency. With the intervention stemming from a situation of social problems and cultural tensions rather than militarised political conflict, there is no state security crutch for the authorities to lean on. Expansive meaning is nonetheless given to the term 'national emergency', in this case amounting to something far more limited in substantive and geographical scope than an existential threat to the life of the (settler) nation. The narratives constructed and justifications proffered by the state for its invasive measures ring hollow in the settler colonial context, as does international law's ode to non-discrimination. Emergency powers deployed in this context are both constitutive and symptomatic of a deep-seated institutionalisation of difference on racial terms.

Over the past two and a half centuries, the story of native/settler relations in Australia is one of territory taken, title extinguished and generations stolen. These are the traces of history that underpin the structure of settler colonial invasion and the racialisation of Indigenous people.[34] While Aboriginal society is constituted on the basis of a historical, territorial and cultural uniqueness that transcends any purported biological categorisation, it was through the language of race that

---

[33] Cera Godinez, 'Stronger Futures?' in Cristy Clark (ed.), *The Politics of Human Rights in Australia: Law Under the Spotlight* (Southern Cross University, 2015) 123–124.

[34] Wolfe, *Traces of History*, 31–60, examining the development of these processes with reference to key legal instruments including the Aborigines Protection Act 1869 and the Aborigines Protection Act (Vic) 1886.

the dynamic of difference cast Aboriginal people as inferior and allowed for their subjugation by force (as part of the primary colonial project of resource exploitation and capital accumulation). In the post-frontier era of colonisation, acts of physical extermination gave way to a more permanent strategy of removal, confinement and assimilation. The settler's law functioned as a facilitator and legitimator of these processes. Aboriginal writer, lawyer and scholar Nicole Watson shows how 'the law facilitated the regulation of a population stigmatised as lacking acceptable social norms. Australian Parliaments have a long tradition of enacting legislation for the purpose of coercing behavioural change in Aboriginal people. It is often preceded by a moral panic buttressed by racist mythology'.[35] The role of law here is ongoing insofar as settler conquest remains a continuing project, and the use of emergency management techniques typically surface at its sharper edges to reinforce and entrench settler sovereignty.

This story of white Australia's racial history (not only in relation to the land's original people, but also 'alien races' in the form of Asian or African migrant settlers and workers[36]) continues to be animated in the words of its Constitution. Section 51(xxvi) reflects nineteenth-century thinking on race in providing Parliament with the power to pass discriminatory laws relating to 'the people of any race for whom it is deemed necessary to make special laws'. A constitutional referendum in 1967 removed the explicit exclusion of 'the aboriginal race' from the state's legislative jurisdiction under Section 51(xxvi). The liberal assumption was that this would pertain to affirmative discrimination for the benefit of Indigenous people in fields where they required special protection or support. The trend of post-1967 High Court jurisprudence in relation to Section 51(xxvi), however, gravitated in a direction whereby the so-called 'race power' can be used to discriminate in either direction: positive measures for the benefit of a racial group; but also negative discrimination, including against Indigenous peoples, 'to regulate and control the people of any race in the event that they constitute a threat or problem to the general community'.[37]

---

[35] Nicole Watson, 'The Northern Territory Emergency Response: The More Things Change, the More They Stay the Same' (2011) 48:4 *Alberta Law Review* 905, 906.

[36] On the coordinated and complementary nature of the white Australia project historically including Aboriginal people through assimilation policies and excluding non-white foreigners through immigration and deportation policies, see Wolfe, *Traces of History*, 55-56.

[37] *Commonwealth v. Tasmania* ['*Tasmanian Dam Case*'] (1983) 158 CLR 1, 158. See further, for example, Sarah Pritchard, 'The Race Power in Section 51[xxvi] of the Constitution' (2011) 15:2 *Australian Indigenous Law Review* 44, 49-50.

The 1967 referendum also decided to repeal Section 127 of the Constitution, which had stated that 'aboriginal natives shall not be counted' among the people of the Australian commonwealth. With the deletion of Section 127, Indigenous people were henceforth to be included as part of the Australian population. While looking like a progressive inclusion in that sense, this was – again – symptomatic of a repressive, controlling and assimilationist inclusion. The idea of assimilation was articulated clearly in 1961 by Australia's Minister for Territories (a distinctly colonial ministerial portfolio with responsibility externally for Papua New Guinea and internally for the Northern Territory), Paul Hasluck:

> The policy of assimilation means in the view of all Australian governments that all Aborigines and part-Aborigines are expected eventually to attain the same manner of living as other Australians and to live as members of a single Australian community enjoying the same rights and privileges, accepting the same responsibilities, observing the same customs and influenced by the same beliefs, hopes, loyalties as other Australians.[38]

The purpose of this assimilation and inclusion was to create a uniform (white) Australian culture and polity by the dissolution of native life into settler society. It is a comprehensive process of cultural, spatial and biological assimilation to 'normalise' Aboriginal societies and economies, and to excise Indigenous claims to self-determination, sovereignty or treaty-making capacities. Colonial development policy relies on a 'perpetual recognition and disavowal of difference' in this sense.[39] Through the emergency intervention policies, we see how an understanding of difference as 'otherness' which lies at the heart of colonial control and assimilation[40] continues to undergird settler-Indigenous relations in Australia generally, and the federal state's approach to Aboriginal communities in the Northern Territory specifically. The emergency marks a stark neo-paternalistic continuation of past iterations of assimilation and their failed civilising missions.[41] All the while, the Australian Constitution

---

[38] Hansard, Commonwealth Parliamentary Debates, House of Representatives, 20 April 1961, 1051.

[39] Arturo Escobar, *Encountering Development: The Making and Unmaking of the Third World* (Princeton, Princeton University Press, 1995) 54.

[40] Odette Mazel, 'Development in the "First World": Alleviating Indigenous Disadvantage in Australia – the Dilemma of Difference' (2009) 18:2 *Griffith Law Review* 475.

[41] JC Altman, 'The Howard Government's Northern Territory Intervention: Are Neo-Paternalism and Indigenous Development Compatible?' (2007) *Centre for Aboriginal*

'remains a relic of institutionalised racism'.[42] It contains no entrenched non-discrimination clause and retains a parliamentary 'race power' that allows for (positive or negative) legislative measures based on racial difference. The result is that equality legislation can be suspended at the sovereign's whim, which – as we will see – was the case in the Northern Territory emergency.

Whereas the board of inquiry report had stressed that any action taken should be locally rather than centrally controlled, the Prime Minister at the time, John Howard, displayed no reticence in acknowledging that the federal government's action was 'highly interventionist [and] represents a sweeping assumption of power', comprising 'exceptional measures to deal with an exceptionally tragic situation'.[43] Through the narrative constructed around its release, more than its actual content, the report 'had provided a strategic moment in which decisive intervention could be made [which] relied heavily on rhetorical tactics and linguistic devices to construct a state of emergency in the minds of the Australian populace'.[44] Howard framed the Indigenous communities 'in our rich and beautiful country' as mired in a primitive state of nature, their children 'living out a Hobbesian nightmare of violence, abuse and neglect'.[45] To recognise life in the Northern Territory as such, evocative of an uncivilised existence, is, Howard claimed, 'not racist. It's simply an empirical fact'.[46] The burden of the civilising mission makes itself vividly clear in his pronouncement that 'without urgent action to restore social order, the nightmare will go on – more grog, more violence, more pornography and more sexual abuse – as the generation we're supposed to save sinks further into the abyss'.[47]

Economic Policy Research 16/2007, 1. See also Peter Sutton, *The Politics of Suffering: Indigenous Australia and the End of the Liberal Consensus* (Melbourne: Melbourne University Press, 2009) 27, 30, describing the emergency intervention as 'punitive and paternalist ... informed by the ethnocentricity of earlier colonial policies'.

[42] Shireen Morris, 'Indigenous Constitutional Recognition, Non-Discrimination and Equality Before The Law: Why Reform is Necessary' (2011) 7:26 *Indigenous Law Bulletin* 7, 7.

[43] John Howard, 'To Stabilise and Protect' (Address to the Sydney Institute, 25 June 2007) (2007) 19:3 *The Sydney Papers* 68.

[44] Deirdre Howard-Wagner, 'From Denial to Emergency: Governing Indigenous Communities in Australia' in Didier Fassin and Mariella Pandolfi (eds.), *Contemporary States of Emergency: The Politics of Military and Humanitarian Interventions* (New York: Zone Books, 2010) 217–218.

[45] Howard, 'To Stabilise and Protect'.   [46] *Ibid.*

[47] *Ibid.* It has been noted that '[t]he question of race was always problematic for John Howard's vision of Australia. When in Opposition, he was silent on the question of apartheid in South Africa and in the late 1980s he was insistent that Chinese immigration

Despite Howard's rhetorical flourishes positing a 'colour blind' society, the intervention amounted to one of the most overtly racialised deployments of emergency powers in recent times. Australia's Racial Discrimination Act 1975 (the domestic incorporation of Australia's obligations under the International Convention on the Elimination of all forms of Racial Discrimination, which also sought to address some of the anomalies remaining after the 1967 referendum) was suspended in Northern Territory Aboriginal communities. The emergency legislation provided that measures taken as part of the intervention were excluded from the operation of Part II of the Racial Discrimination Act (its prohibition on racial discrimination). This was in recognition of the reality that the emergency legislation was prima facie discriminatory in targeting a particular racial group, and thus to enact the legislation the federal government needed to put its national anti-racism legal principles into abeyance. Again, such an approach was not envisaged in any way in the original board of inquiry report. The suspension of the Racial Discrimination Act was effected in a bid to immunise the emergency legislation from legal challenge on the basis of its racial nature. Otherwise, the manner in which the compulsory acquisition of land, the usurping of local community administration, the management of income and the restrictions on alcohol and computer usage only applied to Aboriginal communities on the basis of race may have been legally contestable:

> The provisions of the NTER [Northern Territory Emergency Response] legislation were targeted directly at Indigenous people. As a result, they were clearly open to challenge as being racially discriminatory. By suspending (excluding) the operation of Part II of the RDA, the members of the communities affected by the NTER legislation were effectively denied the protections afforded by the RDA to every other citizen to challenge legislation that they consider to be in breach of the RDA.[48]

to Australia was unsettling and should be significantly reduced.' Drew Cottle and Dawn Bolger, 'John Howard and the Race Question', paper presented to the Australian Political Studies Association Conference, 6–9 July 2008. While Howard is identified here on the basis that he was leading the government at the time the emergency intervention was sanctioned, it must be noted that the mainstream political class was in unison on the necessity of the emergency measures. The intervention was continued under the Labour government that assumed power in 2008, contrary to advice returned from its own independent review on the matter.

[48] Australian Human Rights Commission, 'The Suspension and Reinstatement of the RDA and the Special Measures in the NTER' (Sydney, November 2011) 6.

The intervention measures were also designated as 'special measures' for the purposes of section 8 of the Racial Discrimination Act, which provides the only permissible grounds under the legislation for differential treatment on the basis of race. Defining a policy or practice as a special measure allows for possible discrimination, but only in the sense of 'positive' discrimination or 'affirmative action'. This is understood as applying to proactive policies designed to advance the rights of vulnerable or oppressed groups by redressing historical disadvantage and conferring conditions that are amenable to the realisation of their rights.[49] To be justified, special measures must be necessary to ensure equality where structural exclusion or exploitation has pertained. The measures should be temporary, and be based on prior consultation with affected communities.[50] This paradigm of 'positive' discrimination and participative consultation was far from the reality of the Northern Territory emergency, yet the intervention was framed under the rubric of exempted special measures and this was not in contravention of the prevailing interpretation of the constitutional 'race power'. Research has found the overarching societal consensus on this to be clearly opposed to the Australian government position and by extension aligned with arguments contesting the idea of the emergency intervention as a legitimate special measure, even if it was constituted as a lawful one.[51] Aboriginal elder (and Australian Social Justice Commissioner at the time) Tom Calma argued that suspending the prohibition on racial discrimination and removing basic democratic protections could in no circumstances be justified as necessary or appropriate for the purposes of child protection.[52]

The emergency effectively amounted to the (not unconstitutional) bipartisan passing of racist legislation through Australia's national parliament. Watson argues that 'history remains a powerful influence, resulting in the NTER being based on assumptions of Aboriginal people that are grounded in a racist past'.[53] The effect of the emergency

---

[49] Article 1(4), International Convention on the Elimination of all forms of Racial Discrimination; *Gerhardy v. Brown* (1985) 159 CLR 70 (High Court of Australia).

[50] UN Committee on the Elimination of Racial Discrimination, General Recommendation No. 32, CERD/C/GC/32, 24 September 2009, para. 18.

[51] Cosima Hay McRae, 'Suspending the Racial Discrimination Act, 1975 (Cth): Domestic and International Dimensions' (2012) 13 *Journal of Indigenous Policy* 61, 74.

[52] Tom Calma, 'Indigenous Rights: The Debate over a Charter of Rights' (2008) 33:2 *Alternative Law Journal* 105.

[53] Watson, 'The Northern Territory Emergency Response', 905. See also Nicole Watson and Pat Turner, 'The Trojan Horse' in Jon Altman and Melinda Hinkson (eds.), *Coercive Reconciliation: Stabilise, Normalise, Exit Aboriginal Australia* (Melbourne: Arena, 2007); Nicole Watson, 'Regulating Alcohol: One Step Forward, Two Steps Back?' (2009) 7:11

measures was to nullify the concept of racial equality, and remove – from Indigenous people specifically – any avenues of redress available via the complaint mechanism at the Australian Human Rights Commission. These special measures and exemptions instituted by law heralded, in effect, a derogation from the normative prohibition of institutionalised racial discrimination. The United Nations Special Rapporteur on the situation of human rights and fundamental freedoms of Indigenous people, James Anaya, found aspects of the emergency response to be racially discriminatory.[54] In response, opposition leader Tony Abbott, who would subsequently become Australia's Prime Minister, advised Anaya to stop listening 'to the old victim brigade'[55] and argued that 'sanctimonious nonsense' about rights was not an appropriate response to 'the drunken squalor and dysfunction which characterised these communities before the intervention'.[56]

After much pressure, and after missing a self-imposed deadline in 2009, the government moved to reinstate the Racial Discrimination Act in Northern Territory Aboriginal communities from the end of 2010, through a Welfare Reform Act.[57] This was a partial and somewhat contingent reinstatement, however. While the provision in the 2007 emergency legislation that suspended the application of the Racial Discrimination Act was removed, this would not terminate other provisions elsewhere in the legislation which were racially discriminatory in practice and which would continue to apply. The 2010 amendments did 'not bring an immediate end to all intervention measures that were racially targeted' and excluded pre-existing discriminatory intervention actions from the scope of the reinstated Racial Discrimination Act.[58]

Indigenous Law Bulletin 27; Nicole Watson, 'Of course it wouldn't be done in Dickson! Why Howard's Battlers Disengaged from the Northern Territory Emergency Response' (2009) 8:1 *Borderlands*; Nicole Watson, 'The Northern Territory Emergency Response: Has it Really Improved the Lives of Aboriginal Women and Children?' (2011) 35:1 *Australian Feminist Law Journal* 147.

[54] James Anaya, 'Report of the Special Rapporteur on the Situation of Human Rights and Fundamental Freedoms of Indigenous People', UN Doc. A/HRC/15, 4 March 2010, Appendix B: Observations on the Northern Territory Emergency Response in Australia.

[55] Quoted in Kirrin McKechnie, 'UN Labels Intervention Racist', *Australian Broadcasting Commission*, 27 August 2009.

[56] Quoted in Piers Akerman, 'A Future Free of UN Meddling', *The Sunday Telegraph*, 30 August 2009.

[57] Social Security and Other Legislation Amendment (Welfare Reform and Reinstatement of Racial Discrimination Act) Act 2010.

[58] Australian Human Rights Commission, 'The Suspension and Reinstatement of the RDA', 3, 11.

The government's concerted refusal to include a 'notwithstanding clause' in the amending legislation (to state that the Racial Discrimination Act would prevail, notwithstanding any provisions to its contrary in the Northern Territory Emergency Response legislation) meant that in the case of a clash between the Racial Discrimination Act and any provisions of the amended emergency response legislation, the latter (more recent) provisions would override the former.

Under the 2010 amendments, some special measures were redesigned, but not repealed. They were no longer to be defined as special measures in blanket terms, but the special measures provisions were replaced with 'objects clauses' designed to allow special measures to be implemented in certain circumstances for 'particular purposes'. In this way, compulsory leases of Indigenous land, alcohol restrictions, community store licensing and other facets of the emergency were continued. The disingenuousness of this move on the part of the state – in framing land expropriation as positive discrimination, for example – was clear: 'changes to the compulsory 5 year lease arrangements do not change this directly negative discrimination into a benign special measure'.[59] Although the Racial Discrimination Act was formally reinstated – and although that Act prohibits non-consensual land management or expropriation – the compulsory acquisition of Aboriginal land was able to continue under the emergency intervention provision which allowed the Commonwealth to obtain five-year leases of land in Northern Territory Indigenous communities without consent[60] and under the guise of special measures. Aboriginals still had no legal avenue to contest these emergency measures, and the rationale of the emergency intervention prevailed even after its explicitly racial complexion was covered over.

The other significant state manouevre in the context of the 'reinstatement' of the Racial Discrimination Act was the repackaging, and extension, of compulsory income management as non-discriminatory. Income management provisions were no longer to be characterised as special measures confined to Northern Territory Indigenous society on the basis of race, and instead were to be applied to non-Indigenous welfare recipients in the Northern Territory as well as to both Indigenous and non-Indigenous people in socially disadvantaged areas in other parts of Australia. This would apply particularly to those defined as 'disengaged

[59] Amnesty International, 'Statement to the Senate Standing Committee on Community Affairs: Reinstating the RDA in the NTER Legislation', 11 February 2010.
[60] Section 31(1)(a) of the Northern Territory National Emergency Response Act 2007.

youth' and 'long-term welfare recipients'. On the face of it, the localised and racially contingent policy was converted into a nation-wide and 'race-neutral' (although arguably ageist and classist) policy. There was widespread opposition to this, with demands that the partial restoration of the Racial Discrimination Act in the Northern Territory 'should not be traded off against extension of Income Management to communities across Australia'.[61] Aboriginal groups warned in advance of the high likelihood that this extension would impact disproportionately on Indigenous Australians and that implementation of the measures would continue in a de facto racialised fashion. Initial data bore this out, with the breakdown of those subjected to compulsory income management in the Northern Territory after the reinstatement of the Racial Discrimination Act showing that 87 per cent of those subjected to the measures were still Indigenous people (although they only make up approximately 30 per cent of the territory's population), while in parts of Western Australia and Queensland that figure was as high as 97 per cent.[62]

It is clear that, overall, the 2010 reforms did not amount to a full or unconditional reinstatement of the Racial Discrimination Act. The racialised nature of the emergency continued, albeit less overtly. That a twenty-first-century liberal democratic state would formally suspend its prohibition of institutionalised racism in the first place may appear remarkable, but it is a product of the long tradition of racialised emergency governance in settler colonial contexts. In the intervention's land policies in particular, we can see emergency governance as part of the ongoing dispossession and subjugation that settler colonialism entails. Part of the strategy of this dispossession of native peoples is the 'logic of elimination'[63] by assimilation. Historically, 'Black people in Australia have been subjected to a set of inclusive discourses intended to bring about their assimilation into White Australian society'.[64] The state of emergency operates to intensify the inclusion of the colonised into the settler sovereign's law, as part of the continuing process of settler state formation and preservation.

[61] Australian Council of Social Services, 'Compulsory Income Management: A Flawed Answer to a Complex Issue' (June 2010) 12.

[62] Luke Buckmaster, 'Income management and the Racial Discrimination Act', *Parliamentary Library Research Publications*, 28 May 2012.

[63] Patrick Wolfe, 'Settler Colonialism and the Elimination of the Native' (2006) 8:4 *Journal of Genocide Research* 387.

[64] Wolfe, *Traces of History*, 30.

Law, Land and Settler Sovereignty

Given the misleading premise upon which the Northern Territory emergency was initiated in 2007, clear alternative motives underpinning the intervention come to the surface. Most significant among them is the contention advanced by Aboriginal leaders that 'this government is using child sexual abuse as the Trojan horse to resume total control of our lands'.[65] In a territory with vast untapped mining potential, this points to a reverberation of colonisation. It evokes the 'possessive logic of patriarchal white sovereignty',[66] a vestige of the eighteenth-century imposition of British sovereignty in Australia under the aegis of settlement and *terra nullius*, whereby any analogous sovereign agency of Australia's Indigenous peoples was disavowed. Power dynamics rooted in this encounter have pervaded the country's land policies and cultural interactions since then, and are mirrored in the situation created by the emergency intervention. The work of Watson and others from before the intervention shows the expropriation policies as an ongoing structural process pre-dating the 2007 state of emergency.[67] In this light, the emergency intervention can be seen as continuation rather than rupture. It heralded the escalation of a brand of forced assimilation that has assumed a neoliberal form in seeking to overhaul the existing social order, dismantle the welfare apparatus and absorb Indigenous communities deeper into Australia's market economy. Proponents of such transformations advocate a shift away the communal nature of Aboriginal land title on the basis that its inalienability produces 'dead capital' and obstructs efficient entrepreneurial participation in the economy by Indigenous communities.[68] Mal Brough, the Australian government minister with responsibility for Indigenous affairs who presided over

---

[65] Pat Turner, former head of the (now defunct) Aboriginal and Torres Strait Islander Commission, quoted in Stringer, 'A Nightmare of the Neocolonial Kind'.

[66] Jillian Kramer, 'Protecting White Australia: John Howard's Announcement of the Northern Territory Emergency Response and the Ongoing Colonial Project' (2012) 5 *NEO: Journal for Higher Degree Research in the Social Sciences and Humanities*; Aileen Moreton-Robinson, 'The Possessive Logic of Patriarchal White Sovereignty: The High Court and the Yorta Yorta Decision' (2004) 3:2 *Borderlands* 1.

[67] See, for example, Nicole Watson, 'Howard's End: The Real Agenda Behind the Proposed Review of Indigenous Land Titles' (2005) 9:4 *Australian Indigenous Law Review* 1.

[68] See, for example, Noel Pearson, 'White Guilt, Victimhood and the Quest for a Radical Centre' (2007) 16 *Griffith Review* 11; Noel Pearson and Lara Kostakidis-Lianos 'Building Indigenous Capital: Removing Obstacles to Participation in the Real Economy' (2004) 2:3 *Australian Prospect*; Hernando de Soto, *The Mystery of Capital: Why Capitalism Triumphs in the West and Fails Everywhere Else* (New York: Basic Books, 2000).

the initiation of the intervention in 2007, had made his position in this regard clear when he stated in parliament that Australia's Indigenous people were living in 'little communist enclaves' which revealed the retrograde nature of their economy.[69] The idea of compulsory acquisition and the leasing back of land to members of Indigenous communities – with the right to sell or mortgage the lease – is consistent with the aim of rendering the land a productive asset capable of generating wealth through the credit/debt-based market economy. The legal effect of the intervention's leases is the supplanting of traditional Aboriginal community control of their land with government management. With this, federal entities can deal with the land in Indigenous areas as they see fit, including the granting of sub-leases to commercial enterprises for a wide range of purposes.[70]

In presenting the grounds for the emergency intervention in 2007, John Howard had made repeated references to the need to protect children. Yet the words 'child' and 'children' do not appear once in the emergency response legislation. By contrast, the word 'land' appears 891 times in the Northern Territory National Emergency Response Act 2007 alone. Indigenous communities have seen the intervention as mode of land grab to facilitate mining access to Aboriginal land. The fact that such lengthy and complex legislation was drafted in a very short time period between the publication of the board of inquiry report and the initiation of the intervention – and that over the course of Howard's prior eleven years in office there had been other inquiries into child abuse that garnered no follow-up action – fostered immediate mistrust among Aboriginal communities.[71] For those communities, measures like the compulsory acquisition leases 'seemed to be addressing old agendas; they looked like anti-land rights obsessions masquerading as help and depended for their passage through the Parliament on the threat that those who dared oppose them would be outed as "Friends of

---

[69] Hansard, Commonwealth Parliamentary Debates, House of Representatives, 19 June 2006, 31.

[70] Kirsty Howey, '"Normalising" What? A Qualitative Analysis of Aboriginal Land Tenure Reform in the Northern Territory' (2014) 18:1 *Australian Indigenous Law Review* 4, 18. For an argument that the leases acquired by the government are not primarily about exclusive long-term possession of the land, but more so about the time and space of belonging that property produces and deploys as a tool of governance, see Sarah Keenan, 'Property as Governance: Time, Space and Belonging in Australia's Northern Territory Intervention' (2013) 76:3 *Modern Law Review* 464.

[71] Creative Spirits, 'Northern Territory Emergency Response (NTER) - "The Intervention"', www.creativespirits.info/aboriginalculture/politics/northern-territory-emergency-respon se-intervention.

262   THE COLONIAL PRESENT

the Paedophiles'".[72] Independent diagnoses of the emergency's compulsory acquisition measures as 'an excision of Aboriginal land' were
unequivocal:

> The clear intent is that the compulsory 5 year acquisition of Aboriginal
> land is to be seamlessly turned into a long term arrangement. . . . [the
> leases] diminish the generally recognised key right of Indigenous people
> to permanent recognition, title and control of their ancestral lands. A long
> term lease is tantamount to de facto expropriation of title. The land is
> being returned to reserve status.[73]

Cognisant of such criticism of the land policies, the Australian government deployed a classic colonial tactic in seeking to cast its response to
complex social problems in terms of security, emergency, and 'law and
order', so as to deflect from the land being grabbed. The rhetoric of
officials and ministers was couched heavily in military jargon narrating
the 'intervention' and its mission to 'stabilise', 'normalise' and then 'exit'
the prescribed Indigenous areas. The intervention was operationalised
under the army's command, and the language of the emergency strategy
documents refers to 'boots on the ground', 'command operations' and an
'embedded' media presence. While the intervention fell short of describing Indigenous communities as enemy belligerents, '[i]t looked for all the
world like an invasion of hostile territory to "subdue the natives"'.[74]
I conceptualise this dynamic of the Northern Territory emergency intervention as a form of internal *hypercolonisation*. Deirdre Tedmanson and
Dinesh Wadiwel provide an apt illustration with reference to a joke
which circulated in Australia after the initiation of the intervention that
'Australia was the first member nation of the US President Bush's
'Coalition of the Willing' *to invade itself*.[75] For them, the emergency
measures are a form of racialised combat which reinforce elements of
biopower and population management that have remained integral to
Western traditions of sovereignty.[76] Analogy can certainly be drawn to
other settler colonial environments in which militarised emergency
powers prevail, not least to that which I have described in Palestine. As
David Lloyd and Patrick Wolfe highlight in their analysis of the intersection of pioneer and soldier mythologies across frontier settlement and
neoliberal regimes:

[72] Lawrence, 'The "Emergency Intervention"'.
[73] Amnesty International, 'Statement to the Senate Standing Committee'.
[74] Lawrence, 'The "Emergency Intervention"'.
[75] Tedmanson and Wadiwel, 'Neoptolemus', 19. Emphasis in original.   [76] *Ibid.*, 9.

The settler colonial and the military imaginaries intertwine with great and familiar intimacy, from the stockades of the early colonists and forts of the frontier cavalry to the hilltop Israeli settlements in Palestine that double as military outposts, to the current military intervention into Aboriginal communities in Australia's Northern Territory.[77]

As in Palestine, Indigenous Australian resistance to the emergency has been steadfast in its substance and diverse in its tactics. Aboriginal community groups in the Northern Territory and national Indigenous organisations opposed the intervention from the outset, arguing that its framing was racist and that its paternalistic approach would reduce the communities' own capacity to resolve the complex social problems they faced. They articulated and advocated alternative courses of action to federal intervention that would instead be led by local Aboriginal communities and informed by principles of sustainability and self-determination.[78] The federal state has failed to engage meaningfully with such voices. Watson points out the irony in the fact that only the day before the Australian prime minister made a 'historic' apology to the 'Stolen Generations' of Indigenous people in 2008, Aboriginal people and their supporters had been protesting outside the same parliament building in Canberra demanding an end to the emergency intervention.[79] The emergency's land policies have been central to the mistrust and outrage which with which it has been received by Indigenous society.

> We are the people of the land. The land is our mother. For more than 40,000 years we have been caring for this land. We are its natural farmers. Now, after so many years of dispossession, we find once again we are being thrust towards a new dispossession. Our pain and our fear are real. Our people are being shamed. Under the intervention we lost our rights as human beings, as Australian citizens, as the First People of the Land. We feel very deeply the threat to our languages, our culture and our heritage. Through harsh changes we have had removed from us all control over our communities and our lives. Our lands have been compulsorily taken from us. We have been left with nothing.[80]

---

[77] David Lloyd and Patrick Wolfe, 'Settler Colonial Logics and the Neoliberal Regime' (2016) 6:2 *Settler Colonial Studies* 9, 10, 115.

[78] See, for example, Combined Aboriginal Organisations of the Northern Territory, 'A Proposed Emergency Response and Development Plan to Protect Aboriginal Children in the Northern Territory: A Preliminary Response to the Australian Government's Proposals', 10 July 2007.

[79] Watson, 'The Northern Territory Emergency Response', 906.

[80] Rosalie Kunoth-Monks et al., 'To the People of Australia', 7 February 2011.

In seeking to combat this new dispossession, Indigenous communities have contested the compulsory land lease measures in particular. This has included refusing to sign new leases when the government's original five-year compulsory leases expired in 2012,[81] as well as legal challenges in the Australian courts.[82] Claims by Indigenous plaintiffs as to the unconstitutionality and unjustness of the intervention's land and permit system measures were rejected by the High Court,[83] however, illustrating the limits of legal avenues. A request for urgent action was also submitted to the UN Committee on the Elimination of Racial Discrimination (by a group of twenty Indigenous Australians representing eleven different Northern Territory communities) which argued that the intervention precipitated 'serious, massive and persistent' discrimination against Aboriginal communities and compromised their cultural norms, collective land ownership traditions and social security protections on the basis of race.[84] The limited mandate of UN treaty-monitoring bodies and their lack of traction at higher-level structures of international legal institutions ensured that this urgent request could produce no more than a series of polite (and not so urgent) communications between the Committee and the Australian government,[85] followed by a 'non-binding' recommendation for Australia to bring the intervention into line with international human rights standards.[86]

With the emergency continuing in its 'stronger futures' avatar, and failing to deliver even by its own assimilationist metrics of 'closing

---

[81] Keenan, 'Australian Government Asked to Leave Aboriginal Community'.

[82] See, for example, *Shaw v Minister for Families, Housing, Community Services and Indigenous Affairs* [2009] FCA 1397. For analysis see Keenan, 'Property as Governance'.

[83] *Reggie Wurridjal, Joy Garlbin and the Bawinanga Aboriginal Corporation v. The Commonwealth of Australia and The Arnhem Land Aboriginal Trust* [2009] HCA 2.

[84] Request for Urgent Action under the International Convention on the Elimination of All forms of Racial Discrimination, Submission in Relation to the Commonwealth of Australia, 28 January 2009, paras. 20–29. See also

[85] Letter from Fatimata-Binta Victoire Dah, Chairperson of the Committee on the Elimination of Racial Discrimination, to the Permanent Mission of Australia to the United Nations, 13 March 2009; Response from the Government of Australia to the Committee on the Elimination of Racial Discrimination, 30 July 2009; Letter from Fatimata-Binta Victoire Dah, Chairperson of the Committee on the Elimination of Racial Discrimination, to the Permanent Mission of Australia to the United Nations, 28 September 2009.

[86] Committee on the Elimination of Racial Discrimination, 'Concluding Observations: Australia', UN Doc. CERD/C/AUS/CO/15–17, 13 September 2010, para. 16.

the gap',[87] concerted opposition persists. The National Congress of Australia's First Peoples repeats its calls for the emergency measures to be repealed and the intervention dismantled,[88] while social movement and grass-roots mobilisation against the imposition of land expropriation and market hegemony in the Northern Territory can be seen across the country. Stop the Intervention Collectives continue to organise to challenge the assumptions of emergency discourse and to 'roll back the intervention', campaigning for the federal and territorial governments to instead redistribute resources and control to communities themselves. Indigenous platforms of resistance, despite their diversity, remain clear and resolute in pressing for the logics of racialised emergency and settler sovereign interventionism to give way to those of reparations for dispossession, restitution of a land base, and realisation of self-determination.[89]

---

[87] See, for example, Australian Government Department of the Prime Minister and Cabinet, 'Closing the Gap: Prime Minister's Report 2016'; Monash University Castan Centre for Human Rights Law, 'The Northern Territory Intervention: An Evaluation', July 2015.

[88] Calla Wahlquist, 'Northern Territory Intervention Should be Disbanded, says Indigenous Advocacy Group', *The Guardian*, 8 February 2016.

[89] See further Nicole Watson, 'Justice in Whose Eyes? Why Lawyers Should Read Black Australian Literature' (2014) 23:1 *Griffith Law Review* 44.

9

International Law, Resistance and 'Real' States of Emergency

The script of resistance and liberation is a historical continuum, taken some-times in small, localized, and painful steps.[1]

Emergency doctrine is imbued with a counter-revolutionary spirit. Colonial experience is testament to that. The states of emergency that I have explored in Kenya, Palestine and Australia are stories of imperial or settler state reliance on emergency law to confront different forms of anti-colonial resistance and to reify racial sovereignty. It is in the shadow of those constellations that international law permits a wide margin of appreciation to the state to decide on both the form and substance of an emergency legal regime. This reflects – and sets a continued tone for – a promiscuous approach to any procedural requirements and substantive limitations that purport to preserve the chastity of the state of emergency. It underpins a reflex resort to emergency powers in the processes of governmentality: political administration, population management, security policy and economic orthodoxy. Emergency modalities, as a result, are endemic in the modern state, with international law essentially permitting a margin of discretion to the preservation of colonial-style governance. Coercive functions tend to become embedded in the archi-tecture of state power in a manner that renders them distinct from government, such that they survive and transcend changes of regime or administration. Their overarching function is the preservation and con-solidation of the interests of the ruling class in settler-colonial or post-colonial societies, and of the hegemony of capital in a class-structured order.[2] Seeing emergency doctrine as part of this architecture reveals the

---

[1] Makau Mutua, 'What is TWAIL?', 32.
[2] For elucidation of the state-government distinction, and analysis of the elements of the state system and the composition of state elites in capitalist countries, see Ralph Miliband, *The State in Capitalist Society* (London: Quartet Books, 1969) 49–67.

nature of state power from a socio-legal perspective, and allows a diagnosis of emergency law as fundamental to a 'deep state' apparatus.
The permanence of the state of emergency in contemporary contexts is
a phenomenon that is refracted in particular ways through the colonial
present and post-colonial prisms. While there may not be an unbroken
lineage or seamless continuity from the functions served by emergency
doctrine in former European colonial legal systems, there has equally
been no definitive rupture. Normative and institutional developments
across the legal landscape bear this out. States of emergency continue in
different guises, often with an expanded scope and impact, but with
remnants of the imperial legacy intact. While the mainstream may still
view emergency derogations provisions as an unfortunate but temporary
relapse to be balanced and tempered, the more fundamental quandary
relates not simply to the plausibility of liberal legal management of
emergency powers and the capacity of law to regulate public emergencies,
but to the penetration of sovereignty in a more fundamental manner. As
Rajagopal suggests, the point is not just that emergency doctrine is
tainted by its colonial ancestry, but that it has been 'naturalised' as an
intuitive element of governance.

> [T]he form in which Britain deployed [the concept of emergency] to
> combat anticolonialism has proved to be particularly enduring among
> postcolonial regimes in the Third World, but more perniciously, we do
> not even notice it anymore; colonial policies that were invented as ad hoc
> responses to mass resistance, have thus been made a "natural" part of the
> international legal corpus. Indeed, this culture of emergency is so "natur-
> alized", so deeply rooted among the governing elites that it is hard to see it
> being shaken fundamentally anytime soon.[3]

This raises the question as to whether established rights frameworks that
incorporate emergency derogations on both domestic and international
planes, and allow for extreme measures by state authorities without
oversight or sanction, are fatally flawed. Political challenges from the
masses or the racialised suspect community can be lawfully quelled with
recourse to emergency powers. An important corollary question flows
from this in relation to resistance. Given that emergency doctrine was
developed (if perhaps not quite 'invented', as Rajagopal has it) to nullify
popular resistance to top-down domination, what form can or should
emancipatory resistance to states of emergency take? In the face of a

---

[3] Rajagopal, *International Law from Below*, 182.

doctrine with reactionary qualities designed to negate resistance, what is to be done? How this question of tactical (dis)engagement with law is approached will hinge on the relative weights of law's hegemonic rigidity and its counter-hegemonic potential.

The Limits and Possibilities of (International) Law

Such questions as to the possibilities of resistance are fundamental to any alternative vision to the mutually reinforcing relationship between emergency law and coloniality. They evoke themes that radical and Third World legal scholars continue to grapple with in the broader context of law's role in political asymmetry and socio-economic inequality between various cores and peripheries, as well as its potential (if any) as an emancipatory vehicle. Law's structural deficiencies and regressive features are, by now, well rehearsed. International legal norms and institutions are rightly critiqued as complicit in the facilitation of racialised and class-driven subjugating measures, given the extent to which – particularly in relation to sovereignty and governance – they were shaped by the European imperial project. The contemporary repercussions are clear: it is through reflection on 'the history of the colonial relationship that it becomes possible to understand why these apparently liberatory projects [governance, sovereignty, rights] do not always meet with the success they promise – for they often embody power relations which are simply reproduced by their transference to the non-European world'.[4] The incisive critiques that have penetrated the field of international legal theory from a Marxist perspective drive the point further, suggesting in their most acute articulation that international law as a whole is so inextricably bound up with imperialism as to be inherently incapable of opposing it on any level.[5] From this viewpoint, there is no faith to be placed in the possibility of radical change through the realm of law. Resistance to global inequalities and the domination of international institutions, as such, must occur on other registers.

There is a substantial spectrum of critical scholarship that sees the terrain of law in more ambiguous and uncontainable terms, however. Here we may recall readings of Foucault in which is not possible for law be rendered entirely conservative and impenetrable. Rather, it remains

---

[4] Anghie, 'What is TWAIL: Comment', 39.
[5] China Miéville, *Between Equal Rights: A Marxist Theory of International Law* (Leiden: Brill, 2005).

susceptible 'to the ineradicable and importunate demands of resistance and transgression . . . it is the impelling force of such resistance which is itself formative of Foucault's law'.[6] In this understanding, that is, law cannot be entirely hemmed in by power; the possibility of infiltrating or subverting the hegemonic space endures. E.P. Thompson arrives at a similar (and, by his own admission, surprising) conclusion in his canonical *Whigs and Hunters*. Thompson's historical deconstruction of a particular piece of repressive emergency-type legislation from the eighteenth century does much to confirm traditional Marxist perspectives of the rule of law as merely another front for the rule of class. It suggests that the 'revolutionary can have no interest in law, unless as a phenomenon of ruling-class power and hypocrisy; it should be his aim simply to overthrow it'.[7] The law is deployed – not only instrumentally but also ideologically – in the imposition and legitimisation of class power. This function of law in mediating and reinforcing class relations does not, however, represent the full picture. For Thompson, law has its own logic and evolution which are rooted – at least partly – in some notion of justice. On this basis, and in spite of his trenchant critique through the book of a political oligarchy creating malicious laws in pursuit of self-interested domination, Thompson ultimately concludes that justice cannot always amount to empty rhetoric, lest the law be exposed as sham and lose the instrumental capacity it holds for its own architects. If the law is too obviously partial and unjust, 'it will mask nothing, legitimize nothing, contribute nothing to any class's hegemony'.[8] To function effectively as ideology, the law must appear to be just. And it cannot appear to be just, it is claimed, without occasionally fulfilling its own promise and actually being just.

> We reach, then, not a simple conclusion (law = class power) but a complex and contradictory one. On the one hand, it is true that the law did mediate existent class relations to the hands of the rulers . . . On the other hand, the law mediated these class relations through legal forms which imposed, again and again, inhibitions on the actions of the rulers. . . . The rhetoric and rules of a society are something a great deal more than sham. In the same moment they may modify, in profound ways, the behaviour of the powerful, and mystify the powerless. They may disguise the true realities of power, but, at the same time, they may curb

---

[6] Golder and Fitzpatrick, *Foucault's Law*, 54

[7] E.P. Thompson, *Whigs and Hunters: The Origin of the Black Act* (New York: Pantheon Books, 1975) 259.

[8] *Ibid.*, 263.

that power and check its intrusions. And it is often from with that very
rhetoric that a radical critique of the society is developed.[9]

If the normative claims expressed here apply in the particular context of
eighteenth-century English society – where law had displaced religion as
the primary source of legitimising ideology, and was yet to be overcome
by market liberalism – the question arises as to what extent they speak to
colonial relations and the deeper inequalities forged therein. Can the law
even appear to be just in such circumstances? Thompson was cognisant
of this question and acknowledges that, when transplanted to situations
of gross inequalities on a global plane, 'the equity of the law must always
be in some part sham' and that law is prone to 'become an instrument of
imperialism'.[10] Again, however, he asserts that 'even here the rules and
the rhetoric have imposed some inhibitions on the imperial power', and
invokes the example of India's anti-colonial struggle: 'If the rhetoric was
a mask, it was a mask which Gandhi and Nehru were to borrow, at the
head of a million masked supporters.'[11] From this flows the implication
that for progressive and radical movements to fail to recognise and
mobilise the counter-hegemonic potential in engagement with legal
discourse, in order at least to resist bad laws, is to disarm themselves in
the face of power and to abandon one important site of struggle.

Support for the idea of law as a site of resistance in anti-colonial
struggles, based on similar understandings of its illimitable nature, can
be found in colonial legal histories. In examining law as a locus of
contestation in a transformed political environment, Samera Esmeir
acknowledges prevailing structural counter-revolutionary impulses in
the form of 'legal technology that functions to prevent revolution against
the law and to assert state power'.[12] At the same time, her characterisation of juridical humanity not only performing itself but also producing
its own critique points to law's repression/resistance double move: '[t]his
is why modern law has become such a powerful technology of government *and* a tool of emancipatory struggles'.[13] Law has been both a
conduit of colonial dispossession but also an arena of Indigenous
struggle, constituting a junction at which settler agendas and local interests collide. European law was integral to the conquest and colonisation
process on the one hand, being brought to bear to expropriate native land
and create a peasant wage labour force. On the other hand, however, its

---

[9] *Ibid.,* 264–265.   [10] *Ibid.,* 266.   [11] *Ibid.,* 266.   [12] Esmeir, *Juridical Humanity,* 3.
[13] *Ibid.,* 289. Emphasis added.

chameleonic features offered a mirror by which colonised groups could mobilise the master's tools 'to protect lands and to resist some of the more excessive demands of the settlers for land and labor'.[14]

The colony as a socio-political space in which imperialism's legal structures have been resisted or instrumentalised – or have at least functioned as a pressure valve of sorts – points to law's ambiguities and instabilities; to the existence of cracks in a generally conservative armour. The legal edifice is not a purely coercive monolith, but a disparate canvas over which counter-hegemonic contestations may also be brushed. The problems in this context relate partly to the tools of law themselves, but more so to the equality of arms in their distribution, with access to the canvas for the legal artists of the colonised and subjugated classes often heavily restricted. For all of its inherent structural flaws, however, there is a sense that law retains the potential to serve as a medium through which reactionary state power and draconian emergency measures and security laws can be challenged. This is consonant with the transformative drive that animates the Third World Approaches to International Law movement. While sharply aware of the alienation of the marginalised and oppressed masses from international law and its institutions, and deeply critical of the discipline in that respect, the TWAIL perspective is conscious of the inescapable role played by law in public international affairs. Some elements of such critical legal projects retain a lingering faith in international law as an emancipatory catalyst, rooted in the impression that 'law's liberal promise has lost *much*, though *not all*, of its luster'.[15] Short of any prevailing semblance of a utopia beyond law, TWAIL voices are reluctant to vacate the field.

> Yet legal nihilism cannot be the answer. A pure critique with its stress on inescapable domination loses its edge. It only disarms the poor and marginal peoples of the third world vis-à-vis the imperial project. The language of international law is not structurally apologetic, leaving no room whatsoever for the emancipation project. Such a suggestion, despite its radical tone, is status quo oriented. International law can be, and has been, to whatever degree, effectively deployed on behalf of the poor and the wretched of the earth.[16]

Divergence between the transformative engagement and radical resistance thrusts of critique has long been cause for reflection in the TWAIL

---

[14] Sally Engle Merry, 'Law and Colonialism' (1991) 25:6 *Law & Society Review* 889, 891.
[15] Ruth Buchanan, 'Writing Resistance Into International Law' (2008) 10 *International Community Law Review* 445, 447. Emphasis added.
[16] Chimni, 'The Past, Present and Future of International Law', 503.

community. There is a sense within recent scholarship that TWAIL's duality of engagement with international law – of both resistance and reform – can coalesce to produce the possibility of destabilisation and transformation: to first provide the necessary rupture from established concentrations of power, and to then generate a praxis of (new, or unrealised) justice and universality.[17]

The evolution of international law has traditionally been traced and analysed by lawyers and scholars *from above*, with a distinct focus on formal sources, judicial opinions, treaties and state practice. Such 'elitist historiographies'[18] tend to frame human rights law, for example, as the outcome of the benevolence of north Atlantic states in response to the atrocities of the Second World War. They serve to sideline the legacy of colonialism and exclude the struggles of Indigenous peoples and grass-roots movements in the global South. By contrast, TWAIL scholarship (in addition to unmasking the imperial, racial, material and gendered premises of international law, and as part of its political project to bring about a more just global legal order) implores us to consider the possibilities of influences on international law *from below*. It seeks to demonstrate that even while international law remains predominantly a space of inter-national organisations and states, it can also be a space of social move-ments. Rajagopal, for one, does so by positioning local Third World and transnational social movements at the vanguard of resistance to the contemporary international legal order, and presents a case for the decen-tring of that order from the extant institutional and state-based power structures towards a system that is less elitist, more equitable; less global, more local; and appropriately reflects the role of social movements and quotidian struggles in the development of international norms.[19] Indigen-ous communities in the global South have in some instances successfully resisted the hegemony of the World Bank and other top-down impos-itions, and been able to start remaking international law. Such an approach can be adopted to emphasise the use made of law as a shield of resistance by civil society, as well as its agency in impacting the normative and institutional development of international law from below.

---

[17] Eslava and Pahuja, 'Between Resistance and Reform', 105. For further discussion see John Reynolds and Sujith Xavier, '"The Dark Corners of the World": TWAIL and International Criminal Justice' (2016) 14:4 *Journal of International Criminal Justice* 959.

[18] Terminology borrowed from Ranajit Guha, 'On Some Aspects of the Historiography of Colonial India' in Ranajit Guha and Gayatri Chakravorty Spivak, *Selected Subaltern Studies* (Oxford: Oxford University Press, 1988) 37.

[19] Rajagopal, *International Law from Below*.

Critiques of rights as hegemonic Western construct or newfangled civilising mission are not new. The privileging of human rights discourse in its individualised civil liberties guise has done much to obfuscate the underlying socio-economic roots of power dynamics and conflict in society, and to restrict our ability to combat structural inequalities. The emancipatory force of liberal human rights remains tempered by deference to marketisation and conservative international institutions. There are, nonetheless, experiences to be drawn from the progressive political utilisation of rights norms and language as a counterpunch to repression, inequality and dispossession. In many cases, rights are invoked because they offer a mode of resistance to subjects who are abandoned by the law of the sovereign and excluded from the community to which the law gives rise.[20] Since emergency derogations can serve to blunt even those limited counter-hegemonic edges, the quandary that follows is whether or how the state of emergency itself can be engaged with as a site of progressive legal and political struggle; whether the counter-revolutionary thrust of emergency doctrine can be mitigated from below.

Scripts of Resistance

For some political theorists, Agamben's accounts of biopolitics and emergency present an apocalyptic perspective that 'closes out the possibility of any worthwhile democratic politics'.[21] Whilst this may not be his intention, such foreclosure of politics of dissent can be the implication of Agamben's framing of emergency where it is (mis)understood in the reductive binary version of the state of exception in which sovereign power operates beyond the pale of law. Where we acknowledge a more pluralistic conception of emergency, with a more ambivalent and unruly role for law and legality, cracks emerge and resistance and transformation appear possible. In the context of ongoing crisis politics, often manifesting through the tedium of prosaic and normalised emergency measures, opportunities for action exist. From a vantage point that sees emergency doctrine in contemporary international and constitutional legal regimes as the product of occidental colonial legalism emerging from the interests of state power from above, resistance to states of emergency for the purposes of destabilisation or

---

[20] Anne Orford, 'A Jurisprudence of the Limit', in Anne Orford (ed.), *International Law and its Others* (Cambridge: Cambridge University Press, 2006) 15.

[21] Bonnie Honig, *Emergency Politics* (Princeton: Princeton University Press, 2009) xv.

rupture must necessarily come from below. Whether such resistance holds the potential to then transform the praxis of emergency powers – rather than merely mitigate their effects – is a vexed question.

Resistance to emergency laws and measures, and to the underlying rationale of emergency doctrine, has sprung from varied quarters. It is, however, in the political struggles, civil society and social movements of the global South that we find the most concerted challenges to the state of emergency as itself constitutive of repressive sovereign power. Within the liberal democracies of the global North, opposition to emergency law has tended to amount to moderate reform or accountability initiatives from within the halls of establishment. In the United States, President Nixon's emergency diktats prompted 'liberal-minded American politicians in the 1970s to launch a short-lived and ultimately ineffective battle against the proliferation of emergency powers'.[22] While the exceptional measures implemented in the context of Guantánamo Bay have generated sustained human rights campaigns, successive administrations responsible for those measures were reelected for second terms, and there was little popular resistance to the annual 'Continuation of National Emergency' declarations by George W. Bush and Barack Obama.[23] The submission of the Federal Emergency Management Agency to security politics and its incorporation into the Department of Homeland Security in 2003, without meaningful opposition, further accentuates the point.

In France, there has been only sporadic and ineffectual criticism of the *pouvoirs exceptionnels, état d'urgence* and *état de siège* applications of emergency doctrine.[24] Initiatives from the left beginning in 1972 towards repealing Article 16 of the Constitution faded out and did not form part of the agenda during the Socialist Party's era of dominance through the following decade.[25] Watered down reform proposals put forward by François Mitterrand's Vedel Commission in 1992 to give the

---

[22] Scheuerman, 'The Economic State of Emergency', 1881.

[23] See, for example, Barack Obama, 'Notice: Continuation of the National Emergency with Respect to Certain Terrorist Attacks', *Federal Register*, 30 August 2016.

[24] As noted in Chapter 3, these are provided for under Article 16 of the 1958 Constitution, the *Loi n° 55-385 du 3 avril 1955 relatif à l'état d'urgence*, and Article 36 of the Constitution respectively. See further, for example, Gilles Lebreton, 'Les atteintes aux droits fondamentaux par l'état de siège et l'état d'urgence' (2007) n°6 *Cahier de la Recherche sur les Droits Fondamentaux* 81.

[25] The 'Common Program' of the Left signed by the French Communist Party (PCF) and the Socialist Party (PS) in an alliance formed before the 1973 parliamentary elections included a proposal that Article 16 be repealed.

Constitutional Council supervisory powers in respect of Article 16 were ultimately not implemented. The 2005 state of emergency in the context of social unrest in France's racialised banlieue communities thus saw emergency measures discharged under the *état d'urgence* framework. This prompted the submission of a complaint by the Green Party and a collective of legal academics, challenging the necessity of exceptional powers. The Council of State rejected the complaint and upheld the legality of *l'état d'urgence*.[26] Mild reform came subsequently with a 2008 legislative amendment to Article 16 of the Constitution that allows for review of the conditions of a prevailing emergency by the Constitutional Council after certain time periods,[27] but this is hardly the embodiment of any radical subversion of emergency modalities in conceptual or practical terms. Nor is it linked to any broader political strategy beyond a nominal commitment to legal oversight of executive power.

Opposition to national security emergency measures in Britain has also been relatively marginal, and has likewise revolved for the most part around individual liberties and judicial oversight of executive powers. More fundamental questioning of the state of emergency at a legal-political level can be seen in the post-Belfast Agreement transition in the north of Ireland, where the question arose of what – if any – form an emergency derogation regime should take in the proposed Bill of Rights for Northern Ireland. Based on an experience of emergency powers operating in an oppressive manner and serving as an aggravator of conflict, the political factions of the republican movement have argued for the exclusion of any emergency derogation regime, with rights to be non-derogable and subjected only to narrow limitations clauses where appropriate.[28] In the consultation process, 'concern was expressed about facilitating too easy resort to derogation, particularly given the current international climate. ... It was observed that derogation clauses in existing international regimes ... did not adequately protect people from human rights violations'.[29] It was argued that 'rights should never be

---

[26] Conseil d'État, 'Etat d'urgence: rejet des demandes de suspension de l'exécution des décrets', Communiqué, 14 novembre 2005; Ordonnance du juge des référés du 14 novembre 2005, N°286837.

[27] Article 6, Loi constitutionnelle n° 2008-724 du 23 juillet 2008 de modernisation des institutions de la Ve République (1).

[28] Bill of Rights Forum, 'Final Report: Recommendations to the Northern Ireland Human Rights Commission on a Bill of Rights for Northern Ireland', 31 March 2008, 166–168.

[29] Bill of Rights Forum, Preamble, Enforceability and Implementation Working Group, 'Final Report', March 2008, 15.

derogable, since derogations aggravate and prolong conflict'; on this basis
Sinn Féin and the Social Democratic and Labour Party (SDLP) – as well
as representatives of Northern Ireland's ethnic minority and feminist
civil society groups – took the position that the Bill of Rights should not
allow for emergency derogations.[30]

The lived experience over recent decades in the north of Ireland that
informed such opposition to establishment views on the necessity of a
state of emergency regime in a Western liberal democracy was, significantly, that of a lingering colonial conflict. It is primarily to anti-imperial
and post-colonial struggles in the global South that we must look for
stories of sustained popular resistance to emergency rule. I have alluded to
the diverse modes of resistance to emergency rule in Kenya, Palestine and
Australia. In addition to those spaces, India, for instance, also has a rich
history of such dissent. Resistance to the state of emergency in its various
forms was, over time, a feature of anti-colonial struggle at all levels, but
initiated and driven from below – from peasants and labourers organising
at local levels. The tea plantations in the Assam region, for example,
originally annexed by the East India Company, were sustained by an
indenture system of Indian peasant labourers brought in to replace
African slave labour following the abolition of formal slavery. They were
subject to a process of penal servitude reconstituted as 'exceptional'
labour. Penal contracts were legitimised by exceptional labour legislation
in Assam with the effect that the powers of the planters 'were simultaneously authorized by the state and also a-legal, or outside of and uncon-
trolled by law.'[31] With private owners and landlords effectively vested
with unchecked sovereign discretion, European planter violence was rife.
The discharge of such exceptional powers was met with concerted resistance on the tea plantations 'through violent and non-violent means, using
overt actions (refusing to work, labor strikes, violent confrontations) and
other weapons of the weak (indolence or avoidance, threats, destruction of
property)', as well as through tactical uses of the law in ways 'that did not
simply reinforce the power of the colonial legal system'.[32] This included

[30] Bill of Rights Forum, Preamble, Enforceability and Implementation Working Group,
'Final Report', March 2008, 16–22. The Democratic Unionist Party, the Ulster Unionist
Party and the Alliance Party – as well as representatives from the Northern Ireland's
business sector – argued in favour of emergency doctrine. At the time of writing, the Bill
of Rights drafting process remains unfinished.
[31] Kolsky, *Colonial Justice in British India*, 157–158.
[32] *Ibid.*, 175, 180–182. Kolsky argues that the tea workers 'understood, engaged with, and
sometimes found ways to appropriate the mechanisms of justice to their own ends', and

inundating the regional authorities with complaints and mass strikes to disrupt criminal prosecutions of workers. While the workers' acts of unruliness were typically painted as fanatical and irrational by the planters, their resistance was in fact for the most part calculated, collectively organised, and politically aware. Though such action emerged and continued during the latter part of the nineteenth century, the Indian National Congress was reluctant to adopt the case of the plantation labourers. It was seen as a provincial social issue, not of direct concern to the higher national cause, while the more elitist elements of Indian nationalism retained a distinctly paternalistic view of the peasant masses involved. As such, the everyday resistance on the Assam tea plantations proceeded for some time before any intervention or support from the Indian nationalist leadership was forthcoming.[33] The level of social organisation and political consciousness in the workers' defiance of Assam's exceptional legal regime ultimately could not be ignored by Gandhi and the central leadership, however, and by the early twentieth century was, along with other local peasant movements, incorporated by the Congress into the larger national liberation movement.[34]

Such mass resistance to emergency rule from below proved to be influential on the thrust of Indian emancipation as the century progressed. The immediate catalyst for the British declaration of martial law in Punjab in 1919 was, somewhat ironically, resistance to a prior piece of emergency legislation. In the Emergency Powers Bill 1919 (known also as the Rowlatt Act after the British judge who presided over the committee that recommended the retention of emergency powers), the imperial council provided for the continuation of First World War emergency measures outlined in the Defence of India Regulation Act. This amounted to an attack on civil liberties in the form of censorship and banning, arrest without warrant, indefinite detention without trial, and secretive juryless prosecutions of political dissidents. The passing of the bill into law was viewed by Indian nationalist leaders as a betrayal of assurances given to them by Britain that autonomous Indian political participation would be expanded once the war was over. The Act was

that law 'sometimes offered a language and method of resistance'. See also Nitin Varma, 'Coolie Strikes Back: Collective Protest and Action in the Colonial Tea Plantations of Assam, 1880–1920', in Biswamoy Pati (ed.), *Adivasis in Colonial India: Survival, Resistance and Negotiation* (New Delhi: Orient Blackswan, 2011) 186–215.

[33] Kolsky, *Colonial Justice in British* India, 181.

[34] See Jacques Pouchepadass, *Champaran and Gandhi: Planters, Peasants and Gandhian Politics* (New Delhi: Oxford University Press, 1999).

denounced by Indian nationalists, and triggered unrest and agitation. Resistance to the emergency powers took the form of organised civil disobedience. Shops and markets were closed in protest, demonstrations were mobilised, and the population sought to actively disobey or refuse to adhere to the Act. This culminated in rioting in Delhi, Ahmedabad, Lahore and elsewhere. In Punjab, local leaders were arrested and interned on orders of the Governor, before colonial officials in Amritsar called in military forces who opened fire on crowds, killing Indians in their hundreds.[35] Gandhi was arrested attempting to enter Punjab, and martial law declared. This further provoked the local population, and the repression-dissent cycle intensified. British administrators associated the breaking of one law with the potential for all law to be overthrown:

> Lord Chelmsford suggests, echoing once again a thematic of despotism, [that] every law is a personal and direct manifestation of the sovereign. To call for even the nonviolent disobedience of the Rowlatt Act is to unleash a more general "disturbance" that threatens the authority of the state. Thus, the real need for martial law is not merely to put down this or that outbreak of violence but to restore this authority.[36]

The priority of preserving imperial sovereignty and the perceived necessity of emergency measures to that end are clear. Chelmsford's position was based on a view of the people of India 'in its present state of development' as insufficiently civilised to able to distinguish between specific laws (which may appear to them to be inappropriate) and the overall authority of the state (which should not be in question).[37] The dynamic of difference is clear in the implication that only more civilised people, in a higher state of development, have the capacity to selectively oppose individual (bad) laws while still respecting law, order and authority writ large. Chelmsford's logic linking Indian disobedience of the legislation with a broader antipathy to colonial rule was actually well-founded, however, insofar as resistance to the Rowlatt Act did not occur in isolation or out of mere constitutional fidelity to the rule of law. Resistance to the provisions of this Act were part of a principled opposition to the violence of emergency law more broadly, which itself was

---

[35] See discussion of the Jallianwala Bagh massacre in Chapter 3.
[36] Hussain, *The Jurisprudence of Emergency*, 127.
[37] Letter from the Government of India, Home Department (Political), to Edwin Montagu, Secretary of State for India, No. 2, 3 May 1920, in *Correspondence Between the Government of India and the Secretary of State for India on the Report of Lord Hunter's Committee*, Cmd. 705 [1920] 22, cited in Hussain, *The Jurisprudence of Emergency*, 127.

integral to the struggle toward the overarching political goal of national liberation. Far from being too backward-thinking to be able to discern between the Rowlatt Act specifically and the benevolence of colonial law in general, the Indian self-determination movement understood very well that emergency powers were essential – rather than incidental – to the machinery of colonial rule, and ought to be resisted as such.

Resistance to emergency governance continued during the inter-war period and remained central in the build-up to the launching of the Quit India movement during the Second World War. Another civil disobedience action initiated in October 1940 came as a direct response to new wartime emergency powers. Gandhi's tactics of non-violent resistance included resistance to emergency law: 'Individual satyagrahis, in the beginning personally chosen by him, made public anti-war speeches in defiance of emergency orders.'[38] In 1944, social worker and political activist Hansa Mehta (who had herself been administratively detained along with her husband) wrote an influential pamphlet for the All India Women's Conference strongly indicting Britain's use of emergency powers.[39] The theme of emergency law as an integral element of the ruling structure to be overthrown was continually highlighted by liberation leaders and was a sustained part of the narrative of colonialism's oppressive and anti-democratic nature, culminating in Indian independence in 1947.

Independence was no panacea of course, and the state of emergency remains an important site of resistance for marginalised and peripheral communities in post-colonial India. The legacy of colonial emergency doctrine is keenly felt, particularly in the country's north-eastern regions through the application of the Armed Forces (Special Powers) Act 1958,[40] a permanent emergency statute that vests the military with

---

[38] Geraldine Forbes, *Women in Modern India, Volume 4* (Cambridge: Cambridge University Press, 1996) 203.

[39] Simpson, *Human Rights and the End of Empire*, 88, citing Civil Liberties, Tract No. 4 (Bombay, 1945). After independence, Mehta represented India on the UN Human Rights Committee and was involved in the drafting of the Universal Declaration of Human Rights.

[40] Upon independence, the Indian Constitution consolidated rather than severed the state of emergency precepts. The Armed Forces (Special Powers) Act 1958, modeled on the Armed Forces Special Powers Ordinance promulgated by the British authorities in 1942 to suppress the Quit India Movement, vests the military with extensive emergency powers in a number of Indian states where some form of opposition to centralised rule emerged after decolonisation. The legislation was originally enacted in 1958 to apply to Assam and Manipur; its territorial scope was expanded by an amendment in 1972 to also

unmitigated powers and is symptomatic of the violence of the state against its others. Significantly, the states of the north-east amount to 'India's very own quasi-colony', defined by a 'history of forceful and illegitimate appropriation of entire lands and communities' (and their natural resources) by a paternalistic Indian state, as well as by racial, ethnic and cultural tropes that operate to construct people from the north-east as fundamentally different to 'mainland' Indians.[41] Manipur, described even by Indian government officials in diplomatic interactions as 'less a state and more of a colony of India',[42] has been home to a particularly severe and racialised application of emergency powers in the context of ethnic conflict. Mainstream political actors in India have remained silent on the matter, with resistance to the measures again being driven from below, most visibly and physically embodied by Irom Sharmila (a Manipuri activist who went on hunger strike after the killing of ten civilians by Indian paramilitary forces in November 2000) and the Meira Paibi (a grass-roots women's association in Manipur who use 'their bodies as weapons of protest against a violent and marginalising state').[43] The Armed Forces (Special Powers) Act is the axis around which their politics of resistance revolves. Sharmila remained on hunger strike in detention for sixteen years, being force-fed through her nose, calling for the repeal of the special powers legislation. These movements' persistent but unanswered demands for the termination of the legislation highlight the rootedness of repressive security discourse in Indian law

encompass Meghalaya, Nagaland, Tripura, Arunachal Pradesh and Mizoram. The Act continues to apply in these seven regions. A 1983 amendment extending the legislation to Punjab and Chandigarh was in force until 1997. The Armed Forces (Jammu and Kashmir) Special Powers Act 1990 has applied in the northern state of Jammu and Kashmir since 1990. On the 'exceptionalism of the Northeast', see Duncan McDuie-Ra, 'Fifty-year disturbance: the Armed Forces Special Powers Act and exceptionalism in a South Asian periphery' (2009) 17:3 *Contemporary South Asia* 255. On the 'colonial continuities' of India's national security law generally, see Anil Kalhan, Gerald P. Conroy, Mamta Kaushal, Sam Scott Miller and Jed S. Rakoff, 'Colonial Continuities: Human Rights, Terrorism, and Security Laws in India' (2006) 20:1 *Columbia Journal of Asian Law* 93.

[41] Gaikwad Namrata, 'Revolting Bodies, Hysterical State: Women Protesting the Armed Forces Special Powers Act (1958)' (2009) 17:3 *Contemporary South Asia* 299, 301.

[42] See Wikileaks Cable #76968: U.S. Consulate General Calcutta, 'Northeast Indian State of Manipur Experiences Escalating Violence', 1 September 2006, para. 10. The Consulate General noted that: 'The general use of the AFSPA meant that the Manipuris did not have the same rights of other Indian citizens and restrictions on travel to the state added to a sense of isolation and separation from the rest of India "proper".'

[43] Namrata, 'Revolting Bodies, Hysterical State', 305.

and have garnered solidarity from national social movements and international rights organisations.[44] This has filtered up to the UN Committee
on the Elimination of Racial Discrimination, which in 2007 criticised the
Armed Forces (Special Powers) Act in racial terms, noting the impunity
it grants to the military for acts committed against 'tribal peoples' and
urging India to revoke it.[45] Struggles against the logic of special powers in
India's peripheries continue.

The state of emergency also featured prominently as a weapon of
choice in the legal arsenal of white domination in South Africa.[46] Conscious of this, the anti-apartheid movement identified, from an early
point, sustained challenge to emergency doctrine as a necessary and
integral component of the liberation struggle. What began in 1960 as
small, localised acts of resistance eventually resulted in the UN General
Assembly demanding in 1989 that the apartheid regime unconditionally
abrogate its emergency powers.

In March 1960, a state of emergency was declared by the National
Party's Minister for Justice under the Public Safety Act 1953, on the back
of the Sharpeville protests and police atrocities. As has so often been the
case in colonial situations, the 'public safety' rationale for the necessity of
emergency measures is a misnomer that serves to mask the underlying
imperative of reinforcing settler sovereignty. With the white population
constituting a distinct minority of the 'public', this was very much the
case in South Africa. In the 1950s, the African National Congress had
decisively shifted the focal point of the anti-apartheid movement to the
impoverished masses, departing from the more elitist approach that had
preceded the inclusion of the Communist Party of South Africa and the

---

[44] Human Rights Watch, 'India: Repeal Armed Forces Special Powers Act', 19 August 2008;
Amnesty International, 'India: Authorities Must Release Irom Sharmila Chanu' AI Index:
ASA 20/013/2013, 20 March 2013; Amnesty International, 'The Armed Forces Special
Powers Act: Time For A Renewed Debate in India on Human Rights and National
Security', AI Index: ASA 20/042/2013, 8 November 2013.
[45] Committee on the Elimination of Racial Discrimination, 'Concluding Observations:
India', UN Doc. CERD/C/IND/CO/19, 5 May 2007.
[46] On the apartheid emergency laws, see, for example, A.S. Mathews and R.C. Albino, 'The
Permanence of the Temporary: An Examination of the 90- and 180-Day Detention Laws'
(1966) 83 *South African Law Journal* 16; Cora Hoexter, 'Emergency Law' (1990) 1 *South
African Human Rights Yearbook* 110; Vincent Mntambo, 'Emergency Law' (1991) 2
South African Human Rights Yearbook 83; Gilbert Marcus, 'Civil Liberties Under Emergency Rule' in John Dugard, Nicholas Haysom and Gilbert Marcus (eds.), *The Last Years
of Apartheid: Civil Liberties in South Africa* (New York: Foreign Policy Association, 1992)
32–54.

adoption of the Freedom Charter. Emergency regulations were imposed by the apartheid regime from 1960 to consolidate the racialised legal apparatus of pass laws, segregated education and forced evictions in the face of rising popular dissent and disobedience. The restrictions that the government instituted under the emergency framework made the work of the defence lawyers in the ongoing 'Treason Trial' of prominent anti-apartheid activists increasingly difficult. In April 1960, the lawyers proposed withdrawing from the case in protest. Nelson Mandela recalls how he and his fellow defendants discussed that proposal and – despite 'the serious implications of such a withdrawal and the consequences of our conducting our own defense in a capital case' – decided 'in favor of this dramatic gesture, for it highlighted the iniquities of the State of Emergency'.[47] Mandela and Duma Nokwe took on the work of preparing the defence themselves in the absence of the legal team. It was a tactic that created no tangible threat to the authorities, but amounted to a symbolically significant act of defiance, demonstrating the liberation movement's acute awareness of the nature of the role played by emergency legal doctrine. In its founding manifesto in 1961, the armed wing of the African National Congress, Umkhonto we Sizwe (MK), made explicit reference to the state of emergency: 'virtual martial law has been imposed in order to beat down peaceful, non-violent strike action of the people in support of their rights'.[48] Umkhonto we Sizwe was formed, in essence, to resist the state violence that the emergency served to legitimise.

Formal states of emergency were suspended and reinstated through the subsequent decades of apartheid, bridged by an unbroken chain of security legislation. Political violence, repression and mass detention reached a nadir under the 1985–1986 and 1986–1990 emergencies. Resolute resistance from below to the state of emergency continued, and ultimately came to shape the basis for negotiations within South Africa – as well as international policy – toward the dismantling of apartheid. During this period, channels of communication were opened between the leaderships of the ANC and the National Party. Still imprisoned and in a position of ostensible weakness as such, Mandela – 'a lawyer who discovered that the law was the barrier to change and so moved to politics'[49] – was relentless in his opposition to the state of

---

[47] Mandela, *The Long Walk to Freedom*, 291.
[48] 'Manifesto of Umkhonto we Sizwe', issued by the Command of Umkhonto we Sizwe, 16 December 1961.
[49] Vijay Prashad, 'Mandela, the Unapologetic Radical', *Colorlines*, 6 December 2013.

emergency. Revocation of the emergency was – along with the release of political prisoners, the unbanning of the ANC and the removal of apartheid troops from the townships – an imperative precondition to any negotiation process. For the ANC, there was an 'onus on the government to eliminate the obstacles to negotiations that the state itself had created'.[50] The 1989 Harare Declaration, which articulated the ANC's charter for negotiations, reaffirmed the movement's longstanding position on the state of emergency.

> We recognise the reality that permanent peace and stability in Southern Africa can only be achieved when the system of apartheid in South Africa has been liquidated and South Africa transformed into a united, democratic and non-racial country. We therefore reiterate that all the necessary measures should be adopted now, to bring a speedy end to the apartheid system … Accordingly, the present regime should, at the very least:
> [...]
> End the state of emergency and repeal all legislation, such as, and including, the Internal Security Act, designed to circumscribe political activity.[51]

The Declaration proved to be a striking example of the shaping of international law from below. Stemming from a grass-roots popular liberation movement, this statement of principles on the establishment of a post-apartheid democratic South Africa was adopted by the Organisation of African Unity's Ad Hoc Committee on Southern Africa. It was then endorsed by the Non-Aligned Movement in Belgrade in September 1989. It was invoked with approval by the UN General Assembly in November 1989, in a resolution in which the Assembly 'strongly demands the lifting of the state of emergency'.[52] The following month, the principles laid down in the Harare Declaration formed the basis of the UN Declaration on Apartheid and its Destructive Consequences in Southern Africa. The language on the state of emergency as it appeared in that document was almost identical to the ANC's original declaration.

> The present South African regime should, at the least:
> [...]
> End the state of emergency and repeal all legislation, such as the Internal Security Act, designed to circumscribe political activity.[53]

---

[50] Mandela, *The Long Walk to Freedom*, 663.
[51] Declaration of the Organisation of African Unity Ad Hoc Committee on Southern Africa on the question of South Africa (Harare, 21 August 1989), sections 5, 19.
[52] UN General Assembly Resolution A/RES/44/27, 22 November 1989.
[53] UN General Assembly Resolution A/RES/S-16/1, 14 December 1989.

Mandela continued to demand the revocation of the state of emergency in his meetings with F.W. de Klerk and the National Party's secret negotiating team. On 2 February 1990, de Klerk announced the lifting of the bans on the ANC and the Communist Party, the freeing of political prisoners, and 'the lifting of various restrictions imposed by the State of Emergency'.[54] The following week Mandela was released, but the ANC was unsatisfied with the qualified revocation of the emergency measures. 'The international community applauded de Klerk's bold actions. Amidst all the good news, however, the ANC objected to the fact that Mr. de Klerk had not completely lifted the State of Emergency or ordered the troops out of the townships.'[55] In his speech in Cape Town on the day of his release, Mandela reiterated this position.

> Mr. De Klerk has gone further than any other Nationalist president in taking real steps to normalise the situation. However, there are further steps as outlined in the Harare Declaration that have to be met before negotiations on the basic demands of our people can begin. I reiterate our call for, inter alia, the immediate ending of the State of Emergency and the freeing of all, and not only some, political prisoners.[56]

The ANC continued to agitate for the absolute termination of the emergency. In June 1990, more than thirty years after it had declared its first formal state of emergency, the apartheid regime relented and fully lifted the state of emergency in all provinces bar Natal, where the emergency was revoked four months later. Mandela described this as a 'most important event'[57] in the dismantling of apartheid. The ANC saw the revocation of the emergency in pragmatic, tactical terms: as a loosening of the structures of oppression that allowed for the commencement of negotiation. The significance of the resistance to the state of emergency as a sustained element of the broader revolutionary struggle cannot be underestimated, however. Emergency powers and the apartheid legal system were identified as central agents of white domination. The strategic objective of emancipation from such domination thus necessitated the tactics of legal and political resistance to the state of emergency.[58]

---

[54] Mandela, *The Long Walk to Freedom*, 666.   [55] *Ibid.*
[56] Nelson Mandela, 'Address to a rally in Cape Town', 11 February 1990.
[57] Mandela, *The Long Walk to Freedom*, 697.
[58] Following the dismantling of apartheid, South Africa's much-lauded 'transformative' Constitution does still provide for executive emergency regulations, but makes it more difficult for them to be sustained. A state of emergency declared under by the President under section 37 of the Constitution is limited to a duration of 21 days. It may be extended by the National Assembly for a period of at most three months at a time. The

The central problem with entrenched states of emergency is that extraordinary powers are normalised in the process of maintaining a larger control system. Resistance to such measures in abstraction from the ideological and institutional system which they serve to reinforce is, by definition, superficial. The Indian and South African examples provide a glimpse of how emergency legal regimes may offer a site of effective resistance where framed as part of a broader radical movement. The languages of law and rights can be instrumentally useful in challenging hegemonic modes of governmentality but, given the centrality of emergency doctrine to colonial legal systems – and now to constitutional and international human rights regimes in which some of the dynamics and biases of racialised governance are reproduced – they must serve to complement other languages of resistance. Here, the interaction between strategy and tactics is crucial to bear in mind. The compulsive desire for 'strategic' intervention in legal-political debates often results in the conflation of tactical considerations with strategy. This collapses the distinction between the two concepts, in which 'strategy refers to the achievement of long term, structural (or organic) goals, whereas tactics refers to the achievement of short term, conjunctural ones'.[59]

The repeal of entrenched emergency rule is not a strategic end in itself, but rather one of many potential tactical goals aimed at weakening the foundations of the racial or class power structures that the emergency serves to reinforce. Where emergency governance has become the normal and permanent state of affairs, the norm/emergency divide is blurred beyond distinction and exposed as illusory. The implication that flows from this is that rather than simply demanding a return to a 'normal' rule of law and regulation of capitalist control of land, resources and labour, what is needed is a 'counter politics'[60] not only against the

---

extent and scope of emergency measures under the state of emergency are subject to a range of limitations.

[59] See further Robert Knox, 'Strategy and Tactics' (2010) 21 *Finnish Yearbook of International Law* 193, 227. Knox draws on Antonio Gramsci's distinction between 'organic' ('relatively permanent ... far-reaching historical significance') and 'conjunctural' (occasional, immediate, almost accidental ... of a minor, day-to-day character') phenomena in framing this distinction. See Antonio Gramsci, *Selections from the Prison Notebooks* (London: Lawrence & Wishart, 2003) 177–178. For reflections in the context of Palestine, see John Reynolds, 'Anti-Colonial Legalities: Paradigms, Tactics and Strategy' (2015) 18 *Palestine Yearbook of International Law* 8.

[60] Neocleous, 'The Problem with Normality', 209.

permanent emergency but against the normality of racialised governance and socio-economic inequality, and their underpinning legal structures.

Real States of Emergency

Where emergency powers are a normalised feature of the law, then, the necessary Benjaminian task is not to restore an illusory or usurped historical normalcy, but to 'brush history against the grain' by bringing about 'a real state of emergency'[61] – for fascist rule in Benjamin's 1930s; for imperial-racial rule and capitalist-class hegemony in our early twenty-first century. Every generation 'must strive anew to wrest tradition away from the conformism that is working to overpower it'.[62] Resistance to historically embedded emergency doctrine must create a rupture definitive enough to blast open the continuum of history and carve out a real alternative to normalised emergency governance. Liberal constitutional oversight mechanisms which review the methods by which sovereign power is exercised, but which leave the relationship between the sovereign and its others fundamentally intact, are insufficient in and of themselves. A more radical challenge to the conditions that perpetuate emergency politics is required, one that seeks not mere checks and balances on the permanent emergency, but an overhaul of the system that fosters it. This demands thinking that rejects accepted framings. In the context of counter-terrorism law and policy debates, for example, we cannot move towards a real state of emergency with emancipatory potential by striking an artificial semblance of 'balance' between human liberty and state security, but only rather by escaping the very shackles of the security vs. liberty trade-off narrative, and galvanising sustained opposition to the racialising tendencies of state security discourse.

The rationale behind the reliance on emergency doctrine by sovereign authorities is conservation of the pre-crisis status quo. Where necessary, emergency powers underpin the state's exercise of its claimed monopoly on legitimate violence. The proclamation of a state of emergency in this sense is a concerted play by state institutions to avoid a real emergency for the established order, and to preserve the naturalised condition of racial subordination and social stratification. In order to garner sufficient leverage to effectuate progressive and lasting systemic change, a sustained

---

[61] Benjamin, 'On the Concept of History', 392.   [62] *Ibid.*, 391.

challenge to entrenched emergency discourses and crisis politics in civic and economic life is needed. This mobilisation of agency and resistance can bring about a real state of emergency for centres of institutional power, and offers a potential springboard towards the radical transformation of local and global governance structures.

Traditions of the oppressed, because of their particular relationship to law's violence, project us beyond formalistic legal categories and summon up the revolutionary potential of mass civil disobedience, 'pure' violence or the proletarian general strike.[63] As with the Mau Mau revolt in Kenya, India and South Africa do provide examples where some semblance of the type of real emergency envisaged by Benjamin was created in the context of liberation struggles, but their post-colonial and post-apartheid realities equally show the difficulty, even for cathartic revolutionary processes, in fully uprooting jurisprudential concepts of emergency that have been firmly implanted in political and legal systems. In the current conjectures in those settler colonial spaces that I have analysed, Palestine and Australia, if any 'threat to the life of the nation' exists, it is not to the life of the settler nation, but rather to that of the colonised. Scripts of native resistance continue in a diversity of small, localised and often painful steps, seeking to create a real emergency for the oppressing power, as well as for the domestic and international legal structures that facilitate the oppression.

At the register of international law, the position taken by the UN General Assembly in 1989 in echoing demands that originated in localised social and political activism in apartheid South Africa, including the dismantling of the state of emergency, demonstrates the ontological possibilities of international law from below. If international law is implicated in the normalisation of emergency and its racialised application, to what extent can anti-colonial or Indigenous resistance be written or absorbed into international law? What might amount to a real state of emergency for international law itself, in the sense that the anti-colonial and anti-apartheid movements sought to rupture regimes of normalised emergency? My parting suggestion here is that we might understand initiatives like the Palestinian call for Boycott, Divestment and Sanctions (BDS) as engendering the possible beginnings of a real state of emergency for an established international legal order that remains imperial and

---

[63] Walter Benjamin, 'Critique of Violence' (1921) in *Essays, Aphorisms, Autobiographical Writings* (Edmund Jephcott trans., Peter Demetz ed., New York: Schocken, 1986) 282, 291–292.

state-centric at its core. The Palestinian BDS call[64] invokes the findings of
the International Court of Justice[65] and uses the language of international
law, but in an expansive manner that transcends the conventional focus
of international legal institutions on discrete violations of the laws of war
or individualised human rights. It is based instead on the illegitimacy of
the Israeli occupation, the structures of segregation and apartheid
throughout historic Palestine, and the right of Palestinian refugees to
return. The BDS campaign targets the structural and economic aspects of
settler colonialism that the professional apparatus of UN agencies and
international human rights organisations are too often reluctant to name
and confront. Perhaps most importantly, BDS cuts through the state
centricity and institutional hierarchies of international law, as well as
the bourgeois claims of national elites. It is an organic, diffuse mobilisation of international law – or, to invoke Edward Said, an 'amateur
intellectual' mobilisation, rather than a professional expert application
of traditional international law from above.[66] It is an expression of
popular sovereignty, in contrast to Schmitt's executive decisionist sovereignty and in keeping with Benjamin's vision of the real state of emergency. It elicits a vision that problematises existing structures of racial,
hierarchical and repressive sovereignty. It imagines instead the possibility
of more emancipatory, horizontal and inclusive sovereignties. It imagines
an end to empire's emergency rule.

[64] Palestinian BDS National Committee, 'Palestinian Civil Society Call for Boycott, Divestment and Sanctions', 9 July 2005.
[65] *Legal Consequences of the Construction of a Wall in the Occupied Palestinian Territory*,
Advisory Opinion, 2004 I.C.J. Rep. 136.
[66] Edward W. Said, *Representations of the Intellectual: The 1993 Reith Lectures* (New York:
Vintage, 1996); John Reynolds, 'Disrupting Civility: Amateur Intellectuals, International
Lawyers and TWAIL as Praxis' (2016) 37:11 *Third World Quarterly* 2098.

BIBLIOGRAPHY

Abu Hussein, Hussein and Fiona McKay, *Access Denied: Palestinian Land Rights in Israel* (London: Zed Books, 2003)

Ackerman, Bruce, 'The Emergency Constitution' (2004) 113 *Yale Law Journal* 1029

Adam, Smith, *An Inquiry into the Nature and Causes of the Wealth of Nations* (London: Ward, Lock & Co, 1776)

Afzal-Khan, Fawzia and Kalpana Seshadri-Crooks (eds.), *The Pre-occupation of Postcolonial Studies* (London: Duke University Press, 2000)

Agamben, Giorgio, *Homo Sacer: Sovereign Power and Bare Life (1995)* (Daniel Heller-Roazen trans., Stanford: Stanford University Press, 1998)

Agamben, Giorgio, *Remnants of Auschwitz: The Witness and the Archive* (1998) (Daniel Heller-Roazen trans., New York: Zone Books, 1999)

Agamben, Giorgio, *Means Without End: Notes on Politics* (Vincenzo Binetti and Cesare Casarino trans., Minneapolis: University of Minnesota Press, 2000)

Agamben, Giorgio, *State of Exception* (2003) (Kevin Attell trans., Chicago: University of Chicago Press, 2005)

Ahmad, Aijaz, *In Theory: Classes, Nations, Literatures* (London: Verso, 1992)

Al-Asmar, Fouzi, *To Be an Arab in Israel* (Beirut: Institute for Palestine Studies, 1978)

Al-Ghunaimi, M.T., *The Muslim Conception of International Law and the Western Approach* (The Hague: Martinus Nijhoff, 1968)

Alexandrowicz, C.H., *An Introduction to the History of the Law of Nations in the East Indies (16th, 17th and 18th Centuries)* (Oxford: Clarendon Press, 1967)

Allain, Jean, *International Law in the Middle East: Closer to Power than Justice* (Aldershot: Ashgate, 2004)

Allhoff, Fritz, 'A Defense of Torture: Separation of Cases, Ticking Time-bombs, and Moral Justification' (2005) 19:2 *International Journal of Applied Philosophy* 243

Altman, Jon and Melinda Hinkson (eds.), *Coercive Reconciliation: Stabilise, Normalise, Exit Aboriginal Australia* (Melbourne: Arena, 2007)

Amin, Mohamed and Malcolm Caldwell (eds.), *Malaya, the Making of a Neo Colony* (Nottingham: Spokesman Books, 1977)

Amin, Samir, *Imperialism and Unequal Development* (Hassocks: Harvester Press, 1977)

Amin, Samir, 'The Challenge of Globalization' (1996) 3:2 *Review of International Political Economy* 216

Amin, Samir, 'Imperialism and Globalization' (2001) 53:2 *Monthly Review* 6

Anand, R.P., *New States and International Law* (Delhi: Vikas, 1972)

Anderson, David, *Histories of the Hanged: Britain's Dirty War in Kenya and the End of Empire* (London: Weidenfeld & Nicolson, 2005)

Anderson, David, 'Mau Mau in the High Court and the "Lost" British Empire Archives: Colonial Conspiracy or Bureaucratic Bungle?' (2011) 39:5 *Journal of Imperial and Commonwealth History* 699

Anderson, David, 'Guilty Secrets: Deceit, Denial, and the Discovery of Kenya's "Migrated Archive"' (2015) 80:1 *History Workshop Journal* 142

Anghie, Antony, 'What is TWAIL: Comment' (2000) 94 *American Society of International Law Proceedings* 39

Anghie, Antony, *Imperialism, Sovereignty and the Making of International Law* (Cambridge: Cambridge University Press, 2005)

Anghie, Antony, 'The Evolution of International Law: Colonial and Postcolonial Realities' (2006) 27:5 *Third World Quarterly* 739

Anghie, Antony, 'Rethinking Sovereignty in International Law' (2009) 5 *Annual Review of Law and Social Science* 291

Anghie, Antony, B.S. Chimni, et al., *The Third World and International Order: Law, Politics and Globalization* (Leiden: Martinus Nijhoff, 2003)

Anghie, Antony and B.S. Chimni, 'Third World Approaches to International Law and Individual Responsibility in Internal Conflicts' (2003) 2 *Chinese Journal of International Law* 77

Arai-Takahashi, Yutaka, 'Administrative Discretion in German Law: Doctrinal Discourse Revisited' (2000) 6 *European Public Law* 69

Arden-Clarke, Charles, 'Gold Coast into Ghana: Some Problems of Transition' (1958) 34:1 *International Affairs* 49

Arendt, Hannah, *The Origins of Totalitarianism* (New York: Meridian, 1958)

Arendt, Hannah, *Eichmann in Jerusalem: A Report on the Banality of Evil* (New York: Viking, 1963)

Aristotle, *Politics* (Benjamin Jowett trans., Kitchener: Batoche Books, 1999)

Arold, Nina-Louisa, *The Legal Culture of the European Court of Human Rights* (Leiden: Martinus Nijhoff, 2007)

Authers, Benjamin and Hilary Charlesworth, 'The Crisis and the Quotidian in International Human Rights Law' (2014) 44 *Netherlands Yearbook of International Law* 19

Babington Macauley, Thomas, *The History of England from the Accession of James II, vol. III* (Philadelphia: Porter & Coates, 1855)

Balandier, Georges (ed.), *Le Tiers-Monde: Sous-développement et développement* (Paris: Presses Universitaires de France, 1961)

Banton, Michael, *The Idea of Race* (London: Tavistock, 1977)

Barnett, Donald and Karari Njama, *Mau Mau from Within: Autobiography and Analysis of Kenya's Peasant Revolt* (London: Macgibbon & Kee, 1966)

Barreto, José Manuel (ed.), *Human Rights from a Third World Perspective: Critique, History and International Law* (Newcastle: Cambridge Scholars Publishing, 2013)

Bassiouni, M. Cherif, 'The Institutionalisation of Torture under the Bush Administration' (2006) 37 *Case Western Reserve Journal of International Law* 389

Baxi, Upendra, 'Voices of Suffering and the Future of Human Rights' (1998) 8 *Transnational Law and Contemporary Problems* 125

Baxi, Upendra, *The Future of Human Rights* (2nd edn., Oxford: Oxford University Press, 2006)

Bedjaoui, Mohammed, *Towards a New International Economic Order* (Paris: UNESCO, 1979)

Belknap, Michael R., 'The New Deal and the Emergency Powers Doctrine' (1983) 62 *Texas Law Review* 67

Bellamy Foster, John and Robert W. McChesney, 'Monopoly-Finance Capital and the Paradox of Accumulation' (2009) 61:5 *Monthly Review* 1

Benjamin, Walter, *Reflections: Essays, Aphorisms, Autobiographical Writings* (Edmund Jephcott trans., Peter Demetz ed., New York: Schocken, 1986)

Benjamin, Walter, *Selected Writings, Vol. 4: 1938–1940* (Harry Zohn trans., Howard Eiland and Michael W. Jennings eds., Cambridge, MA: Harvard University Press, 2003)

Bennett, Huw, 'Soldiers in the Court Room: The British Army's Part in the Kenya Emergency under the Legal Spotlight' (2011) 39:5 *Journal of Imperial and Commonwealth History* 717

Berman, Bruce and John Lonsdale, *Unhappy Valley: Conflict Kenya and Africa* (Nairobi: Heinemann, 1992)

Bernard, Semmel, *Jamaican Blood and the Victorian Conscience: The Governor Eyre Controversy* (Boston: Houghton Mifflin, 1962)

Bhagwati, Jagdish N. (ed.), *New International Economic Order: North-South Debate* (Cambridge, MA: MIT Press, 1977)

Bhargava, B.S., *The Criminal Tribes: A Socio-Economic Study of the Principal Criminal Tribes and Castes in Northern India* (Lucknow: Universal Publishers, 1949)

Bhatia, Amar, 'The South of the North: Building on Critical Approaches to International Law with Lessons from the FourthWorld' (2012) 14 *Oregon Review of International Law* 131

Bhuta, Nehal (ed.), *The Frontiers of Human Rights: Extraterritoriality and its Challenges* (Oxford: Oxford Universty Press, 2015)

Bignall, Simone and Marcelo Svirsky (eds.), *Agamben and Colonialism* (Edinburgh: Edinburgh University Press, 2012)

Binchy, D.A. (ed.), *Corpus Iuris Hibernici* (Dublin: Dublin Institute for Advanced Studies, 1988)

Bisharat, George, 'Land, Law, and Legitimacy in Israel and the Occupied Territories' (1994) 43 *The American University Law Review* 467

Bolt, Christine, *Victorian Attitudes to Race* (London: Routledge, 1971)

Bossuyt, Marc J., *Guide to the Travaux Préparatoires of the International Covenant on Civil and Political Rights* (Dordrecht: Martinus Nijhoff, 1987)

Boylan, Henry, *Theobald Wolfe Tone* (Dublin: Gill and Macmillan, 1981)

Branche, Raphaëlle, 'The Case of France in Algeria, 1954–1962' (2007) 89 *International Review of the Red Cross* 543

Brunet, Jean-Paul, *Police Contre FLN: Le drame d'octobre 1961* (Paris: Flammarion, 1999)

Buchanan, Ruth, 'Writing Resistance Into International Law' (2008) 10 *International Community Law Review* 445

Bukharin, Nikolai, *Imperialism and World Economy* (1917) (London: The Merlin Press, 1972)

Burchell, Graham, Colin Gordon and Peter Miller (eds.), *The Foucault Effect: Studies in Governmentality* (Chicago: University of Chicago Press, 1991)

Burin, Frederic S. and Kurt L. Shell (eds.), *Politics, Law, and Social Change: Selected Essays of Otto Kirchheimer* (New York: Columbia University Press, 1969)

Butler, Judith, *Precarious Life* (London: Verso, 2004)

Butler, Judith, 'Human Shields' (2015) 3:2 *London Review of International Law* 223

Calma, Tom, 'Indigenous Rights: The Debate over a Charter of Rights' (2008) 33:2 *Alternative Law Journal* 105

Cameron, Chloe, 'Recognising Human Rights in Australia's Third World: A Critical Analysis of the Displacement and Dispossession Caused by the Federal Government's Northern Territory Emergency Response' (2011) 4:2 *Queensland Law Student Review* 71

Campbell, Colm, *Emergency Law in Ireland, 1918-1925* (Oxford: Clarendon Press, 1994)

Capua, J.V., 'The Early History of Martial Law in England from the Fourteenth Century to the Petition of Right' (1977) 36:1 *Cambridge Law Journal* 152

Carey, John M. and Matthew Soberg Shugart (eds.), *Executive Decree Authority* (New York: Cambridge University Press, 1998)

Carey, Roane and Jonathan Shainin (eds.), *The Other Israel* (New York: The New Press, 2002)

Carlson, Scott N. and Gregory Gisvold, *Practical Guide to the International Covenant on Civil and Political Rights* (Ardsley, NY: Transnational, 2003)

Carothers, J.C., 'Frontal Lobe Function and the African' (1951) 97 *Journal of Mental Science* 12

Carothers, J.C., *The African Mind in Health and Disease* (Geneva: World Health Organization, 1953)

Carothers, J.C., *The Psychology of Mau Mau* (Nairobi: Government Printer, 1954)

Carr, Cecil T., 'Crisis Legislation in Britain' (1940) 40 *Columbia Law Review* 1309

Cavanaugh, Kathleen A., 'Policing the Margins: Rights Protection and the European Court of Human Rights' (2006) 4 *European Human Rights Law Review* 422

Césaire, Aimé, *Discourse on Colonialism* (1955) (Joan Pinkham trans., New York: Monthly Review Press, 1972)

Chandler, David, 'The Revival of Carl Schmitt in International Relations: The Last Refuge of Critical Theorists?' (2008) 37:1 *Millennium: Journal of International Studies* 27

Charlesworth, Hilary, 'International Law: A Discipline of Crisis' (2002) 65:3 *Modern Law Review* 383

Chatterjee, Partha, *The Politics of the Governed: Reflections on Popular Politics in Most of the World* (New York: Columbia University Press, 2004)

Childress, Diana, *Augusto Pinochet's Chile* (Minneapolis: Twenty-First Century Books, 2009)

Childs, Peter and Patrick Williams, *An Introduction to Post-Colonial Theory* (Hemel Hempstead: Prentice Hall, 1997)

Chimni, B.S., *International Law and World Order: A Critique of Contemporary Approaches* (New Delhi: Sage, 1993)

Chimni, B.S., 'Third World Approaches to International Law: A Manifesto' (2006) 8 *International Community Law Review* 3

Chimni, B.S., 'The Past, Present and Future of International Law: A Critical Third World Approach' (2007) 7 *Melbourne Journal of International Law* 499

Chimni, B.S., 'Capitalism, Imperialism and International Law in the 21st Century' (2012) 14:1 *Oregon Review of International Law* 17

Chossudovsky, Michel, *The Globalization of Poverty: Impacts of IMF and World Bank Reforms* (London: Zed Books, 1997)

Clayton, Anthony, *Counter-Insurgency in Kenya 1952-60: A Study of the Military Operations against the Mau Mau* (Nairobi: Transafrica, 1976)

Clough, Marshall, *Mau Mau Memoirs: History, Memory, and Politics* (Boulder, CO: Lynne Rienner, 1998)

Cobain, Ian, *Cruel Britannia: A Secret History of Torture* (London: Portobello, 2012)

Coetzee, J.M., *Waiting for the Barbarians* (London: Secker & Warburg, 1980)

Coetzee, J.M., *Diary of a Bad Year* (London: Harvill Secker, 2007)

Cohen, Amichai and Stuart Cohen, *Israel's National Security Law: Political Dynamics and Historical Development* (London: Routledge, 2011)

Colby, Elbridge, 'How to Fight Savage Tribes' (1927) 21 *American Journal of International Law* 279

Cook, S.B., *Imperial Affinities: Nineteenth-Century Analogies between India and Ireland* (New Delhi: Sage, 1993)

Cooper, Frederick and Ann L. Stoler (eds.), *Tensions of Empire: Colonial Cultures in a Bourgeois World* (Berkeley: University of California Press, 1997)

Corfield, Frank, *The Origins and Growth of Mau Mau: an Historical Survey* (Nairobi: Government of Kenya, 1960)

Cotter, Cornelius P., 'Constitutionalizing Emergency Powers: The British Experience' (1952-1953) 5 *Stanford Law Review* 382

Cowell, Frederick, 'Sovereignty and the Question of Derogation: An Analysis of Article 15 of the ECHR and the Absence of a Derogation Clause in the ACHPR' (2013) 1 *Birkbeck Law Review* 135

Criddle, Evan (ed.), *Human Rights in Emergencies* (Cambridge: Cambridge University Press, 2016)

Cripps, Kyllie, 'Indigenous Family Violence: From Emergency Measures to Committed Long-Term Action' (2007) 11:2 *Australian Indigenous Law Review* 6

Cronin, Seán, *For Whom the Hangman's Noose was Spun: Wolfe Tone and the United Irishmen* (Dublin: Repsol, 1991)

Crossman, Virginia, 'Emergency Legislation and Agrarian Disorder in Ireland, 1821-41' (1991) 27:108 *Irish Historical Studies* 309

Crusto, Mitchell F., *Involuntary Heroes: Hurricane Katrina's Impact on Civil Liberties* (Durham, NC: Carolina Academic Press, 2015)

Curtis Jr, L.P., *Apes and Angels: The Irishman in Victorian Caricature* (Newton Abbot: David & Charles, 1971)

da Costa, Karen, *The Extraterritorial Application of Selected Human Rights Treaties* (Leiden: Martinus Nijhoff, 2013)

Dallmayr, Winfried R. and Robert S. Rankin, *Freedom and Emergency Powers in the Cold War* (New York: Appleton-Century-Crofts, 1964)

Darcy, Shane and John Reynolds, 'An Enduring Occupation: The Status of the Gaza Strip from the Perspective of International Humanitarian Law' (2010) 15:2 *Journal of Conflict and Security Law* 211

David, Saul, *The Indian Mutiny, 1857* (London: Viking, 2002)

De Hart, William C., *Observations on Military Law* (New York: Wiley & Putnam, 1846)

de la Campa, Roman, E. Ann Kaplan and Michael Sprinker (eds.), *Late Imperial Culture* (London: Verso, 1995)

Denham, Mark E. and Mark Owen Lombardi (eds.), *Perspectives on Third World Sovereignty: The Postmodern Paradox* (London: Macmillan, 1996)

Dershowitz, Alan, *Why Terrorism Works: Understanding the Threat, Responding to the Challenge* (New Haven: Yale University Press, 2003)

de Soto, Hernando, *The Mystery of Capital: Why Capitalism Triumphs in the West and Fails Everywhere Else* (New York: Basic Books, 2000)

Dicey, A.V. *Introduction to the Study of the Law of the Constitution* (8th edn., London: Macmillan & Co., 1915)

Dickson, Brice, 'The Detention of Suspected Terrorists in Northern Ireland and Great Britain' (2009) 43 *University of Richmond Law Review* 927

Donohue, Laura K., *Counter-Terrorist Law and Emergency Powers in the United Kingdom, 1922-2000* (Dublin: Irish Academic Press, 2000)

Drescher, Seymour, 'The Ending of the Slave Trade and the Evolution of European Scientific Racism' (1990) 14:3 *Social Science History* 415

Dugard, John, Nicholas Haysom and Gilbert Marcus (eds.), *The Last Years of Apartheid: Civil Liberties in South Africa* (New York: Foreign Policy Association, 1992)

Dugard, John and John Reynolds, 'Apartheid, International Law, and the Occupied Palestinian Territory' (2013) 24:3 *European Journal of International Law* 867

Dutton, Geoffrey, *The Hero as Murderer: The Life of Edward John Eyre, Australian Explorer and Governor of Jamaica, 1815-1901* (Sydney: Collins, 1967)

Dyzenhaus, David (ed.), *Law as Politics: Carl Schmitt's Critique of Liberalism* (Durham, NC: Duke University Press, 1998)

Dyzenhaus, David, *Legality and Legitimacy: Carl Schmitt, Hans Kelsen and Hermann Heller in Weimar* (Oxford: Clarendon Press, 1997)

Dyzenhaus, David, 'The Puzzle of Martial Law' (2009) 59 *University of Toronto Law Journal* 1

Eaves, John, *Emergency Powers and the Parliamentary Watchdog: Parliament and the Executive in Great Britain, 1939-1951* (London: Hansard Society, 1957)

Egerton, R.B., *Mau Mau: An African Crucible* (New York: The Free Press, 1989)

Elias, T.O., *Africa and the Development of International Law* (Leiden: Sijthoff, 1972)

Elias, T.O., *New Horizons in International Law* (Leiden: Sijthoff, 1979)

Elkins, Caroline, *Imperial Reckoning: The Untold Story of Britain's Gulag in Kenya* (London: Pimlico, 2005)

Caroline Elkins, 'Looking Beyond Mau Mau: Archiving Violence in the Era of Decolonization' (2015) 120:3 *American Historical Review* 852

Elliott, Marianne, *Wolfe Tone: Prophet of Irish Independence* (New Haven: Yale University Press, 1989)

Escobar, Arturo, *Encountering Development: The Making and Unmaking of the Third World* (Princeton, Princeton University Press, 1995)

Eslava, Luis and Sundhya Pahuja, 'Between Resistance and Reform: TWAIL and the Universality of International Law' (2011) 3:1 *Trade, Law & Development* 103

Eslava, Luis, *Local Space, Global Life: The Everyday Operation of International Law and Development* (Cambridge: Cambridge University Press, 2015)

Esmeir, Samera, *Juridical Humanity: A Colonial History* (Stanford: Stanford University Press, 2012)

Etkes, Dror and Hagit Ofran, *Breaking the Law in the West Bank: Israeli Settlement Building on Private Palestinian Property* (Jerusalem: Peace Now, 2006)

Evans, Peter, *Law and Disorder: Scenes of Life in Kenya* (London: Secker & Warburg, 1956)

Fairman, Charles, 'The Law of Martial Rule' (1928) 22 *American Political Science Review* 591

Fairman, Charles, 'Martial Rule, In the Light of Sterling v. Constantin' (1934) 19 *Cornell Law Quarterly* 20

Fairman, Charles, 'The Law of Martial Rule and the National Emergency' (1942) 55 *Harvard Law Review* 1253

Fakhri, Michael, 'Law as the Interplay of Ideas, Institutions, and Interests: Using Polanyi (and Foucault) to ask TWAIL Questions' (2008) 10 *International Community Law Review* 455

Falk, Richard, Friedrich Kratochwil and Saul H. Mendlowitz (eds.), *International Law: A Contemporary Perspective* (Boulder: Westview Press, 1985)

Falk, Richard, Balakrishnan Rajagopal and Jacqueline Stevens (eds.), *International Law and the Third World: Reshaping Justice* (London: Routledge-Cavendish, 2008)

Fanon, Frantz, *The Wretched of the Earth* (1961) (Constance Farrington trans., London: Penguin, 1967)

Fanon, Frantz, *Toward the African Revolution: Political Essays* (Haakon Chevalier trans., New York: Grove Press, 1970)

Farrell, Michelle, *The Prohibition of Torture in Exceptional Circumstances* (Cambridge: Cambridge University Press, 2013)

Fassin, Didier and Mariella Pandolfi (eds.), *Contemporary States of Emergency: The Politics of Military and Humanitarian Interventions* (New York: Zone Books, 2010)

Fatovic, Clement, 'The Political Theology of Prerogative: The Jurisprudential Miracle in Liberal Constitutional Thought' (2008) 6:3 *Perspectives on Politics* 488

Finlason, W.F., *The History of the Jamaica Case* (London: Chapman & Hall, 1868)

Fisch, Jörg, *Die europäische Expansion und das Völkerrecht* (Stuttgart: Jahrhundert bis zur Gegenwart, 1984)

Fisch, Jörg, 'International Law in the Expansion of Europe' (1986) 34 *Law and State: A Biannual Collection of Recent German Contributions* 7

Fisch, Jörg, 'The Role of International Law in the Territorial Expansion of Europe, 16th–20th Centuries' (2000) 3:1 *International Center for Comparative Law and Politics Review* 4

Foley, Tadhg and Maureen O'Connor (eds.), *Ireland and India: Colonies, Culture and Empire* (Dublin: Irish Academic Press, 2006)

Forbes, Geraldine, *Women in Modern India, Volume 4* (Cambridge: Cambridge University Press, 1996)

Foucault, Michel, *The History of Sexuality Volume I: An Introduction (1976)* (Robert Hurley trans., London: Allen Lane, 1979)

Foucault, Michel and Colin Gordon (eds.), *Power/Knowledge* (Colin Gordon et al. trans., New York: Pantheon Books, 1980)

Foucault, Michel, *Society Must Be Defended: Lectures at the Collège de France, 1975-76* (1997) (David Macey trans., London: Penguin, 2004)

Foucault, Michel, *Security, Territory, Population: Lectures at the College de France 1977-1978* (New York: Palgrave Macmillan, 2007)

Foucault, Michel, *The Birth of Biopolitics: Lectures at the College de France, 1978-79* (Graham Burchell trans., Michel Senellart ed., New York: Palgrave MacMillan, 2010)

French, David, *The British Way in Counter-Insurgency, 1945–1967* (Oxford: Oxford University Press, 2012)

Füredi, Frank, 'The Social Composition of the Mau Mau Movement in the White Highlands' (1974) 1 *Journal of Peasant Studies* 486

Füredi, Frank, *The Mau Mau War in Perspective* (Nairobi: Heinemann, 1989)

Füredi, Frank, *Colonial Wars and the Politics of Third World Nationalism* (London: I.B. Tauris, 1994)

Furnivall, J.S., *Progress and Welfare in South-East Asia: A Comparison of Colonial Policy and Practice* (New York: Secretariat, Institute of Pacific Relations, 1941)

Furnivall, J.S., *Colonial Policy and Practice: A Comparative Study of Burma and Netherlands India* (Cambridge: Cambridge University Press, 1948)

Gaikwad, Namrata, 'Revolting Bodies, Hysterical State: Women Protesting the Armed Forces Special Powers Act (1958)' (2009) 17:3 *Contemporary South Asia* 299

Gathii, James Thuo, *War, Commerce, and International Law* (New York: Oxford University Press USA, 2010)

Gavaghan, Terence, *Corridors of Wire: A Saga of Colonial Power and Preventive Detention in Kenya* (London: Terence Gavaghan, 1994)

Gélinas, Jacques B., *Freedom from Debt: The Reappropriation of Development Through Financial Self-Reliance* (1994) (Arnold Bennett and Raymond Robitaille trans., London: Zed Books, 1998)

Ghai, Yash, Robin Luckham and Francis Snyder (eds.), *The Political Economy of Law: A Third World Reader* (New Delhi: Oxford University Press, 1987)

Gibbons, Luke, *Transformations in Irish Culture* (Cork: Field Day, 1996)

Gikoyo, Gucu G, *We Fought for Freedom* (Nairobi: East African Publishing House, 1979)

Golder, Ben and Peter Fitzpatrick, *Foucault's Law* (Abingdon: Routledge, 2009)

Gordon, Neve, *Israel's Occupation* (Berkeley: University of California Press, 2008)

Gott, Gil, 'The Devil We Know: Racial Subordination and National Security Law' (2005) 50 *Villanova Law Review* 1073

Graham, Colin, *Deconstructing Ireland: Idenity, Theory, Culture* (Edinburgh: Edinburgh University Press, 2001)

Gramsci, Antonio, *Selections from the Prison Notebooks* (London: Lawrence & Wishart, 2003)

Green, Maia, 'Mau Mau Oathing Rituals and Political Ideology in Kenya: A Re-analysis' (1990) 60:1 *Africa* 69

Greenberg, Karen (ed.), *The Torture Debate in America* (New York: Cambridge University Press, 2006)

Greenberg, Karen J. and Joshua L. Dratel, *The Torture Papers: The Road to Abu Ghraib* (Cambridge: Cambridge University Press, 2005)

Greer, Steven, *'The Margin of Appreciation: Interpretation and Discretion under the European Convention on Human Rights'* (Strasbourg: Council of Europe, 2000)

Gregory, Derek, *The Colonial Present* (Malden, MA: Blackwell, 2004)

Gregory, Derek, 'Palestine and the "War on Terror"' (2004) 24:1 *Comparative Studies of South Asia, Africa and the Middle East* 183

Grewe, Wilhelm G., *The Epochs of International Law* (1984) (Michael Byers trans., Berlin: Walter de Gruyter, 2000)

Gross, Emanuel, 'Human Rights, Terrorism and the Problem of Administrative Detention in Israel: Does a Democracy Have the Right to Hold Terrorists as Bargaining Chips?' (2001) 18:3 *Arizona Journal of International and Comparative Law* 721

Gross, Oren, '"Once More unto the Breach": The Systemic Failure of Applying the European Convention on Human Rights to Entrenched Emergencies' (1998) 23 *Yale Journal of International Law* 437

Gross, Oren, 'The Normless and Exceptionless Exception: Carl Schmitt's Theory of Emergency Powers and the "Norm-Exception" Dichotomy' (2000) 21 *Cardozo Law Review* 1825

Gross, Oren, 'Chaos and Rules: Should Responses to Violent Crises Always Be Constitutional?' (2003) 112 *Yale Law Journal* 1011

Gross, Oren, 'Are Torture Warrants Warranted? Pragmatic Absolutism and Official Disobedience' (2004) 88 *Minnesota Law Review* 1481

Gross, Oren and Fionnuala Ní Aoláin, 'From Discretion to Scrutiny: Revisiting the Application of the Margin of Appreciation Doctrine in the Context of Article 15 of the European Convention on Human Rights' (2001) 23 *Human Rights Quarterly* 625

Gross, Oren and Fionnuala Ní Aoláin, *Law in Times of Crisis: Emergency Powers in Theory and Practice* (Cambridge: Cambridge University Press, 2006)

Guha, Ranajit and Gayatri Chakravorty Spivak, *Selected Subaltern Studies* (Oxford: Oxford University Press Press, 1988)

Guha, Ranajit (ed.), *VI Subaltern Studies* (Delhi: Oxford University Press, 1989)

Gunneflo, Markus, *Targeted Killing: A Legal and Political History* (Cambridge: Cambridge University Press, 2016)

Hafner-Burton, Emilie M., Laurence R. Helfer and Christopher J. Fariss, 'Emergency and Escape: Explaining Derogations from Human Rights Treaties' (2011) 65:4 *International Organization* 673

Hahn, Michael J., 'Vital Interests and the Law of GATT: An Analysis of GATT's Security Exception' (1991) 12 *Michigan Journal of International Law* 558

Hall, Stuart, 'Conclusion: The Multi-Cultural Question' in Barnor Hesse (ed.), *Un/settled Multiculturalisms: Diasporas, Entanglements, Transruptions* (London: Zed Books, 2000)

Hammond, John L., *Gladstone and the Irish Nation* (London: Longmans, 1938)

Hamzić, Vanja, 'Mir-Said Sultan-Galiev and the Idea of Muslim Marxism: Empire, Third World(s) and Praxis' (2016) 37:11 *Third World Quarterly* 2047

Hardt, Michael and Antonio Negri, *Multitude: War and Democracy in the Age of Empire* (New York: Penguin, 2004)

Hart, H.L.A., *The Concept of Law* (Oxford: Oxford University Press, 1961)

Hartman, Chester and Gregory D. Squires (eds.), *There is No Such Thing as a Natural Disaster: Race, Class, and Hurricane Katrina* (New York: Routledge, 2006)

Harvey, David, *The Enigma of Capital and the Crises of Capitalism* (Oxford: Oxford University Press, 2010)

Hay McRae, Cosima, 'Suspending the Racial Discrimination Act, 1975 (Cth): Domestic and International Dimensions' (2012) 13 *Journal of Indigenous Policy* 61

Herzl, Theodor, The Jewish State *(1896)* (Raleigh: Hayes Barton Press, 2006)

Higgins, Rosalyn, 'Derogation under Human Rights Treaties' (1976) 48 *British Yearbook of International Law* 281

Hilferding, Rudolf, *Finance Capital: A Study of the Latest Phase of Capitalist Development* (1910) (Tom Bottomore ed., Morris Watnick and Sam Gordon trans., London: Routledge, 1981)

Hillyard, Paddy, *Suspect Community: People's Experience of the Prevention of Terrorism Acts in Britain* (London: Pluto, 1993)

Hobson, John A., *Imperialism: A Study* (London: James Nisbet, 1902)

Hoexter, Cora, 'Emergency Law' (1990) 1 *South African Human Rights Yearbook* 110

Hofnung, Menachem, *Democracy, Law and National Security in Israel* (Brookfield, VT: Dartmouth, 1996)

Holland, Denys C., 'Emergency Legislation in the Commonwealth' (1960) 13 *Current Legal Problems* 148

Holland, Robert, *Britain and the Revolt In Cyprus, 1954-1959* (Oxford: Oxford University Press, 1998)

Holland, Robert (ed.), *Emergencies and Disorder in the European Empires After 1945* (Abingdon: Frank Cass, 1994)

Holmes, Michael and Denis Holmes (eds.), *Ireland and India: Connections, Comparisons, Contrasts* (Dublin: Folens, 1997)

Honig, Bonnie, *Emergency Politics* (Princeton: Princeton University Press, 2009)

Hovell Devoka, 'The Gulf between Tortious and Torturous: UK Responsibility for Mistreatment of the Mau Mau in Colonial Kenya' (2013) 11 *Journal of International Criminal Justice* 223

Howey, Kirsty, '"Normalising" What? A Qualitative Analysis of Aboriginal Land Tenure Reform in the Northern Territory' (2014) 18:1 *Australian Indigenous Law Review* 4

Hunt, Alan and Gary Wickham, *Foucault and Law: Towards a Sociology of Law as Governance* (London: Pluto, 1994)

Hussain, Nasser, 'Towards a Jurisprudence of Emergency: Colonialism and the Rule of Law' (1999) 10 *Law & Critique* 93

Hussain, Nasser, *The Jurisprudence of Emergency: Colonialism and the Rule of Law* (Ann Arbor: University of Michigan Press, 2003)

Hussain, Nasser, 'Hyperlegality' (2007) 10 *New Criminal Law Review* 514

Hyam, Ronald, *Britain's Imperial Century, 1815-1914: A Study of Empire and Expansion* (Basingstoke: Palgrave Macmillan, 2002)

Ignatiev, Noel, *How the Irish Became White* (New York; Routledge, 1995)

Ismael, Tareq Y. (ed.), *The International Relations of the Middle East in the Twenty-First Century* (Aldershot: Ashgate, 2000)

Jackson, John H., *The World Trading System: Law and Policy of International Economic Relations* (2nd edn., Cambridge, MA: MIT Press, 1997)

Jeffery, Keith and Peter Hennessy, *States of Emergency: British Governments and Strikebreaking Since 1919* (London: Routledge, 1983)

Jiryis, Sabri, *The Arabs in Israel* (New York: Monthly Review Press, 1976)

Jiryis, Sabri, 'The Arabs in Israel 1973-79' (1979) 8:4 *Journal of Palestine Studies* 31

Johns, Fleur, Richard Joyce and Sundhya Pahuja (eds.), *Events: The Force of International Law* (Abingdon: Routledge, 2011)

Johnson, James, *A Tour in Ireland: With Meditations and Reflections* (London: S. Highley, 1844)

Joseph, Bernard, *British Rule in Palestine* (Washington: Public Affairs Press, 1948)

Joseph, Sarah, Jenny Schultz and Melissa Castan, *The International Covenant on Civil and Political Rights: Cases, Materials, and Commentary* (Oxford: Oxford University Press, 2004)

Kahan, Rebecca M., 'Constitutional Stretch, Snap-Back, and Sag: Why Blaisdell was a Harsher Blow to Liberty than Korematsu' (2005) 99 *Northwestern University Law Review* 1279

Kalhan, Anil, Gerald P. Conroy, Mamta Kaushal, Sam Scott Miller and Jed S. Rakoff, 'Colonial Continuities: Human Rights, Terrorism, and Security Laws in India' (2006) 20:1 *Columbia Journal of Asian Law* 93

Kanwar, Vik, 'International Emergency Governance: Fragments of a Driverless System' (2004) *Critical Sense* 41

Kariuki, Josiah Mwangi, *'Mau Mau' Detainee* (Nairobi: Oxford University Press, 1963)

Kaye, J., *Kaye and Malleson's History of the Indian Mutiny of 1857-8* (London: Longmans, Green & Co., 1907-11)

Keenan, Sarah, 'Property as Governance: Time, Space and Belonging in Australia's Northern Territory Intervention' (2013) 76:3 *Modern Law Review* 464

Kelly, Fergus, *A Guide to Early Irish Law* (Dublin: Dublin Institute for Advanced Studies, 1988)

Kelly, Joseph B. and George A. Pelletier, 'Theories of Emergency Government' (1966) 11 *South Dakota Law Review* 42

Kennedy, David, 'Law and the Political Economy of the World' (2013) 26 *Leiden Journal of International Law* 7

Khalidi, Walid, 'Plan Dalet: Master Plan for the Conquest of Palestine' (1988) 18:1 *Journal of Palestine Studies* 4

Kitson, Frank, *Low Intensity Operations: Subversion, Insurgency and Peacekeeping* (London: Faber & Faber, 1971)

Kitson, Frank, *Bunch of Five* (London: Faber & Faber, 1977)

Klein, Naomi, *The Shock Doctrine: The Rise of Disaster Capitalism* (New York: Metropolitan Books, 2007)

Knox, Robert, 'Strategy and Tactics' (2010) 21 *Finnish Yearbook of International Law* 193

Kolsky, Elizabeth, *Colonial Justice in British India: White Violence and the Rule of Law* (Cambridge: Cambridge University Press, 2010)

Kooijmans, Pieter Hendrik, *The Doctrine of the Legal Equality of States: An Inquiry into the Foundations of International Law* (Leiden: A.W. Sijthoff, 1964)

Koskenniemi, Martti, *From Apology to Utopia: The Structure of International Legal Argument* (Helsinki: Lakimiesliiton Kustannus, 1989)

Koskenniemi, Martti, 'International Law and Hegemony: A Reconfiguration' (2004) 17:2 *Cambridge Review of International Affairs* 197

Koskenniemi, Martti, 'International Law as Political Theology: How to Read *Nomos der Erde*?' (2004) 11:4 *Constellations* 492

Koskenniemi, Martti, *From Apology to Utopia: The Structure of International Legal Argument* (Reissue with a New Epilogue, Cambridge: Cambridge University Press, 2005)

Koskenniemi, Martti, 'Histories of International Law: Dealing with Eurocentrism' (2011) 19 *Rechtsgeschichte* 152

Koskenniemi, Martti, *The Politics of International Law* (Oxford: Hart, 2011)

Kostal, R.W., *A Jurisprudence of Power: Victorian Empire and the Rule of Law* (Oxford: Oxford University Press, 2005)

Kratochvíl, Jan, 'The Inflation of the Margin of Appreciation by the European Court of Human Rights' (2011) 29:3 *Netherlands Quarterly of Human Rights* 329

Kretzmer, David, *The Legal Status of the Arabs in Israel* (Boulder: Westview Press, 1990)

Kretzmer, David, *The Occupation of Justice* (New York: SUNY Press, 2002)

Laski, Harold, *The Crisis and the Constitution: 1931 and After* (London: Hogarth Press, 1932)

Lauterpacht, Elihu, 'The Contemporary Practice of the United Kingdom in the Field of International Law – Survey and Comment' (1956) 5:3 *International Law Quarterly* 405

Lawrence, Carmen, 'The "Emergency Intervention" in Northern Territory Indigenous Communities' (2008) 7 *The New Critic*

Lazar, Nomi Claire, *States of Emergency in Liberal Democracies* (Cambridge: Cambridge University Press, 2009)

Lazreg, Marnia, *Torture and the Twilight of Empire: From Algiers to Baghdad* (Princeton: Princeton University Press, 2008)

Leadam, Isaac S., *Coercive Measures in Ireland, 1830-1880* (London: National Press Agency, 1886)

Leakey, Louis, *Defeating Mau Mau* (London: Methuen & Co, 1954)

Lebow, Richard Ned, *White Britain and Black Ireland: The Influence of Stereotypes on Colonial Policy* (Philadelphia: Institute for the Study of Human Issues, 1976)

Lee, H.P., *Emergency Powers* (Sydney: Law Book Co., 1984)

Legg, Andrew, *The Margin of Appreciation in International Human Rights Law: Deference and Proportionality* (Oxford: Oxford University Press, 2012)

Lenin, V.I., *Imperialism: The Highest Stage of Capitalism: A Popular Outline* (1917) (New York: International Publishers, 1939)

Lennon, Joseph, *Irish Orientalism: A Literary and Intellectual History* (Syracuse, NY: Syracuse University Press, 2004)

Lentin, Ronit, '*Femina sacra*: Gendered Memory and Political Violence' (2006) 29:5 *Women's Studies International Forum* 463

Lentin, Ronit (ed.), *Thinking Palestine* (London: Zed, 2008)

Lentin, Ronit, 'Palestinian Women: From *Femina Sacra* to Agents of Active Resistance' (2011) 34:2 *Women's Studies International Forum* 165

Lentin, Ronit, 'Palestine/Israel and State Criminality: Exception, Settler Colonialism and Racialization' (2016) 5:1 *State Crime* 32

Levinson, Sanford (ed.), *Torture: A Collection* (Oxford: Oxford University Press, 2004)

Lloyd, David, 'Settler Colonialism and the State of Israel: The Example of Palestine/Israel' (2012) 2:1 *Settler Colonial Studies* 59

Lloyd, David and Patrick Wolfe, 'Settler Colonial Logics and the Neoliberal Regime' (2016) 6:2 *Settler Colonial Studies* 109

Locke, John, *Two Treatises of Government* (1690) (Cambridge: Cambridge University Press, 1960)

Lonsdale, John, 'Mau Maus of the Mind: Making Mau Mau and Remaking Kenya' (1990) 31:3 *Journal of African History* 393

Luban, David, 'Liberalism, Torture, and the Ticking Bomb' (2005) 91 *Virginia Law Review* 1425

Luban, David, 'Carl Schmitt and the Critique of Lawfare' (2010) 43 *Case Western Reserve Journal of International Law* 457

Lugard, Frederick, *The Dual Mandate in British Tropical Africa* (Hamden, CT: Archon Books, 1965)

Lustick, Ian, *Arabs in a Jewish State: Israel's Control of a National Minority* (Austin: University of Texas Press, 1980)

Luxemburg, Rosa, *The Accumulation of Capital* (1913) (Kenneth J. Tarbuck ed., Rudolf Wichmann trans., London: Penguin, 1972)

MacDermott, John Clarke, 'Law and Order in Times of Emergency' (1972) 17 *Juridical Review* 1

MacDougall, Hugh A., *Racial Myth in English History* (New England: Harvest House, 1982)

Macharia, Kinuthia and Muigai Kanyua, *The Social Context of the Mau Mau Movement in Kenya (1952-1960)* (Oxford: University Press of America, 2006)

Mackenzie, Fiona, *Land, Ecology and Resistance in Kenya, 1880–1952* (Edinburgh: Edinburgh University Press, 1998)

Majdalany, Fred, *State of Emergency: The Full Story of Mau Mau* (London: Longmans, 1962)

Major, Andrew J., 'State and Criminal Tribes in Colonial Punjab: Surveillance, Control and Reclamation of the "Dangerous Classes"' (1999) 33 *Modern Asian Studies* 657

Makdisi, Saree, *Palestine Inside Out: An Everyday Occupation* (New York: W.W. Norton & Co., 2008)

Malik, Kenan, *The Meaning of Race: Race, History, and Culture in Western Society* (New York: New York University Press, 1996)

Maloba, Wunyabari O., *Mau Mau and Kenya: An Analysis of a Peasant Revolt* (Bloomington: Indiana University Press, 1993)

Mandela, Nelson, *The Long Walk to Freedom* (London: Abacus, 1994)

Mansoor, M., *The Story of Irish Orientalism* (Dublin: Hodges Figgis, 1944)

Mansour, Camille, 'Israel's Colonial Impasse' (2001) 30:4 *Journal of Palestine Studies* 83

Maran, Rita, *Torture: The Role of Ideology in the French-Algerian War* (New York: Praeger, 1989)

Marks, Susan, 'Civil Liberties at the Margin: the UK Derogation and the European Court of Human Rights' (1995) 15 *Oxford Journal of Legal Studies* 69

Marshall, P.J., 'Empire and Authority in the later Eighteenth Century' (1987) 25:2 *Journal of Imperial & Commonwealth History* 105

Marx, Karl, *The Eighteenth Brumaire of Louis Bonaparte* (1852) (Moscow: Progress Publishers, 1934)

Marx, Karl and Friedrich Engels, *On Colonialism* (Moscow: Foreign Languages Publishing House, 1960)

Marx, Karl and Friedrich Engels, *Marx and Engels on Ireland* (Moscow: Progress Publishers, 1971)

Marx, Karl and Friedrich Engels, *On Colonies, Industrial Monopoly and Working Class Movement* (Copenhagen: Futura, 1972)

Masters, Cristina, '*Femina Sacra*: The "War on/of Terror", Women and the Feminine' (2009) 40:1 *Security Dialogue* 29

Mathews, A.S. and R.C. Albino, 'The Permanence of the Temporary: An Examination of the 90- and 180-Day Detention Laws' (1966) 83 *South African Law Journal* 16

Maus, Ingeborg, 'The 1933 "Break" in Carl Schmitt's Theory' (1997) 10 *Canadian Journal of Law & Jurisprudence* 125

Mazel, Odette, 'Development in the "First World": Alleviating Indigenous Disadvantage in Australia – the Dilemma of Difference' (2009) 18:2 *Griffith Law Review* 475

Mbembe, Achille, *On the Postcolony* (Berkeley: University of California Press, 2001)

Mbembe, Achille, 'Necropolitics' (2003) 15:1 *Public Culture* 11

McClintock, Anne, *Imperial Leather: Race, Gender, and Sexuality in the Colonial Contest* (London: Routledge, 1995)

McCormick, John P., *Carl Schmitt's Critique of Liberalism: Against Politics as Technology* (New York: Cambridge University Press, 1997)

McCulloch, Jock, *Black Soul White Artifact: Fanon's Clinical Psychology and Social Theory* (Cambridge: Cambridge University Press, 1983)

McDuie-Ra, Duncan, 'Fifty-year Disturbance: The Armed Forces Special Powers Act and Exceptionalism in a South Asian Periphery' (2009) 17:3 *Contemporary South Asia* 255

Mehozay, Yoav, 'The Fluid Jurisprudence of Israel's Emergency Powers: Legal Patchwork as a Governing Norm' (2012) 46:1 *Law & Society Review* 137

Memmi, Albert, *The Colonizer and the Colonized* (1965) (Howard Greenfeld trans., London: Earthscan Publications, 1990)

Meredith, Martin, *The State of Africa* (London: Free Press, 2005)

Meron, Theodor, *Human Rights and Humanitarian Norms as Customary Law* (Oxford: Clarendon, 1989)

Merry, Sally Engle, 'Law and Colonialism' (1991) 25:6 *Law and Society Review* 889

Mickelson, Karin, 'Rhetoric and Rage: Third World Voices in International Legal Discourse' (1998) 16 *Wisconsin International Law Journal* 360

Miéville, China, *Between Equal Rights: A Marxist Theory of International Law* (Leiden: Brill, 2005)

Miliband, Ralph, *The State in Capitalist Society* (London: Quartet Books, 1969)

Mntambo, Vincent, 'Emergency Law' (1991) 2 *South African Human Rights Yearbook* 83

Montesquieu, *The Spirit of the Laws* (1748) (Cambridge: Cambridge University Press, 1989)

Morash, Christopher and Richard Hayes (eds.), *Fearful Realities: New Perspectives on the Famine* (Dublin: Irish Academic Press, 1996)

Moreton-Robinson, Aileen, 'The Possessive Logic of Patriarchal White Sovereignty: The High Court and the Yorta Yorta Decision' (2004) 3:2 *Borderlands* 1

Morris, Gillian S., 'The Emergency Powers Act 1920' (1979) *Public Law* 317

Morris, Shireen, 'Indigenous Constitutional Recognition, Non-Discrimination and Equality before the Law: Why Reform Is Necessary' (2011) 7:26 *Indigenous Law Bulletin* 7

Morsink, Johannes, *The Universal Declaration of Human Rights: Origins, Drafting, and Intent* (Philadelphia: University of Pennsylvania Press, 1999)

Morton, Stephen, *States of Emergency: Colonialism, Literature and Law* (Liverpool: Liverpool University Press, 2013)

Moor, Louise and A.W.B. Simpson, 'Ghosts of Colonialism in the European Convention on Human Rights' (2005) 76:1 *British Yearbook of International Law* 121

Müller, Amrei, 'Limitations to and Derogations from Economic, Social and Cultural Rights' (2009) 9:4 *Human Rights Law Review* 557

Muñoz Heraldo, *The Dictator's Shadow: Life under Augusto Pinochet* (New York: Basic Books, 2008)

Mutua, Makau, 'The African Human Rights Court: A Two-Legged Stool?' (1999) 21 *Human Rights Quarterly* 343

Mutua, Makau, 'What is TWAIL?' (2000) 94 *American Society of International Law Proceedings* 31

Nakkara, Hanna Dib, 'Israeli Land Seizure under Various Defense and Emergency Regulations' (1985) 14:2 *Journal of Palestine Studies* 13

Neal, Andrew W., 'Normalisation and Legislative Exceptionalism: Counterterrorist Lawmaking and the Changing Times of Security Emergencies' (2012) 6:3 *International Political Sociology* 260

Nelson, Cary and Lawrence Grossberg (eds.), *Marxism and the Interpretation of Culture* (Basingstoke: Macmillan, 1988)

Neocleous, Mark, 'The Problem with Normality: Taking Exception to "Permanent Emergency"' (2006) 31 *Alternatives* 191

Neocleous, Mark, 'From Martial Law to the War on Terror' (2007) 10:4 *New Criminal Law Review* 489

Neocleous, Mark, *Critique of Security* (Edinburgh: Edinburgh University Press, 2008)

Ní Aoláin, Fionnuala, 'The Cloak and Dagger Game of Derogation', in Evan Criddle (ed.), *Human Rights in Emergencies* (Cambridge: Cambridge University Press, 2016)

Nicholls, Anthony and Erich Matthias (eds.), *German Democracy and the Triumph of Hitler* (New York: St. Martin's Press, 1971)

Nigam, Sanjay, 'Disciplining and Policing the "Criminals by Birth", Part 1: The Making of a Colonial Stereotype – the Criminal Tribes and Castes of North India' (1990) 27:2 *Indian Economic Social History Review* 131

Nigam, Sanjay, 'Disciplining and Policing the "Criminals by Birth", Part 2: The Development of a Disciplinary System, 1871–1900' (1990) 27:3 *Indian Economic Social History Review* 257

Nolte, Georg, 'General Principles of German and European Administrative Law – A Comparison in Historical Perspective' (1994) 57:2 *Modern Law Review* 191

O'Brien, John Paul Jones, *Treatise on American Military Laws* (Philadelphia: Lea & Blanchard, 1846)

Odumosu, Ibironke T., 'The Law and Politics of Engaging Resistance in Investment Dispute Settlement' (2007) 26:2 *Penn State International Law Review* 251

Ohlin, Jens David and Larry May, *Necessity in International Law* (Oxford: Oxford University Press, 2016)

Okafor, Obiora Chinedu, *Re-defining Legitimate Statehood: International Law and State Fragmentation in Africa* (The Hague: Martinus Nijhoff, 2000)

Okafor, Obiora Chinedu, 'Critical Third World Approaches to International Law (TWAIL): Theory, Methodology, or Both?' (2008) 10 *International Community Law Review* 371

Oliviero, Katie E., 'The Immigration State of Emergency: Racializing and Gendering National Vulnerability in Twenty-First-Century Citizenship and Deportation Regimes' (2013) 25:2 *Feminist Formations* 1

Olson, Mancur, *The Rise and Decline of Nations: Economic Growth, Stagflation, and Social Rigidities* (New Haven: Yale University Press, 1982)

Omi, Michael and Howard Winant, *Racial Formation in the United States: From the 1960s to the 1990s* (New York: Routledge, 1994)

Ophir, Adi, Michal Givoni and Sari Hanafi (eds.), *The Power of Inclusive Exclusion: Anatomy of Israeli Rule in the Occupied Palestinian Territories* (New York: Zone Books, 2009)

Orford, Anne, *Reading Humanitarian Intervention: Human Rights and the Use of Force in International Law* (Cambridge: Cambridge University Press, 2003)

Orford, Anne (ed.), *International Law and its Others* (Cambridge: Cambridge University Press, 2006)

Overton, John, 'The Origins of the Kikuyu Land Problem: Land Alienation and Land Use in Kiambu, Kenya, 1895– 1920' (1988) 31 *African Studies Review* 109

Page, James, *Ireland: Its Evils Traced to Their Source* (London: Seeley & Burnside, 1836)

Pahuja, Sundhya, 'Technologies of Empire: IMF Conditionality and the Reinscription of the North/South Divide' (2000) 13 *Leiden Journal of International Law* 749

Pahuja, Sundhya, *Decolonising International Law: Development, Economic Growth and the Politics of Universality* (Cambridge: Cambridge University Press, 2011)

Pakenham, Thomas, *The Year of Liberty: The Great Irish Rebellion of 1798* (London: Hodder & Stoughton, 1969)

Palley, Thomas I., 'The Limits of Minsky's Financial Instability Hypothesis as an Explanation of the Crisis' (2010) 61:11 *Monthly Review* 28

Pantazis, Christina and Simon Pemberton, 'From the "Old" to the "New" Suspect Community: Examining the Impacts of Recent UK Counter-Terrorist Legislation' (2009) 49:5 *British Journal of Criminology* 646

Pappé, Ilan, *The Ethnic Cleansing of Palestine* (Oxford: Oneworld, 2006)

Pati, Biswamoy (ed.), *Adivasis in Colonial India: Survival, Resistance and Negotiation* (New Delhi: Orient Blackswan, 2011)

Pearson, Noel, 'White Guilt, Victimhood and the Quest for a Radical Centre' (2007) 16 *Griffith Review* 11

Perrine, Aaron, 'The First Amendment Versus the World Trade Organization: Emergency Powers and the Battle in Seattle' (2001) 76 *Washington Law Review* 635

Polanyi, Karl, *The Great Transformation: The Political and Economic Origin of Our Time* (New York: Farrar & Reinhart, 1944)

Pollock, Frederick, 'What is Martial Law?' (1902) 18 *The Law Quarterly Review* 152

Porter, Andrew (ed.), *Oxford History of the British Empire, Volume III: The Nineteenth Century* (Oxford: Oxford University Press, 1999)

Pouchepadass, Jacques, *Champaran and Gandhi: Planters, Peasants and Gandhian Politics* (New Delhi: Oxford University Press, 1999)

Poulett Scrope, George, *How is Ireland to Be Governed?* (London: James Ridgway, 1846)

Power, Patrick C., *The Courts-Martial of 1798-99* (Kilkenny: Irish Historical Press, 1997)

Prashad, Vijay, *The Darker Nations: A People's History of the Third World* (New York: New Press, 2007)

Prashad, Vijay, *The Poorer Nations: A Possible History of the Global South* (London: Verso, 2012)

Prashad, Vijay, *The Death of the Nation and the Future of the Arab Revolution* (Oakland: University of California Press, 2016)

Prashad, Vijay (ed.), *Letters to Palestine: Writers Respond to War and Occupation* (London: Verso, 2014)

Prince, Raymond H., 'John Colin D. Carothers (1903-1989) and African Colonial Psychiatry' (1996) 33 *Transcultural Psychiatry* 226

Quigley, John, 'Israel's Forty-Five Year Emergency: Are There Time Limits to Derogations from Human Rights Obligations?' (1994) 15 *Michigan Journal of International Law* 491

Quigley, John, *The Case for Palestine: An International Law Perspective* (2nd edn., Durham: Duke University Press, 2005)

Radhakrishna, Meena, *Dishonoured by History: "Criminal Tribes" and British Colonial Policy* (Hyderabad: Orient Longman, 2001)

Rajagopal, Balakrishnan, *International Law from Below: Development, Social Movements and Third World Resistance* (Cambridge: Cambridge University Press, 2003)

Ramakrishna, Kumar, *Emergency Propaganda: The Winning of Malayan Hearts and Minds, 1948-1958* (London: Routledge, 2002)

Ramraj, Victor V. (ed.), *Emergencies and the Limits of Legality* (Cambridge: Cambridge University Press, 2008)

Ramraj, Victor V., Michael Hor and Kent Roach (eds.), *Global Anti-Terrorism Law and Policy* (Cambridge: Cambridge University Press, 2005)

Randall, James G., *Constitutional Problems under Lincoln* (Urbana: University of Illinois Press, 1926)

Raulff, Ulrich, 'An Interview with Giorgio Agamben' (2004) 5:5 *German Law Journal* 609

Razack, Sherene H., (ed.), *Race, Space, and the Law: Unmapping a White Settler Society* (Toronto: Between the Lines, 2002)

Reinach, Théodore, *De l'état de siège: Étude historique et juridique* (Paris: F. Pichon, 1885)

Reiterer, Markus A., 'Article XXI GATT - Does the National Security Exception Permit "Anything Under the Sun"?' (1997) 2 *Austrian Review of International and European Law* 191

Reynolds, John, 'The Long Shadow of Colonialism: The Origins of the Doctrine of Emergency in International Human Rights Law' (2010) 6:5 *Osgoode Comparative Research in Law and Political Economy* 1

Reynolds, John, 'The Use of Force in a Colonial Present, and the Goldstone Report's Blind Spot' (2010) 16 *Palestine Yearbook of International Law* 55

Reynolds, John, 'The Political Economy of States of Emergency' (2012) 14:1 *Oregon Review of International Law* 85

Reynolds, John, 'Anti-Colonial Legalities: Paradigms, Tactics and Strategy' (2015) 18 *Palestine Yearbook of International Law* 8

Reynolds, John, 'Disrupting Civility: Amateur Intellectuals, International Lawyers and TWAIL as Praxis' (2016) 37:11 *Third World Quarterly* 2098

Reynolds, John and Sujith Xavier, '"The Dark Corners of the World": TWAIL and International Criminal Justice' (2016) 14:4 *Journal of International Criminal Justice* 959

Reza, Sadiq, 'Endless Emergency: The Case of Egypt' (2007) 10:4 *New Criminal Law Review* 532

Rodney, Walter, *How Europe Underdeveloped Africa* (London: Bogle-L'Ouverture, 1972)

Rodríguez, Dylan, *Forced Passages: Imprisoned Radical Intellectuals and the U.S. Prison Regime* (Minneapolis: University of Minnesota Press, 2006)

Román, Ediberto, 'Race as the Missing Variable in Both the Neocolonial and Self-Determination Discourses' (1999) 93 *Proceedings of the American Society of International Law*

Roosevelt, Franklin D., *On Our Way* (New York: John Day, 1934)

Rosberg, Carl and John Nottingham, *The Myth of 'Mau Mau': Nationalism in Kenya* (New York: Praeger, 1966)

Rossiter, Clinton L., *Constitutional Dictatorship: Crisis Government in the Modern Democracies* (Princeton: Princeton University Press, 1948)

Roth, Brad, 'Governmental Illegitimacy and Neocolonialism: Response to Review by James Thuo Gathii' (2000) 98 *Michigan Law Review* 2056

Roustang, Francois and Mark Ensalaco, *Chile under Pinochet: Recovering the Truth* (Philadelphia: University of Pennsylvania Press, 2000)

Roy, Sara, *The Gaza Strip: The Political Economy of De-development* (3rd edn., Beirut: Institute for Palestine Studies, 2016)

Sachs, Wolfgang (ed.), *The Development Dictionary: A Guide to Knowledge as Power* (London: Zed, 2010)

Said, Edward W., *Orientalism* (London: Penguin, 1978)

Said, Edward W., *The Question of Palestine* (New York: Times Books, 1979)

Said, Edward W., 'Representing the Colonized: Anthropology's Interlocutors' (1989) 15:2 *Critical Inquiry* 205

Said, Edward W., *Culture & Imperialism* (New York: Vintage, 1993)

Said, Edward W., *Representations of the Intellectual: The 1993 Reith Lectures* (New York: Vintage, 1996)

Sands, Philippe, *Torture Team: Rumsfeld's Memo and the Betrayal of American Values* (New York: Palgrave Macmillan, 2008)

Sarat, Austin (ed.), *Sovereignty, Emergency, Legality* (Cambridge: Cambridge University Press, 2010)

Schabas, William, *The European Convention on Human Rights: A Commentary* (Oxford: Oxford University Press, 2015)

Scheuerman, William E., *Carl Schmitt: The End of Law* (Oxford: Rowman & Littlefield, 1999)

Scheuerman, William E., 'The Economic State of Emergency' (1999–2000) 21 *Cardozo Law Review* 1869

Scheuerman, William E., 'Carl Schmitt and the Road to Abu Ghraib' (2006) 13 *Constellations* 108

Schmitt, Carl, *Political Theology: Four Chapters on the Concept of Sovereignty* (1922) (George Schwab trans., Cambridge, MA: MIT Press, 1985)

Schmitt, Carl, *The Nomos of the Earth in the International Law of the Jus Publicum Europaeum* (1950) (G.L. Ulmen trans., New York, Telos Press, 2006)

Schwarz, Henry, *Constructing the Criminal Tribe in Colonial India: Acting Like a Thief* (London: Wiley-Blackwell, 2010)

Shafir, Gershon, *Land, Labor and the Origins of the Israeli-Palestinian Conflict, 1882–1914* (Cambridge: Cambridge University Press, 1989)

Shalakany, Amr A., 'Arbitration and the Third World: A Plea for Reassessing Bias under the Specter of Neoliberalism' (2000) 41:2 *Harvard International Law Journal* 419

Shamsul Alam, S.M., *Rethinking Mau Mau in Colonial Kenya* (Basingstoke: Palgrave Macmillan, 2007)

Shapiro, Michael J., *Violent Cartographies: Mapping Cultures of War* (Minneapolis: University of Minnesota Press, 1997)

Sharpe, R.J., *The Law of Habeas Corpus* (Oxford: Clarendon Press, 1976)

Shehadeh, Raja, *The Law of the Land: Settlement and Land Issues under Israeli Military Occupation* (Jerusalem: PASSIA, 1993)

Shenhav, Yehouda, 'The Imperial History of "State of Exception"' (2006) 29 *Theory and Criticism* 205

Shetreet, Simon, 'A Contemporary Model of Emergency Detention Law: An Assessment of the Israeli Law' (1984) 14 *Israel Yearbook on Human Rights* 182

Short, Anthony, *The Communist Insurrection in Malaya, 1948–60* (London: Frederick Muller, 1975)

Sigona, Nando, 'The Governance of Romani People in Italy: Discourse, Policy and Practice' (2011) 16:5 *Journal of Modern Italian Studies* 590

Silberstein, Laurence J. (ed.), *New Perspectives on Israeli History: The Early Years of the State* (New York: New York University Press, 1991)

Simpson, A.W.B., *In the Highest Degree Odious: Detention without Trial in Wartime Britain* (Oxford: Oxford University Press, 1992)

Simpson, A.W.B., 'Round Up the Usual Suspects: The Legacy of British Colonialism and the European Convention on Human Rights' (1996) 41 *Loyola Law Review* 629

Simpson, A.W.B., *Human Rights and the End of Empire: Britain and the Genesis of the European Convention* (Oxford: Oxford University Press, 2001)

Simpson, A.W.B., 'Emergency Powers and Their Abuse: Lessons from the End of the British Empire' (2004) 33 *Israel Yearbook of Human Rights* 219

Singha, Radhika, *A Despotism of Law: Crime and Justice in Early Colonial India* (Delhi: Oxford University Press, 1998)

Sinha, S.P., *New Nations and the Law of Nations* (Leiden: Martinus Nijhoff, 1967)

Skogly, Sigrun I., 'Structural Adjustment and Development: Human Rights – An Agenda for Change' (1993) 15:4 *Human Rights Quarterly* 751

Smith, Anthony D., *The Ethnic Origin of Nations* (Oxford: Blackwell, 1986)

Snyder, Frederick and Surakiart Sathirathai (eds.), *Third World Attitudes to International Law: An Introduction* (Dordrecht: Martinus Nijhoff, 1987)

Spickard, Paul (ed.), *Race and Nation: Ethnic Systems in the Modern World* (New York: Routledge, 2005)

Spivak, Gayatri, *The Post-Colonial Critic: Interviews, Strategies, Dialogues* (Sarah Harasym ed., London: Routledge, 1990)

Stephen, Leslie, *The Life of Sir James Fitzjames Stephen* (London: Smith, Elder, & Co., 1895)

Strawson, John, 'Reflections on Edward Said and the Legal Narratives of Palestine: Israeli Settlements and Palestinian Self-Determination' (2002) 20:2 *Penn State International Law Review* 363

Strawson, John, 'British (and International) Legal Foundations for the Israeli Wall: International Law and Multi-Colonialism' (2004-2005) 13 *Palestine Yearbook of International Law* 1

Sultany, Nimer, 'Unmasking Juridical Humanity' (2013) 4:1 *Transnational Legal Theory* 157

Sutton, Peter, *The Politics of Suffering: Indigenous Australia and the End of the Liberal Consensus* (Melbourne: Melbourne University Press, 2009)

Svensson-McCarthy, Anna-Lena, *The International Law of Human Rights and States of Exception* (The Hague: Martinus Nijhoff, 1998)

Syatauw, J.J.G., *Some Newly Established Asian States and the Development of International Law* (The Hague: Martinus Nijhoff, 1961)

Tal, David, *War in Palestine, 1948: Strategy and Diplomacy* (London: Routledge, 2004)

Tedmanson, Deirdre and Dinesh Wadiwel, 'Neoptolemus: The Governmentality of New Race/Pleasure Wars' (2010) 16:1 *Culture and Organization* 7

Thénault, Sylvie, 'L'état d'urgence (1955-2005). De l'Algérie coloniale à la France contemporaine: destin d'une loi' (2007) n° 218 *Le Mouvement Social* 63

Thiong'o, Ngũgĩ wa, *Weep Not, Child* (Nairobi: Heinemann, 1964)

Thiong'o, Ngũgĩ wa, *The River Between* (Nairobi: Heinemann, 1965)

Thiong'o, Ngũgĩ wa, *A Grain of Wheat* (Nairobi: Heinemann, 1967)

Thompson, E.P., *Whigs and Hunters: The Origin of the Black Act* (New York: Pantheon Books, 1975)

Tilley, Virginia et al. (ed.), *Beyond Occupation: Apartheid, Colonialism and International Law in the Occupied Palestinian Territories* (London: Pluto, 2012)

Townshend, Charles, 'Martial Law: Legal and Administrative Problems of Civil Emergency in Britain and the Empire, 1800-1940' (1982) 25 *The Historical Journal* 167

Townshend, Charles, *Britain's Civil Wars: Counter Insurgency in the Twentieth Century* (London: Faber & Faber, 1986)

Travers, Robert, *Ideology and Empire in Eighteenth-Century India: The British in Bengal* (Cambridge: Cambridge University Press, 2007)

Trebilcock, Michael J. and Robert Howse, *The Regulation of International Trade* (3rd edn., New York: Routledge, 2005)

Tümay, Murat, 'The "Margin of Appreciation Doctrine" Developed by the European Court of Human Rights' (2008) 5:2 Ankara Law Review 201

Umozurike, U.O., International Law and Colonialism in Africa (Enugu: Nwamife,
1979

Vagts, Detlev F., 'Hegemonic International Law' (2001) 95 American Journal of
International Law 843

Valdes, Juan Gabriel, Pinochet's Economists: The Chicago School in Chile (Cambridge: Cambridge University Press, 1995)

Van Harten, Gus, 'TWAIL and the Dabhol Arbitration' (2011) 3:1 Trade Law &
Development 131

Veracini, Lorenzo, Settler Colonialism: A Theoretical Overview (London: Palgrave
Macmillan, 2010)

Vitoria, Francisco de, De Indis et de Ivre Belli Relectiones (1532) (Ernest Nys ed.,
John Pawley Bate trans., Washington, DC: Carnegie Institution of Washington, 1917)

Waibel, Michael, 'Two Worlds of Necessity in ICSID Arbitration: CMS and LG&E'
(2007) 20 Leiden Journal of International Law 637

Waibel, Michael et al. (eds.), The Backlash against Investment Arbitration: Perceptions and Reality (The Hague: Kluwer, 2010)

Wallerstein, Immanuel, The Modern World-System, vol. I: Capitalist Agriculture
and the Origins of the European World-Economy in the Sixteenth Century
(London: Academic Press, 1974)

Wallerstein, Immanuel, The Modern World-System, vol. II: Mercantilism and the
Consolidation of the European World-Economy, 1600–1750 (New York:
Academic Press, 1980)

Wallerstein, Immanuel, The Modern World-System, vol. III: The Second Great
Expansion of the Capitalist World-Economy, 1730–1840's (San Diego: Academic Press, 1989)

Wallerstein, Immanuel, The Modern World-System, vol. IV: Centrist Liberalism
Triumphant, 1789–1914 (Berkeley: University of California Press, 2011)

Watson, Nicole, 'Howard's End: The Real Agenda Behind the Proposed Review of
Indigenous Land Titles' (2005) 9:4 Australian Indigenous Law Review 1

Watson, Nicole, 'The Northern Territory Emergency Response: Has it Really
Improved the Lives of Aboriginal Women and Children?' (2011) 35:1
Australian Feminist Law Journal 147

Watson, Nicole, 'The Northern Territory Emergency Response: The More Things
Change, the More They Stay the Same' (2011) 48:4 Alberta Law Review 905

Watson, Nicole, 'Justice in Whose Eyes? Why Lawyers Should Read Black Australian Literature' (2014) 23:1 Griffith Law Review 44

Weheliye, Alexander G., Habeas Viscus: Racializing Assemblages, Biopolitics and Black
Feminist Theories of the Human (Durham: Duke University Press, 2014)

Weizman, Eyal, *Hollow Land: Israel's Architecture of Occupation* (London: Verso, 2007)

Westlake, John, *Chapters on the Principles of International Law* (Cambridge: Cambridge University Press, 1894)

Whittington, Keith E., R. Daniel Kelemen and Gregory A. Caldeira (eds.), *The Oxford Handbook of Law and Politics* (Oxford: Oxford University Press, 2008)

Williams, David Owen, 'Racial Ideas in Early Victorian England' (1982) 5:2 *Ethnic and Racial Studies*

Williams, Michael, 'The Relations of Environmental History and Historical Geography' (1994) 20 *Journal of Historical Geography* 12

Williamson, John (ed.), *The Political Economy of Policy Reform* (Washington: Institute for International Economics, 1994)

Wills, Claire, 'Language Politics, Narrative, Political Violence' (1991) 13 *Oxford Literary Review* 20

Wolfe, Patrick, *Settler Colonialism and the Transformation of Anthropology: The Politics and Poetics of an Ethnographic Event* (London: Cassell, 1999)

Wolfe, Patrick, 'Settler Colonialism and the Elimination of the Native' (2006) 8:4 *Journal of Genocide Research* 387

Wolfe, Patrick, *Traces of History: Elementary Structures of Race* (London: Verso, 2016)

Yang, Anand A., *Crime and Criminality in British India* (Tucson: University of Arizona Press, 1985)

Yourow, Charles, *The Margin of Appreciation Doctrine in the Dynamics of European Human Rights Jurisprudence* (Dordrecht: Martinus Nijhoff, 1996)

Žižek, Slavoj, *Welcome to the Desert of the Real* (London: Verso, 2002)

Žižek, Slavoj, 'A Permanent Economic Emergency' (2010) 64 *New Left Review* 85

Zuckeman, Ian, 'One Law for War and Peace? Judicial Review and Emergency Powers between the Norm and the Exception' (2006) 13 *Constellations* 523

Zurayk, Elia T., *The Palestinians in Israel: A Study in Internal Colonialism* (London: Routledge, 1979)

ACKNOWLEDGEMENTS

The roots of this book are in Palestine, and so my acknowledgements must start there. My thanks to the Al-Haq family for their warmth of heart, their commitment to the work they do, and the opportunities they gave me as a young researcher. There are many amazing thinkers whom I have worked with in or through Palestine, and who encouraged or inspired me in their own untold ways to pursue this work. Here I want to acknowledge Wesam Ahmad, Reem Bahdi, Frank Barat, George Bisharat, Eitan Bronstein, Grazia Careccia, Dylan Cantwell-Smith, Angela Davis, John Dugard, Noura Erakat, Richard Falk, Daphna Golan, Ardi Imseis, Hassan Jabareen, Shawan Jabarin, Ronnie Kasrils, Mudar Kassis, Ronit Lentin, Darryl Li, David Lloyd, Michael Lynk, Dania Majid, Mazen Masri, Lisa Monaghan, Fadi Quran, Rina Rosenberg, Iain Scobbie, Emily Schaeffer, Michael Sfard, Charles Shamas, Raja Shehadeh, Hadeel Abu Hussein, Patrick Wolfe and Rafeef Ziadeh. And all of those Palestinians who, as Rafeef so eloquently puts it, wake up every morning to teach us life.

The book is the culmination of my doctoral research, undertaken at the National University of Ireland, Galway. The Irish Centre for Human Rights has fostered a unique environment for postgraduate research since its early years, largely thanks to Bill Schabas, Vinodh Jaichand, Ray Murphy, Joshua Castellino and Elvira Dominguez-Redondo. Their generosity of spirit and intellect set me on the path originally, Shane Darcy helped keep me on the straight and narrow, and Ekaterina Yahyaoui provided a valuable and insightful reading of my thesis. Heartfelt thanks to Joe Powderly and Niamh Hayes, who took me in off the street when I first landed back to Galway from the Middle East, and to Josh Curtis for many a late-night whiskey and early-morning coffee in St. Mary's Road. Also to Helen Nic an Rí, Michael Higgins, Edel Hughes, Jane O'Sullivan, Nick McGeehan, Peter Fitzmaurice, Aoife Duffy and all of the Galway crew for their friendship and provocations over the years. I am especially indebted to Michelle Farrell, who was a vital sounding board in working through many of the ideas in the book and offering me detailed criticism and comments on the manuscript. Thanks as well to resident rebels in England, Michael Kearney and Dave Keane, for their hospitality on many a conference or archive trip across the water and for insights that have sharpened my academic work more broadly. My biggest debt of gratitude for the substantive work that went into this book is to my doctoral supervisor, Kathleen Cavanaugh. She guided me through the process with wisdom and geniality, keeping me relatively close to the path whilst always maintaining patience with my frequent detours and helping me to understand how to harness such meanderings productively.

I'm also lucky to have worked with and learnt from a great gang of scholars on my travels, particularly at events and workshops organised by the Toronto Group for the Study of International, Transnational & Comparative Law, the Third World Approaches to International Law movement, the Institute for Global Law & Policy, and the Law & Society Association Collaborative Research Network on International Law & Politics. Numerous colleagues, comrades and fellow travellers have been generous enough to read or listen to some aspect or other of the work contained in this book, and offer important input in various different shapes and forms. Both this research and my understanding of the field of international law more generally have benefited tremendously from their remarkable knowledge and radical thinking, as well as their camaraderie. So my thanks here to Michelle Burgis-Kasthala, Irina Ceric, Matt Craven, Ayça Çubukçu, Luis Eslava, Michael Fakhri, Christopher Gevers, Markus Gunneflo, Ioannis Kalpouzos, Vik Kanwar, Rob Knox, Martti Koskenniemi, Paavo Kotiaho, Tor Krever, Vidya Kumar, Tyler McCreary, Vasuki Nesiah, Paul O'Connell, Gearóid Ó Cuinn, Obiora Okafor, Reecia Orzeck, Sundhya Pahuja, Maïa Pal, Rose Sydney Parfitt, Balakrishnan Rajagopal, Nahed Samour, Adrian Smith, Owen Taylor, Riaz Tayob and Ntina Tzouvala, and especially to Cairo co-conspirators Amar Bhatia, Usha Natarajan and Sujith Xavier. I am particularly grateful to Tony Anghie for his engagement and encouragement over the lifetime of this project, his critical eye and constructive provocations as my doctoral examiner, and his generosity in writing the foreword for this book.

For the financial support that allowed me to embark upon and sustain the precarious life of postgraduate research, I am much obliged to the Irish Research Council and the National University of Ireland. Angela Melchiorre and my colleagues at the European Inter-University Centre in Venice created a hospitable and dynamic environment for teaching and research during my time there. Michael Doherty and my colleagues at the National University of Ireland, Maynooth have been a wonderful social and intellectual support network since I took up my post there in the Department of Law. Hayley Egan helped with crucial research assistance in the final stages of this book project, for which I am immensely grateful. At Cambridge University Press, Elizabeth Spicer, Finola O'Sullivan, Lorenza Toffolon and their team have been a pleasure to work with.

Finally, for their immeasurable support, strength and entertainment over the years, special thanks to my friends and family in Dublin and beyond, to my parents Liam & Jo, and my brothers Dave & Jimmer.

And most of all to Vani: maestra, compagna, stella.

INDEX

A. and Others v. the United Kingdom
(Belmarsh case), 184–89
Aboriginal Land Rights Act, Northern
Territory (1976) Australia, 246–48
Ackerman, B., 57
Act for Confiscation of Villages (1858)
Britain, 85–86
Act for More Effective Suppression of
Local Disturbances and
Dangerous Associations (1833)
Ireland, 78–79
Act for the Better Protection of
Person and Property (1881)
Ireland, 79–80
Acts of Union (Britain), 78
aesymneteia, regime of, 68–69
Africa, 158–60, 190–91
African Charter on Human and
Peoples' Rights, 189–91
*The African Mind in Health and
Disease* (Carothers), 158
African National Congress, 281–82
African-Americans, 45–46
Agamben, G., 36, 41–43, 200–1
emergency framing by, 273–74
homo sacer from, 40–41, 57
inclusion exclusion from, 210
law double-structure from, 47
state of exception from, 39–40, 203–
4, 209–10
Agamben and Colonialism (Bignall and
Svirsky), 41–42
Ago, R., 112–13
Aksoy v. Turkey, 181
Al-Assad v. Minister of Interior, 237
Alexandrowicz, R., 217–20
Algeria, 8–9, 69

Allied powers, 111–12
Amritsar massacre, 71–72, 76, 89–90
Anarchical and Revolutionary Crimes
Act (1919), 91–92
Anaya, J., 256–57
Anderson, D., 149–52
Anghie, A., 16–17, 26, 47, 59–60
colonialism work of, 51–52
doctrines of sovereignty from,
47–48
dynamic of difference from, 97–98
anti-colonial rebellion, 41–42, 104–5,
116–17, 144–46, 270–71
apartheid regime, 281–82
Arab Revolt (1936), 92–93
Arabs, 223–26
architecture of enmity, 195–96
Arden-Clark, C., 106–7
Arendt, H., 41–42, 52–53
Armed Forces (Special Powers) Act,
279–81
Armenia, 133–35
assimilation, 252–53
Australia, 35, 60–61, 256–57, 262–63
Constitution of, 252–54
indigenous people in, 244–45,
248–49
racial history of, 252–59
authoritarian regimes, 47

Balfour Declaration, 214–16
bank bailouts, 94–95
Barak, A., 238–39
barbarism, 63–64
Barcelona Traction case, 26
bare life, 202–5, 209–10
Baring, E., 146, 154–56, 160

BDS. *See* Boycott, Divestment and Sanctions
Beckett, S., 64
Beddoe, J., 62–63
Bedjaoui, M., 24–26, 97–98
Begin, M., 223–25
Belgium, 128
Bengal Criminal Law Amendment Acts (1925), 92
Bengal Emergency Powers Ordinance of 1931, 92
Bengal State Prisoners Regulation, 81–82, 84–86
Ben-Gurion, D., 225–26
Benjamin, W., 9–10, 32–33, 286
Berda, Y., 207–10
Bhandar, B., 213–14
Bignall, S., 41–42
Bill of Rights, for Northern Ireland, 275–76
Bishara, A., 232–33
Black Protest Committee, 245
bombing towns by Israel, 199
Boycott, Divestment and Sanctions (BDS), 242–43, 287–88
Brannigan & McBride v. the United Kingdom, 181, 183–84, 186–88
Bretton Woods institutions, 94–95
Brexit, 60
Britain, 90–91, 131–32, 177, 241
  colonial emergency measures of, 14–15, 105, 133–35
  colonial legal history of, 68–69
  as colonial state, 55, 70, 72–73, 156–57, 221
  Commission on Human Rights draft derogation clause in, 124
  Defence (Emergency) Regulations repealed by, 223
  emergency in, 104–5, 223, 275–76
  emergency power in, 101, 133–35
  Gordon hanging and, 75–76
  human rights and, 33, 117–18
  imperial law of, 52–53
  imperialism of, 60
  India and colonial rule of, 82–85
  Ireland and, 62–64, 178–81, 78
  Jamaican reign of terror by, 107–8

Kenya and rule of, 142–43, 167
  Mau Mau society and, 161
  peasants in, 79–80, 106–7
  state of emergency by, 30–31, 148–49
  strikes in, 101–3
  torture by, 138–43
British East India Company, 81–82
British empire, 17–18, 104–5, 139–41, 176
  Article 15 invoked by, 133–35
  British Guiana, 130–33
  British India, 81–82
  emergency rule in, 48
  Greece complaints against, 173
  hostile populations against, 76
  imperial hegemony of, 60
  racialised hegemony of, 74–75
  rebellions against, 116
  special powers of, 105–6
  theory of law in, 168–69
British forces, 149–50, 152–54
  in Kenya, 138–39, 144–46, 156–57
Brogan & Others v. the United Kingdom, 181–83
Brough, M., 260–61
Bush, G. W., 155, 274
Butler, J., 15–16, 201–2

camps, 49, 116, 150–51
  detention, 151–52, 154–56
  internment, 33, 41–42, 141–42
capital accumulation, 98–99
capitalism, 94–99
Caribbean sugar plantations, 45
Carothers, J.C., 158–59
censorship, 108
Ceylon, 76
Charles I (king of England), 72
Chelmsford, Lord, 277–79
Cherokee Nations v. Georgia, 57–58
child abuse, 261–62
Chile, 124–25
Chimni, 22–23, 26
Churchill, W., 113–15
civil rights, 181–83
class status, 95–97, 268–70
class subjugation, 94–97

coal strike, 101–3
Cockburn, A., 75–76
Coercion Bill, 80
Coetzee, J.M., 12–13, 210
Cold War, 21–23
collective criminality, 87–89, 152–54
Collective Punishment Ordinance, 147–48
Collective Punishment under Emergency Regulations, 141–42
colonial emergency, 138–39, 189–90, 268
  of Britain, 14–15, 105, 133–35
  legacy of, 279–81
Colonial Office (Britain), 128–30
colonial territories, 21–22, 128–37, 139–41
  lawlessness in, 50–51
  legal system of, 52–53
  state of emergency in, 130–31
colonialism, 16–20, 62–63, 81–82, 96.
    See also post-colonialism
  Anghie work on, 51–52
  anti-colonial resistance and, 177
  boomerang effect and, 91–92
  bureaucratic violence in, 207–9
  capitalism relationship with, 96–97
  in counter-terrorism, 191–92
  in Cyprus, 176–77
  dispossession, 270–71
  emergency measures and, 107–8
  expansionary settlement and, 195–96
  history, 36, 66–67
  human rights and, 31–32
  human settlements and, 196
  humanity and, 54–55
  in international law, 23–24
  law, 14–15, 55–56, 68–69, 107–8
  legislation, 77–78
  liberal international law in, 98–99
  liberal legal regime, 53–54
  mutations, 30–31
  occupation, 206
  power dynamics, 28
  present, 20
  racist ideology of, 17–18
  rule, 39–40, 72–73, 82–85
  rule of law and, 37–38
  settler, 18–19
  sovereignty, 13–14, 141–42
  space, 49–50
  state, 97–98
  taxation, 76
  violence, 206–7
  wars, 104–5
  Zionist settlements in, 214–15
colonised populations, 45–46, 49
Committee of Displaced Persons from Iqrit, Rama and Others v. Government of Israel, 228
Committee of Ministers, 117, 119–20
Commonwealth Games, 244–45
communism, 107–8, 131–32
compulsory acquisition measures, 261–62
concept of necessity, 46–47
Conference of Senior Officials, 120–21
conflict, low-intensity, 168–69
conflict zones, 135–37
constitutional law, 238
Council of Europe, 178
counter-hegemony, 168–69, 267
counter-revolutionary spirit, 266–67
counter-terrorism, 12–13, 15–16, 188–89, 191–92, 195–96
  British law on, 241–43
Crime and Outrage Act (1847) Britain, 79–80
criminal tribes, 45–46, 87–90
Criminal Tribes Act (1871), 89–90, 92
criminality, 87–90, 111–12
Crown of Ireland Act (1542) Britain, 62
cultural superiority, 28
Curfews Law, 172
Cyprus, 172, 176–77
Cyprus case, 171–81

Darwish, M., 199–201
dead land concept, 220–21
decolonisation, 24–26
Defence of India Act (1915, 1939), 92–93, 277–78
Defence of the Realm Act (DORA), 90–91, 101

Defence (Emergency) Regulations,
    34–35, 221–29
  British repeal of, 223
  Iqrit case and, 228
  Israel and, 221, 223–25, 228–29,
    236–37
  Supreme Court challenge against,
    236–37
Department of Homeland Security,
    U.S., 274
derogation, 33–34, 118–19, 122, 124
  of emergency, 111–12, 115, 121–22,
    189–91
  European Court validity of, 183–84
  state of emergency and, 164–65, 190
Derogation Order, 184
despotism of law, 82–84
detainees, 164–65
detention, 108, 188–89, 235
detention camps, 151–52, 154–56
Detention of Persons Law, 165–66, 172
Dicey, A. V., 73–74
discrimination, 160–61, 188–89, 243.
    See also Racial Discrimination Act
dispossession, 213–14, 227–28, 270–71
doctrines of sovereignty, 47–48
DORA. *See* Defence of the Realm Act
Dowson, O., 118–19
Dweikat, M., 217–18
Dyer, General, 71–72
Dyzenhaus, D., 46–47

East Jerusalem, 241–43
economic regulations, 100–3
Eitan, R., 218–19
*El-Ard v. Commissioner of the Northern
    District*, 237
Elkins, C., 141, 154–56
Elon Moreh, 217–20
Elon Moreh case, 218–19
emergency, 18–19, 93, 104–8, 236–43
  codes, 90–91, 223
  colonial Britain and, 14–15, 105
  governance, 11, 13–14, 31–32
  indigenous communities normalised
    by, 246–48
  interventions, 35, 245–51, 262–63
  law and coloniality of, 268

law and order upheld in, 105–6
  modalities, 212, 221–22, 243
  political economy of, 93–104
  public, 124–25
  regulatory powers in, 233
  role of law in, 97–98
  use of force calculated in, 162
emergency doctrine, 28–29, 47, 82–84
  British empire governance with, 17–18
  colonial history and, 36, 66–67
  within colonial legal system, 14–15
  counter-hegemonic resistance to, 267
  counter-revolutionary spirit and,
    266–67
  enactment of, 101–3
  evolution of, 70
  Fenian revolution and, 80
  in France, 68–69, 274–75
  in hegemonic control systems, 20
  national security through, 35
  occupation through, 213
  pre-crisis status quo of, 286–87
  racial elements of, 31
  restrictive measures in, 38–39
  violence and, 167
emergency laws, 12–13, 55, 78–79,
    248–49
  class repression in, 96–97
  Muslim persecution from, 8–9
  racist ideology and, 37
emergency measures, 107–8, 221, 229–
    36, 249–50, 258
emergency power, 12–15, 68–69, 165–67
  in Britain, 101, 133–35
  colonial rule using, 39–40
  colonial sovereignty and, 13–14
  economic regulations from, 100–3
  legislative normalisation of, 77–93
  martial law and, 46–47, 71
  methodology of governance with,
    15–16
  pre-emptive measures in, 105–6
  racialised deployment of, 255
  regulations in, 103
  ruling regimes deploying, 30
  in twilight zones, 165–66
Emergency Powers Act (1920), 101–3
Emergency Powers Act (1970s), 70–71

Emergency Powers Bill (1919). *See* Rowlatt Act
Emergency Powers (Detention) Law, 233–34
Emergency Powers (Colonial Defence) Order in Council 1939, 92–93, 108
Emergency Powers Ordinance, 146–47
Emergency Powers Regulations, 172
emergency regulations, 151–52, 154–56, 162, 223, 232–33, 241, 281–82
emergency rules, 20–21, 111–13, 277–78, 285–86
Emergency Scheme for Kenya Colony, 146–47
Emergency Whipping Act (1942–1943) Britain, 92–93
enemy aliens, 113–15
enemy civilizations, 58
Engels, F., 96–97
England, medieval, 48, 72
English law, 61–62, 84
environmental demonstrations, 8
equality, socio-economic, 93–94
equity of law, 268–70
Esmeir, S., 52–55, 270–71
état d'urgence, 274–75
ethno-psychiatry theories, 157–60
ethno-racial privilege, 196–98
Europe, 24–26, 98, 189–90
European Commission of Human Rights, 171–78
European Convention on Human Rights, 31–33, 115, 118–19, 178–81
  adoption of, 125–26
  Article 15 of, 121–22, 126–27, 131–35, 173, 176–78
  articles of, 122
  British colonies extension of, 131–32
  civil rights issues in, 181–83
  in colonial territories, 128–37
  drafting process of, 117
  emergency legal regimes and, 132–33
  human rights limitations in, 120–21
  Protocol 11 of, 171
  working draft of, 117–18
European Court of Human Rights, 33–34, 170, 183–85
Eustathiades, 176–77

Fanon, F., 16–18, 54–55, 159–60, 206–7
Farrell, M., 40, 210
fascism, 31–32, 107–8, 111
Federal Emergency Management Agency, U.S., 274
federal intervention, 248–49
Fenian revolution, 80
Finlason, W., 75–76
Fisch, J., 50–51
Fitzjames Stephen, J., 61–62, 81–82, 89–90
five-year sunset clause, 250–51
Foreign Office (Britain), 128–30, 140–41
Forfeiture of Lands Bill, 151–52
Forfeiture Order, 141–42
Foucault, M., 38, 42–43, 47–48
France, 7–8, 68–69, 124, 274–75
  imperialism in, 68–69
  militarism of, 17–18
  Muslims in, 8–9
French Revolution, 68–69
frontal lobe hypothesis, 158
fundamental rights, 119–20
Füredi, F., 105, 149–50, 160–61

Gandhi, M., 92–93, 276–79
Gavaghan, T., 154–57
Gaza Strip, 58, 199–203, 210
  Israel on status of, 199, 201
  state of exception in, 212
Genocide Convention, 111
Germany, 174–75
  Nazi regime, 39–42
  Weimar Constitution, 40, 100
Givoni, M., 209–10
Gladstone, J. L., 80
Gold Coast experiment, 106
Goldstone Report, 200–1
Good Friday Agreement, 184
Gordon, N., 203–4
Gott, G., 57–58
government, 15–16, 42–43, 47, 104–8, 184
  human rights respect of, 128–30
  land acquisition by, 246–48
Governor Eyre case, 75–77

Greece, 173
Gregory, D., 195–98, 200–2
Grenada, 130–31
Griffith-Jones, E., 154–56, 166

Habeas Corpus Suspension Acts (1848-49, 1866-69), 79–80
Hall, S., 60
Hanafi, S., 204–5, 208–11
Handyside v. the United Kingdom, 171–78
Hanslope files, 139–41, 143–44
Harare Declaration, 282–83
Hasluck, P., 252–53
Hassan v. the United Kingdom, 135–37
hegemony, 20, 41–42, 60, 168–69, 267
    militarised, 196–98
    racialised, 74–75
Heinous Offences Act (1857) Britain, 85–86
Henry II (king of England), 62
Henry VIII (king of England), 72
Herzl, T., 202–3
Hoffman, Lord, 185
Hola Camp killings, 152–54
Holland, D., 133–35
homeland security, 10–11. *See also* Department of Homeland Security, U.S.
hominis sacri, 40–42
homo sacer, 40–41, 57
Hong Kong, 131–32
hostile populations, 76
House of Lords, 184–89
Howard, J., 254–55, 261–62
human rights, 111, 117–22, 124, 178–81
    African Charter violators of, 190–91
    African instruments for, 190–91
    Britain and, 33, 117–18
    collective guarantee of, 118–19
    colonial governments respect for, 128–30
    colonial special powers and, 104–5
    colonialism and international, 31–32
    counter-hegemonic tendencies in, 168–69
    declaratory principle of, 116
    emergency and international law on, 32–33

emergency measures and, 186–88
emergency rules and, 112–13
European Convention limitations of, 120–21
Foreign Office on, 128–30
Greece complaints about, 173
international law and, 112–13
international protection of, 113–15
law of, 125, 272
margin of appreciation doctrine and, 170–71
prevented realization of, 12–13
socio-economic roots and, 273
states of emergency influencing, 14–15, 163–64
universal, 93–94, 126–27
Universal Declaration of Human Rights applied for, 128
utopian ideologies and, 114
Human Rights Act (1998) Britain, 184
Human Rights Committee, 234–35
human settlements, 196
Hume, J., 78–79
Hussain, N., 15–18, 42–43, 56, 84–85
    Ameer Khan ruling and, 86
    rule of law from, 61–62
hyperlegality, 15–16, 241

imaginative geographies, 195
imperialism, 20, 61–62, 191–92, 195–96
    British hegemony and, 60
    capitalism relationship with, 94–96
    equity of law and, 268–70
    in France, 68–69
    international relations governed by, 16–17
    law of, 52–53, 87–89
    legal structures of, 271–72
    race and, 82–84
imperialist-racial formations, 58
imperial-racial rule, 286
In the Matter of Ameer Khan, 86
inclusion exclusion, 209–10
income management provisions, 258–59
indentured labour, 45, 276–77
India, 60–61, 87, 92–93, 277–79
    British, 81–82
    British colonial rule in, 82–85

Constitution of, 279
martial law in, 72–73, 89–90
Quit India movement in, 92, 279
Indian Councils Act (1861), 85–86
Indian Revolt, 85–86
indigenous communities, 35, 246–50,
    254
  child abuse and, 261–62
  international law remaking by, 272
  intervention resistance of, 263
  land leases contested by, 264
  market economy for, 260–61
Indigenous people, 21–22, 51–52, 258
  in Australia, 244–45, 248–49
  racialisation of, 251–52
industrial disputes, 103
inequalities, 21–22, 98–99, 273
institutionalised racism, 259
insurgency tactics, 168–69
intent to regularise, 236–43
International Bill of Human Rights, 123
International Covenant on Civil and
    Political Rights, 31–32, 115, 123–
    26, 234–35
  Article 4 of, 126–27
International Covenant on Economic,
    Social and Cultural Rights
    (ICESCR), 115
international law, 14–15, 28, 32–33, 47–
    48, 122
  colonial patterns in, 23–24
  European colonial project and, 24–26
  evolution of, 272
  politics and, 161–69
  racialisation of, 65–67
  rights and obligations under, 161–62
international legal studies, 23–24
international relations, 16–17
internment camps, 33, 41–42, 141–42
intervention resistance, 263
Iraq, 135–37
Ireland, 18–19, 60–61, 64, 276–77
  agitation suppression in, 78–79
  Britain and, 62–64, 178–81, 78
  Coercion Bill for, 80
  Crown of Ireland Act, 62
  Emergency Powers Act in, 70–71
  martial law rebellions and, 78

Northern Ireland, 183–84, 275–76
  racial differential of, 62–63
  security policy in, 178–81
Ireland v. United Kingdom, 181–84
Irish Republican Army, 178–81
Israel, 201–2, 210–11
  absentee property doctrine of, 230–31
  Anti-Terror Law, 241–43
  Arab population centers inside,
    223–25
  Association for Civil Rights in Israel
    (ACRI), 238
  bare life and occupation by, 204–5
  Citizenship Law (1952) in, 199–201
  counter-terrorist law in, 241–43
  Defence (Emergency) Regulations
    and, 221, 223–25, 228–29, 236–37
  emergency modalities of, 34–35,
    221–22
  Emergency Regulations (Absentees'
    Property) Law 1948, 230–31
  Emergency Regulations (Cultivation
    of Waste Lands) Law 1951, 231
  Emergency Regulations (Requisition
    of Property) Law 1948, 230–31
  Emergency Regulations (Security
    Zones) Law 1949, 232
  Gaza Strip and, 199, 201
  international law in, 216–17
  Jewish state, 213–16
  land seizure by, 217–20
  militarised hegemony of, 196–98
  military hyperregulation in, 241
  Palestine and, 213, 225–27
  Palestinians in, 196–98, 200–1, 241–43
  security concerns of, 234–35
  sovereign power of, 204
  state of emergency in, 18–19, 238–40
  state-sanctioned torture by, 154–56
  Supreme Court, 219–20, 236–37
  violent actions of, 213
Italy, 18–19

Jallianwala Bagh massacre. See
    Amritsar massacre
Jamaica, 72–75, 107–8
Jewish National Fund, 232
judicial oversight, 178

juridical humanity, 52–55
juridical-security apparatus, 34–35
justness, 268–70

Kariuki, J., 145, 151–52
KAU. *See* Kenya African Union
KCA. *See* Kikuyu Central Association
Kenya, 60–61, 130–33, 143
   British forces in, 138–39, 144–46,
     156–57
   British rule of, 142–43, 167
   Colony Emergency Committee
     (EMCOM) in, 146–47
   emergency declaration in, 166
   internment camps in, 141–42
   Preservation of Public Security
     Ordinance in, 166–67
   protocol extension in, 130
   state of emergency in, 33, 138, 143–
     44, 146, 163–64, 167
Kenya African Union (KAU), 144–46
Kenyatta, J., 145
Khalidi, W., 232
Kikuyu Central Association (KCA),
   144–46
Kikuyu (*Gĩkũyũ*) people, 144–46, 150–
   51, 156–57
   discrimination against, 160–61
   resistance by, 148–49
Killearn, Lord, 104–5
Kitson, F., 168–69
Kolsky, E., 81–84
Koskenniemi, M, 26, 52, 161, 216
Kostal, R., 17–18, 72–73, 75–76, 107–8

land leases, 264
land seizure, 217–20, 246–48, 261–62.
   See also dispossession
Latin America, 191
Law and Administration Ordinance,
   223–25, 233–34
law and order, 105–6, 262–63
law enforcement, 15–16, 207–9
The Law in These Parts (documentary
   film), 217–18
Law of Return (1950) Israel, 199–201
Lawless v. Ireland, 178–81
lawlessness, 50–51, 69

lawmaking process, 13–14, 70
laws, 36, 47, 238, 268, 270–71
   Anti-Terror, 241–43
   class power and, 268–70
   counter-terrorist, 241–43
   Curfews, 172
   dead land concept and, 220–21
   despotism of, 82–84
   discriminatory, 243
   emergency and role of, 97–98
   English, 61–62, 84
   equity of, 268–70
   of human rights, 125, 272
   natural, 51–52
   of occupied territories, 217–18
   positive, 52–53
   theory of, 168–69
   Third World colonial, 107–8
League of Nations, 97–98, 214–15
Lebow, R. N., 62–63
legal regimes, 132–33, 157–58, 161–62
legal system, 38–39, 41–42, 50–51, 90–
   91, 228–29
   of British colonial state, 70
   of colonial territories, 52–53
   emergency doctrine in, 14–15
   of imperialism, 271–72
   of Palestine, 243
   scholarship on, 23–24
legislation, 14–15, 77–93, 250–51
Lennox-Boyd, A., 154–56, 160
Lentin, R., 203–5
L'état de siege, 68–69
liberty restrictions, 225–26
Limitation Act (1980) Britain,
   139–41
Lloyd, D., 262–63
low-intensity conflict, 168–69
Luban, D., 36
Lyttelton, O., 160

Macaulay, T., 45, 63, 81–84
MacDonald, R., 101–3
Macleod, I., 141
Macpherson, J., 106
Majdalany, F., 145
Major, A., 87
Makanga, E., 154

Malaya, 103–4, 132–33
Mandela, N., 2, 281–82, 284
Marais case, 76
margin of appreciation doctrine, 33–34,
     170–71, 174–75
  Cyprus case and, 178–81
  European Court of Human Rights
     and, 170
market economy, 260–61
Marshall v. the United Kingdom,
     186–88
martial law, 73–74, 77–78, 95, 148–49
  emergency power and, 46–47, 71
  in India, 72–73, 89–90
  Ireland rebellions and, 78
  liberalisation of, 77
  in Medieval England, 48, 72
  in Phillipines, 70
  in Punjab, 277–78
  purpose and deployment of,
     71–77
  state of emergency and, 30–31, 69–
     70
Marx, K., 78, 96–97, 100
Marx-Longuet, J., 80
Mary I (queen of England), 95
Mathari Mental Hospital, 158
Mau Mau society, 143, 149–50, 156–57,
     159–61
  oathing campaigns of, 147–48, 160
  revolt of, 144–46
Mbembe, A., 49–50, 55–56, 206
  necropolitics from, 207–9
  sovereignty claims and, 206–7
Mehta, H., 279
Meira Paibi, 280
mental capacity, 158–59
mental illness, 159–60
Mickelson, K., 22–23
Miéville, C., 203–4
militarised hegemony, 196–98
Military and State Offences Act (1857)
     Britain, 85–86
military hyperregulation, 241
military rule, 223, 225–26, 228
Mitterrand, F., 274–75
MK. *See* Umkhonto we Sizwe
Morton, S., 210

Mosley, O., 113–15
Moyn, S., 114
Muhamed, A., 217–18
Muslims, 8–9, 45–46, 89, 188–89
Mutua, M., 190
*Mutua & others v. The Foreign and
     Commonwealth Office*, 138–41
Mwea camps, 154–56

nation, defining, 176, 186
national emergency, 7–8, 251
national security, 39–40, 57–58, 93,
     113–15
  in Australia, 262–63
  through emergency doctrine, 35
  Israeli concerns of, 234–35
  post-emergency context and, 15–16
native sovereignty, 60
natives, 87–89, 103–4
natural law, 51–52
naval vessels, 241
Nazi regime, 39–42
necessity, concept of, 46–47
necropolitics, 49, 207–9
necropower, 49–50, 206–7
Nehru, J., 92–93
neo-colonial world, 19–20
Netanyahu, B., 243
New International Economic Order, 27
Ngũgĩ wa Thiong'o, 157, 160–61
Nkrumah, K., 106–7
Nokwe, D., 281–82
Non-Aligned Movement, 282–83
non-state terrorism, 191–92
non-violent resistance, 279
North Borneo, 134
Northern Territory, Australia, 35,
     258–61
  emergency intervention in, 245–51,
     262–63
  Little Children are Sacred report,
     248–49
  national emergency in, 251
  Stronger Futures legislation, 250–51
  Welfare Reform Act (2010), 257–58
Northern Territory Emergency
     Response (NTER), 246, 250–51,
     255

Northern Territory National
    Emergency Response Act (2007),
    261–62
north-south divide, 22–26
NTER. *See* Northern Territory
    Emergency Response

oathing campaigns, 147–48, 160
Obama, B., 274
occupied territories, 135–37, 211–13,
    228–29
  laws of, 217–18
  military rule in, 223
  Palestinians in, 233–34
  state land and, 219–20
open-air prison, 199–201
Operation Anvil, 162
Operation Cast Lead, 199
Operation Defensive Shield, 204
Operation Progress, 154–56
Ophir, A., 209–10
oppression, 10–11, 160–61, 212, 287
O'Rorke, M. S., 152–54
Oslo II Accord, 204
Ottoman Land Law, 217–20

Palestine, 34–35, 58, 60–61, 206–7, 235
  BDS in, 287–88
  dispossession experienced by, 213–
    14, 227–28
  emergency modalities and legal
    system of, 243
  Emergency Regulations and,
    223
  indiscriminate violence against,
    209–10
  Israel and, 213, 225–27
  Israel and people of, 196–98, 200–1,
    241–43
  Jewish state and, 215
  juridical order in, 210–11
  militarised hegemony of, 196–98
  occupied territories and, 233–34
  Ottoman Land Law and, 217–18
  Plan Dalet and, 232
  as space of exception, 198–212
  state of emergency and, 212
  unlawful combatants of, 216–17

Palestine (Defence) Orders in Council,
    92–93, 223
Pan Malayan Federation of Trade
    Unions (PMFTU), 103–4
Panic in Whitehall, 105–6, 146
Pappé, I., 212
peasant uprising, 74–75, 95, 144–46
peasants, 79–80, 106–7
Penal Codes, 89–90
penal contracts, 276–77
Peres, S., 226–27
Peretz, D., 227–28
permanent emergency, 10–16
Philippines, 70
Pilgrimage of Grace rebellion, 72
Pindaris, 89
Plan Dalet, 232
PMFTU. *See* Pan Malayan Federation
    of Trade Unions
police state scenario, 245
politics, 40–41, 93–104, 206–7, 216
population management, 31–32, 71
Porot, A., 158
Portugal, 128
positive law, 52–53
post-colonialism, 15, 42–43, 64
  theory, 19–20, 49
pre-emptive measures, 39–40, 105–6
Preservation of Public Security
    Ordinance, 166–67
Prevention of Crime Act (1883)
    Ireland, 80
Prevention of Infiltration
    (Offences and Jurisdiction) Law,
    232–33
prison camps, 150–51
private land, 217–18
property rights, 220–21
Protection of Life and Property Act
    (1871) Ireland, 79–80
psychological assessment,
    159–60
public emergency, 124–25, 131–32
public order, 151–52
Public Records Act (1958), 140–41
Public Safety Act (1953), 281–82
public security, 167
Punjab, martial law in, 277–78

Queensland, 244–45
Quit India movement, 92, 279

R v. Nelson and Brand, 75–76
race, 43–44, 60, 62–63, 255–56
  Australian history of, 252–59
  conflict of, 58
  construction of, 64
  groups by, 30
  hierarchy of, 43, 45
  imperialism and, 82–84
  markers of, 39–40
  Nazi policy on, 41–42
  necropower and, 49–50
  sovereignty of, 29, 34–35, 56–64
  state of emergency and, 29–30, 37,
    66–67
Races of Britain (Beddoe), 62–63
Racial Discrimination Act, Australia,
    35, 253–54, 257–59
  amendments to, 258
  racism and, 256, 259
  suspension of, 255
racialisation, 28, 43–44, 65–67, 230–31
  colonised populations and, 45–46
  of hegemony, 74–75
  of indigenous people, 251–52
  otherness and, 60–61
  sovereignty, 66–67
racism, 35, 256–57, 259
racist ideology, 17–18, 37, 57–58, 60
  emergency doctrine and, 31
  emergency law and, 37
  emergency rule and, 20–21
  mental illness and, 159–60
Radcliffe, T., 95
Rajagopal, B., 106–7, 267
Ramat, A., 217–18
rational model of bureaucracy, 207–10
Razack, S., 43–44
regional defence, 218–19
Regulating Act (1773) Britain, 84
Regulation 18B (Britain), 113–15
Regulation 125 (Israel), 226–27
Regulation XXII (Britain), 89
regulatory system, 98, 103, 233
repressive inclusion, 210–11
resistance, 263, 277–79
  anti-colonial, 177
  counter-hegemonic, 267
  by Kikuyu (*Gĩkũyũ*) people, 148–49
  Latin America, 191
  to state of emergency, 274, 285
Restoration of Order in Ireland Act
    (1920), 80
Roman dictatorship, 68–69
Roman law doctrine, 39–40
Rossiter, C., 99–101
Roth, B., 16–17
Rowlatt Act, 277–79
Rubinstein, Justice, 239–40
rule of law, 52–53, 61–62, 207–9, 213
  colonialism and, 37–38
  emergency legal framework and,
    161–62
  state of emergency and, 14, 30–31
ruling regimes, 30

Said, E., 19, 195, 200–1, 225–26,
    287–88
  occupied territories and, 228–29
Salah, R., 232–33
Sandys, D., 163–64
Sarat, A., 38–39
Sarawak, 134
savage life, 49–50
Scheuerman, W., 99–103
Schmitt, C., 36, 99–100
SDLP. *See* Social Democratic and
    Labour Party
security, 15–16, 171, 178–81, 225–26,
    232. *See also* national security
  homeland, 10–11
  Israeli concerns of, 234–35
  public, 167
self-determination, 171–78, 264–65
Sepulveda, J. G., 51–52
settlement of the land of Israel (*Yishuv
    Eretz Yisrael*), 213–14
settlements, West Bank, 220
settler colonialism, 18–19, 213–14,
    232–33, 251
settler colonies, 35, 60–61
sexual abuse, 249–50, 260–61
Shaked, A., 241–43
Shamgar, M., 219–20

Shapira, Y. S., 223
Sharett, M., 223–25
Sharmila, I., 279–81
Sharon, A., 217–20
Shenhav, Y., 207–10
Simpson, B., 90–91, 128–30, 132–33,
    145, 151–52
  criminal tribes from, 87–89
  Cyprus case comments of, 178–81
  emergency law description of, 78–79
Singapore, 132–33
Singha, R., 87–89
Sinn Féin, 275–76
slavery, 45
Social Democratic and Labour Party
    (SDLP), 275–76
social movements, 191
socio-economics, 87–89, 93–94, 268, 273
South Africa, 12–13, 281–85, 287–88
  Constitution of, 284
sovereign power, 200–1, 204
sovereignty, 14, 37, 47–48, 201–2, 260–
    61
  claims, 206–7
  colonialism, 13–14, 141–42
  international law and, 14, 59–60
  native, 60
  of race, 29, 34–35, 56–64
  racialisation, 66–67
  racist ideology in, 57–58
  state of emergency and penetration
    of, 267
space of exception, 198–212
Spanish-Indian relations, 59–60
spatial division, 206–7
special powers, 104–6, 147–48
Spivak, G., 19, 55
Squatter Resistance movement, 144–46,
    152–54
state land, 219–20
state legal powers, 9–10
state of emergency, 29, 93–94, 133,
    148–49
  capitalist expansion and, 95
  capitalist liberal democracy and,
    99–100
  checks and balances of, 165
  colonial sovereignty in, 141–42

in colonial territories, 130–31
colonialism and rule of law in,
    37–38
counter-terrorism emergencies and,
    188–89
derogation and, 164–65, 190
emergency measures under, 229–36
European Commission of Human
    Rights and, 173–74
as government tool, 184
human rights influenced by, 14–15,
    163–64
imminence of threat in, 186–88
industrial disputes and, 103
international law and, 126–27,
    287–88
internment camps under, 33
Irish regime, 276–77
irreconcilable detainees and, 164–65
Israel and, 18–19, 238–40
in Kenya, 33, 138, 143–44, 146, 163–
    64, 167
Latin America resistance to, 191
in Malaya, 103–4
martial law and, 30–31, 69–70
in North Borneo, 134
oppressed communities and rule of,
    10–11
Palestine and, 212
race and, 29–30, 37, 66–67
resistance to, 274, 285
rule of law and, 14, 30–31
settler colonial policies in, 232–33
in South Africa, 281–85
sovereignty penetration and, 267
state legal powers in, 9–10
transitional measures in, 239–40
in Uganda, 132–33
underlying war on terror, 18–19
universalising of, 123–28
unlawful expropriation and, 218–19
state of exception, 41–42, 49–50, 203–4,
    209–10
in Gaza Strip, 212
Roman law doctrine and, 39–40
selective law enforcement in, 207–9
State Offences Act (1857) Britain, 85–86
state powers, 73–74

State Prisoners Act (1858) Britain, 85–86

Stoler, A. L., 60

Strasbourg Court, 170–71

Strawson, J., 214–15

subversive activity, 164–65, 185

Sumi Cho, 57–58

super-emergency measures, 241

Suppression of Terrorist Outrages Act (1932), 92

Supreme Court (Israel), 219–20, 236–37

Supreme Court (U.S.), 57–58

Svirsky, M., 41–42

Syria, 8–9

territorial regime, 48

terrorism, 46–47, 104–5, 186

Terrorism Act (2000) Britain, 184

theory of law, 168–69

Third World, 20–29
  colonial law and, 107–8
  international law in, 23–24, 26, 96–97, 271–72

Third World Approaches to International Law (TWAIL), 23–26, 271–72

Thompson, E. P., 268–70

Thuggee Act (1836) Britain, 89

Torres Strait Islander, 244–45

torture, 40, 138, 141–42
  Britain denying legal responsibility of, 139–43
  Israeli state-sanctioned, 154–56

totalitarianism, 113–15

tribal peoples, 156–57, 279–81

Trinidad, 108

Turkey, 134

TWAIL. See Third World Approaches to International Law

Uganda, 132–33

Umkhonto we Sizwe (MK), 281–82

United Nations Conference on Climate Change, 8

United Nations General Assembly, 24–26

Universal Declaration of Human Rights, 116–20
  Article 29 of, 124
  human rights applied in, 128

universal human rights, 93–94, 126–27

universalism, 16–17

unlawful combatants, 216–17

Utopian ideologies, 114

Vallat, F. A., 173–74

violence, 167, 206–10, 213

Vitoria, F., 51–52, 59–60

Wadiwel, D., 262–63

Waiting for the Barbarians (Coetzee), 12, 210

war on terror, 8–9, 12, 107–8, 133–35, 212
  architecture of enmity and, 195–96
  state of emergency underlying, 18–19

Waruhiu, Chief, 148–49

Watson, N., 251–52, 256–57, 260–61, 263

Weber, M., 207–9

Weep Not, Child (Ngũgĩ wa Thiong'o), 160–61

Weheliye, A., 43

Weimar Constitution, Germany, 40, 100

Weizman, E., 22–23, 217–20

West Bank, 202–4, 210, 241–43
  colonial occupation of, 206
  settlements of, 220

Westlake, J., 65

Whigs and Hunters (Thompson), 268–70

White Britain and Black Ireland (Lebow), 62–63

Wolfe, P., 43–44, 262–63

World Zionist Congress, 225–26

Yom Kippur war, 233

Young, A., 162

Ziadah, R., 213–14

Zionism, 211–15

Lightning Source UK Ltd.
Milton Keynes UK
UKHW021108121219
355233UK00021B/458/P